Francis S. Wagner

HUNGARIAN CONTRIBUTIONS
TO WORLD CIVILIZATION

alpha
publications

ibrary of Congress Cataloging in Publication Data

Wagner, Francis Stephen, 1911-
   Hungarian Contributions to World Civilization.

   1. Hungary — Civilization.
   2. Civilization — Hungarian influences.
   3. United States — Civilization — Hungarian influences.
   4. Intellectuals — Hungary — Biography.
   5. Magyar Tudományos Akadémia, Budapest — History — Sources.
   6. American Philosophical Society, Philadelphia — History — Sources.
   I. Title.
   DB920.5.W34

REPRINT BY HUNYADI M M K
HAMILTON, ONTARIO
1991

Printed in the United States of America
Library of Congress Catalog Card Number 77-73767
ISBN 0-912404-04-3

Produced by Alpha Publications, Inc.
1079 De Kalb Pike, Center Square, Pennsylvania
U.S.A.

CONTENTS

Preface

Since the conclusion of World War II, an entirely new era has begun in the life of mankind. This has made possible for the very first time and on truly global proportions the interchange of ideas, a powerful gateway to heretofore unthinkable progress. One may challenge the values of the political and socioeconomic phenomena of this historic epoch on various grounds. But the fact remains that its almost limitless worldwide communication has opened up completely new vistas for humanity as a whole and has altogether broadened our perspective on all branches of human knowledge. In these epoch-making efforts I firmly believe we ought to prepare a balance sheet of all nations in order to show their places in the evolution of the world's civilizations. In other words: let us put into historical perspective the intellectual contributions of all separate ethnic entities, without which effort no positive steps can be taken to achieve interethnic (international) cooperation aiming at lasting peace and justice.

To my knowledge, my present treatise is the very first experiment in this direction and it tries to determine the place of a nation in the universal history of human civilizations. Owing to this, my treatise is necessarily of a pioneering nature with all of its virtues and deficiencies. One of my greatest shortcomings is that during the whole process of source and data collection as well as their evaluation and composition I have been compelled to be overselective for several different but understandable reasons.

The first encouragement to publish this book came from U.S. Representative Frank Horton of New York who kindly inserted my preliminary study "Hungarian Contributions to American Culture" in the September 30, 1975 issue of the *Congressional Record*. In the course of my research I found such a wealth of material on the topic that I extended my research into a book.

ACKNOWLEDGMENTS

I am grateful to all those who in any way influenced or assisted me in the preparation of this volume. Among them are Professor N. F. Dreisziger of the Royal Military College of Canada who kindly put at my disposal some data about distinguished Canadians of Hungarian birth.

Special thanks are in order to Mr. Maurice Schulman, Head of Archives and Research at the U.S. Olympic Committee headquarters in New York City, for generously providing access to a treasure trove of published and unpublished information.

My wife, Irene, has assisted untiringly with proofreading and our daughter, Christina, besides writing two chapters of the book, has edited the manuscript with great care and expertise.

The assistance and encouragement of the aforementioned individuals helped materialize this project.

F.S.W.

PART I — MAIN PHASES IN INTELLECTUAL GROWTH

1

Presently there are about sixteen million Hungarians all over the world. Out of this total number approximately ten and a half million live in the Middle Danube Valley, the People's Republic of Hungary (an area of 35,919 square miles — 93,000 square kilometers), over three and a half million in its neighboring countries (several tens of thousands in Austria; 750,000 in Czechoslovakia; 170,000 in the Soviet Union's Carpatho-Ruthenia; nearly 2,500,000 in Romania, and roughly 500,000 in Yugoslavia). Included in their total number are over 1,500,000 immigrants scattered over the five continents, the majority of them — that is about 1,000,000 — dwell in the United States of America.

Even recently there has been much dispute about their ethnic origin and ancient home though historians, linguists and archaeologists almost unanimously agree that the Magyars are of Finno-Ugrian origin both ethnically and linguistically and that their ancient home some milleniums ago was somewhere in the Kama River region between the Ural Mountains and the Volga River. Some scholars assert linguistic and cultural affinity with the Sumerians. By all means, the problem of their origin cannot be regarded as completely solved since, for instance, folklore and mythology point to important Asian analogies science has until now failed to interpret and utilize.

Magyars (Hungarians), at least linguistically, belonged to the group of Finno-Ugrian peoples. These peoples formed a nomadic pastoral society and were relatively advanced in animal (especially horse) breeding, knew the primordial forms of agriculture, could make earthenware and could weave and spin. Their transformation from a clan system into a more developed tribal organization took place under the hegemony of Turkish tribes. Henceforth the Magyars became acquainted with a higher civilization and their tribal unions participated in various nomadic empires during their centuries-long wanderings between their ancient habitations and their present home in the Danube area. The Conquest of the Danube region occurred in the closing years of the ninth century A.D. Up to this point of time the pagan Magyars believed in animism. Other principal elements of their primitive faith seemed to be their belief in the duality of the soul and body, the cult of the dead, the spirits of good and evil, and a very primitive form of the immortality of the soul. Prior to reaching the Danube area the wandering tribes met and assimilated a number of different peoples and cultures (Turkish, Iranian, etc., and much later German, Slavic, Italian . . .) so when they appeared in the Carpathian Basin, the Magyars happened to be quite a mixture of many ethnic entities and their respective cultures but the dominant feature of their language, culture, and lifestyle remained Magyar. Furthermore, their wanderings acquainted the Magyar tribes with the then already well-established religions such as the Christian, Jewish and Islamic. In the light of all written sources these early Magyars' attitude to other religions and races seemed to be quite tolerant if not friendly. This tolerant attitude can be considered a causative why during and after the Conquest the institution of slavery did not materialize. On the contrary, their mutually beneficial relationship resulted in the integration of foreign elements into the Magyar nation. This process went on incessantly during the reign of the House of Árpád (ca. 890-1301).

In the time of the Magyar Conquest Slavs, Germans and some other peoples already lived there. The Magyars, characteristically, did not enslave them as did earlier the Huns and the Avars to native population. The economic order of the Magyars was built on the contemporary feudal system and not on the barbarian exploitation of subjugated peoples. And, furthermore, while the Huns and the Avars occupied primarily the Great Hungarian Plains, the central base of the Magyar Conquest lay in Dunántúl (Transdanubia): that is, in the very neighborhood of Western cultural sphere. These circumstances, as well as the specific concept of the nomadic nation as practiced by the Magyars, helped develop the fate of this area in the centuries to come. In the formative period the old, nomadic nation concept of the Magyars embraced all separate racial (nationality) groups who lived on the territories under Magyar military and political supremacy. This fairly elastic concept of nation saved the Magyars in their long and tragic struggles against the Tatars, Turks and others as well as helping to absorb their invaders' strengths and rejuvenate the whole nation.

2

For decades after the Conquest, Hungarian warriors on swift horses forayed into the disintegrating Carolingian empire and defeated its slow feudal cavalry by employing a military strategy and tactics entirely unknown in the West: sudden, unexpected attack followed by pretended retreat which ended up in hand-to-hand combat, etc. Finally, in 955 the Augsburg Disaster put an end to their lightning raids leaving the Hungarians with but two alternatives: to continue their seminomadic lifestyle and perish as did their predecessors the Huns and the Avars, or adapt themselves to the feudal socioeconomic conditions of Western Europe through the adoption of Christianity. The Hungarians were compelled to choose the latter alternative. King (Saint) Stephen I (1000-1038) founded the Christian kingdom and simultaneously took into account the characteristics of his people. Upon their conversion to Christianity, the Magyars began the process of adapting themselves to the Latin-speaking culture of feudal Europe. Since then until the conclusion of World War II the country remained a kingdom and its cultural life more or less developed within the framework of Western (Christian) civilization. This profound change was carried out by the kings of the House of Árpád with the aid of foreign priests and missionaries (Slavic, German, French, Italian, and other) who disseminated Christianity in Hungary. Hungarians also started attending foreign schools. In this initial phase of cultural evolution theology and certain branches of history writing — annals, chronicles, legends and gestas — came to the fore of intellectual efforts. This age regarded philosophy as "ancilla theologiae." This was the case especially in Hungary where native scholars for centuries excelled neither in theology nor in philosophy although they made quite important contributions to historical writing.

Historical writing by native authors for centuries bore many signs of foreign influence, particularly in the case of structure and to a lesser extent with respect to the reflection of medieval universality. It is worth mentioning that medieval Hungarian historians did not follow the practice of annalists and chroniclers so fashionable in contemporary Germany and other parts of the West. In Hungary the accepted form of writing was rather the so-called gesta in which a topical and not chronological arrangement of events dominated. Even those writings which bore the word "chronicle" in their titles should be regarded as gestas in this country's Middle Ages. It should also be noted that Hungarian gestas (historias) were the works of court historians. Therefore, dynastic interests rather than ecclesiastical viewpoints guided the authors in their works. This in itself explains why these medieval writings idolized even the pagan age and heroes of the Magyars. Quite unlike the German annals and chronicles, these Hungarian gestas were true national *historias* in the medieval sense. From a methodological point of view, these early forms of historiography were influenced by French, German, Italian, and English models up to the Age of Renaissance when the country's historical science tended to follow and imitate the works of the Italian masters. Until the reign of King Matthias Corvinus (1458-1490), gesta and chronicle writing was almost exclusively the profession of clergymen who in a number of cases were officially designated as court historians. In addition to the royal chancery, some ecclesiastical bodies (monasteries, cloisters, etc.) were entrusted with notarial functions and were thus the precursors or early forms of record offices (public archives) for issuing documents or diplomas and conducting verification procedures.

The individual character of the Magyars did not allow their accommodating themselves to medieval universalness as did, for instance, the

Germans. Partly owing to this national characteristic, these centuries passed without any signficant contributions to the history of intellectual life. Yet, these silent centuries already showed some signs of future promise. The most famous library of that time, the still existing Benedictine Library of Pannonhalma, was founded in 1001, and the first reference to a Hungarian college in Veszprém (established in the eleventh century) was made as early as 1276. However, the Age of Humanism and the Renaissance, much more than the centuries of medievalism, helped inspire the genius of the Magyars for unlimited intellectual growth.

3

In the second half of the Middle Ages (1301-1526) the country's cultural aspirations rose significantly higher. This was all the more understandable in the light of the Tartar invasion (1241) because it almost nullified the cultural achievements of Christianity by destroying nearly all the monasteries, their schools and libraries. Hungarians quickly rebuilt these cultural centers; historical writing flourished once again and even theology came by its native scholars which had been unthinkable during the age of the Árpáds.

As from the thirteenth century on, many young Hungarians frequented the universities of Paris, Padova, Bologna and mainly the universities of the neighboring countries: primarily those of Cracow, Prague and Vienna. The University of Vienna had 4,600 Hungarian students between its foundation in 1363 and the Battle of Mohács in 1526. Progress in the sciences is shown by the mere fact that several universities were founded in the last two centuries of the Middle Ages: the University of Pécs in 1367 and the University of Ó-Buda in 1389. When these short-lived universities ceased to exist, the Archbishop of Esztergom, Joannes (János) Vitéz (1408-1472), founded the so-called Academia Istropolitana in Pozsony (Bratislava) in 1467. Somewhat later, in 1497, Konrad Celtis established the Sodalitas Litteraria Danubiana (Danubian Scholarly Society) in Ó-Buda and Vienna presumably in the pattern of Italy's Academia Platonica. The membership, consisting of Hungarian, German, Czech and Italian humanists, arranged symposia to discuss scholarly topics.

The Renaissance court of King Matthias I (1458-1490), among its many-sided activities, asserted the primacy of mundane glory and interests over transcendentalism. Historical as well as belletristic works reflected a specific philosophy of man which did not have much in common with the Christian attitude of preceding centuries. Janus Pannonius (1434-1472), Bishop of Pécs and a member of the royal court of

King Matthias I, attained European fame as a humanist poet and was also very popular in Italy. Janus Pannonius was the first poet who sang on beauties of Hungary's scenery and her people's patriotism. The humanistic trend was an import from Italy. In 1486, Antonio Bonfini (1434?-1503) became a member of the royal court of Matthias I at Buda and was commissioned there by the King to rewrite in Renaissance spirit the country's past.

King Matthias' library was one of the great libraries of contemporary Europe. Its holdings of some 3,000 to 5,000 volumes in Greek and Latin represented heretofore hardly cultivated branches of human knowledge: philosophy, mathematics, physics and the social sciences. What remains of the Matthias' humanist library known as "Corvina" — 168 codices — resides in thirty cities of Europe and the United States. Hungary has only forty-three of the codices.

The Gutenberg Bible was the first great book printed. The printing of the Bible was probably completed late in 1455 at Mainz, Germany by Johann Gutenberg (ca. 1400-1468). Not so many years later, in 1472, Andreas (András) Hess set up in Buda the first Hungarian printing shop with the aid of Vice-Chancellor László Karai and printed the first Hungarian book, *Chronica Hungarorum* in 1473. It was evidently in the Age of Renaissance that the country, for the very first time and through the ministrations of King Matthias' royal court, entered the cultural community of Western nations as an equal member.

4

The Reformation and Counter-Reformation were turning points in the intellectual development of the nation. The adoption of the Reformation coincided with the dual oppression of the nation by the Turks and the Habsburg dynasty which determined the fate of Hungary for at least the next two centuries from cultural, political and socioeconomic points of view. The conquest of the country by the Turks and the anti-Hungarian policy of the Habsburgs put a prolonged halt to Hungarian cultural development. In the dawn of the Modern Age, Hungary suffered the most devastating defeat by the Turks at Mohács in 1526. After the Mohács Disaster the country was torn into three parts: its western and northern parts constituted the Habsburg Kingdom, the eastern part formed the Principality of Transylvania which enjoyed semi-independence from the Ottoman Empire, while the central part of the country remained under Turkish occupation for a century and a half. This division of Hungary helped develop a specific feudal system by perpetuating the serfdom and the egoistic efforts of the nobility until the 1848-1849 revolution and fight for freedom. The Western-oriented foreign policy of the Habsburg Empire was chiefly responsible for the long-lasting Turkish occupation of East Central Europe which had a devastating result on Hungary. It affected first of all the ethnic structure of its population. During the reign of King Matthias I in the second half of the fifteenth century, the population amounted to 4,000,000 of which roughly 80% were Hungarians; and at the end of the Turkish conquest, more correctly in 1720, due to the continuous struggles with the Turks and their deportations by them to the Orient, the population had dwindled to 2,570,000 and the Hungarians became a minority in their own country. Had Hungary as the defender of the West not stopped the onslaught of Islamic Turkey, the Turks would have overrun a Europe exhausted by religious wars, and as Thomas Babington Macaulay (1800-1859) said: "The Koran would now be taught in Oxford."

The settlement policy of the Vienna Court in the eighteenth century aggravated the already disastrous conditions by favoring non-Magyar, chiefly German, minorities and creating nationality islands across the country in order to divide and rule.

Faced with the above-mentioned conditions both the Reformation and Counter-Reformation tried to save the cultural heritage of the nation. The Reformation proved to be an effective counterbalance to germanizing Habsburg Catholicism. There was a period of two decades when three fourths of the population were converted to Protestantism. The memorial to the Reformation erected in Geneva perpetuates Stephen Bocskay, Prince of Transylvania, who battled for and gained for Protestantism equality under the law. While contemporary Europe generally accepted the principle that each country should adhere to a single religion, in Transylvania under the rule of Hungarian princes the situation was quite different. The Diet of 1564 proclaimed that each and every town and province in Transylvania should be given the free choice of its own religion, and according to the Diet of 1571 three nations and four accepted religions (receptae religiones) — the Catholic, Lutheran, Calvinist and Unitarian — were recognized in Transylvania. The Transylvanian Diet was the first legislative body in Europe to enact religious freedom. The Reformation greatly intensified religious fervor not only among the Protestants but among Catholics too by way of reaction and as self-defense. In a matter of decades, owing to the application of the principle "cuius regio eius religio" in the process of conversion, Hungary again became a predominantly Catholic country.

Because of the lack of higher educational institutions in the sixteenth century, more and more Hungarian students resumed the old custom of frequenting foreign universities. Protestants went above all to the University of Wittenberg which during the sixteenth century was attended by more than 1,000 Hungarian students; and a fair number of Hungarian youths studied at the universities of Bologna, Padova, Vienna, and Cracow. In the seventeenth century only Lutherans studied at Wittenberg, the Calvinists on the other hand went to the universities at Heidelberg, Basel, Utrecht and Leiden in the Netherlands, and sometimes to England (Oxford).

From a cultural point of view, the introduction of the vernacular language in all branches of knowledge should be regarded as the greatest and truly unsurpassable accomplishment of the Reformation. Beginning with the Bible translations, by the end of the eighteenth century several thousand foreign books had been translated into Hungarian. Gáspár Károli's complete Bible translation in 1590 represented a milestone in translation literature. Gáspár Károli can be valued with Hieronymus and Martin Luther among the greatest Bible translators of the world.

Interestingly, the leader of the Counter-Reformation, Cardinal Péter Pázmány (1570-1637) created the modern prosaic style and founded the country's most prestigious university (Péter Pázmány University, now Lóránd Eötvös University, Budapest) in 1635.

During this period, cultural life developed under the influence of the Italian Renaissance and German Protestantism. Due mainly to the efforts of the Reformed Church, a peculiar political and cultural attitude developed through the centuries following the Battle of Mohács in 1526. This attitude combined the country's historical heritage with Western civilization.

In spite of the disadvantageous circumstances of the Turkish Age, more and more individuals became engaged in promoting knowledge. Miklós Oláh (1493-1568), later Archbishop of Esztergom, wrote a remarkable, very reliable historico-geographical description *Hungaria* (ca. 1536, publ. in Belgium). As a friend and to some extent a co-worker of Desiderius Erasmus (d. 1536) he rose to the stature of a great celebrity. His protégé, Andreas (András) Dudith (1533-1589), Bishop of Pécs who later left the Catholic Church to become a Calvinist then a Unitarian traveled throughout Europe and developed working relationships with outstanding humanists. Dudith can be regarded as a polyhistor who, as a prolific author of Latin works, scrutinized then timely questions of theology, classical literature as well as natural history.

5

After Ferenc Rákóczi's War of Independence (1703-1711), conditions fundamentally changed. Scholars and scientists began interpreting the world in terms of human values and experiences. This new, rationalistic anthropocentrism produced in the field of the humanities a real transition from church history to political history which in Hungary commenced with the activities of Mátyás Bél (1684-1749) whom the Slovaks also claim. In accordance with the teachings of his German masters — Francke, Cellarius, Ludwig, Gundling — at the pietist University of Halle, Mátyás Bél interpreted history as a part of political science (Staatenkunde). György Pray (1723-1801) was especially influenced by the works of Mátyás Bél and established the school of critical historiography for which Queen Maria Theresa conferred upon him the title of "historiographus Hungariae." Pray's school of historical criticism affected the elite of the whole Danube area. In the second half of the eighteenth century it became quite evident that Hungary entered the period of change from semi-feudalism to capitalism — more aptly phrased to a bourgeois socioeçonomic order. Her intellectual life already seemed more and more interwoven with the threads of the rationalist philosophy of the Enlightenment and with the ideas of the French and the American revolutions. These foreign influences helped shape the concept of nation as a historical entity and put it in the focus of scholarly as well as public attention. Many a new literary product of that age, affected by the progressive trends of the contemporary West, expressed to some degree anticlerical, chiefly anti-Catholic, mentality. A major step toward spreading ethnocentric knowledge and laicism was taken by the issuance in 1777 of *Ratio educationis*. József Ürményi, Dániel Tersztyánszky and Pál Makó were commissioned by Queen Maria Theresa to prepare this all-important educational reform plan which in essence placed public education under strict government control and introduced rationalism at all levels of schools. Accordingly, in the service of utilitarianism, curricula of mathematical and natural sciences, physics, stenography, the reading of newspapers, bookkeeping, physical education, etc., were prescribed. New districts of school administration were set up under the leadership of high-ranking government officials. This reform plan, preceding by some years the initiation of Josephinism, acknowledged and materialized the principle of state-church separation. This whole process of educational reforms took place partly under the influence of Rousseau and partly in the spirit of the French Enlightenment.

The disillusioned progressive intelligentsia and the nobility turned against the policy of the Vienna Imperial Court but their movements could not become politically large-scale — partly because most of the progressive elements were intimidated by the events of the French Revolution. But the essence of the Enlightenment, the idea of progress remained the chief goal of all human activities: social, economic, political and above all, cultural. Characteristically, the ideas of the French Enlightenment came to Hungary through Viennese channels due to the modernization trends of Maria Theresa and her son, Joseph II. The struggles of the leaders for the Hungarian intellectual revival and progress was closely tied to a fight against the authority of the Catholic

Church. This attitude since then has survived in the cultural activities of all the generations to come.

6

The scientific thinking so characteristic of the Renaissance and even more of the Enlightenment was not nurtured by the scholars in the coming decades. The central issue in the Age of Reforms (1825-1848) was the struggle for self-fulfillment of all ethnic minorities throughout the Habsburg Monarchy but especially in Hungary. All nations and ethnic minorities happened to be more or less involved in these self-realization movements and wanted to actualize their political aims primarily through the promotion of their native languages and literatures. Naturally, emotional prejudices on all sides came to the fore in public life and as a result objective research and publication on the whole was at a standstill for decades. It would have been an urgent priority to rewrite national histories in an objective manner. But instead, scholarly efforts deviated to illusory goals by the invention of fantastical hypotheses in order to satisfy public demand — namely, the self-centeredness of a rapidly elevating fever of nationalism. The romantic interest, for example, in discovering the ancient home and the origins of the Magyars ran so high in those decades that Alexander (Sándor) Kőrösi Csoma (1784-1842), the world-renowned founder of Tibetan philology, as early as his student years decided to visit the remnants of the "Asiatic Magyars" in the heart of that continent. He, as it is known, was unsuccessful in his quest to locate those Magyars on his romantic journey.

In these years of stagnation an extraordinary event occurred which proved to be epoch-making in Hungary's intellectual growth. In 1825 at the initiation of Stephen (István) Széchenyi (1791-1860), the Hungarian Academy of Sciences was founded, through which the country gradually entered the mainstream of the American and world civilization. It is most interesting to note that the Academy of Sciences initiated its first foreign contact not with the then already flourishing royal institutions of continental Europe and Great Britain but with the Benjamin Franklin-founded and Philadelphia-based American Philosophical Society. In order to explain this unusual phenomenon in an age when intercontinental travels were dangerous and lasting for many months, let us reveal in the following its historical background.

The peoples of the European continent have always had an interest in America. The first accounts of the New World were published almost immediately following its discovery. These post-Columbian Western writings, preoccupied with the bright economic promise of the newly discovered land, contained hardly any spiritual elements. Such early works, as well as the 16th- and 17th-century geography and history books, were based on matter-of-fact descriptions. But the power of imagination so characteristic of needy Europeans early created an economic wonderland on the other shore of the Ocean. These stories, combined with the deep-rooted conviction that America's wealth was close to the legendary treasures of India and the Spice Islands, had prepared the foreign mind for wonders, for an enthusiastic approach towards the American economy, where anything miraculous could happen.

At the same time in Central and Eastern Europe a new notion of America was being born, diametrically opposed to those commercial views. It occurred on the frontier of Christian civilization where small nations had stood guard in the path of the expansion of the Ottoman Empire. In their historic struggle against Turkish "paganism", literary men of these small nations subjected to Turkish occupation became disillusioned by the inept diplomacy of the Christian great powers and riveted their eyes upon the New World. The Hungarian Miklós Istvánffy (1583-1615) displayed the essential characteristics of these publications when in his *Historia Regni Hungarici* he said that America was simply discovered "for the glory of Christianity" (p. 16). In the decades to come, many Hungarian Protestant sources especially referred to the New World, though very briefly. Gáspár Miskolczi Csulyák made mention of America, New England and New Plymouth in his *Angliai Independentismus* (English Independentism, Utrecht, 1654, p. 41). The famed Samuel Köleséri[1] went further in the "Preface" of his collection of sermons by citing Thomas Hooker, an English Puritan author who emigrated into America, among his sources.

A few years later, in 1694, the first Hungarian book about America appeared, a translation of Increase Mather's (1639-1723) *De succéssu evangelii apud Indos Occidentales, in Nova Anglia, etc.*[2]

Since the last quarter of the 18th century, the earlier developed idea of the "bulwark of Christendom" was consistently being replaced by the content of the American Revolution, focused on the Declaration of Independence and the Constitution itself. The American freedom concept with all its well-known requisites (state-church separation, relatively classless society, republicanism, free enterprise, etc.) obviously attracted the political and cultural philosophy of the European cultural élite. The land of opportunity and its promise of a brilliant future captivated, among others, the French-born Michel-Guillaume de Crevecoeur who already in 1782, in the early formative period of the American nation said: "Here individuals of all nations are melted into a new race of men, whose labours and posterity will one day cause great change in the world. Americans are the western pilgrims, who are carrying along with them that great mass of arts, sciences, vigor, and industry, which began long since in the east; they will finish the great circle."[3]

The portrait of America has varied from time to time, keeping pace with general requirements of the cultural progress of mankind. Benjamin Franklin happened to be the first American of great cultural importance whose inventions helped create a very impressive image of scientific America. Through the invention of the lightning rod he became the No. 1 scientist of the world in the eyes of contemporary Europeans. A professor of mathematics at the University of Buda, Pál Makó (1723-1793), author of the first Hungarian book on electricity, showed high regard for Franklin's scientific accomplishments.[4] The rise in Franklin's popularity was so spectacular that many contemporary poets sang enthusiastically about his newly invented lightning rod.[5]

So it was not surprising that Hungarian men of science wished so eagerly to become acquainted with Franklin's land of liberty and prosperity, and to establish lasting, mutual relationships. Sándor Bölöni Farkas (1795-1842), a prolific scholar, did the pioneer work through his widely publicized travel notes[6] of his brief sojourn in the New World (September 4 to November 24, 1831), during which he traveled 2,450 miles by land and water. America, this "happy country" was chosen by Providence to demonstrate "whether human society is able to establish a good administration through free elections in the service of the happiness of mankind" (pp. 28-29). When Bölöni Farkas returned to Europe, he bade America farewell in these ardent words: "God bless you, glorious country! Be the immortal guardian of the noblest heritage of mankind! Stand as an everlasting model of encouragement for the souls of the enslaved!" (p. 343)

Apart from the American system of democracy, the cultural life of Franklin's Philadelphia made the deepest impact upon the thinking of Bölöni Farkas. Let us illustrate this with some excerpts:

"Many a traveler says and writes that Philadelphia is the most beautiful city of the world . . . But the various divisions of science stand in the most beautiful light in the city of Philadelphia. It seems this city is the place of education for men of science, the cradle of scientific activities . . . The American Philosophical Society founded in 1743 by Franklin is foremost among all scientific societies with its outstanding library, natural history and other collections. The goal of this Society is: to disseminate useful and scientifically important knowledge. Its rooms are permanently open for reading and discussion. Foreigners are hospitably received. Its sessions are held every first and third Friday of the month. Lectures delivered at these sessions are published annually . . ." (pp. 327-328)

After arriving home early in 1832, that is long before the first publication of his travel notes in the spring of 1834, Bölöni Farkas discussed his American experience with many of his acquaintances, including a lifelong friend, Gábor Döbrentei, then the powerful secretary of the Hungarian Academy of Sciences (Magyar Tudós Társaság).[7]

With the help of Count Stephen Széchenyi (1791-1860), founder and then vice president and treasurer of the Hungarian Academy of Sciences — known to his most prominent countrymen as a leading pro-American figure — these and similar actions contributed directly to promoting the idea of a cultural exchange with representative foreign institutions. As a result of these discussions, the noted mathematician and astronomer, Academician Károly (Charles) Nagy, sailed to Bölöni Farkas' "happy country," and sent a letter, dated Philadelphia, Pa., December 25, 1832, to Peter Duponceau, president of the American Philosophical Society of Philadelphia. It is interesting to note that despite the transportation difficulties of that age, the Hungarian Academy sought to establish its first foreign contact with an overseas institution.*

Academician Nagy in his above-cited three-page letter informed President Duponceau about the founding, legal status, organizational structure, office staff, by-laws and planned activities of the Academy. Then at the end of the letter Nagy described his mission in the following words:[8]

"I can take upon myself to declare to you, that the Hungarian Academy, anxious to entertain scientific relations with foreign academies and learned societies, feels the duty to recommend itself in the friendly affections of the Philosophical Society of Philadelphia, and expresses its wishes for an uninterrupted connection between these two bodies, and asserts that the Hungarian Academy will be the first in the communication of all its proceedings and transactions with the Philosophical Society. The Hungarian Academy would be highly honoured by the friendly assent of the Society, and I should feel very happy in being the messenger . . ."

Peter Duponceau reacted very quickly to this letter. The next day, December 26, 1832, he prepared the following Resolution[9] to exchange publications with the Hungarian Academy of Sciences:

---

*To the American Philosophical Society of Philadelphia, Pa., for granting me permission to use the following unpublished documents from its library collections, I wish to express my warm gratitude.

"A letter from Mr. Charles Nagy, stating that he is a member of the Hungarian Academy of Sciences, established at Pest, by an act of the Diet with the Royal Sanction in the year 1829, that the said Society is desirous of corresponding with similar institutions throughout the world and particularly with the American Philosophical Society; whereupon

Resolved; that Mr. Nagy be informed that this Society is equally desirous of establishing a regular and constant communication with the Hungarian Academy of Sciences, and that a copy of the New Series of our Transactions be transmitted to him by the Librarian with a request that he will be so good as to present it in our name to the Academy, and that a copy of this Resolution be at the same time sent to him duly attested by the Secretary."

Afterwards, in the light of some archival materials, these steps were taken. According to the minutes of the January 4, 1833 Stated Meeting of APS, a donation to APS was also made by "M. Nagy of the Hungarian Academy of Sciences." At the same meeting, John Vaughan, the librarian "read a letter from M. Nagy giving an account of the Hungarian Academy of Sciences . . . Resolved, that the President be requested to reply to the letter addressed through him to the Society . . . On the motion of Mr. Vaughan. Resolved, that a copy of the Transactions of this Society (new series) be presented through M. Nagy to the Hungarian Academy of Sciences."

The January 18, 1833 minutes (Stated Meeting, APS) said that: "The President reported that he had executed the duty devolved upon him in relation to the letter of M. Nagy."[10]

The minutes of the February 1, 1833 meeting, furthermore, indicated that "A letter from Mr. C. Nagy was read by Mr. John Vaughan, relative to the telescopes made by Mr. Ploessel of Vienna." This two-page letter which broadened the recently initiated relationships between the two bodies, was written in New York, January 5, 1833, by Nagy to Vaughan, librarian of the APS. He described the contemporary level of European instrument making, including microscopes, with emphasis on Ploessel of Vienna:

"Of course, requests were sent from all parts of Europe for obtaining one of his (Ploessel) unequalled microscopes. — The results of this comparative enquiry are published, and I shall have the pleasure to send you a copy together with the catalogue of Ploessel . . . The easiest manner to send some objects to Hungary is, by addressing them to the Austrian Embassy . . . London with the note — for the Hungarian Academy of Sciences . . ."[11]

The activity of Academician Nagy was greatly appreciated by the Philadelphia institution and at its April 19, 1833 meeting, he became a "duly elected member of that Society."[12]

In acknowledging that honor, Nagy sent a three-page letter to John

Vaughan, from Pest, August 20, 1833. This letter clearly reflects the many-sided nature of cordial relations between the two institutions. It even deals with the tragic fate of some Polish revolutionary officers. These are the most interesting excerpts from the letter:

"In returning from some travels in different parts of our country, I found the letter of the Secretary of the Philosophical Society and your kind lines together. I feel very greatly honoured having been elected member of your highly distinguished and learned Society. No greater pleasure could occur to me. My sincerest thanks to you my dear Sir for the hearty kindness you had in proposing me . . . The catalog of the optician Ploessel is unfortunately out of print . . . Since my return this artist made an important discovery in the construction of telescopes . . ." Then Nagy described at length and illustrated that newly invented telescope. ". . . The books I collected for the Library of the (American Philosophical) Society — among them the Hungarian Bible you wished for — together with some minerals I shall send probably with the same Austrian frigate who takes the unfortunate Poles for America. You know probably that about 400 Poles — all officers from the late Revolutionary Army — who resided in Austria are to be sent off in your country: a very strange thing, without asking the Americans to send them a large number of exiled poor soldiers!! . . . With the present opportunity I send you for the Society 1) a good Chart of Hungary — in the German tongue — a larger one is now to be prepared in the Hungarian language, (the old ones are not accurate enough) as soon as it is completed (in two years I hope, one sheet is published already) I shall send it for the Society, 2) an exact copy of the Moon with its mountains . . . 3) The Report of the 10th congregation of the said German Society (Society of German Naturalists), held at Vienna past year in September as I was in your happy country . . . The Hungarian Academy of Sciences will send you next time some of its publications . . . I found a very interesting collection of minerals, almost all in beautiful specimens, well arranged. I think we could have it . . . if the Society wishes to multiplicate or to grow its fine . . . collection, I shall feel very happy in being an instrument to contribute to its extent . . . You would extremely oblige me dear Sir by sending the National Gazette or any other of your best Philadelphia daily papers . . ."[13]

On November 11, 1833, when the Hungarian Academy sent its first *Yearbook* (*A Magyar Tudós Társaság Évkönyvei. I. 1831-1832.* Pest, Trattner-Károlyi nyomt., 1833), as well as two copies of its *Bylaws* (*Rendszabás*) and one copy of its *Directory* (*Névkönyv*) to Philadelphia, the accompanying letter, signed by President Count József Teleki and Secretary Gábor Döbrentei, emphasized that "The Hungarian Academy of Sciences is sending you its first Yearbook and desires that by love of sciences and arts all mankind may be spiritually united in the great society of kinship."[14]

Undoubtedly, in the initial stage of these growing relations between the two institutions, Károly Nagy and his counterpart, John Vaughan, played the most distinguished role. In the September 1, 1835 letter, written from Vienna, to John Vaughan, Nagy spoke about a very important publication: "In presenting to the Society this volume, it is my duty, I feel, to explain its object and content. This is the first Arithmetic in the Hungarian language intended for Academies and Universities — this science as all others being taught to this day in Latin . . ." Then in this two-page accompanying letter, he reviewed at length the math book consisting of 12 chapters.

His next letter available in the Archives of the American Philosophical Society Library was again addressed to his partner, John Vaughan, dated Vienna, May 23, 1838. Finally, Nagy was in a position to report to Vaughan that: "The telescope inclosed was brought to me the day of 21 May and I send it to your nephew this day to London, in hope it will arrive at least to the end of June in New York or Philadelphia. I inclose 3 small catalogues of names of the Hungarian Academy of Sciences with the calendar for 1838.[15] All expenses and price of the telescope will be paid by your nephew . . . My best and heartiest compliments to Mr. Duponceau . . ."

Also, from Vienna, according to the August 10, 1839 accompanying letter, Academician Nagy sent to the Philosophical Society "2 copies of his calendar for 1840 with useful tables (in Hungarian); printed for the Hungarian Academy of Sciences in Pest."

Károly Nagy, being himself an excellent mathematician and astronomer, was well aware of the fact that Hungarian linguistic and belletristic publications, for understandable reasons, could not play a leading role in the foreign exchange program. He, therefore, constantly switched to more practical subjects. In line with his realistic policies, he notified John Vaughan, in a letter from Vienna, March 10, 1841, that he had sent to Philadelphia, among other things, "the calendar for 1841 and a description of the oldest university in Hungary." Then, he said: "Some pendulum experiments are going on under my direction. I shall have the pleasure in communicating the results to the Society; the experiments closed, I would send the invariable pendulum itself to Philadelphia for continuation, you may inform me, when this idea is agreeable to the Society."[16]

Due to the 1848-49 revolutionary events in Austria, the highest institution of Hungarian science was compelled to weaken or even sever its carefully built up foreign relations. And it might not be entirely accidental that its 1852 shipment (containing volumes 3-7 of the Yearbook) was mailed on March 15, the anniversary of the uprising.[17]

The exchange program of the Hungarian Academy of Sciences has increased greatly since those pioneering years. Nowadays, as stated by István Rusznyák, President, Hungarian Academy of Sciences, "its exchange relations involve more than 1,700 institutions of some 86 states."[18] But among all the foreign institutions, the Benjamin Franklin-founded American Philosophical Society was the first with which the Hungarian Academy of Sciences established a fruitful relationship.

8

The Uprising and the War of Independence of 1848-1849 ended in complete defeat for Hungary's cause. Owing to the lessons drawn from this political struggle for independence, it dawned on the intelligentsia that there had accumulated by then numerous shortcomings in cultural policy. The Academy's activities, for instance, were one-sidedly philological. Now they saw clearly that the various other branches of the sciences had been neglected for decades. Psychologically, therefore, it was natural that after the devastating defeat, politicians and scholars rivet their eyes upon the more fortunate periods of history and start organizing a centralized mode of research for the first time in history.

The advance of capitalism and the country's constitutional bonds with Austria influenced the development of scientific life between the Austro-Hungarian Compromise of 1867 and the collapse of the Dual Monarchy in 1918. The expansion of capitalism served the progress of the mathematical and natural sciences of this era and proved a healthy stimulus to the advancement of the arts and humanities. Three newly founded universities were added to the network of higher educational institutions. Of the former, the University of Szeged excelled in the mathematical and natural sciences. Positivism featured quite strong in the Age of Dualism (1867-1918) when specialization began in Hungary. By the turn of the nineteenth and twentieth centuries the country's progress in sciences, arts and sports equalled to a European standard.

9

The conclusion of World War I and the Treaty of Trianon (June 4, 1920) entirely changed Hungary's position in the family of nations. The country's dismemberment caused serious economic and political problems and perpetuated its financial crisis. As a means of self-aid — psychologically quite understandably — the official cultural policy favored idealistic trends to save the national spirit from collapse. As a consequence, the official line emphasized the promotion of the

humanities over most of the branches of sciences. Yet the most outstanding cultural politician between the wars, Kunó Klebelsberg, did
much in organizing scientific research at universities and at independent
institutes such as the Tihany Institute of Biological Research. In spite of
the industrious work of many devoted scholars and scientists, their
research lacked the coordination by a national institution. Consequently
there was no systematic planning of research prior to the end of the
World War II.

10

As an aftermath of World War II, Hungary fell into the Soviet Union's
sphere of influence and became one of its neighbors. The new constellation not only determined the political fate of the country but its intellectual orientation as well. It is an established fact that up to this point in
time there had been no direct — if any — lasting Russian effect on
Hungary's cultural life which had hitherto developed exclusively under
Western influences. Since the conclusion of the war, the country's
intellectual evolution has precisely mirrored the main phases and
characteristics of the political changes taking place there and in the
Kremlin-dominated areas as a whole. Directives issued by the Central
Committee of the Hungarian Communist Party have triggered all political and cultural changes and intellectual workers have been compelled
to conduct their research accordingly. The reorganization of the Hungarian Academy of Sciences by Law No. XXVII of 1949 made possible
the planning and coordination of all high-level intellectual activities
under the guidance and supervision of the Academy. Undoubtedly, it
has been the greatest achievement in scientific organization and management as well as in planning research. The central planning and
coordination necessarily are closely associated with the country's
economic plans. In line with this policy, research institutes are required
to solve first of all those problems which are in one way or other
connected with the topics of current economic demands and requirements. This utilitarian approach can lead to ignoring the primacy of
basic research over industry-focused interests and application. Were
that to happen, the advancement of knowledge the world over would
suffer a severe setback.

---

[1] See Sámuel Köleséri, *Szent Irás Rámájára Vonatott Fél-Keretyén.* Debrecen, 1677. Cf.
László Országh, "Misztótfalusi Kis és az első magyar könyv Amerikáról," *Magyar
Könyvszemle,* vol. 74, no. 1, 1958. p. 22.
[2] L. Országh, *op. cit.,* pp. 22-41.
[3] *Letters from an American farmer, etc.* London, 1782. See also Francis S. Wagner, "The
image of America in foreign books," *Free World Review,* vol. 5, no. 4, Winter 1959-1960,
28-31.

⁴*A mennykőnek mivoltáról való böltselkedés mellyet deák nyelven irt, és most feles másolásokkal és toldalékokkal megjobbitott Makó Pál, magyarázta pedig Révai Miklós.* Posonyban és Kassán, Landerer Mihály költségével és betüivel, 1781. See its review by Oszkár Szimán, "Az első magyar nyelvű könyv az elektromosságról," *Fizikai Szemle,* vol. 10, no. 8, Aug. 1960, pp. 252-255. At the same time the enlightened Piarist, Elek Horányi, applied Franklin's theory of electricity in teaching Antal Grassalkovich and Ignác Almássy. Cf. *Merkur v. Ungarn,* 1786, p. 977.

⁵See, for instance, Lőrinc Orczy's poem (1718-1789) in Oszkár Szimán's above-quoted article.

⁶S. Bölöni Farkas, *Utazás Észak Amerikában.* Kolozsvárt, Ifjabb Tilsch János tulajdona, 1834. 346 p. Its 2nd and 3rd eds. were publ. in 1835.

⁷For more information about their friendship see Dr. Elemér Jancsó, "Bölöni Farkas Sándor élete és munkássága" (pp. 3-54) in Sándor Bölöni Farkas, *Nyugateurópai utazás.* Bevezetéssel ellátta: Dr. Jancsó Elemér. Kolozsvár, Minerva Rt., 1943. 180 p. (Erdélyi Ritkaságok).

⁸⁻⁹See orig. documents in APSL (American Philosophical Society Library, Philadelphia, Pa.). The building of the Library of the Hungarian Academy of Sciences in Budapest was so badly damaged at the end of World War II that its relevant sources were almost completely destroyed (Communication of the MTA Könyvtára under No. 7058-59, June 3, 1959, addressed to me.

¹⁰Duponceau's letter, dated January 5, 1833, was addressed to Charles Nagy in New York who brought it to Pest where it was read at the June 10, 1833 weekly session of the Hungarian Academy of Sciences presided over by Stephen Széchenyi, Vice President of the Academy. In the letter Duponceau stated that the *Transactions* of the American Philosophical Society, dating back to 1770, had been sent to the Hungarian Academy. (See *A Magyar Tudós Társaság Évkönyvei.* Vol. 2. 1832-1834. Buda, Magyar Kir. Egyetem nyomt., 1835. p. 5.) The same session of the Academy acknowledged the receipt of the book shipment of Dr. Jacob Mease, Secretary of the American Philosophical Society, and entrusted Széchenyi with the task of answering Duponceau's letter. The original Hungarian draft of Széchenyi's letter was published in Béla Majláth, *ed., Gróf Széchenyi István levelei.* Vol. 2. Budapest, 1891, pp. 15-16. (See its English translation under "Document. Széchenyi and Cultural Exchange." A letter to Pierre Du Ponceau. By G. Barany in *Journal of Central European Affairs,* vol. 20, no. 3, Oct. 1960, pp. 312-313.)

¹¹John Vaughan's 2-page reply of March 26, 1833, housed also in the APSL, is quite illegible due to unknown causes. Its conclusion reads as follows: "We look up to you for a continuance of your interesting correspondence . . ."

¹²APSL. Stated Meeting, 19th April, 1833. Peter Duponceau, president, APS, was elected a foreign corresponding member of the Hungarian Academy of Sciences at its fourth general assembly, November 15, 1833. See *A Magyar Tudós Társaság Évkönyvei.* Vol. 2. 1832-1834. Buda, Kir. Egyetem nyomt., 1835, p. 47.

¹³The November 15, 1833 meeting of the APS, see its minutes in the APSL, dealing with the Nagy letter, says: "A letter was read from M. Nagy of Pest in Hungary acknowledging the honor done him by his election as a member of this Society, and communicating some particulars in relation to a telescope made by Plössel, optical instruments maker."

¹⁴Orig. manuscript in the APSL. See also Francis S. Wagner, "Széchenyi and the nationality problem in the Habsburg Empire," *Journal of Central European Affairs,* vol. 20, no. 3, Oct. 1960, p. 294. — At the May 24, 1834, weekly meeting arranged by the Hungarian Academy, Count Stephen Széchenyi who just returned from England, reported that the first volume of the *Yearbook* was sent to Philadelphia through an English merchant. Cf. *A Magyar Tudós Társaság Évkönyvei.* Vol. 2. 1832-1834, etc., p. 72.

¹⁵*Magyar tudós társasági Névkönyv, astronómiai napkönyvvel és kalendáriummal 1838-ra Nagy Károly r. tagtól.* Budán, 124 p. See also *Tudománytár.* Literatura. Vol. 2. Buda, 1838, p. 96.

¹⁶APS at its November 19, 1841 Stated Meeting dealt with Nagy's invariable pendulum and adopted a favorable Resolution which was sent to the scientist in Vienna. Cf. orig. document in the APSL.

¹⁷The shipment was acknowledged by the APS at its November 5, 1852 meeting.

¹⁸See István Rusznyák's introductory words in György Rózsa, *ed., The Library of the*

Hungarian Academy of Sciences, 1826-1961. Budapest, Akadémiai Kiadó. 1960. p. 5-6. — For a general review of the foreign contacts of the Hungarian Academy of Sciences and its Library see also Ferenc Schedel (Toldy), *Az académiai könyvtár rövid története s mibenléte.* Buda, 1848, Egyet. ny., 31 p.; Gyula Haraszthy, *A 130 éves Akadémiai Könyvtár.* 1956. p. 23; Jenő Berlász and Mária Németh, *Az Akadémiai Könyvtár múltja és jelene.* 1956. p. 30; Mária Szentgyörgyi, "A Magyar Tudományos Akadémia Könyvtárának nemzetközi kapcsolatai," *A Könyvtáros,* vol. 7, no. 6, November 1957, pp. 416-418; Dóra F. Csanak, "Az Akadémiai Könyvtár története a szabadságharcig," *Magyar Könyvszemle,* vol. 75, no. 1, 1959, pp. 47-73.

Győrffy, György, *The original landtaking of the Hungarians.* Budapest: Hungarian National Museum, 1975.

Hajdú, Péter, ed., *Uráli népek: nyelvrokonaink kultúrája és hagyományai.* Budapest: Corvina, 1975.

Gabriel, Astrik L., *Garlandia. Studies in the history of the mediaeval university.* Frankfurt a.M.: Knecht, 1969.

Gabriel, Astrik L., *The mediaeval universities of Pécs and Pozsony; commemoration of the 500th and 600th anniversary of their foundation, 1367-1467-1967.* Notre Dame, Ind.: Mediaeval Institute, University of Notre Dame, 1969.

Kardos, Tibor, ed., *Janus Pannonius: tanulmányok.* Budapest: Akadémiai Kiadó, 1975.

Horváth, János, *A magyar irodalmi műveltség kezdetei: Szent Istvántól Mohácsig.* Budapest: Magyar Szemle Társaság, 1944.

Horváth, János, *Az irodalmi műveltség megoszlása: magyar humanizmus.* Budapest: Magyar Szemle Társaság, 1944.

Eckhardt, Sándor, *A francia forradalom eszméi Magyarországon.* Budapest: Franklin Társulat, 1924.

Domanovszky, Sándor, ed., *Magyar művelődéstörténet.* 5 v. Budapest: Magyar Történelmi Társulat, 1939-42.

Kornis, Gyula, *Hungary and European civilisation.* Budapest: Royal Hungarian University Press, 1938.

Nékám, Lajos, *The cultural aspirations of Hungary from 896 to 1935.* Budapest, 1935.

A companion to Hungarian studies, with a pref. by Count Stephen Bethlen. Budapest: Society of the Hungarian Quarterly, 1943.

Radisics, Elemér, ed., *A Dunatáj, történelmi, gazdasági és földrajzi adatok a Dunatáj államainak életéből.* Budapest: Gergely R. r.t., 1946.

Várkonyi, Nándor, *Dunántúl.* Budapest, Magvető Kiadó, 1975.

Köpeczi, Béla, *A magyar kultúra harminc éve, 1945-1975.* Budapest: Kossuth Könyvkiadó, 1975.

Sőtér, István, *A sas és a serleg: akadémiai arcképek.* Budapest: Akadémiai Kiadó, 1975.

A Magyar Tudományos Akadémia másfél évszázada, 1825-1975. Főszerkesztő Pach Zsigmond Pál. Írta Kónya Sándor (et al). Budapest: Akadémiai Kiadó, 1975.

Information Hungary. Erdei, Ferenc, ed., Budapest: Akadémiai Kiadó, 1968.

PART II—THE MATHEMATICAL AND THE NATURAL SCIENCES

Mathematics

In mathematics, physics and several branches of the natural sciences, Hungarians displayed remarkable creative genius. Since the closing years of the fifteenth century they have assumed an active role in Europe's intellectual life. At the outset Hungarian scientists seemed to be only very industrious disciples. Georgius (György) of Hungary published his *Arithmetica* in the Netherlands in Latin as early as 1499 which is regarded as one of the very first books ever written on the subject. But the Turkish occupation of a century and a half hindered any real progress. Following the country's liberation from the Turkish yoke, György Maróthi (1715-1744), a Debrecen schoolmaster, wrote a model Hungarian mathematical textbook (*Arithmetica*, 1743) which for many decades served as a guide for teachers and beginning students of mathematics. Until the appearance of the Bolyais, father and son, the period should be considered rather a preparatory one.

Mathematician-astronomer Miksa Hell (1720-1792) was the son of Mátyás Cornelius Hell, chief mathematician of the Selmec mines. Having graduated from Vienna University's Faculty of Philosophy, he taught at Lőcse (now Levoca, Czechoslovakia), Zsolna (now Zilina, Czechoslovakia), and Kolozsvár (now Cluj, Romania). He helped establish and modernize observatories at the University of Nagyszombat (now Trnava, Czechoslovakia), in Kolozsvár, Eger (Hungary), and Vienna where he was appointed director of the observatory. Miksa Hell was regarded a great authority by European astronomers for his mathematically well-based observations which are partly described in his astronomy yearbook *Ephemerides astronomicae ad anni . . . ad meridianum Vindobonense*, published between 1757 and 1793. His many-sided interests (astronomy, mathematics, geography, history, etc.) are reflected in the prolificness of his publications. Miklós Konkoly-Thege (1842-1916) although a versatile scientist, was above all an astronomer. In 1871 he built his own Ógyalla (now Stará Dala, Czechoslovakia) meteorological and geomagnetic observatory which was recognized throughout the world. Among his several inventions are the Konkoly-Thege diagrams which are still used today. A. Kopff, former president of the Astronomische Gesellschaft, in 1942 acknowledged the uniqueness of Konkoly-Thege's accomplishments when he stated that . . . . "Konkoly-Thege was the first to conduct astrophysical investigations and is now considered the founder of this young discipline." Jenő Gothard (1857-1909) under the influence of Konkoly-Thege became an astronomer and constructed his private observatory at his estate in Hereny, Vas County, near the city of Szombathely. (See his article "A herenyi astrophysikai observatorium leírása és az abban tett megfigyelések 1881-ben" in *A Magyar Tudományos Akadémia Értesítője*, no. 3, 1882, p. 1-35). Gothard was one of the fathers of astrophysics. He designed and constructed a number of photographic and spectroscopic instruments and furthered the growth of amateur photography. According to J. M. Eder: . . . "a Hungarian amateur (Jenő Gothard) has fought for and established the right of photography in the domain of astronomy."

Research in mathematics and pure geometry starts with the Bolyais. Farkas Bolyai (1775-1856), the father, studied in Göttingen where he forged a lifelong friendship with Karl Friedrich Gauss (1777-1855), the greatest mathematician of all time. Having finished his studies Farkas Bolyai returned to Marosvásárhely (Transylvania) and via frequent correspondence with Gauss they continued their fruitful cooperation. Farkas Bolyai was the first to recognize the significance of axiomatic methods in his Latin-language *Tentamen* (1832-1833), and made several strikingly new, innovative statements on integral calculus as well as the theory of sets. He tried unsuccessfully to prove Euclid's parallel postulate. Educated by his father, Farkas Bolyai, and trained in the spirit of Karl Gauss, János Bolyai (1802-1860) wrote his *Absolute Science of Space (Appendix scientiam spatii absolute veram exhibens)* in Latin as an *Appendix* to the first volume of *Tentamen*. János Bolyai succeeded in proving that both his father and K. Gauss attempted in vain, showing that Euclid's parallel postulate was not necessary and that a whole system of geometry could be based on the pseudosphere of Beltrami. János Bolyai had already proven the 5th Euclidean postulate (the axiom of parallelism) around 1820 — much earlier than the Russian Nikolai Ivanovich Lobacnevskii (1793-1856) in 1829. Bolyai referred to this discovery in a letter addressed to his father, Farkas Bolyai, on November the 3rd, 1823 exulting that . . . "I have created a new world from nothingness — Semmiből egy új, más világot teremtettem . . ." Bolyai's revolutionary paper on absolute geometry opened new horizons in physics and even in philosophy. His discovery refuted the Kantian concept of "a priori space." Thus János Bolyai with the Russian Nikolai Ivanovich Lobachevskii was the founder of non-Euclidean geometry.

The epoch-making significance of Bolyai's discovery was recognized only years later when mathematical thought had adequately advanced and various schools had come into existence.

In Hungary the last quarter of the nineteenth century meant the breakthrough in mathematical thinking. After the decades — long standstill following the work of the Bolyais, two brilliant schools of mathematics were founded. One school of mathematicians grouped around the professors of the Budapest University of Technical Sciences (Műegyetem) and the other school was developed at the University of Kolozsvár which later transferred to Szeged. In the first school Jenő Hunyadi (1838-1889), a pioneer of linear algebra, accomplished great results in the theory of conic sections which earned him an international reputation. Gyula König (1849-1913) also recognized internationally for his proofs of some basic theses of the theory of sets.

In the other school of mathematics, at the University of Kolozsvár, Gyula Farkas (1847-1930) excelled chiefly in mechanics and his investigations into linear disparity expanded the horizons of mathematical thought.

During the first years of the twentieth century, many young mathematicians appeared on the scene as the products of the then already famous Hungarian mathematical schools. Lipót Fejér and Frigyes Riesz should be the first of these to be mentioned, all the more because both of them created by means of a long line of gifted disciples a school of mathematics.

Lipót Fejér (1880-1959) is considered one of the country's foremost mathematicians. He spent the 1899-1900 academic year in Berlin and there, under the influence of H. A. Schwarz, his attention turned to the Fourier's series. He published his first treatise of major importance in 1900 entitled *Sur les fonctions bornées et intégrables* (Paris). Many of his studies were published in German. Fejér laid the foundations for the modern theory of trigonometric series, thereby giving impetus to research in analysis. He taught mathematics first at Kolozsvár then at Budapest University. For his international renown Fejér was elected member of the division of mathematics and physics of the Göttingen Scientific Society, the Bavarian and Polish academies of sciences and the Calcutta mathematical society, to mention a few. Lipót Fejér was one of four of the most outstanding European scientists invited to the Chicago World Exhibition in 1933.

Frigyes Riesz (1880-1956) finished his university studies at Budapest, Zürich and Göttingen. Professor of mathematics at the University of Kolozsvár (later Szeged) from 1911 to 1945 and then at Budapest University until his death, Riesz had a great part in making Szeged one of the world centers of mathematical research. Together with Alfréd Haár (1885-1933) he began in 1922 the periodical *Acta Scientiarum Mathematicarum* in which many famous papers were published. Frigyes Riesz' most known achievement was the so-called Riesz-Fischer theorem in the domain of the theory of real functions. His role is widely acknowledged in the development of abstract spaces, Riesz is also well known as one of the founders of functional analysis, a branch of modern mathematics. His monograph *Les systèmes d'équations linéaires à une infinité d'inconnues* (Paris, 1913) is considered a turning point in the field of functional analysis. His work co-authored by Béla Szőkefalvi-Nagy (*Leçons d'analyse fonctionelle* . . .) was a bestseller on world market and was translated into several languages.

József Kürschák (1864-1933) as a pupil of Gyula König, started his research and was associated with the Budapest University of Technical Sciences (Műegyetem) since 1891. Kürschák's research fields include investigations into determinants, matrices and the theory of numbers which brought him worldwide recognition. He took part in preparing mathematical curricula for the school reforms transpiring at the turn of the century.

One of the greatest mathematicians of our time, John von Neumann, was born in 1903 in Budapest (d. 1957, Washington, D.C.). Von Neumann attended the famous Lutheran High School (Evangélikus Gimázium) at Budapest. Then he studied chemistry at the Eidgenössische Technische Hochschule in Zürich and took his degree in 1926. Von Neumann obtained his Ph.D. in mathematics in Budapest in 1927. Afterwards studying in Göttingen, Berlin and Hamburg he went to Princeton University in 1931 as a lecturer but in a short time he was functioning as professor of mathematical physics. In 1933 he joined the newly founded Institute for Advanced Study, Princeton, New Jersey, as research professor of mathematics and remained a member of the Institute until his death. In 1945 von Neumann was appointed director of the Electronic Computer Project, Institute for Advanced Study, Princeton, N.J., which under his guidance developed several major electronic computers. After some basic research his attention turned to quantum mechanics and his monograph *Mathematical Foundations of Quantum Mechanics* (1932) has remained the standard treatise on the subject. Von Neumann's interest extended to several questions of applied mathematics and he was one of the founders of the theory of games, a momentous accomplishment. The application of the theory of games to economics is likewise of great significance. Its results were published in cooperation with economist Oskar Morgenstern under the title *Theory of Games and. Economic Behavior* (1944). Von Neumann's research work decisively influenced the progress in the theory of computing machines and automata. During World War II von Neumann took part in the development of the atomic bomb, and because of his achievements became a member of the U.S. Atomic Energy Commission.

Károly Jordán (1871-1959) did pioneering work in the fields of mathematical statistics and the calculus of probabilities (*Statistique mathématique*. Paris, 1927).

Between the world wars and afterwards, many noted mathematicians emigrated to Great Britain and especially to the United States. Among them, Pál Dienes (1882-1952) went to England and became professor at Birkbeck College. His monograph *The Taylor Series; An Introduction to the Theory of Functions of a Complex Variable* (New York, 1957) is still widely used and appreciated. John G. Kemeny (b. 1926), president of Dartmouth College, has been active in several fields of mathematical research, namely in mathematical analysis, business mathematics and in investigations into Markov processes. Pál Erdős (b. 1913) completed his studies in Budapest, and since 1934 has lived in Great Britain and the United States. His main fields of interest include the theory of numbers along with the calculus of probabilities, etc. His international distinction is based on more than 500 publications.

Since the conclusion of World War II a great number of internationally famed mathematicians have been working in a multiplicity of spheres, classical and applied alike. For example, Pál Turán (b. 1910), professor at Budapest University, is especially versed in the theory of numbers and mathematical analysis. Turán discovered an entirely new method of analysis (*Eine neue Methode in der Analysis und deren Anwendungen*, 1953) which has been translated into English and Chinese.

Following a line of great tradition, many a Hungarian mathematician has extended the work of Frigyes Riesz — foremost among them his one-time closest associate, Béla Szőkefalvi-Nagy (b. 1913). Szőkefalvi-Nagy was trained by his father, Gyula, also a noted mathematician, and by Frigyes Riesz with whom he collaborated for many years. He has been professor of mathematical analysis at Szeged University since 1948. During 1964 he was guest professor at Columbia University, New York City, and in 1970 at Indiana University. He is a leading world authority on functional and mathematical analysis. Several of his treatises have been published in English, German, French, Russian and Chinese. His first standard work appeared in Berlin in 1942 under the title *Spektraldarstellung linearer Transformationen des Hilbertschen Raumes*. Szőkefalvi-Nagy received an honorary doctorate from the Dresden University of Technical Sciences and from the Turku University, and was elected (foreign) member of the Academy of Sciences of the Soviet Union.

Algebra has played a prominent role in contemporary research. Alfréd Rényi (b. 1921) and László Rédei (b. 1900) and their associates have achieved international fame in this discipline. Rédei's main fields of investigation embrace many algebraic and geometrical problems, most importantly the theory of numbers. His major work, (*Algebra*, 1954), was published in English as well as German. In addition to Rédei, internationally valued work in geometry has been done by a great many other specialists, among them György Hajós (b. 1912), Ottó Varga (b. 1909), László Fejes Tóth (b. 1915) and Pál Szász (b. 1901). They rank high and follow the best traditions of Hungarian science as once represented by Béla Kerékjártó (1898-1946) who produced lasting results in the theory of topological groups and in projective geometry. László Fejes Tóth was guest professor at Freiburg (1960-1961) and at the University of Wisconsin (USA, 1963-1964).

Rózsa Péter (b. 1905) has distinguished herself as a researcher in the foundations of mathematics and has carried on noteworthy investigations into recursive functions. Her *Rekursive Funktionen* (1951, 1957) has been translated into English (*Recursive Functions*. 3d rev. ed., 1967), Russian and Chinese. Since 1937 Ms. Péter has been on the editorial boards of *The Journal of Symbolic Logic* (Princeton, New Jersey) and since 1955 of the *Zeitschrift für mathematische Logik und Grundlagen der Mathematik* (issued in East Germany). Her *Játék a végtelennel: matematika kívülállóknak* (*Playing with infinity* . . . New York: Simon & Shuster, 1961, 1962) has reached a magnitude of 20 editions in 10 languages.

László Kalmár (b. 1905) deals chiefly with mathematical logic, cybernetics and several other practical topics of applied mathematics about which he has published several papers at home and abroad. It should also be mentioned that Alfréd Rényi with his co-workers has applied with outstanding success the calculus of probabilities and the methods of mathematical statistics to many practical problems.

György Pólya (b. 1887) obtained his doctorate in mathematics in Budapest then continued his studies at Göttingen and Königsberg. In 1914 as an associate and in 1928 as professor he joined the teaching staff of the Eidgenössische Technische Hochschule in Zürich, Switzerland. Since 1940 Pólya has lived in the United States, and taught first at Brown then at Stanford universities. Significant results have been produced by Pólya in the theory of real and complex functions, probability calculus, and the methodology of mathematical problem-solving. His collection of mathematical problems (co-authored by Gábor Szegő) entitled *Aufgaben und Lehrsätze aus der Analysis* (2 v., 1925, 1959) is considered an indispensable textbook.

Gábor Szegő (b. 1895) studied at Budapest and Vienna (Austria) universities then taught at Berlin and Königsberg. Since 1934 Szegő has resided in the United States and been on the faculties of Washington and Stanford universities. He pursued important studies in the fields of mathematical analysis and the orthogonal functions. In 1965 Szegő became an honorary member of the Hungarian Academy of Sciences.

It is impossible for lack of space to survey in toto, however superficially, the activities of those Hungarian mathematicians who have greatly contributed to the history of their science. It is an established fact that noted mathematics professors of Hungarian descent can be found all over the world and especially in the United States. Before closing this chapter we would like to answer one important question as to the future contingent of first-class Hungarian mathematicians. One prediction can safely and easily be made in a very promising direction, and it is underlined by the simple fact that since 1945 the mathematical olympic games of the high-school students of the Soviet Union and all other European socialist countries has been made a permanent institution in the service of training and directing young mathematicians. It is noteworthy to state that Hungary's high-school students have won these mathematical contests every single year as individuals as well as team workers. This fact in itself seems to be a guarantee of the past and present achievements in the future of Hungarian mathematics.

Bolyai-levelek. Bucharest: Kriterion, 1975.

Bonola, Roberto, *Non-Euclidean geometry; a critical and historical study of its developments.* New York: Dover Publications, 1955.

Gauss, Karl Friedrich, *Briefwechsel Carl Friedrich Gauss und Wolfgang Bolyai.* New York: Johnson Reprint Corp., 1972.

Livanova, Anna Mikhailovna, *Tri sudby.* Moskva: Znanie, 1969.

Stäckel, Paul Gustav, comp., *Wolfgang und Johann Bolyai: geometrische Untersuchungen.* New York: Johnson Reprint Corp., 1972.

Rados Gusztáv, *Kürschák József emlékezete* (MTA emlékbeszédek, Budapest, 1934).

Jordán, Károly, *Chapters on the classical calculus of probability.* Budapest: Akadémiai Kiadó, 1972.

Benedick, Jeanne, *Mathematics illustrated dictionary; facts, figures, and people including the new math.* New York: McGraw Hill, 1965.

Herland, Leo Joseph, *Dictionary of mathematical sciences.* 2d ed., rev. and enlarged. London-Toronto, 1966.

Langford, Thomas A., *Intellect and hope; essays in the thought of Michael Polanyi.* Durham, N.C., 1968.

The Universal encyclopedia of mathematics. London: Allen & Unwin, 1964.

Physics

The country's physicists have also made extraordinary strides in the international advancement of their scientific branch. Despite the unfavorable circumstances prevailing immediately upon the death of the Renaissance king, Matthias Corvinus, there were always individuals even in the darkest times of the Turkish occupation whose scientific activities helped the European community of scientists. Let us count among those individuals, for instance, Izsák Czabán (Zabanius) the first known advocate of atomic theory in his *Existentia atomorum* (1667). János Pósaházi (d. 1686), one of the masters of the famous Sárospatak School where Johann Amos Comenius, the world famous Czech educator taught for years (1650-1654), compiled an early bestseller of his age on physics in 1667 entitled *Philosophia naturalis*. Pósaházi who had studied at Utrecht and Franeker through this book helped educate future generations of mathematicians in his native land and elsewhere in Europe.

Somewhat later, in 1678, Márton Szilágyi Tönkő from Debrecen authored the first monograph on Cartesian physics in Hungary.

Gradually, Debrecen became an important cultural center of the nation. One of the century's foremost physicists, András Segner (1704, Pozsony-1777, Halle) began his higher educational studies at the Debrecen College in 1724. A year later he enrolled in the Medical Faculty at Jena and simultaneously studied mathematics and physics there. In 1730 he obtained his medical diploma and immediately began his medical practice in Pozsony. The following year Segner began practicing medicine at Debrecen as the city physician. Afterwards between 1733 and 1755 Segner worked as professor of physics, mathematics and chemistry at Göttingen University and then taught physics, mathematics and astronomy at Halle, Germany. Segner achieved noteworthy results in fluid mechanics as well as in the mechanics of solids. Among his multi-faceted endeavors, the domain of hydraulics is registered in the history of science as the most important. András Segner happened to be the first scientist who introduced into investigations the notion of surface tension of liquids and invented the so-called Segner wheel, the ancestor of reaction-type turbines which he first described in 1740 in his Göttingen treatise under the title *Programma quo theoriam machinae cuiusdam hydraulicae praemittit*. Euler's turbine equations which established the theoretical foundations for the development of turbines were based upon Segner's experimental accomplishments. Furthermore, Segner also excelled as an outstanding mathematician of that age by producing, among other things, the first proof of Descartes' theory of signs. In return for his theoretically as well as practically important inventions, Segner was elected member of the Royal Society in 1739, and of the Berlin Academy in 1747, and of the Göttingen Royal Scientific Society in 1751. The St. Petersburg Academy also elected Segner as its member in 1754. Karl Keller, a Segner biographer ("Johannes Andreas Segner" in *Beitrag zur Geschichte der Technik und Industrie*, 1913, p. 54-72) and all the leading historians of technology regarded Segner as the father of the turbine.

Some decades later Segner was followed and even surpassed by Ányos Jedlik (1800, Szimő — 1895, Győr) a Benedictine monk, a genius in experimental physics. Between 1840 and 1878 Jedlik taught physics at Budapest University. At the beginning of his scientific career he dealt with chemistry, electrochemistry and electricity. Later, in addition to electricity, Jedlik engaged in optical experiments. During the years 1827-1828, Jedlik conducted experiments which finally resulted in the invention of the first electromotor in the history of technology. This electromotor worked on the basis of electromagnetic effect. With this invention Ányos Jedlik became the first physicist-technologist who as early as 1827 successfully transformed electrical energy into revolving motion. Jedlik made several improvements on his electromotor in order to demonstrate that the electromotor is suitable for driving vehicles, and in 1855 he designed a model for an electric motorcoach. In the second half of 1850, Jedlik developed the first unipolar machine. In connection with relevant experiments he discovered — six years earlier than either Werner Siemens and Charles Wheatstone did — the principle of the dynamo and then constructed the first model of his dynamo-electric motor. His unipolar machine seems to be of utmost importance all the more because J. Noegerrath invented his unipolar generator for practical use a full half century later in 1905.

Ányos Jedlik's third extremely important invention was the construction of his "electrostatic machine", a high-capacity electric condenser. For this invention, as recommended by Werner Siemens himself, the "Medal for Progress" was awarded to Jedlik at the 1873 Vienna World Exhibition. This equipment was an early form of impulse-generators which are now applied in nuclear engineering research. His experiments on light interference conducted already in the 1860's were also regarded as pioneer enterprises. The epochal character of Jedlik's lifework was highly valued by Loránd Eötvös, his successor in professorship at Budapest University. Eötvös did much in Europe's professional circles to have the priority of Jedlik's inventions acknowledged.

Out of his fifty-three years as physics teacher, Jedlik spent 38 years at the university level. During his educational career he wrote the first physics textbook in 1850 and with his successor, Loránd Eötvös, educated the subsequent generations of the country's physicists.

Loránd Eötvös' (1848-1919) university studies including his doctoral degree were completed at Heidelberg under such professors as Kirchoff, Bunsen and Helmholtz. Very soon he became the greatest Hungarian scientist of theoretical and experimental physics. In 1872 Eötvös was appointed to the chair of theoretical physics at Budapest University. From 1870 on for about two decades Eötvös examined capillary phenomena and worked out an entirely new method for measuring surface tension: the widely used Eötvös' reflection method. Through theoretical reasoning Eötvös recognized the correlation between surface tension and molecular weights of liquids measured at different temperatures. In doing so he discovered the so-called Eötvös Law (1866). The Eötvös' Law was declared by Albert Einstein to be one of the pillars of his theory of relativity. For many years Eötvös studied the problem of gravity and designed the world-renowned Eötvös Torsion Balance (Pendulum) which measured the minute changes of gravity and determined the distribution of masses in the earth's crust. The Eötvös Torsion Balance is still used all over the world for gravity measurements and for exploring natural resources. His ingenious method of measurements won him the prestigious Göttingen Benecke Prize. His method was subsequently improved upon by his disciples and the American Dicke.

Eötvös finally extended his research into the field of electromagnetism and designed appropriate instruments for this purpose. He also called geophysicists' attention to the presence of Coriolis force and thus gave new proof of the earth's rotation. Eötvös' contribution to science has always been highly valued by the international community. In remembrance of the eightieth anniversary of the first measurements by the Eötvös Torsion Balance (1891) the Hungarian Academy of Sciences sent commemorative photographs and literature to the world's leading geophysicists of today. Sigmund Hammer's letter of thanks is typical and reflects fully the deep appreciation of Eötvös' work existing even in our decade. Sigmund Hammer, professor of geology-geophysics at the University of Wisconsin, said in his letter addressed to professor György Barta of Hungary: "I deeply appreciate your thoughtfulness and kind generosity in sending me photographs and literature celebrating the 80th Anniversary of the beginning of active field operations by the Eötvös Torsion Balance. I will prize these very highly for the rest of my life. The World owes a great debt to your illustrious Countryman. As a small return for your great kindness to me, I am enclosing a reproduction of the Torsion Balance map which led to *the first* oil field discovery by geophysicists in the western hemisphere. I have distributed this little map to hundreds of my students and co-workers in geology and geophysics. It was traced from Dr. Barton's paper 'The Eötvös Torsion Balance Method of Mapping Geologic Structure', Technical Publication No. 50, American Institute of Mining and Metallurgical Engineers,

1930.'' (Cf. *Magyar Tudomány*, June 1972, p. 395-396). The use of the Eötvös Torsion Balance has been a landmark in geological research and prospecting and was instrumental in the discovery of oil fields in Texas, Venezuela, the Zala oil fields in Hungary, etc.

Eötvös founded a school of geophysics. His assistant at Budapest University between 1883 and 1893 was Radó Kövesligethy (1862-1934), himself a world famous seismologist whose monographs on mathematical and astronomical geography (1899) and on the universe (1906), as well as his Latin-language *Seismonomia* (Modena, 1906), are still highly valued and his findings positively discussed at today's international symposia.

Since Eötvös' work, his countrymen's studies in gravitation, geomagnetism and seismology have been notable. Among them the achievements of László Egyed (b. 1914), head of the Budapest University's Institute of Geophysics, deserve special mention. He has contributed much in the spirit of Eötvös to the science of geophysics. The international community of geophysicists has focused growing attention on Egyed's investigations into the inner layers of the earth. In connection with the latter, László Egyed developed an entirely new theory relating to the expansion of the earth's inner structure. His main works on geophysics (1956) and earthquakes (1966) have been interpreted in several foreign languages.

Since the end of World War II, research has focused rather on experimental physics for the simple reason that scientific tasks in present-day Hungary are quite parallel with national economic plans. No wonder physical research is under the supervision of the Hungarian Academy of Sciences at its Central Institute for Physical Research as opposed to being concentrated at university institutes. Since the mid-thirties experimental physicists have undergone part of their training at the well-equipped laboratories of the United Incandescent Lamp and Electric Factory (Egyesült Izzólámpa és Villamossági Rt., Budapest), and more recently have received training in cooperation with several foreign institutes, above all, at the United Atomic Research Institute of Dubna in the U.S.S.R.

It is worth mentioning that the world's first crypton bulb was manufactured by the United Incandescent Lamp and Electric Factory.

The task of describing principal achievements in contemporary physics is a time- and space-consuming enterprise. Therefore, I will restrict my discussion to internationally renowned physicists, though there are many other physicists who have also obtained remarkable results who enjoy but national recognition.

The late Károly Novobátzky (b. 1884) worked out a uniform space theory and the electrodynamics of insulating materials. Novobátzky founded a new school of theoretical physics.

Lajos Jánossy (b. 1912) worked abroad as a physicist — between 1934 and 1950 in Berlin, London, Manchester and from 1947 to 1950 as the head of the laboratory for cosmic radiation at the Dublin Institute for Advanced Studies. He developed the mathematical apparatus of the theory of cosmic radiation. Jánossy's monographs on cosmic radiation, theory of relativity, quantum theory and the problem of the application of the calculus of probabilities in physics were published first in English, later in German, Russian, Bulgarian, and Hungarian.

In nuclear physics the late Pál Gombás (b. 1909); Lajos Jánossy; Lénárd Pál; Ervin Fenyves (b. 1924) and György Marx (b. 1927) have done valuable research work at the U.S.S.R.'s United Atomic Research Institute of Dubna.

Ágoston Budó (b. 1914) and István Kovács (b. 1913) excell in the study of the structure of molecular spectra and arouse the interest of scientists outside Hungary.

György Marx deals highly successfully with the physics of elementary particles, worked out the theory of neutrino emission of the earth and sun. His work on quantum mechanics has appeared, in addition to Hungarian, in Czech and Russian.

Between the world wars and afterwards many well-trained physicists left the country and found excellent opportunities abroad, especially in the United States, to continue their already well-known physical research work.

Cornelius Lánczos (b. 1893) is one of the outstanding physicists and mathematicians of our age. His works on mathematical physics, Fourier series and linear differential operators were published in Great Britain and the United States. For many years Lánczos was a close collaborator and assistant of Albert Einstein and made valuable contributions to the theory of relativity. His monograph entitled *The Einstein decade, 1905-1915* (New York: Academic Press, 1974) is an indispensable survey and characterization of his master's work.

Since 1933 Michael Polanyi (b. 1891) has lived in England. His manifold areas of expertise embrace physicochemistry, sociology and philosophy which is a very rare phenomenon in our age of specialization. Polanyi's investigations into the structure of metals and the adsorption of gases are significant. Interestingly, since about 1945 Polanyi's interest has been devoted to the problems of epistemology and the philosophy of science and in recent years his research, lecturing and publishing in these fields have earned him a world reputation.

Hungarian-born physicists, Edward Teller (b. 1908), the "father of the hydrogen bomb," Leo Szilard (1898-1964), and Eugene P. Wigner (b. 1902) worked closely with Enrico Fermi and helped persuade Albert Einstein to write his historic letter in 1939 to President F. D. Roosevelt that meant the start of the U.S. atomic-bomb project (The Manhattan

Project). These Hungarian physicists received the highest honors that science and the United States can bestow and they rank among the architects of the atomic age.

Teller studied at Budapest, Karlsruhe, Munich, and Leipzig and emigrated to America in 1935. By 1941 he was part of the research group of Enrico Fermi that produced the first nuclear chain reaction. In 1958 Teller was appointed director of the U.S. second weapons laboratory at Livermore, California. He also functioned as professor of physics at the University of California at Berkeley. In 1962 the U.S. Atomic Energy Commission conferred the Enrico Fermi Award on Edward Teller.

Leo Szilard since the beginning of the twenties has been associated with the Institute of Theoretical Physics at the University of Berlin. In the year of the Nazi takeover (1933) Szilard left Berlin and after a brief stay in Vienna went to London. In 1937 he joined the staff of Columbia University in New York. Between 1942 and 1945 he conducted research in nuclear physics at the University of Chicago and helped Enrico Fermi's team design the first nuclear reactor which commenced operation at the University of Chicago on December 2, 1942. His work was highly instrumental in initiating the Manhattan Project which developed the first atomic bomb. After the first use of the atomic bomb Szilard became so disillusioned that he advocated the peaceful use of atomic energy and international control of nuclear weapons. As a consequence, he received the Atoms for Peace Award in 1959.

Evidently, Hungarian physicists have scored considerable successes in world relations in this century, and two of them — Eugene P. Wigner and Dennis (Dénes) Gábor were awarded the Nobel Prize for Physics. Eugene P. Wigner like John von Neumann attended the Lutheran High School in Budapest. He started his career as a chemical engineer but very soon his interest turned to theoretical physics which he taught at the Berlin Technische Hochschule then at Princeton University and the University of Wisconsin. In 1936 he evolved the theory of neutron absorption which was utilized in constructing nuclear reactors, after which he worked out his law of parity conservation. In the years of World War II, Wigner was in charge of the group concerned with the theory of chain reaction and the basic design for the plutonium-producing reactors at Hanford, Washington. For some years professor of theoretical physics at Princton University after the war, he was subsequently appointed a member of the General Advisory Committee to the U.S. Atomic Energy Commission. In 1963 Wigner won the Nobel Prize for Physics for his extraordinary contributions to nuclear physics including his formulation of the law of conservation of parity. Eugene Wigner has published extensively on theoretical and nuclear physics, and is the author of *Group Theory* and *Symmetries and Reflections: Scientific Essays*, and over 200 papers in physics. In addition to authoring, he has edited several books, among them *Survival & the Bomb; Methods of Civil Defense* published in 1969 (Chapter 4, entitled "Human Behavior in Disaster: the Siege of Budapest" contributed by Francis S. Wagner). Dennis Gábor (1900, Budapest) completed his studies in electrical engineering at Budapest and Charlottenburg, Berlin. From 1927 to 1933 he worked as a research engineer in Berlin for the Siemens-Halske firm. The years 1934 to 1948 found him working at Rugby in the British Thompson Houston Company's research laboratory. In 1949 Gábor joined the staff of the Imperial College of Science and Technology, and in 1958 he became professor of applied electron physics there. He also conducted research on high-speed oscilloscopes, physical optics, television as well as on communication theory. He won the Nobel Prize for Physics in 1971 for his invention of holography, a system of lenseless three-dimensional photography which can be applied in an abundance of fields including computer technology, topographic mapmaking and medicine. His papers on holography are among his most important publications.

Maria Telkes (b. 1900, Budapest) has lived in the United States since the early twenties and devoted her research mostly to energy conversion. She has long been acknowledged as a pioneering authority in the use of solar energy. Telkes has been associated with several prestigious U.S. research organizations, among them Westinghouse, the Massachusetts Institute of Technology, the University of Pennsylvania, and the University of Delaware.

Joseph Lindmayer, formerly with the Hungarian Academy of Sciences, has also conducted research in solar energy utilization. In his other field of interest he published the *Fundamentals of semiconductor devices* (Princeton, N.J., Van Nostrand, 1965. 486 p.). One-time department head of semiconductor physics of the Sprague Electric Company Research Center in North Adams, Mass., Lindmayer is currently branch manager of the Communication Satellite Corporation's Comsat Laboratories in Bethesda, Maryland.

One of the great physicists of our age, Zoltan Bay (b. 1900) is also a native of Hungary.* He was graduated (Ph.D., 1926) from the university of Budapest. From 1926 to 1930 he conducted research in the Physikalisch-Technische Reichsanstalt and in the Physikalisch-chemisches Institut of the University of Berlin. His experiments culminated in the first spectroscopic proof that active nitrogen gas contains free nitrogen atoms. In 1930 he obtained the chair of Theoretical Physics at the University of Szeged (Hungary). In 1936 he was invited to head

---

*This biographical sketch contains excerpts from a separate work of the author entitled *Fifty Years in the Laboratory; A Survey of the Research Activities of Physicist, Zoltan Bay*, by Francis S. Wagner.

the Research Laboratory of the United Incandescent Lamps and Electric Co. (Tungsram) in Budapest. Among several patents he developed the pioneer patent for electroluminiscence in 1939.

During World War II he was commanded by the Hungarian government to work on radar. Completely isolated from foreign literature, he developed the Hungarian military radar. After that he worked out an equipment to detect radar echoes from the moon. Hindered by the devastations of the war this work simultaneously with the independent similar work by the U.S. Army Signal Corps (led by J.H. De Witt), led to success in early 1946. These two experiments are now considered to be the starting accomplishments of Radar Astronomy. However, the Hungarian experiment, by introduction of the principle of repetition and long time integration, went one step further in the direction of later development. All modern radar astronomy systems take advantage of integration, first demonstrated in Bay's design.

While chief of the Tungsram Laboratory, Bay also headed the Institute of Atomic Physics established in 1938 at the Budapest University of Technical Sciences. In his research at the Institute of Atomic Physics, Bay introduced for the first time the principle of secondary electron multiplication in atomic counting, increasing thereby the speed of counting by 3 orders of magnitude. The new concept served as the basis for all subsequent high speed counting, e.g. for scintillation counters. By applying the new counters Bay worked out the first nanosecond coincidence circuits in 1943.

In 1948 Bay left Hungary for the United States. He continued his fast coincidence work at The George Washington University in Washington, D.C. By introduction of the principle of the differential coincidence circuit he could reduce the resolving time to a small fraction of a nanosecond, surpassing in that respect all other contemporary coincidence circuits. The application of his circuitry and that of his coincidence theory led to important results in the measurements of very short time intervals.

In 1955 Bay joined the National Bureau of Standards in Washington D.C. There he first conducted research into ionization by high energy particles in matter. By developing new techniques he improved the accuracy of the measurements of important constants and helped to clarify the theory of the ionization process.

After the advent of lasers around 1960, Bay's interest turned towards a new possibility of measuring the speed of light. In the course of his investigations he concluded that his new experimental design permitted the measurement of optical frequencies (a first in experimental physics) and that this opened the way to the first practical realization of a new measurement system in which the units of time and length are connected through the speed of light. This represents a breakthrough in measurement science.

Because the proposal urged for many years by Bay is now very close to being internationally accepted though the topic at the time of this writing has not been conclusively resolved, it seems appropriate to treat this subject in more detail in an Appendix.

Chemistry

Up to the middle of the nineteenth century, progress was very slow in chemistry, one of the reasons being that the country's industrial development did not show any encouraging signs and Hungary for a long period of time did not raise even its agricultural production to a considerable level. It is by no means surprising that under these circumstances chemistry could not be regarded as an independent branch of science but was associated with medicine. The first Hungarian book on chemistry was written by a physician, Ferenc Nyulas (1758-1808). His book dealt with the chemical analysis of medicinal waters of Transylvania (*Az erdélyországi orvosi vizeknek bontásáról*. Kolozsvár, 1800). Nyulas thus adopted and popularized the trend of chemical analysis. In addition, Ferenc Nyulas was one of the discoverers of manganese and described it long before Klaproth. In spite of Nyulas' work, chemistry remained a neglected branch of scientific activities for decades afterwards. Only a few individuals like János Irinyi (1819-1895) devoted some research to it. Irinyi conducted experiments which led to the invention and improvement of phosphorous matches.

Real progress came only in the second half of the nineteenth century, and was ushered in by Móric Preysz (1829, Sopron—1877, Budapest) who studied at Pest and in Vienna. Preysz demonstrated as early early as 1861 that the post-fermentation of the Tokaji wine (popularized in the United States under the name "Tokay") can be prevented if it is heated in a closed vessel at temperature of 70-80 C° which is then kept airtight. He demonstrated this method of preventing post-fermentation in Tokaji wine at the 1862 general meeting of the winemaking society of the Hegyalja region (Hegyaljai Bormívelő Egyesület) thus preceding by years Louis Pasteur (1822-1895) who presented his process of pasteurization only in 1865. The scientific world could not take cognizance of Móric Preysz' process because his relevant articles appeared in Hungarian periodicals ("Vélemény és indítvány a borok megtörésének elhárítására Nézve," *Gazdasági Lapok*, 1859; "Néhány szó azon módokról, melyek a bor romlásának meggátolására szolgálnak,"

Gazdasági Lapok, 1862; "A tokaji bor Utóerjedésének meggátlásáról," *Termtud. Közl.*, 1865).

Systematic and organized research in chemistry began with Károly Than (1834, Óbecse — 1908, Budapest). Obtaining his doctorate in chemistry in 1858 he then spent a year in Heidelberg as Bunsen's disciple after which his attention turned to physical chemistry and gasometry. From 1860 Than taught chemistry at Pest University, and in 1872 he established the No. 1 Institute of Chemistry at Pest University which in a while raised to European fame. Károly Than was instrumental in founding the *Magyar Kémiai Folyóirat* (Hungarian Periodical of Chemistry) in which outstanding and innovative articles have been published ever since. He was the first to discover carbonoxysulphide in the gases of the Harkány medicinal waters and later derived it experimentally. His methods for gas analysis were precise and his methods for volumetric analysis were internationally acclaimed and accepted. Furthermore, Than proved the atomic structure of electricity and his definition of chemical affinity was adopted verbatim as a model. As the founder of up-to-date higher education in chemistry in the country, Than established a school which trained the next generation of chemists. His main works include treatises on the unity of the volumetry of molecular weights (*A molekulasúlyok térfogatának egységéről*. Budapest, 1888); rudiments of qualitative chemical analysis (*A qualitativ chemiai analysis elemei*. Budapest, 1895).

In the second half of the nineteenth century the country's industrialization process — though being in an embryonic phase — brought about progress in several branches of the applied sciences, among them the field of chemical technology. Vince Wartha (1844-1914), a Bunsen disciple and from 1867 on professor of chemical technology at Budapest University of Technical Sciences, kept abreast of Western scientific advances. He specialized in the application of theoretical results in, for instance, wine chemistry, city water supply, ceramic manufacture, to mention a few. Vince Wartha pioneered in the analysis of eosin and devised a very good method for manufacturing eosin-glazed pottery. Vilmos Zsolnay (1828-1900) introduced Wartha's process in his porcelain and faience factory at Pécs in 1867 and started decorating earthenware with eosin glaze. As a result the Zsolnay products became world famous within a very short period of time.

Vince Wartha published many books and articles in his native Hungarian and German in Hungary and elsewhere. His first monograph appeared as early as 1867 in Zürich under the title *Die qualitative Analyse mit Anwendung der Bunsenschen Flammenreaktionen* which was translated into French in 1877.

The most talented member of Károly Than's school was Lajos Winkler (1863-1939) whose doctoral dissertation discussed the determination of oxygen dissolved in water (*A vízben feloldott oxigén meghatározása*, 1888). The method, described in his dissertation, is known as "Winkler's iodometric determination" and has become a classic in chemical analysis. Lajos Winkler acquired world fame by many of his accomplishments: interception of ammonia in tartaric acid solution, laying down new foundations for weight analysis, determination of the "Winkler's correlation" between the stability and inner friction of gases, etc. Owing to Winkler's determination of iodide and bromide, the analytics of halogens has since been considered in a world context to be a distinctively Hungarian branch of science. Winkler's process for iodine and bromine determination is even now widely applied. Several leading Hungarian chemists of the twentieth century were trained by Winkler. He published over 200 articles in foreign and Hungarian periodicals. His handbook dealing with chemical laboratory investigations was internationally acknowledged (*Untersuchungsverfahren für das chemische Laboratorium*. Stuttgart, 1936).

Elemér Schulek (1893-1964) was Lajos Winkler's assistant from 1918. In 1926 as a Rockefeller fellow Schulek made a study tour of the United States and some European countries to investigate their pharmaceutical industries. Appointed the head of the Chemistry Division of the National Institute of Health in Budapest in 1927, and in 1944 professor of inorganic and analytical chemistry at Budapest University, Elemér Schulek achieved meritorious results in the chemistry and application of halogen cyanides and interhalogens. His use of his own methods to research the systems of hydrogen peroxide and sulphuric acid is also noteworthy. Schulek, according to his critics, created solid foundations for the up-to-date analysis of drugs. His publications appeared in English, German, and Hungarian. One of his major works was published under the title *Az általános kvantitatív analitikai kémia elvi alapjai és módszerei*. (Co-author: Zoltán László Szabó. Budapest, 1966 — Theoretical foundations and methods of general quantitative analytical chemistry).

Aladár Buzágh (1895-1962) graduated from the Budapest University of Technical Sciences and was appointed research assistant at Budapest (Péter Pázmány) University. Professor Wolfgang Ostwald, the founder of colloid chemistry, invited Buzágh to Leipzig to become his assistant where Buzágh worked until 1925. Buzágh improved Ostwald's colloid chemistry research results and established the Ostwald-Buzágh sediment rule, as well as the Ostwald-Buzágh continuity theory. In 1939 Aladár Buzágh made a lecture tour of the United States. He also elaborated a quantitative method for measuring adhesion. His publications on colloid chemistry (*Kolloidik. Eine Einführung in die Kolloidwissenschaft*. Dresden, 1936; *Colloid Systems*. London, 1937) met with a very favorable reception throughout the world.

Colloid chemistry has been for decades in the focus of Hungarian scientists, a case in point being Richard Zsigmondy who as early as 1925 received a Nobel Prize for chemistry for the elucidation of the heterogeneous nature of colloidal solutions.

Most industrially developed countries of the world granted patents for József Varga's (1891-1956) inventions in mineral oil industry. Interestingly, József Varga participated in Hungary's public life between 1939 and 1943 in his capacity as minister of industry, later as minister of commerce and transportation, and finally as a member of parliament. At the beginning of his career, Varga occupied himself with the utilization of bauxites in the manufacture of cement. He obtained his most significant results in the preparation of synthetic gasoline and propellants. He is especially remembered in professional circles for the high-pressure hydrogenation of coal, and mineral oil. In this field his internationally valued discovery was the so-called "Varga-Effect" (hydrogen sulphide effect). After the conclusion of World War II Varga invented the hydrocracking process named after him for the hydrogenation of mineral oils and tars containing much asphalt under medium pressure. For the further development of his hydro-cracking process the Hungarian-East German Varga Research Society was formed. Varga published many articles in Hungary and abroad dealing with the results of his investigations. His two-volume set *Kémiai technológia* (Chemical technology, prepared with Károly Polinszky. Budapest, 1953-1961) deserves special mention.

Géza Zemplén (1883-1956) received his doctorate from the Budapest University in 1904. Afterwards he joined the research staff of Emil Abderhalden (1877-1950) in Berlin and studied the chemistry of enzymes. Later, also in Berlin, Zemplén became a close associate of Emil Fischer (1852-1919) and with Fischer engaged in the synthesis of amino acids. Géza Zemplén founded the first school of organic chemistry in Hungary. He performed internationally acknowledged research in the fields of carbohydrates and glycosides. He invented the Zemplén saponification method and a new technique for sugar decomposition bearing his name. His extensive treatise of carbohydrates (*Kohlenhydrate*. Berlin, Wien, 1922. XXIV, 1101 p.) ranks among his most important publications.

Best known in biochemistry, Albert Szent-Györgyi (b. 1893, Budapest) studied at the Budapest and Cambridge universities. Working at Cambridge University (1927, 1929) and at the Mayo Foundation, Rochester, Minnesota (1928) he isolated hexuronic acid (now called ascorbic acid or Vitamin C) from plant juice and adrenal gland extracts. Between 1931 and 1945 he taught medical chemistry at Szeged University. Szent-Györgyi was awarded the 1937 Nobel Prize in physiology and medicine for his discoveries in connection with the biological combustion processes with special reference to vitamin C and the catalysts of fumaric acid. He was the first to isolate vitamin C from paprika. Szent-Györgyi discovered a protein in muscle that he named "actin." In 1945 he was appointed professor of biochemistry at Budapest University. Emigrating to the U.S. in 1947, he became director of the Institute of Muscle Research at the Marine Biological Laboratory at Woods Hole, Mass. At the Institute he conducted investigations into the biochemistry of muscular action and into the causes of cell division, obtaining highly important results in the fields of cell respiration, the theory of cell oxidation, etc. He published many books and articles on biochemistry in English, German, and Hungarian. Among his most essential works are *On Oxidation, Fermentation, Vitamins, Health, and Disease* (1940), *Chemical Physiology of Contractions in Body and Heart Muscle* (1953), and *Introduction to a Submolecular Biology* (1960).

Since the mid-thirties Szent-Györgyi has exerted great influence upon his disciples in Hungary and elsewhere. Several of his closest research associates have produced internationally recognized studies: Bruno F. Straub (b. 1914), for one, ranks high among Szent-Györgyi's former assistants. A great number of biochemists — including the late Imre Szörényi (1901-1959) and particularly Bruno Straub — have engaged in protein research. As a Rockefeller fellow, Straub worked at Cambridge University from 1937 to 1939. After the war he taught biochemistry at Szeged (1945-1949) then medical chemistry at the Budapest University of Medical Sciences. In 1971 he was appointed Director General of the newly organized Szegedi Biológiai Kutató Központ (Szeged Biological Research Center of the Hungarian Academy of Sciences). Bruno Straub and his associates have significantly enriched our knowledge with their internationally valued investigations into the structure of enzymes, muscular action, cell respiration and protein synthesis. His *Biokémia*. (Budapest: Medicina, 1958. 600 p.) has been translated into a multitude of foreign languages, including German and Russian.

Biochemist Mihály Gerendás (1908-1976) graduated from Szeged University where he worked under the guidance of Albert Szent-Györgyi. In the meantime in 1938 Gerendás was an associate of professor Wartburg in Berlin. He was appointed to teach biochemistry at Budapest University in 1942. Gerendás conducted important investigations into the physiology of blood clotting and prepared bleeding reducing agents. Gerendás' therapy-oriented research produced several useful remedies and his literary activities served the same purpose, as was the case with his substantial contribution entitled *Thrombin-Fibrinprodukte und ihre Anwendung* (Budapest, 1963).

George Charles Hevesy (b. 1885, Budapest — 1966) developed isotopes as tracers in chemical research which earned him the 1943

Nobel Prize for Chemistry. Hevesy also discovered a new element: hafnium, a member of the zirconium ores. He studied and did research work in Berlin, at the University of Freiburg, and in 1911 Hevesy started working in Manchester under the direction of Ernest Rutherford (1871-1937), the famed British physicist, during which time Hevesy was encouraged to explore the application of radioactive isotopes as tracers. In 1912 he joined Friedrich Paneth's staff in Vienna where he greatly improved his isotopic tracer technique. The results of his lifework are summarized in his following publications: *Das Element Hafnium* (Berlin, 1927); *Artificial activity of hafnium and some other elements* (Copenhagen, 1938); *Radioactive indicators; their application in biochemistry, animal physiology and pathology* (New York, 1948); *Adventures in radioactive research; the collected papers of G. H.* (New York, 1962). In recognition for his unique accomplishments in radioactivity research György Hevesy was awarded in addition to the Nobel Prize the Faraday, Copley and Bohr Medals, the Enrico Fermi Prize, and the Atoms for Peace Award.

There are several chemists in present-day Hungary who have contributed to the advancement of chemical knowledge in quite different branches. Physical chemist Géza Schay (b. 1900) and his collaborators have produced excellent results in catalysis, reaction kinetics, gas chromatography and various aspects of nuclear chemistry and the rubber industry. They succeeded, among other things, in establishing correlations between the structure and reactivity of unsaturated conjugated and aromatic compounds. His major works include *Hochverdünnte Flammen* (Berlin, 1930); *Theoretische Grundlagen der Gaschromatographie* (Berlin, 1960), which was published also in Russian and Hungarian, and *Fizikai kémia* (Budapest, 1945, 1970; with Gyula Gróh and Tibor Erdey-Grúz).

László Erdey (1910-1970) received his Ph.D. in electrochemistry at the Budapest University in 1938, and in 1949 became professor of chemistry at the Budapest University of Technical Sciences. His research and publishing activities embraced the most important aspects of analytical chemistry. He invented several new research methods such as ascorbinometry and the application of luminescent indicators. With the assistance of his co-workers Ferenc and Jenő Paulik, Erdey invented the derivatograph, a device which is used the world over for simultaneously measuring the weight and thermal effects of the same single specimen. Erdey published several books and many articles in various languages. His multivolume set (*A kémiai analízis súlyszerinti módszerei*. Budapest, 1960. 3 v.) is regarded as a standard work in gravimetric analysis. Its English edition, *Gravimetric analysis*, appeared first in New York in 1963 as volume 7 of the International Series of Monographs on Analytical Chemistry, and in 1965 in Oxford under the same title as a

3-volume edition. 1973 saw the publication of his book, *Ascorbinometric titrations*.

Győző Bruckner (1900) studied at the Budapest University of Technical Sciences and at Szeged University. In 1930 Bruckner received a state grant to work in F. Pregl's Institute of Microanalysis in Graz, Austria. He taught at Szeged until 1949 then at Budapest University. Bruckner and his associates helped elucidate the chemical structure of peptides and proteins. His main work is *Szerves kémia* (Organic chemistry, 1952, 1955, 1964).

Zoltán Földi (1895), László Vargha (1903) and their colleagues excelled in the synthesis of substances used in the pharmaceutical and canning industries.

In pharmacology Béla Issekutz (b. 1886) and Miklós Jancsó (1903-1966) scored outstanding successes. Issekutz' investigations into the physiology of the thyroid gland and the action mechanism of insulin are especially well known. He discovered many important medicines, among them the widely used diuretic Novurite. Issekutz authored a standard work on the history of pharmacology entitled *Die Geschichte der Arzneimittelforschung* (1971).

Miklós Jancsó's studies on the reticuloendothelial system are significant contributions (*Speicherung, Stoffanreicherung in Retikuloendothel und in der Niere*. 1955). In addition, the activities of Jancsó, like that of Issekutz, are of significance because both focused their research work on the production of entirely new natural and synthetic drugs and revealed the relationship between their chemical constitution and effect.

László Zechmeister (b. 1889), an internationally famed expert in organic chemistry, also studied in Zürich. In the years 1920 and 1921 he conducted industrial chemical research in Hungary and from 1921 to 1923 in Copenhagen. From 1923 to 1940 Zechmeister held a professorship in chemistry at the Medical Faculty of the University of Pécs, Hungary, after which he emigrated to the United States where he was professor of chemistry at the California Institute of Technology in Pasadena from 1940 to 1959. Most of Zechmeister's experiments were conducted in the following laboratories: Chemisches Laboratorium der Eidgenössischen Technischen Hochschule, Zürich; Kaiser-Wilhelm-Institut für Chemie, Berlin-Dahlem; Royal Veterinary and Agricultural Academy, Copenhagen; Chemical Institute of the Medical Faculty, The University of Pécs, Hungary; Gates and Crellin Laboratories of Chemistry, California Institute of Technology, Pasadena, California. The major fields of investigation in which he became internationally famous include carotenoids, carbohydrates, vitamins, organic compounds, plant physiology and chemical genetics, chromatographic methods and reduction methods. The *Bibliography of papers published by L. Zechmeister and co-authors in the fields of chemistry and biochemistry, 1913-1958*

(Wien: Springer, 1958. 22 p.) lists 257 published items (books and periodical articles). To list a few of them: *Carotinoide; ein biochemischer Bericht über pflanzliche und tierische Polyenfarbstoffe* (Berlin, 1934); *Cis-trans isomeric carotenoids, vitamins A, and arylpolyenes* (New York, 1962); *Principles and practice of chromatography* (New York, 1943, first published in German); *Progress in chromatography, 1938-1947* (London, 1950). Many of his works between 1923 and 1940 were published in his native Hungarian.

Koloman Laki (b. 1909, Szolnok, Hungary) received his Ph.D. in organic chemistry and biochemistry from the University of Szeged in 1936. He belonged to the inner circle of the study group headed by Albert Szent-Györgyi. Before coming to the United States Laki was professor of the Faculty of Medicine of the Budapest University. For years he has been the chief of the Laboratory of Biophysical Chemistry, the National Institutes of Health, Bethesda, Maryland. He is the author of well over 100 scientific papers. His monographic publications include *Fibrinogen* (New York: M. Dekker, 1968. 398 p.); *Contractile proteins and muscle* (New York: M. Dekker, 1971. 606 p.) and *The biological role of the clot-stabilizing enzymes: transglutaminase and factor XIII* (Editor: K. Laki. New York: New York Academy of Sciences, 1972. 348 p.). This collective volume contains papers presented at a conference sponsored by the New York Academy of Sciences and held on November 18-19, 1971. Recently, Koloman Laki received an honorary doctor's degree from the Lajos Kossuth University of Debrecen.

Gábor Fodor (b. 1915, Budapest) graduated from the Technische Hochschule in Graz, Austria in 1934, and obtained his Ph.D. in chemistry from the University of Szeged in 1937. For years he was associated with the University of Szeged as professor of chemistry and headed the research laboratory of stereochemistry of the Hungarian Academy of Sciences in Budapest. Fodor was awarded the Kossuth Prize twice (1950, 1954) for chemistry. In 1961 he was an Overseas Fellow of the Churchill College, Cambridge, Great Britain. He has participated in many international conferences in Europe and North America. He published three books and more than 200 scientific papers in stereochemistry and organic compounds in which fields Gábor Fodor is regarded one of the world's leading authorities. His multivolume monograph *Szerves kémia* was translated into German entitled *Organische Chemie* (Berlin: Deutscher Verlag der Wissenschaften, 1965-). Since 1967 he has taught and conducted research as a professor of West Virginia University, Morgantown.

George A. Olah (b. 1927, Budapest) graduated from the Budapest University of Technical Sciences in 1949 where he held assistant and associate professorship between 1949 and 1956. In the meantime George Olah was the Associate Director of the Chemical Research Institute of the Hungarian Academy of Sciences, 1954-1956. Since 1965 Olah has been associated with the Cleveland-based Case Western Reserve University as professor of chemistry. He published more than 450 scientific papers and has 60 patents issued in his name. Olah's contributions to chemistry cover a wide field of electrophilic organic reactions, particularly carbonium ions, Friedel-Crafts chemistry, aliphatic and aromatic substitutions, and hydrocarbon chemistry. George Olah has demonstrated unusual breadth and originality as evidenced by his major research accomplishments which may be summarized: 1/ the pioneering of new techniques and solvent systems (of the superacid type) which allow the study of reactive intermediates, particularly carbonations, as long-lived stable species in solutions; 2/ the application of physical methods such as nuclear magnetic resonance and Raman spectroscopy to the study of these systems; 3/ Fourier transform carbon-13 nmr and X-ray Photoelectron spectroscopic study of organic ions; 4/ extensive structural and mechanistic studies involving a large variety of organic systems; 5/ studies in Friedel-Crafts chemistry, including new catalyst systems, new reactions (such as acylations, formylations with formyl fluoride, nitration with nitronium salts, new alkylation methods, etc.) and selective substitution methods; 6/ study of electrophilic aromatic substitution reactions; 7/ study of electrophilic aliphatic substitution and addition reactions and in general single bond reactivity; 8/ new approaches in petroleum chemistry particularly relating to the superacid catalyzed processes of saturated hydrocarbons; 9/ study of biologically related alkylating, acylating and phosphorylating systems; 10/ studies relating to organofluorine and phosphorus compounds; 11/ inorganic chemical studies of ionic complexes and strong acid systems.

Camille Sándorfy (b. 1920, Budapest) of the University of Montreal and a member of the Royal Society of Canada has acquired international recognition for his research in quantum chemistry and molecular spectroscopy. His major contributions include *Electronic spectra and quantum chemistry* (Englewood Cliffs, N.J.: Prentice Hall, 1964, 385 p. Tr. from the French original).

John C. Polanyi (b. 1929) is the son of the late Michael Polanyi. He has been working at the University of Toronto, Canada. Winner of numerous Canadian and international awards in chemical research, he is a member of the Royal Society of Canada. He published many items in his field. The *Chemical kinetics* (London-Baltimore, Md., 1972. 322 p.) appeared under his editorship.

Botany

Because of the military expansion of the Turkish Empire, sixteenth-century Hungary relapsed into its pre-Renaissance stagnation and only isolated forces of cultural and scientific advancement were at work. Cultural activities, if any, were rather concentrated on the timely issues of the Reformation and Counter-Reformation. But some of the clergymen, historians and physicians — all of these being polyhistors to an extent — diverted some of their energies to biological sciences. Thus did Péter Melius Juhász (1536-1572) who studied at Wittenberg in 1556 and from 1561 up to his death was the bishop of the Reformed Church in Debrecen. Besides his official activites Melius Juhász found time to author the first Hungarian-language book on botany and medicine. His book carries the then popular title *Herbárium* (Kolozsvár, 1578) in which two hundred and fifty plants of Debrecen and its vicinity are described using Hungarian terminology.

József Benkő (1740-1814), another minister of the Reformed Church, was active as historian and botanist. He organized a botanical garden and compiled his *Flora Transilvanica*.

János Földi (1755-1801) embraced a variety of subjects in his short career. He was known as physician, naturalist, linguist and poet. Földi prepared an early criticism of Hungarian botany *(Rövid kritika és rajzolat a magyar füvésztudományról*. Vienna, 1793). He planned to prepare a comprehensive work on natural history but was able to finish only the first part of his animal taxonomy *(Állatok országa*, 1801) following the system of Carolus Linnaeus *(Természeti história a Linné systémája szerint*. Pozsony, 1801).

Pál Kitaibel (1757-1817) was the country's first natural scientist in a modern sense, engaging in botany, ecology, plant geography, balneology, and mineralogy. Kitaibel described 275 plant species with illustrations in his main work *Descriptiones et icones plantarum rariorum Hungariae* (Vienna, vols. 1-3, 1799-1812). More than fifty plants bear his name. Kitaibel discovered about half the plant species characteristic of the Hungarian flora.

János Xántus (1825-1894) was one of several thousand to set foot in America after the abortive Hungarian Revolution of 1848-1849. During his stay in America from 1851 to 1864, Xántus rose from obscurity to international fame as a pioneer in the natural history of the United States: he collected and classified 390 zoological and botanical species — mainly vertebrates — entirely new to science. His collections were deposited for the most part in the Smithsonian Institution but a generous portion was housed in the Hungarian National Museum in Budapest. János Xántus made a significant contribution to geography as well. He also dealt extensively with some topics of ethnography, including the life and customs of the American Indians. Having returned to his native Hungary, Xántus organized the renowned Budapest Zoological and Botanical Garden and was named its first director.

Árpád Paál (1889-1943) completed his studies in Budapest and in 1929 was already a full professor of botany at Budapest University. A pioneer of plant physiology and one of the first specialists in plant hormone research, his most important works appeared in Hungarian and German.

Sándor Jávorka (1883-1961) also a graduate of the Budapest University, had great influence on the botanists dealing with Central Europe. For a while Jávorka worked in the University's Botanical Garden then for many years in the Botanical Division of the Hungarian National Museum. He made several study trips to the Carpathian Basin and the Balkan Peninsula which helped him elucidate many fundamental questions of floristics and phytogeography. Having discovered more than one hundred plants of which about forty bear his name, his plant identification handbooks are still widely used by scientists interested in the plant life of the Danube Valley and the Balkan Peninsula. We refer above all to his monographs: *A magyar flóra (Flora Hungarica*. 3 vols., Budapest: Studium, 1925);*A magyar flóra képekben (Iconographica florae hungaricae* . . . Budapest, 1929-1934, abstracts of preface in English, German, French, Italian, Czech, Romanian, and Croatian); *Kerti virágaink; középeurópai dísznövények színes atlasza* (Col. atlas of Central Europe's ornamental plants. Budapest: Mezőgazdasági Kiadó, 1962. 154 p., 116 col. plates); *Erdő-mező virágai; a magyar flóra színes kis atlasza* . *Függelékben: az Északi Kárpátok virágai* (Col. atlas of the Hungarian flora, and the flowers of the Northern Carpathian Mountains. Budapest: Mezőgazdasági Kiadó, 1958. 208 p., 120 plates, map. This was translated into Slovak under the title *Kvety lesov a lúk* (Bratislava, 1966. 256 p.).

István Győrffy (1880-1959), professor of botany at Kolozsvár and Szeged universities, is known as one of the world's outstanding bryologists. He issued and edited several important publications such as the *Bryophyta regni Hungariae* and the *Folia Cryptogamica*. At the chairs of botany in both universities Győrffy organized highly professional research groups dealing with cryptograms. He studied chiefly the anatomy, composition and identification of mosses. István Győrffy was especially versed in the bryology of the High Tatra Mountains and that of Transylvania. One of his monographs was published about the flora of the High Tatra Mountains under the title *Die Pflanzenwelt der Hohen Tatra* (Késmárk-Budapest: Verlag "Turistik und Alpinismus," 1922. 79 p., with illus.).

Pál Greguss (b. 1889) studied biology in Budapest and Prague, specializing in plant taxonomy, genetics and xylotomy. He took part in many international conferences in Europe and one in Canada. Greguss published extensively in English and German as well as Russian. As a xylotomist he achieved a world reputation through his publications and lectures delivered at international symposia. His well-known publications include the *Xylotomy of living conifers* (Budapest, 1972. 329 p.), *Identification of living gymnosperms on the basis of xylotomy* (Budapest, 1955. 263 p., *Opreditel' drevesiny golosemennykh po mikroskopicheskim priznakam* in the Russian translation). Greguss' research in paleobotany (*Tertiary angiosperm woods in Hungary*. Budapest, 1969. 151 p., illus., maps, 93 plates) met with the approbation of the professional community.

It is interesting to note that several of Györffy's and Greguss' disciples rose to international fame in hydrobiology—for example Tibor Hortobágyi, professor of botany at the Gödöllő University of Agricultural Sciences, Gábor Uherkovich, research associate of the Hungarian Academy of Sciences in Pécs, and István Kiss, professor of biology at Szeged Pedagogic College. Hortobágyi studied the phytoplankton of India's Yamuna River (*Phytoplankton organisms from three reservoirs on the Jamuna River, India*. Budapest: Akadémiai Kiadó, 1969. 80 p., illus., 30 plates), and the microvegetation of Lake Balaton. Gábor Uherkovich researched the freshwater microbiology of the Tisza River (*A Tisza lebegő paránynövényei; a Tisza fitoszesztonja*. Szolnok: Damjanich János Múzeum, 1971, 282 p., 143 tables) and Finland's flora in a multivolume set entitled *Zur Chlorococcalen-Flora Finnlands* (Helsinki: Societas pro fauna et flora Fennica, 1968-1973. Summaries also in English). Both Hortobágyi and Uherkovich command a place among Europe's leading algologists. They have delivered lectures at international symposia and seminars in most European countries.

Educated at Budapest and Berlin universities in biology and chemistry, Rezső Soó (b. 1903) furthered his studies at Tihany Biological Institute (1927-1929) before being appointed professor of botany at Debrecen then at Kolozsvár and Budapest universities. Soó's research and literary activities have focused on phytogeography, plant taxonomy and phytogenesis. It should be noted that Soó was the first scientist in Hungary to engage in phytosociological research. He devised an entirely new system of phytotaxonomy. In 1947 Soó began publication of a multivolume set on the plant communities of the Carpathian Basin (*Conspectus des groupements végétaux dans les bassins carpathiques* (Debrecen: Institut botanique de l'Université à Debrecen). His six-volume standard work, *A magyar flóra és vegetáció rendszertani-növényföldrajzi kézikönyve* (Synopsis systematico-geobotanica florae vegetationisque Hungariae. Budapest: Akadémiai Kiadó, 1964-1973), is based on his two-volume *A magyar növényvilág kézikönyve* which was prepared on the grounds of Sándor Jávorka's works. Soó's works are considered the best handbooks ever written on Central Europe's flora and vegetation. He published about 500 items in addition to his reports on his many study trips including Cuba and Transylvania. Bálint Zólyomi's (b. 1908) professional career has been connected chiefly with the Museum of Natural Sciences (Természettudományi Múzeum, Budapest). Since 1967 he has been a member of the leadership of the International Union of Biological Sciences. Zólyomi has been engaged in phytosociological, ecological, forest typological and pollen analytical studies. Soó, Zólyomi and Imre Máthé (b. 1911) have solved significant problems of sytematics and have achieved a high degree of success in cross-breeding.

Leslie Oláh (b. 1904 in Kassa — now Kosice, Czechoslovakia) has had a long and distinguished career. In his native land he was the head of the Institute of Plant Genetics in Budapest (1938-1945) and professor of botany at the Faculty of Economics of the Budapest University of Technical Sciences (1942-1945). Simultaneously, Oláh was the director of the University's Institute of Agrobotany. After leaving Hungary, he occupied leading positions in his field at La Plata University (Argentina, 1948-1953). From 1954 to 1957 he was head of the Treub Laboratory and professor at the University of Indonesia (Buitenzorg-Bogor, Java), then professor at Duquesne University (Pittsburgh, Pennsylvania, 1958-1959) and finally at Southern Illinois University, Carbondale, Illinois from 1959 to 1972.

Oláh's scientific interests embraced cytology, genetics, cytogenetics and electron microscopy. His research topics include cytological and cytogenetical research in plants (Solanum, Triticum, Digitalis, Corypha, Rafflesia, and Dodecatheon genera), investigations into the behavior of digitonin-treated cells in tissue cultures, cytotaxonomical research in the Dodecatheon genus, ultrastructural studies on the effect of digitonin on microtubules in plant cells, to mention just a few. Leslie Oláh was the first scientist ever to conduct research on several rare endemic plants, for which purpose he led field expeditions to several regions of the world (Sumatra, 1954; Java and Celebes, 1956; Lesser Sunda Island, 1957; India, etc.). He delivered papers at numerous international conferences in Europe, the Americas, and Asia. Since 1930 Oláh has published several books and hundreds of periodical articles in the Hungarian, English, German, and Spanish languages.

Zoology

Having already referred to the publication of the first Hungarian-language animal taxonomy, János Földi's (1755-1801) *Állatok országa* (Animal world, 1801), we whould like to note that János Salamon Petényi (1799-1855) deserves special mention for having been instrumental in founding scientific ornithology.

Imre Frivaldszky (1799, Bacskó—1870, Jobbágyi) accompanied Pál Kitaibel on his study trips. Though Frivaldszky graduated in medicine from Pest University in 1823, his interest was in botany and zoology, especially the latter's branch of entomology. Frivaldszky organized several scientific expeditions to the Balkan Peninsula and Turkey to study their fauna. He also merits attention for discovering Haberlea, a new genus. In one of his more important works he discussed the characteristics of the fauna of the Middle Danube Valley as early as 1870 (*Jellemző adatok Magyarország faunájához*. Pest).

János Frivaldszky (1822, Rajec—1895, Budapest), himself a noted entomologist, took part in the expeditions of his uncle, Imre. Several insects were discovered by him and named after him. János Frivaldszky was the first speleologist in greater Hungary and he was the first Hungarian to devise a system of ornithology. Frivaldszky published many items in Hungary and abroad. His *Aves Hungariae* (Budapest, 1891) remains a standard work.

Géza Entz (1842-1919), professor of zoology at Kolozsvár and Budapest universities, conducted decades-long research on the Protozoa. He acquired international fame for his discovery of symbiosis between unicellular animals (Protozoa) and plans (Algae). Many of his works appeared in foreign journals, such as his "Über Infusorien des Golfes zu Neapel" (*Mitteilungen aus der zoolog. Station zu Neapel*, Leipzig, 1884).

The other Géza Entz (1875, Kolozsvár—1943, Budapest), also a noted zoologist and university professor like his namesake, taught in Hungary and Utrecht. In 1929 he was appointed director of the Tihany Biological Institute. With his associates he started the hydrobiological investigation of Lake Balaton. His two-volume *Beiträge zur Kenntniss der Peridineen* (1926-1927) as well as his studies in hydrobiology are deemed very useful to this day.

István Apáthy (1861-1922) a preeminent zoologist of his age, graduated from Budapest University where from 1885 to 1886 he taught at the Chair of Zoology. Between 1886 and 1889 he conducted research in Italy at the Naples Zoological Station. In 1890 Apáthy became professor of zoology at Kolozsvár and later at Szeged. He fathered the theory of neurofibrillary continuity which influences even our present-day knowledge of histology. He also made significant contributions to microtomy. In addition to his scientific work Apáthy engaged in belleslettres, sociology and was known as a publicist.

Many of his more important works were published in German, which was then the language of science — for instance, his *Die Mikrotechnik der thierischen Morphologie* (2 vols., Braunschweig-Leipzig, 1896-1901), "Das leitende Element des Nervensystems und seine topographischen Berichtungen zu den Zellen" (*Mitteilungen aus der Zoologischen Station zu Neapel*, Leipzig, 1888).

One of the last polyhistors, Ottó Herman (1835-1914), studied at Miskolc and at the Vienna Polytechnikum. While working under the guidance of another polyhistor natural scientist, Sámuel Brassai (1800-1897), he organized a famous zoological collection. Ottó Herman's three-volume work on the spider fauna of Hungary (*Magyarország pókfaunája*. Budapest, 1876-1879) and his works in ethnography, linguistics, archaeology (especially his studies of prehistoric man) and ornithology, to mention his major fields of accomplishment, earned him global repute. The 2nd International Ornithological Congress held in 1891 in Budapest, shifted Herman's interest to ornithology. He was the most active member of that international congress and was inspired to organize the Hungarian Ornithological Center (Magyar Ornitológiai Központ) in 1893. His book on birds (*A madarak hasznáról és káráról*, 1901) is remarkable.

Entomologist and ethnographer Lajos Biró (1856-1931) made several study trips — first to New Guinea in 1895 where he spent seven years, then to Greece (1906) and Bulgaria (1928), etc. The collections of his one-man expedition to New Guinea are especially highly valued now.*

József Gelei (1885-1952) was one of Apáthy's disciples at Kolozsvár University. From 1924 on he was professor of zoology and comparative anatomy at Szeged. Gelei is regarded an international authority on the studies of protozoa, cytology and the microtomy of vertebrates. Several of his works were published abroad, among them *Das erregungsleitende System der Ciliaten* (Lisbon, 1935), *Feinstrukturen einzelliger Organismen* (Jena, 1943).

Zoltán Kaszab (b. 1915) graduated from the Budapest University and since 1937 has functioned chiefly as scientist and later head of the Department of Zoology of the Museum of Natural Sciences in Budapest. Since 1963 Kaszab has been general editor of a monumental monographic series issued by the Hungarian Academy of Sciences dealing

---

*Cf. Sándor Asztalos, *Biró Lajos, a nagy magyar utazó* (Budapest, 1953, and T. Bodrogi and L. Boglár edited *Opuscula ethnologica memoriae Ludovici Biró sacra* (Budapest, 1959) in which his ethnological research is evaluated.

with Hungary's animal world (*Magyarország állatvilága*). Between 1963 and 1968 Kaszab led six zoological expeditions to Mongolia and discovered a staggering number — some 2,500 — of animal species. He published over 250 items in Hungary and abroad. Szilárd Donhoffer (b. 1902) and Kálmán Lissák (b. 1908) have done extensive research work in animal physiology. Donhoffer's successful research into the nervous and hormonal control of energy and Lissák's work on a variety of questions including hormone metabolism are well-known.

Great traditions in experimental biological research exist in Hungary. In line with those traditions, the Hungarian Academy of Sciences on April 2, 1971 opened its Szeged Biological Center (MTA Szegedi Biológiai Központja) which with its ultra-modern research facilities holds its own among the world's top institutions. The Szeged Biological Center's research is conducted on an interdisciplinary basis with chemists, physicists, mathematicians and scientists representing several other branches of science. The Szeged Biological Center consists of four institutes: namely, of biophysics, biochemistry, genetics and phytophysiology. Its first director was Brunó F. Straub, a world authority on biological sciences. The Center has been cooperating foremost with the leading biological research institutions of the socialist countries.*

Agricultural Sciences — Veterinary Medicine

During the last decades of the eighteenth century, a great number of books on agricultural sciences were printed. It was quite a natural phenomenon because the intellectual movement of the Enlightenment and the transition from semi-feudalism to the early phases of capitalism pushed new forms of agricultural production to the fore. During this period the Faculty of Agriculture was organized at the Pest-Buda University. The first professor of the Faculty was Lajos Mitterpacher (1734-1814) who in his *Elementa rei rusticae* (1777-1794) summarized at a high contemporary level all branches of agricultural sciences. In 1782, Emperor Joseph II issued a decree setting up the Veterinary Institute at the Pest-Buda University's Faculty of Medicine. Sándor Tolnay (1747-1818), the head of this newly established Institute, published several works on the prevention of animal diseases.

*For further details see Gábor Farkas' article "Megnyílt az MTA Szegedi Biológiai Központja" (*Magyar Tudomány, July-August, 1971, pp. 423-429*).

In the closing phase of the Enlightenment, entirely new institutions came into being. Around 1780 Sámuel Tessedik (1742-1820), a Lutheran pastor of Szarvas (Békés County, Hungary), founded a practical school for farming in his hometown—predating by years the founding of such schools in any country of Europe. In addition, he was literarily very active, publishing much to promote agricultural knowledge. Sámuel Tessedik's enterprise was widely known and praised as a model for agricultural schools. Patterned after it, the Keszthely (Hungary) Academy of Agriculture, called "Georgikon", was established in 1797 by György Festetics. A similar academy of agricultural sciences was founded at Magyaróvár (Hungary) in 1818. Both institutions are extant.

Ágoston Haraszthy (1812-1869) played a very important role in America's economic growth by importations of cuttings from Europe for really fine varieties of grapes. On the 100th anniversary of his death, Gov. Ronald Reagan, of California, paid tribute to Haraszthy in these zealous words: "Colonel Ágoston Haraszthy can well be called the Father of the Wine Industry in California . . . Ever since that time, from the 300 varieties of grapes he brought to California and planted, the wine industry of our Golden State has been improving until in the past few decades California wines have become renowned around the world as second to none. Eighty-five percent of the wine produced and consumed in America comes from California, with California vineyards producing 160 million gallons of wine a year . . . . we certainly acknowledge our debt to Colonel Haraszthy for launching the industry into worldwide fame."*

On the same occasion, Maynard A. Amerine, professor of enology, University of California at Davis, also discussed the importance of Ágoston Haraszthy's activities for the development of viticulture in California. According to professor Amerine's opinion: "In retrospect, we can not measure with accuracy the total influence of Haraszthy on the California grape and wine industry, but it was very great. His enthusiasm for grape growing and wine making must have influenced many settlers."**

Péter Treitz (1866-1935) and Elek 'Sigmond (1873-1939) were the architects of modern agricultural science in Hungary. The agrarian crisis that was chronic around the turn of the nineteenth and twentieth centuries presented new problems for soil science. In Hungary, alkaline soil hindered the development of intensive farming. Péter Treitz applied geological methods to the improvement of alkaline soil while 'Sigmond applied chemical ones. Both Treitz and 'Sigmond are responsible for laying the foundations for the study and improvement of alkaline soil.

*Message from Gov. Ronald Reagan, of California, publ. in the Congressional Record. Proceedings and Debates of the 91st Congress, First session, Thursday, June 19, 1969.
**Ibid.

Nowadays Lajos Kreybig (1879-1956) has earned recognition for investigating the biological problems of soil fertility. Gyula Magyar (1880-1945) was among the very first scientists to improve plants by applying scientific horticultural methods and Mátyás Mohácsy (b. 1881) a renowned pomologist, was a pioneer of growing fruit through modern methods.

Paralleling the general advancement of the agricultural sciences since around the turn of the past century, veterinary medicine has also shown great progress. The most important role in the latter trend was that of Professor Ferenc Hutÿra (1860, Szepeshely — 1934, Budapest) whose activities helped elevate the Budapest Veterinary College to the rank of a university. His research into pathology of contagious diseases of animals earned him and his country an international reputation in veterinary science. His successful investigations helped clarify greatly and control such animal diseases as glanders, swine fever, swine erysipelas, and several others. Among his many works let us single out one of his foreign-language publications under the title *Spezielle Pathologie und Therapie der Haustiere* (2 vols., Jena, 1905) which was later revised and partly enlarged by co-authors Rezső Manninger and János Mócsy. It was published in several editions in English, Italian, Russian, Spanish, Turkish, and Finnish languages.

Hutÿra's co-worker, József Marek (1868-1952), shared in the extraordinary accomplishments of his master. János Mócsy (b. 1895), also an internationally recognized scientist of veterinary medicine, obtained highly significant results in the therapy of ovine scabies, while Sándor Kotlán (b. 1887) is well known for creating a new method for preventing coccidiosis in fowl.

Rezső Manninger (b. 1890), doctor of veterinary medicine, university professor and vice-president of the Hungarian Academy of Sciences is an international authority on bacteriology and epidemiology. He acquired a world reputation for inventing an immunization procedure against swine erysipelas. He was instrumental in the establishment of the National Institute of Animal Hygiene (Országos Állategészségügyi Intézet) in Budapest. Manninger enriched veterinary literature particularly with his monograph on bacteriology, immunology and general epidemiology (*Állatorvosi bakteriológia, immunitástan és általános járványtan*. Budapest, 1960).

Medical Sciences

János Balsaráti Vitus (1529-1575) had been associated with Wittenberg and some Italian universities, subsequently practicing medicine for a while in Rome. He authored the *De remediis pestis prophylacticis* as well as the *Magyar Chirurgia* (Hungarian surgery). Balsaráti Vitus' contemporary, Tamás Jordán of Kolozsvár, was the first physician to study typhoid fever.

Károly Rayger (1641-1707), a Pozsony physician was the first in medical literature to describe influenza scientifically (1677) and for this accomplishment Károly Rayger was appointed a Court physician and became one of the few Hungarian scientists named to the prestigious Academia naturae curiosorum (Academia Leopoldina) founded in Vienna, 1652. Rayger wrote several items for the journal of the Academia.

Ferenc Miskóltzi (1697-1771), well-known surgeon and physician of the city of Győr, prepared a surgery handbook (*Manuale chirurgicum, avagy chirurgiai utitárs*. Győr, 1742) which was generally based on the book of E. Norr, a famous German surgeon. Several sections of Miskóltzi's work are noteworthy, especially the one on embryology which is significant from a biological standpoint.

János Dániel Perliczy (1705-1778) studied at German, Dutch and French universities. He graduated from Utrecht University. Between 1731 and 1754 Perliczy was head physician of Nógrád County, Hungary. He published several volumes on medicine, among them the *Medicina pauperum* . . . (Buda, 1740), a greatly informative and widely read Hungarian-language treatise with a Latin title. Perliczy also contributed articles in the annals of Berlin scientific societies. In order to improve public health conditions, Perliczy sent a memorandum to Empress Maria Theresa in 1751 in which he recommended the founding of a faculty of medicine and academy of sciences. As a consequence of the Vienna Imperial Court's failure to respond to his request, Perliczy with the aid of Ferenc Merkhot and others founded the Eger (Hungary) School of Medicine.

István Hatvani (1718-1786), a polyhistor-physician, as early as the middle of the eighteenth century applied the theory of probability to the field of hygiene.

István Weszprémi (1723-1799) published his pioneering work entitled *Tentamen de Inoculate peste* in London in 1755. Weszprémi's *Tentamen* advocated for the first time in history inoculation (antitoxic therapy) for the purpose of producing immunity to the fatal epidemic of the time: the plague. Weszprémi also prepared over the years 1774 to 1787 a multivolume set, in Latin, entitled *Succincta medicorum Hun-*

53

gariae et Transylvaniae biographia which is a collection of bio-bibliographical data on medical researchers and practicing physicians in Hungary and Transylvania. Weszprémi's Hungarian-language books on pediatrics (1760) and midwifery (1786) were also of great significance in the time of their publication.

The Hungarian-born Ignác Fülöp Semmelweis (1818, Buda — 1865, Vienna) made one of the greatest discoveries in the universal history of medicine. Semmelweis' forebears lived in the Hungarian village of Szikra, as early as the seventeenth century. His two brothers fought against Austria in the Hungarian War of Independence of 1848-1849. His education up to and including his third year of medical studies was in Buda and Pest. He finished his medical studies at Vienna University. Afterwards Semmelweis was attached to the Vienna Hospital which was divided into two parts: the First Division (Clinic), comprised of medical students and physicians, and the Second Division (Clinic) made up of midwives and physicians not engaged in surgery immediately prior to attending maternity patients. The mortality from puerperal fever had shown a remarkable difference between the First Division and the Second. This fact was clearly observed and strikingly delineated by Semmelweis himself in the following statistical table:*

	First Division			Second Division		
Year	Cases	Deaths	Per Cent	Cases	Deaths	Per Cent
1841	3,036	237	7.7	2,442	86	3.5
1842	3,287	518	15.8	2,659	202	7.5
1843	3,060	274	8.9	2,739	164	5.9
1844	3,157	260	8.2	2,956	68	2.3
1845	3,492	241	6.8	3,241	66	2.0
1846	4,010	459	11.4	3,754	105	2.7
	20,042	1,989	9.92	17,791	691	3.38

Evidently, as observed by Semmelweis over those six years, the average mortality in the First Division was three times that of the Second. It was simply cadaverous material from autopsies adhering to the hands of those physicians in the First Division subsequently attending mothers in childbed. The cause was cadaveric poison and that alone, which was further demonstrated by the fact that, with the exception of

---

*Cf. William J. Sinclair, *Semmelweis: His life and doctrine; a chapter in the history of medicine*. Manchester, 1909. p. 29.

the introduction of chlorine disinfection, no other change had been made in the conditions prevailing in the First Division. By requiring physicians of the first group to scrub with chlorine disinfectant, the cause of puerperal fever had been removed and its effect, puerperal mortality, disappeared. Until then the system of instruction for midwives was such that neither the group II physicians nor their pupils, the midwives, had so frequent an occasion as those in group I to come into contact with cadavers, thereby contaminating their hands. Semmelweis' fight against childbed fever led to one of the greatest discoveries of all time: that disease was spread by germa (bacteria) and no other causes. For his discovery in 1847 of a new etiology of childbed fever, Semmelweis is honored not only as "the Saviour of Mothers" but as one of the greatest physicians of all time.

In 1851 Semmelweis was named head of obstetrics at Rókus Hospital in Pest and was appointed professor of gynecology at Pest University. On the advice of his physician friend, Lajos Markusovszky (1815-1893), Semmelweis wrote about his lifework first in the Hungarian medical journal, *Orvosi Hetilap* (1858), and later published a book in German: *Die Aetiologia, der Begriff und die Prophylaxis des Kindbettfiebers* (Pest, 1861). Semmelweis' collected works (*Gesammelte Werke*) were edited by Tibor Győry and reprinted under the title *Semmelweis' gesammelte Werke* (Jena: Fischer, 1905; Wiesbaden: Sändig, 1967).

The Lenhossék family promoted medical science for three generations. University professor Mihály Ignác Lenhossék (1773, Pozsony — 1840, Buda) published Latin and German works of great import on medical biology. His *Physiologia medicinalis* (Pest, 1816, and 1818, 5 vols.) influenced a generation of physicians in Hungary and abroad. His son, József Lenhossék (1818, Buda — 1888, Budapest) was professor of topographical anatomy at Pest. His research into the anatomy of the spinal cord was internationally appreciated. József Lenhossék was also well known as an anthropologist for which the French Academy awarded him the prestigious Monthyon prize. Among his non-Hungarian publications we should list his *Neue Untersuchungen über den feineren Bau des zentralen Nervensystems des Menschen* (Vienna, 1855), and *Mémoire sur la structure intime de la möelle espiniére* (Paris, 1859).

Mihály Lenhossék (1863, Pest — 1937, Budapest) was József's son. Director of the No. 1 Institute of Anatomy at Budapest University from 1899 to 1934, he was a pioneer of neuron theory. Mihály Lenhossék also earned reputation through his well-prepared university textbooks on histology as well as anatomy. He published several books in German.

The Korányis also occupy a position among the most eminent figures of modern medicine. Frigyes Korányi (1827-1913) functioned as the director of the No. 1 Clinic of Internal Medicine (in Budapest) until his retirement in 1908 where he engaged in laboratory research as well as chemical, bacteriological, and Roentgen investigations. Author of a comprehensive work on tuberculosis (1880), Frigyes Korányi pointed out the relationship between certain diseases and the social conditions. He founded Hungary's first t.b.-clinic at Budakeszi and authored over 150 publications in addition to contributing to several foreign handbooks on internal medicine.

His son, Sándor Korányi (1866-1944), was acknowledged throughout the world as a leading authority on physiology, gerontology and renal pathology. Honored by several foreign universities and medical institutions, Sándor Korányi also became an honorary member of the prestigious Academia Leopoldina. The following are just some of his highly valued works: "Beiträge zur Theorie und Therapie der Niereninsuffizienz (in *Berliner klinische Wochenschrift*, 1899); *Physikalische Chemie und Medizin* (2 vols., Leipzig, 1907-1908); *Funktionelle Pathologie und Therapie der Nierenkrankheiten* (Berlin, 1929, in Hungarian 1930, Budapest).

Endre Hőgyes (1847-1906) obtained his medical diploma at Budapest and was associated as a professor with Kolozsvár and Budapest universities. In 1879 Hőgyes discovered the mechanism of associated ocular motions. In 1890 he modified Pasteur's procedure for preventive inoculation against rabies and his new method has since been adopted world-wide. Endre Hőgyes was also instrumental in the founding of the Budapest Pasteur Institute. His research work was highly appreciated in Hungary and abroad alike, and his foreign language publications were widely read, for example "Le virus rabique des chiens des rues dans ses passages de lapin à lapin", published in *Ann. de l'Inst. Pasteur, Paris*, 1888; *Die experimentelle Basis der antirabischen Schutzimpfungen Pasteur's* (Stuttgart, 1899).

Tivadar Huzella (1886-1950), histologist and biologist, professor of anatomy, later histology, at Debrecen and Budapest universities. He was honored for his extraordinary achievements by election to the presidency of the 3rd International Congress of Experimental Cytology at Cambridge in 1933. Huzella pursued research into intercellular substances and cellular structure. His main works attracted international interest, above all his *Der Mechanismus der Kapillarkreislaufs und der Sekretion im Bindegewebe* (Berlin, 1925) as well as his general biology (*Általános biológia*. Budapest, 1933).

Tibor Verebélÿ (1875-1941) as a professor of surgery and director of the No. 1 Surgical Clinic of the Budapest University founded an important school of surgery. He did significant research on the surgery of tumors, vascular- and neurosurgery, and applied successful surgical treatment in the case of gastric ulcers. His four-volume set of university lectures on surgery were a veritable backbone in the curriculum of his school of surgery (*Sebészklinikai előadások*. Budapest, 1930-1934).

Géza Hetényi (1894-1959) was assistant to professor Sándor Korányi at the No. 3 Clinic of Internal Medicine in Budapest. In 1947, Hetényi was appointed full professor of Internal Medicine at Szeged University. His research on the metabolism of patients suffering from liver diseases and diabetes is of enormous significance. Hetényi spearheaded successful research into the pathogenesis of ulcerous diseases, discovering the central role of the nervous system in the development of such diseases. His research team also revealed and proved scientifically that the histamine released by the gastric mucous membrane plays a very important part in the development of ulcers. One of his main works dealing with the pathology and therapy of ulcers (*A fekélybetegségek időszerű kérdései*. Budapest, 1958) also appeared in German.

Antal Babics (b. 1902) and his co-workers, especially Ferenc Rényi-Vámos (b. 1910), have performed valuable research into the anatomy of the lymphatic vessels of most organs and their work elucidated from entirely new angles the structure of renal ducts, the renal pelvis, and inspired new surgical procedures.

György Ivánovics (b. 1904) has spent the bulk of his career at Szeged University where in 1940 he became director of its Institute of Microbiology. In 1960 Ivánovics pursued his research at Harvard University and in 1965-1966 at Glasgow University, in both places as guest professor. Ivánovics has dealt with the general biology of bacteria, genetics, virus research and chemotherapy. While engaged in studying the variability of the tubercle bacillus (Mycrobacterium tuberculosis) the Ivánovics team discovered completely new laws. His monograph *Chemotherapie der bakteriellen Infektionen* (1944) has been widely read. In addition to several Hungarian-language books Ivánovics has authored well over 200 scientific papers published in Hungary and abroad.

Kálmán Lissák's (b. 1908) name deserves special mention for his outstanding work in nerve physiology which has been internationally recognized.

Zoltán Zsebők (b. 1908) spearheaded research of utmost significance resulting in advances in lung surgery.

In medicine-oriented biological research, János Szentágothai (b. 1912) is regarded as a leading world authority. His results are all the more noteworthy because the country's biological research for a long time focused only on taxonomy and some related zoological and botanical topics, although experimental biology was popular to a certain extent in the various branches of the medical sciences. The experimental studies of János Szentágothai resulted in forward strides in the functional analysis and nervous correlations of histological structures.

Founder of a new school of experimental pathology, János Szentágothai has been a leading figure at international congresses since the conclusion of the second World War and has published extensively in foreign journals. Because Hungarian medical research has since its very beginnings exhibited a high level, it follows that scientists of Hungarian extraction should be among Nobel Prize laureates. As early as 1914 Róbert Bárány won the Nobel Prize in physiology-medicine for his work on the physiology and pathology of vestibular apparatus. Albert Szent-Györgyi whose studies in biochemistry have already been discussed won the 1937 Nobel Prize in medicine for his work on biological combustion. The most recent laureate of the Nobel Prize in physiology and medicine was Georg von Békésy (1899-1972) for his research into the mechanism of stimulation of the human inner ear. Békésy obtained a Ph.D. in physics from the Budapest University in 1923. Until 1946 he worked in the Research Laboratory of the Budapest Telephone Department of the Hungarian Post Office and simultaneously, between 1939 and 1946, he was professor of experimental physics at the Budapest University. Then for a while he pursued his research in Stockholm at the Karolinska Institutet. In 1947 Georg von Békésy emigrated into the United States where up to his death he was associated with the psychoacoustic laboratory of Harvard University where he fully elucidated the energy conversion process taking place in the cochlea. Although a physicist, he received honors for his contributions from a variety of disciplines: among the many, the Gold Medal of the American Otological Society (1957), the Gold Medal of the Acoustical Association of America (1961), and even honorary M.D. degree by the Münster and Bern universities. Békésy's landmark auditory-physiological research accomplishments are described in detail in his *Experiments in Hearing* (1960).

After emigrating from Hungary Frigyes Verzár (b. 1886) became professor at Basel, Switzerland. Excelling in biochemistry, Verzár is best known for his work on blood grouping and the chemistry of absorption and of vitamins.

Hungarians have been traditionally active in morphological studies. In this time-honored tradition dating back to István Apáthy and Mihály Lenhossék, Ferenc Kiss, professor of human anatomy at Szeged and later Budapest, compiled in cooperation with associates a most modern anatomic atlas. Kiss' atlas of anatomy has been issued in all the Western languages as well as in Russian and has been acknowledged by the international community of morphologists as a topflight contribution.

Lajos Nékám (1868-1957) taught a whole generation of dermatologists as director of the Clinic of Dermatology from 1906 and professor of dermatology at Budapest University up to his retirement.

His investigations on poikiloderma and the appearance of myeloid leukemia in the skin are of great significance. His main work *Corpus Iconum Morborum Cutaneorum* (Budapest, 1938) is still regarded as a sourcebook.

Béla Schick (1877-1967), the father of modern pediatrics and co-discoverer with Clemens von Pirquet of the new medical science of allergy, was born in Boglár, Hungary, and died in New York City. He is best known for the Schick test for diphtheria.

Andrew Sass-Kortsak is professor of pediatrics at the University of Toronto, Canada, and is a ranking member of the staff of the Research Institute of the Hospital for Sick Children.

World-renowned Dezső Kassay (b. 1899) took his degree in medicine at the University of Szeged, spending two and a half years in its Department of Pathology, subsequently. He was certified in surgery and otolaryngology in 1927 by the University of Pécs. He took a six-month postgraduate course in Vienna and Graz in 1928. Kassay was chief of otolaryngology respectively, at Hódmezővásárhely from 1930 to 1941, at Nagyvárad in 1941, and from 1941 to 1950 at the White-Cross Children's Hospital of Budapest. In 1948 he was awarded a UNESCO fellowship to conduct research in Philadelphia, Boston and New York. Then Kassay returned to Hungary to assume chairmanship of the Department of Bronchology and Otolaryngology from 1950 to 1956 at the Budapest University. Kassay escaped from Hungary in 1956. Upon his arrival to the United States in 1957, he was offered a fellowship by the Rockefeller Foundation. In 1957 he was appointed professor of bronchoesophagologic research at the Jackson Clinic of Philadelphia's Temple University. Later he worked in the Lankenau Hospital of Philadelphia as researcher and physician and several other medical institutions all situated in Philadelphia. Named honorary member of the American and International Bronchoesophagologic Associations in 1948 and 1960, he was also named member of the Philadelphia Bronchoscopic Club in 1957. Fascinated by mechanics from early childhood, he invented an instrument which prevented bleeding during and after tonsillectomies. He also created a bronchoscope with proximal illumination that was far better than previous attempts by Brünings and Haslinger. On the basis of his scientific observations and findings he created the "Kassay-Lankenau Authentic Lung Reproduction." This lung model is distributed all over the world to universities, teaching institutions and physicians by the Medical Plastic Laboratory, Inc. of Gatesville, Texas. Among his surgeries his 1950 circular resection of a thoracic part of the trachea with András Bikfalvi bears the distinction of being the first in Hungary and one of the first of its kind anywhere. Dezső Kassay also developed a simple method for bronchoscopy in newborns and infants. He published 86 scientific papers in Hungarian, English, German and

French, three books in Hungarian, and one in English entitled *Clinical Applications of Bronchology* (New York: McGraw-Hill Company, 1960). Dezső Kassay retired in 1972 after an illustrious scientific career and distinguished medical practice.

One of the giants of modern day medicine and psychology, Hans Selye (b. 1907 in Vienna of mixed Hungarian and Austrian parentage), attended the Hungarian-language secondary school of the St. Benedictine Order in Komárom for eight years, continuing his studies in Prague, Paris and Rome. Later awarded a Rockefeller research fellowship, he was associated with the Johns Hopkins University at Baltimore, Maryland. A Canadian resident for the past few decades, Selye has held a professorship at the University of Montreal and has served as director of the University's Institute of Experimental Medicine and Surgery.

In 1936, Selye's revolutionary concept of stress opened up entirely new avenues of treatment for several diseases, including coronary thrombosis, brain hemorrhage, hardening of arteries, certain types of blood pressure and kidney failures, arthritis, peptic ulcers, and to a certain degree even cancer. His theory of stress was introduced to the layman in Selye's *The Stress of Life* (New York: McGraw Hill, 1959). Recently, Selye has been working on a new theory relating the process of aging to the body's disposition of calcium, which research holds the potential of countless medical applications.

Known as the father of the stress theory, Selye has published several dozen books and many hundreds of scientific papers. He has delivered papers at a great many international conferences in the Americas, Europe, and Asia.

Major contributions to pharmacological research and allied fields have been made by Stephen Szára (b. 1923 in Pestújhely near Budapest) who obtained his M.D. from the Budapest University of Medical Sciences in 1951. Known in professional circles the world over for his discovery of the hallucinogenic effect of N.N-Dimethyltryptamine (DMT) on human beings while he was on the staff of Budapest State Mental Hospital, Szára followed up his work in the United States, first as a visiting scientist then as a staff member of the intramural research program at the National Institute of Mental Health in Bethesda, Maryland, and Washington, D.C., with the collaboration of Nobel Prize laureate Julius Axelrod and others. Their research team clarified the metabolism of this compound and proved that DMT may be endogenously formed toxin which may play a role in some forms of schizophrenia.

In 1970 Stephen Szára accepted an administrative position with the extramural program of the National Institute of Mental Health, taking responsibility for directing clinical and basic research support (grants and contracts) for biomedical studies on marihuana and narcotic drugs.

One of the most intriguing accomplishments of this research has been the discovery that marihuana lowers intraocular pressure. Nowadays further basic and clinical investigations are underway to explore the potentials of marihuana and of its ingredients as a new and effective therapeutic agent for the successful treatment of glaucoma. These pioneering studies and other relevant findings are described in detail in a 915-page, 2-volume monograph under the editorship of Stephen Szára (*Pharmacology of marihuana*. New York: Raven Press, 1976). According to reviewers, this collective work is the most complete and up-to-date discussion by the world's leading specialists on the pharmacology of marihuana.

Szára has filled important positions in his field both in Hungary and the United States. Since 1974 he has been chief of the Biomedical Research Branch of the Division of Research at the National Institute on Drug Abuse in Rockville, Md.

In addition to his monographs, Stephen Szára has published about 70 papers, the overwhelming majority of them in English, in his profession's leading periodicals and has taken an active part in a number of international scientific symposia.

Professor László Kátó has long been associated with the University of Montreal, Canada, and is the head of the Department of Experimental Leprosy in the Institute of Microbiology and Hygiene. He authored with Béla Gözsy the *Studies on phagocytic stimulation* (Montreal, 1957. 135 p.) and several other important publications.

One of the world's major figures in orthodontics, the Hungarian-born Miklós Cserépfalvi (b. 1905) attended universities at Prague (1924-1926), Vienna (1926-1928), Paris (1928-1930), Debrecen (1930-1932), Budapest (1932-1935) obtaining an M.D. in 1932 and a D.D.S. in 1935. He emigrated to the United States and attended the Georgetown University School of Dentistry between 1957 and 1959 where he earned another D.D.S. His American postgraduate specialty training is in the fields of oral surgery and orthodontia. Cserépfalvi's appointments include directorship of the Central Institute of Orthodontics and Dental Research in Budapest. During 1957 and 1958 he was a research associate of the Rockefeller Foundation. Since 1959 he has been engaged in private practice in Washington, D.C., and from 1960 on he has been a staff member of the world famous Children's Hospital there.

Miklós Cserépfalvi's research work has resulted in internationally acknowledged accomplishments which have been published in Hungarian, Swiss, German, French, Spanish, and — for the past two decades — English periodicals. He has lectured about his work at international conferences in the U.S.A., Mexico, Venezuela, Argentina, France, Spain, and Portugal, among other places. Cserépfalvi has simplified and improved orthodontic methods, three of his recent articles especially focusing on his pioneering methodology: "Experimental homogenous transplantation of human teeth obtained from human cadavers", *Journal of Oral Implant and Transplant Surgery*, vol. 12, 1966; "Transplantation of a Preserved Human Tooth to a Monkey: Preliminary Report of a Case", *Journal of Dental Research*, vol. 47, no. 4, 1968; "Pulp Viability and the Homotransplantation of Frozen Teeth", *Journal of Dental Research*, vol. 51, no. 1, 1972.

Technical Sciences

Up to the second half of the nineteenth century there were only sporadic gains in the history of technical sciences in Hungary. Evidently, the first specialist of great consequence was Faustus Verancsics (1551-1617), bishop of Csanád, whose uncle was Antal Verancsics, archbishop of Esztergom. He completed his studies through the aid of his uncle. In 1609 Faustus Verancsics resigned his bishopric to devote his full time to scientific studies. He concentrated primarily on architecture and technology. His famous book entitled *Machinae Novae Fausti Verantii* (Venice, 1616) described contemporary machines including his own illustrated invention of the water turbine, parachute and some other technical innovations.

Sámuel Mikoviny (1700-1750) as the head of the mining officer training school at Selmecbánya (now Banska Stiavnica, Czechoslovakia) educated several famous specialists for mining engineering. Mikoviny is considered an early pioneer of mining mechanization for his water management inventions (including his first invention, the changeover paddle wheel). In 1794 during the French Revolution, when the Paris École Polytechnique was established, Fourcroy, in his address to the Convention, was of the opinion that Mikoviny's methods and the Selmecbánya type of school should be held as a pattern for the newly founded French school.

József Károly Hell (1713-1789) studied under Sámuel Mikoviny and invented many useful devices in mining engineering. Hell was the first to construct a compressed air-operated mining machine (machina hydraulica pneumatica, 1753). In 1749 he invented a water column pumping machine and in 1756 put into operation a ventilator he designed. All these were of a revolutionary nature at that time in mining machinery. The Hell-invented "water column" machine installed in 1749 was a predecessor of our modern mining machines. Hell's main work appeared in Vienna in 1711, *Berechnung der Luftmaschine*.

Farkas (Wolfgang) Kempelen (1734, Pozsony — 1804, Vienna) pursued studies mainly in philosophy and jurisprudence in Győr (Hungary) and Vienna. Under his guidance was constructed the Royal Castle of Buda. From 1786 to 1798 Kempelen worked as a councillor at the Royal Hungarian Chancery. He was multi-faceted genius: he improved the steam engine, designed a prototype of the steam turbine, and as early as 1778 invented a talking machine as well as a typewriter for the blind. Kempelen's most famous invention was the so-called automaton chess player which was described in detail in *Leipziger Magazin für Naturkunde, Mathematik und Oekonomie* (1784). Its structure is not completely known because it was rumored that the machine was destroyed in 1854 by a fire in Philadelphia, Pennsylvania. Edgar Allan Poe based one of his novels on Kempelen's invention of a chess playing machine. Kempelen also invented the world's first talking machine which uttered a few sentences in 1790. He is the founder of experimental phonetics and physiological acoustics. In 1791 he published his main work in Vienna which was recently reprinted under the same title: *Mechanismus der menschlichen Sprache nebst Beschreibung einer sprechenden Maschine* (Stuttgart-Bad Cannstatt: F. Frommann, 1970. XIV, 456 p., illus.)

Antal Péch (1822-1895) was Hungary's most gifted mining engineer in the past century. Péch's research into crustal movements proved to be of epochal significance. His valuable papers appeared primarily in *Bányászati és Kohászati Lapok* (Journal of Mining and Metallurgy) which he founded. One of his major publications describes the principles and practical rules of ore dressing (*Az ércek előkészítésének elvi és gyakorlati szabályai*. Pest, 1869).

Metallurgist Antal Kerpely (1837-1907), for many years a professor at Selmecbánya, attained world fame through several patented inventions. As an engineer at the Ruszkabánya Metallurgical Works Kerpely obtained a patent for his novel process to free iron from (sulphur, phosphor and copper) contaminations. In 1884 he obtained a patent for his regenerative puddling furnace. His books and articles were avidly pored over by professionals around the world for its new inventions like the air heater and for designs of his like iron smelting plants. His periodical *Berichte über die Fortschritte der Eisenhüttentechnik* (Leipzig, 1866-1896) was unique and well-known by iron metallurgists everywhere as was his handbook on iron metallurgy (*A vaskohászat gyakorlati és elméleti kézikönyve*. 2 vols., Selmecbánya, 1873-1874); *Die Anlage und Einrichtung der Eisenhütten* (Leipzig, 1873-1884).

János Zámbó (b. 1916) and his study group obtained excellent results in the analytical examination of mining plants, while Gusztáv Tarján (b. 1907) and his associates made outstanding contributions to the solution of ore dressing and enrichment. Sándor Geleji (1898-1967) significantly improved the treatment of malleable metals. László Gillemot (b. 1912) and his co-workers deserve credit for several innovations and they resolved several problems of welding and reaction kinetics in connection with titanium production. Much research has been done on the structure and colloid chemical properties of bentonites. Aladár Buzágh's research above others raised the value of Hungary's bentonites in the world market which is reflected in the upward spiraling export statistics in the past decades. A systematic study of Hungary's mining technology is provided by Gusztáv Tarján's article on mining, ore and coal preparation ("Bányászat, érc- és szénelőkészítés") in Lajos Ligeti, ed., A magyar tudomány tíz éve, 1945-1955 (Budapest: Akadémiai Kiadó, 1955. pp. 283-287).

Sándor Rejtő (1853-1928) while a professor at the Budapest University of Technical Sciences established, partly using devices and instruments of his own design, the University's widely known Laboratory for Testing Materials. Rejtő's theory of the behavior of structural materials produced an international echo. He developed entirely new theses of mechanical technology (inner friction, lasting changes of form) and devised a unique microscope as well as tensiometer for material testing. Sándor Rejtő also worked out a novel technique for the malleable transformation of metals. His inventions and innovations were introduced into many industrially developed countries. For his successful research work, the New York Congress (held September 3-7, 1912) of the International Association for Testing Materials elected him its honorary chairman. Rejtő published many items, monographs as well as articles, in the field of mechanical technology in Hungarian and foreign languages. One of his outstanding books on mechanical technology appeared in German under the title, Einige Prinzipien der theoretischen Mechanischen Technologie der Metalle (Berlin, 1927).

Having completed his studies at the Budapest University of Technical Sciences, Donát Bánki (b. 1859) was assistant professor there from 1879 to 1880 and full professor from 1899 until his death in 1922. With the aid of János Csonka he constructed the world-renowned Bánki-Csonka engine whose most significant innovation was the first petrol (gasoline) carburetor for which they obtained a patent in 1893. A year later Bánki obtained a patent for the first high-pressure combustion engine (internal combustion engine). Bánki's water-turbine, named after him, opened new vistas in the development of hydroelectric power plants. The major foci of his literary endeavors encompassed the theory of gas engine and the basic principles of designing steam and hydraulic engines. One of his chief works on hydraulics and hydraulic engines (Gyakorlati hydraulika és hydrogépek; jegyzet, vols. 1-2, Budapest, 1901-1902) is still in the form of university lecture notes. His Neue Wasserturbine (Berlin, 1917) captured the interest of technologists even decades after his death (Cf. the relevant study by Charles Arthur Mockmore and Fred Merryfield entitled *The Banki Water-Turbine* (Corvallis, Engineering Experiment Station, Oregon State System of Higher Education, Oregon State College, 1949. 30 p.).

János Csonka was born on January 22, 1852 in Szeged, Hungary.

His father, Vince, was a well-known master machine builder-smith, who spoke fluent Latin, and who with the help of his apprentices and assistants constructed a wide variety of mechanisms from windmills and watermills to medical instruments. János Csonka was an autodidact. Unlike his brother who became a chemical engineer, he did not enroll in any university but spent several years traveling and working in Western Europe, particularly in Paris, London, Vienna and Zürich. While an employee of well-known factories there he studied the technology of machine construction, preparing numerous notes and sketches and perfecting his knowledge of languages. In 1876 he accepted a position in Budapest as head of the training shop at the József Nádor Műegyetem (Budapest University of Technical Sciences). The youngest of many applicants for the job, who included several engineers with extensive backgrounds in industry, Csonka occupied this position for 48 years and was instrumental in the education of two generations of engineers.

In 1883 he built a new type of gas engine for the training shop. He manufactured each part himself, even the mold for cylinder casting. In contrast to other contemporary gas-engines, this one was already a four-cycle engine with intake and discharge valves. Subsequently he built several newer and better engines, some of which could be fueled either by gas or gasoline.

In 1887 János Csonka was joined in his work by Donát Bánki, who later became a distinguished professor at the university. Their collaboration proved to be exceptionally fruitful. One of their inventions was the gas and kerosine hammer (1888), later manufactured by the Berlin Anhaltische Maschinenbau A.G. In 1893, as we have already referred to, they produced the Bánki-Csonka engine. A measure of their progress is the fact, that they patented engines at a time when the original patent of the Otto engine still exerted strong restrictions on engine manufacturers. The most significant feature of the Bánki-Csonka engine was a constant fuel lever atomizer which they constructed in 1891 and which they named "carburetor." It was operated by the suction effect produced by the piston. The first model already had float valve control, a needle valve and a butterfly valve. (Their carburetor was patented half a year before Maybach — who is sometimes erroneously considered its inventor — built his first similar device.) The classic simplicity of this invention — its functioning automatically and with scarcely any moving parts — insured its general acceptance. Today, almost a century after it was conceived by Csonka, it is still an essential part of all gasoline engines. The Bánki-Csonka engine was simple and in efficiency and operational safety it surpassed the original Otto engine as well as all contemporary ones. It had a vertical cylinder, an enclosed crank case, and the use of valves was far in advance of other designs. The engines but employed the asymmetric crank shaft design of Westinghouse steam engines, a never before utilized concept in gasoline engines which was consequently incorporated into combustion engines throughout the world. Another remarkable innovation of this engine was the "automatic tube ignition", which eliminated the then customary flame ignition, a perennial fire hazard. As a result, the new and highly combustible fuel — gasoline — could now be safely used. As an even more important innovation, they raised the compression ratio, which led to lower fuel consumption.

János Csonka ranks among the first to employ aluminum in the construction of gasoline engines and to use the high voltage magneto ignition for gasoline engines.

In 1896 the collaboration between Bánki and Csonka became less intimate and in 1898 ceased altogether. Csonka now concentrated his attention on the construction of various vehicles of transportation. The engine-powered tricycles built by him for the Hungarian Postal Management in 1900 were in use for 20 years. He built the first Hungarian automobile in 1902, a car with two cylinders. He designed and built the very first four-cylinder automobiles in Hungary in 1904. He designed various four-cylinder automobiles in 1906-1912, which proved their excellent quality in several international competitions.

At the age of 73 János Csonka retired from the university, and opened a workshop for the construction of gasoline engines. Under the leadership of two of his sons, János and Béla, it grew into a significant industrial plant: the "Csonka János Gépgyár" ("János Csonka Machine Factory"). It was nationalized in 1948 and from it developed what is known today as the "Kismotor- és Gépgyár" ("Small Engine and Machine Factory"). János Csonka continued to work intensely until just a few days before his death on October 27, 1939.

Although János Csonka never received any formal training as a mechanical engineer he was nonetheless awarded that title when the Hungarian Chamber of Engineers invited him to become a member under the so-called "genius clause." He was the first ever to be so invited.

Mechanical engineer and inventor Károly Zipernowsky (1853-1942) started his career as a pharmacist. He then enrolled in the Budapest University of Technical Sciences from which he graduated in 1878 in electrical engineering. Between 1893 and 1924 Zipernowsky worked as professor on the faculty of electrical engineering at the University. He preceded his contemporaries in the production and utilization of alternating currents. With the help of Miksa Déri (1854-1938) Zipernowsky constructed in 1883 a self-induction alternating current generator. In 1889, once again with the scientific collaboration of Miksa Déri, he obtained a patent for a multiphase current distribution system. In his work, *Zipernowsky Károly saját és másokkal közös, szabadalmazott találmányai* (His patented inventions . . . Budapest, 1900) he described 40 of his inventions, among them a single-track electric railway. But his most significant invention in the field of electrical engineering was jointly produced and credited with Miksa Déri (1854-1938) and Ottó Titusz Bláthy (1860-1939): the transformer in 1885. See their study under the title "Secondary generators and transformers" in the *Electrical Review* (London, 1885, 1886).

As mentioned above, Ottó Titusz Bláthy belonged to the giants of electrical engineering and helped invent the world's first transformer thus making possible the conduction and distribution of electric currents over long distances. Bláthy also was the first in the world to successfully apply the parallel switch of alternating currents (Cf. Cerchi power plants, Rome, Italy). The first watt meter of alternating currents (1885), and the first adequate turbine regulator were fashioned according to Bláthy's patents. One of his single-phase engines is housed in the Deutsches Museum in Munich. The number of his Hungarian and foreign language publications amounts to about fifty. The Vienna and Budapest technical universities awarded him a honorary doctor's degree in 1917.

Kálmán Kandó (1869-1931) was a pioneer in railway electrification. The electric engine he designed (Kandó-engines) made possible railway electrification. Between 1896 and 1898 Kandó constructed the first high-voltage three-phase electric railway (Evian-les-Bains). Then he converted Italy's Valtellina Railway into an electric line (1898-1902). Due to the technical accomplishments of the Valtellina Railway the Italian government with the aid of U.S. capital established the Società Italiana Westinghouse and started manufacturing Kandó's electric locomotives. The Kandó system of railway electrification was so successful that it was called "Sistema Italiana." Kandó spent some years in the United States as consultant to Westinghouse. His literary activity centered on railway electrification. Among his articles dealing with Italy's railway electrification are "Der Betrieb der Valtellina-Bahn mit hochgespannten Drehstrom" (*Zeitschrift d. Vereins Deutscher Ingenieure*, 1903), "Neue elektrische Güterzugslokomotive der Italianischen Staatsbahnen" (*Zeitschrift d. Vereins Deutsche Ingenieure*, 1909).

Following the American Civil War, but especially in the last quarter of the nineteenth century, the rapid advance of American industry and technology exerted a great impact on men of science everywhere. During this period Benjamin Franklin was gradually replaced in the foreign image by Thomas A. Edison, perhaps the most prolific inventor of the

United States and the world. Tivadar Puskás (1844-1893) traveled to the United States in order to discuss with Edison the idea of telephone exchange. According to Edison's statement, "Puskás was the first man in the world who raised the idea of telephone exchange." For several years Tivadar Puskás was Edison's close associate and European representative. Puskás developed the principle and the very first form of telephone exchange and invented the "telephonic newspaper" (telephonograph, telediffusion, telefonhírmondó). Puskás' idea of broadcasting formed an organic part of the universal history of telecommunication. The original form of Puskás' invention was displayed at the Paris Electrical Exhibition in 1881. It was Puskás who constructed the telephone exchange in Boston in 1878, and the first European telephone exchange in Paris in 1879. In 1887 he introduced the multiplex switch boxes which had an epochal significance in the further development of telephone exchange. In 1892-1893 Puskás obtained an Austrian patent right to his invention, the "telephonic newspaper,"—a system of news distribution to a network of subscribers which functioned as a wire news system and the precursor of the radio—which commenced operation in Budapest as early as 1893. The historic event was described recently by David L. Woods as follows: "The real pioneering genius who created these concepts of modern radio and television programming was Tivadar Puskás, who established the first operational broadcasting organization in 1893." (David L. Woods, "Semantics versus the 'First' Broadcasting Station," *J. Broadcasting*, vol. 11, 1967, no. 3, pp. 199-207). Some of Puskás ideas are included in his article, "Organisation und Einrichtung einer Telephonzeitung" (*Zeitschrift für Elektrotechnik*, 1893).

Dénes Mihály (1894-1953), a well-known mechanical engineer, is listed among the world's leading scientists of electronic image transmission.

Th. Knaur fully describes Mihály's work in the *Fernsehbuch*. Mihály began his historic photoelectric and sound recording investigations as early as 1912. In August 1928 he introduced the first television (transmissions of static photographs and very simple moving objects) to about 250,000 visitors at the official exhibition arranged by the German Post Office in Berlin. In November of the same year (1928) Mihály transmitted motion pictures. The historic culmination of Mihály's accomplishments came at 11 p.m. on March 8, 1929 when the Berlin-Witzleben radio station broadcast the first moving television program in history.

Physicist Kálmán Tihanyi (1897-1949) in his Hungarian and 1928 British and French patent applications described the archtype of today's television picture tube. F. Schroeder, professor of the Berlin Technical College, gives a detailed account in his *Die neue Entwicklung insbeson-*

dere der deutschen Fernsehtechnik (Berlin, 1937) of the development of our modern picture tube, stating that the first (1926, 1928) description of the heavy-duty charge storage tube was made by Kálmán Tihanyi while its engineering was the work of V. K. Zworykin in the RCA Laboratory in 1933. Schroeder emphasizes that the inventor of the charge storage principle was Tihanyi while Zworykin applied Tihanyi's principle.

At the turn of the last century a great invention was made in the telecommunication industry. Antal Pollák (1865, Szentes — 1943, Budapest) and József Virág (1870, Földvár — 1901, Budapest) obtained a patent for their telegraph apparatus which was able to communicate 5,000 signs per minute. For details see Antal Pollák's main work *40,000 szó óránként* (40,000 words per minute. Budapest, 1934) and József Virág's study "A Pollák-Virág-féle betűíró gyorstelegráf" (*Magyar Mérnök- és Építész Egyl. Közl.*, 1901).

Theodore von Karman (1881, Budapest — 1963, Aachen, Germany), the world-famous scientist of aerodynamics graduated from the Budapest University of Technical Sciences in 1902 and was appointed as an assistant there to professor Emil Schimanek and Donát Bánki. Some years later von Karman earned international reputation by his contribution to heat and quantum theory: his modification in collaboration with M. Born of Peter Debye's modification of Einsten's theory "that atomic heat diminishes more rapidly for low temperatures than is indicated by experiment" secured increased scientific acceptance of the theory. (Cf. M. Born and Th. v. Karman's study in *Physik. Zeitschr.*, vol. 13, 1912, p. 297 as quoted by Florian Cajori, *A History of Physics*. New York: McMillan Co., 1929, p. 317).

Subsequently to spending several years in German aeronautical engineering research positions, Von Karman was appointed director of the Guggenheim Aeronautics Laboratory at the California Institute of Technology in 1930, and in 1936 he became a U.S. citizen. In 1945 he was made director of the Science Advisory Group of the United States Army Air Forces. Later he was chief of the Scientific Advisory Board and subsequently headed technical missions to examine German research projects in supersonic aerodynamics and guided missiles. Between 1944 and 1945 Von Karman had a leading role in the development of the B-36, B-47 and B-52 as well as the Atlas, Titan, and Minuteman rockets. His aeronautical innovations include experiments with helicopters and gliders which he conducted during World War I from 1915 to 1918 as the chief of research in the aviation corps of the Austro-Hungarian Army and as advisor to the Junkers airplane company in Germany from 1922 to 1928. He made unique contributions to the theory of elasticity, the strength of materials, aircraft structures, aerodynamics, hydrodynamics as well as thermodynamics. Von Karman originated the boundary surface theory and the theory of wing surface design and dimensioning for supersonic aviation. Because of his wide-ranging work in aeronautics Von Karman is often remembered as the father of supersonic flight. Von Karman's most important studies in mathematics, mechanics, aerodynamics, as well as a comprehensive survey of his research and theories together with a well-compiled bibliography, are published in his *Collected Works*. Rhode-St. Genèse, Belgium: Von Karman Institute for Fluid Dynamics, 1975. VII, 388 p., illus. Bibliography: pp. 373-385).

Miksa Hermann (1868-1944) and Károly Láng (1877-1938) are considered the architects of the theory and application of rolling. Later their theory was improved by Theodore Von Karman.

Albert Fonó (b. 1881) carried out extensive research on converting heat energy into mechanical energy and was granted the first patent for the propulsion of an airplane by jet engines.

László Verebélÿ (1883-1959) and Ferenc Ratkovszky (1900-1965) bettered to a considerable degree Kandó's electric locomotive.

Á. Géza Pattantyús (1885-1956) achieved lasting results in his research in hydrodynamics.

In the field of automation, Ottó Benedikt (b. 1897) designed the autodyne amplifier whose performance among control apparatus is superb.

Antal Kherndl (1842-1919) studied in Budapest and Karlsruhe. Obtaining his diploma in mechanical engineering at the Zürich Polytechnikum, he became assistant there to the world-famous Carl Culmann, professor of statics and founder of graphostatics. Antal Kherndl devoted all his life to statics, evolving a theory of bridge construction and even improving upon Culman's methods in graphostatics.

Kherndl's assistant, Győző Mihailich (1877-1966), and his research associates — especially Károly Széchy — carrying on Kherndl's work in bridge construction and excelling in, among other topics, the study of shell construction. In addition to bridge building, Győző Mihailich is well-known for his research in reinforced concrete construction. Mihailich contributed many innovative articles to foreign journals — *Beton und Eisen*, and *Bautechnik*, for instance. His book on reinforced concrete structures (*Vasbetonszerkezetek*. Budapest, 1922) is still regarded an important handbook today.

Károly Széchy (1903-1972) studied civil engineering at the Budapest University of Technical Sciences and in London. Széchy specialized in bridge and tunnel construction. He prepared the general designs of the Árpád Bridge (Budapest) and directed its construction work. Széchy also directed the reconstruction of the Budapest bridges destroyed during the siege of the capital city at the end of World War II. He also organized and directed Budapest subway constructions. In 1958 and 1964 Széchy lived in Egypt as guest professor of Cairo University. In 1968 he accepted a guest professorship at the University of Western Ontario (Canada). With the aid of his co-workers Széchy solved several problems of bridge building as well as of the construction of shell structures. His work on foundation errors (*Alapozási hibák*. Budapest, 1957, 2d ed., 1962) has been translated into English, Russian, German, Spanish, French and Czech languages, while his book on tunnel construction (*Alagútépítéstan*. Budapest, 1961) has appeared in English, French and German.

József Petzval (1807, Szepesbéla — 1891, Vienna) received his engineer's diploma from the Institute of Engineering (Mérnöki Intézet) of Pest University in 1828. Between 1828 and 1835 Petzval was employed as a city engineer of Pest. From 1832 to 1836 he worked as a lecturer and then full professor of mechanics and higher mathematics at Pest University, afterwards accepting a full professorship at Vienna University where he worked until 1877. Petzval invented and constructed in 1840 the double system of lenses which were employed in the Voigtländer cameras. According to a note found in Petzval's literary legacy, he should be held the inventor of the modern system of anastigmatic lenses. Interestingly enough, the somewhat altered form of the Petzval objective is still used in most modern movie cameras and slide projectors. Around 1860, using a device he himself constructed, Petzval made reliable photogrammetric measurements. His experiments are summarized in his following two books: *Bericht über die Ergebnisse einiger dioptrischen Untersuchungen* (Pest, 1843), and *Bericht über optische und dioptrische Untersuchungen* (Sitzungsberichte, Vienna, 1857). His older brother, Ottó (1809-1883), likewise an engineer-mathematician and graduate of Pest University, taught higher mathematics there between 1858 and 1883. In addition to mathematics Ottó Petzval was versed in hydraulic engineering.

Ödön Riszdorfer (1893-1944), the inventor of a new photographic camera, in October of 1930 in Budapest was granted patent rights to an invention which is the basis of the automatic and semi-automatic exposure control employed in modern cameras. On July 30, 1934, Riszdorfer signed a contract with Eastman Kodak of Rochester (USA) on the manufacture of his semi-automatic camera. This was the Super Kodak Six-20 which has been on the world market since 1938.

Mechanical engineer Oszkár Asbóth (1891, Pankota — 1960, Budapest) played a prominent role in helicopter research. Having completed his studies between 1909 and 1913, Asbóth was engaged in airplane construction at Arad, Szabadka and Wiener-Neustadt. While experimenting with airscrews at the Fischamend experimental institute during World War I he developed the so-called Asbóth-airscrews. Pursuant to his experimentation Asbóth himself constructed helicopter and as early as September 9, 1928 made the first successful helicopter flight witnessed by many foreign experts. Asbóth's successes in helicopter research lent new impetus to relevant research throughout the world. Asbóth's accomplishment has been acknowledged by the scientific community the world over, including the prestigious Fédération Aéronautique Internationale which awarded him the Paul Tissandier diploma in 1954. See Asbóth's works *Az első helikopter* (The first helicopter. Budapest: Népszava, 1965. 252 p., illus., ports.) and *Géprepülés* (Budapest: Zrínyi Kiadó, 1957. 278 p.).

András Mechwart (1834-1907), a mechanical engineer, in 1859 joined the small Budapest workshop of Abraham Ganz, a Swiss foundry master who emigrated into Hungary. Together they developed this small workshop into the world famous Ganz Works. Mechwart invented the flour rolling mill thereby introducing the revolutionary refined milling which earned Hungary's milling industry international renown.

Pál Csonka (son of János Csonka, the eminent inventor) was born on July 8, 1896 in Budapest. He prepared for his university examinations while on combat duty in World War I. At the same time he successfully developed new techniques for military sound measurement to locate enemy artillery. As a result of this work, at the age of 22 he was offered the position of professor at the Schallmessschule in Vienna. In 1920 he received his diploma in architectural engineering at the József Nádor Műegyetem (Budapest University of Technical Sciences). In the same year he submitted a plan in the largest postwar design competition to redevelop the Margitsziget (Margit Island) in Budapest, and to the great surprise of many, finished ahead of his professors receiving 2nd prize. After several successful design competitions he was invited to lecture on mathematics at the Budapest University of Technical Sciences. Later he taught the subject of statics. In 1936 he was appointed to the chair of statics at that university. His lectures were noted for their convincing simplicity. He knew well how to make an abstract subject interesting and attractive for his students. He became one of the most popular professors at the university, his expertise was widely acknowledged. During the period of persecutions of the World War II era, Csonka saved the lives of several of his colleagues, and actively resisted the government's efforts to relocate the university in Germany. In 1956 he was elected member of the Revolutionary Committee during the Hungarian Uprising. During those days he insisted that no person be removed from his job or otherwise disciplined without due process of law. After the suppression of the uprising disciplinary proceedings were started against him. He was dismissed from his position. Later he served as a consultant and led the research group on statics of the Hungarian Academy of Sciences.

His scientific work started long before he joined the university faculty. It is published in journals, conference reports, in the form of books and in publications of the Hungarian Academy of Sciences. In 1975 the number of items of his publications passed 730, among them over 200 scientific papers in foreign languages, mostly in English and German, the rest in Hungarian. By 1975 Pál Csonka delivered over 180 scientific lectures (in addition to his university lectures) in many countries, although for decades he was not allowed to leave Hungary.

His most important contributions are the following: He extended the theory of buckling of Shanley (1952). In a series of papers Csonka discussed the lateral buckling of beams (1955); this work attracted considerable international attention. He was the first to construct a theory for a chain of beams (1935). His theory started intensive research activity in this field. He introduced a new step (which he named "distortion") in the relaxation calculation of multi-story frames (1948), thereby simplifying such calculations since his method converges faster than any other method. Pál Csonka introduced the concept of proportional frame (1955). Several of his articles are devoted to the problem of membrane shells. He designed new methods to solve such problems. One of these is the method of undetermined shape (1958). He developed new types of shell structures, named after him in the literature. His relevant publications include *Membranschalen* (Berlin: W. Ernst, 1966. VII, 92 p. illus.).

In 1954 he received a Kossuth Prize. He is honorary member of international organizations, such as the International Association for Shell Structures (IASS). Csonka was honored with external membership in the Polish Society for Theoretical and Applied Mechanics (1969), and by an honorary degree from the University of Dresden, East Germany, in 1975.

Charles F. Pulvári (b. 1907) graduated from the Budapest University of Technical Sciences in 1929. Up to 1949, when he emigrated to the United States, Pulvári held several leading positions in Hungary in the field of electrical engineering and was granted many patents for his unique achievements. From 1953 until his recent retirement, Pulvári was professor of electrical engineering at the Catholic University of America in Washington, D.C., and head of its Solid State Research Laboratory. He produced more than twenty patented inventions in the United States including the "Electric Automatic Circuit Breaker with Reclosing Means"; "Method and Apparatus for Recording and Reproducing Intelligence"; "Electrical Condensers". For decades Pulvári has been a principal investigator of many U.S. (Navy, Air Force, etc.) scientific and technological projects. He authored around 40 professional studies appearing in U.S. periodicals and presented a number of papers at U.S. and international conferences. He is still active in a consulting capacity.

Geography

The Age of the Renaissance proved to be quite fruitful in many aspects. It embraced the work of a well-known humanist which marked the beginning of geographical literature in the Middle Danube Valley. This pioneer was a Transylvanian Saxon, Johannes Honterus (1498-1549). Honterus' *Rudimenta* (1530), a treatise on cosmography, appeared in numerous editions and was a bestseller throughout Europe. Márton Szepsi Csombor (1595-1623), himself a child of the Renaissance, traveled all over Europe and published his widely read itinerary *Europica varietas* . . . (Kassa, 1620) in which he advocated human liberty and social progress.

Sámuel Mikoviny (1700-1750) attained European fame by his introduction of astronomical studies into scientific cartography. In the world arena of cartography as early as the second half of the eighteenth century a Hungarian mapmaker had attained the highest level of execution. It was geodesist and hydraulic engineer Antal Balla (1739-1815) whose administrative and hydrographic maps of Hungary (Tisza-Berettyó Valley, Danube branch at Pest, Pest County, etc.) were studied as models by future generations of international cartographers. Aside from this Antal Balla was first to draw a plan for a navigable Danube-Tisza Canal. (See his *Cum propositione Navigationem Danubialem cum Tibiscale per erectionem canalis navigabilis . . . connexionis*, 1791.)

Lajos Lóczy (1849-1920) earned his engineer's diploma at the Zürich Technical University. He was ostensibly the first scientist in Hungary who systematically trained himself in geology and geography. In the years 1877 to 1880 Lóczy participated in Béla Széchenyi's Asiatic expeditions. His relevant observations and discoveries received worldwide recognition. Concerning the genesis of the Mid-Asiatic deserts, Lóczy surprised the world with an entirely new hypothesis. Lóczy successfully proved that the stone and sand materials of the deserts in the Middle Asia are not the remnants of the sea bottom. He theorized that they are the process of accumulation, which opinion has been shared by scientists since. Lóczy's investigations into the geological nature of South-East India's mountain ranges are also of a pioneering character. For details see his description of China's physical geography in *A khinai birodalom természeti viszonyainak és országainak leirása* (Budapest, 1886).

Two-time prime minister of Hungary Pál Teleki (1879-1941) gained international fame and a prestigious prize from France by compiling in 1909 an atlas to the history of cartography of the Japanese Islands (*Atlasz a japán szigetek cartográphiájának történetéhez*. Budapest, 1909). One of its recent reprints in German appeared under the title *Atlas zur Geschichte der Kartographie der Japanischen Inseln* (Nendeln, Liechtenstein, 1966. 184 p.).

Pál Teleki's prize-winning treatise of the historical survey of geographical thought (*A földrajzi gondolat története*. Budapest, 1917) added significantly to his international reputation. He also wrote a standard work on America's economic geography (*Amerika gazdasági földrajza*. Budapest, 1922), and compiled a much-used ethnographic map of historical Hungary based on population density (*Magyarország néprajzi térképe a népsűrűség alapján*. Budapest, 1919).

Teleki and Jenő Cholnoky (1870-1950) exerted possibly the greatest influence on the education of geographers engaged in Central European studies. Jenő Cholnoky was instrumental in solving several problems in physical geography in the Danube Basin. Both geographers spawned a great number of gifted disciples. Béla Bulla (1906-1962) followed the path of Jenő Cholnoky and carried out important investigations into the Middle Danube Valley's physical geography as well as geomorphology, elucidating its glacial epoch and climatic morphology. Márton Pécsi (b. 1923) surpassed even his predecessors in the area's physical geography research. Tibor Mendöl (1905-1966) was one of Europe's best-trained scientists in the methodology of settlement geography. Mendöl's very first monographic publication (*Szarvas földrajza*. Debrecen, 1928) was regarded a model for studies in settlement geography and history.

Pál Zoltán Szabó (1902-1963) dealt chiefly with karst hydrology while Sándor Radó (b. 1899) published notable works in economic geography and earned an international reputation as a cartographer.

The Kogutowicz family occupies a special niche in the long line of noted geographers. Manó Kogutowicz (1851-1908), founder of scientific cartography in the Middle Danube area, prepared its first county atlas in 1885. In 1890 Kogutowicz established the Hungarian Institute of Geography (*Magyar Földrajzi Intézet*), a center of high-level geographers' and cartographers' training. His son, Károly Kogutowicz (1886-1948), longtime professor at Szeged University, wrote works of lasting value in anthropogeography and the best book to date on the regions of the Dunántúl and the Little Alföld (*Dunántúl és Kisalföld*. Budapest, 2 vols., 1928-1932). Károly Kogutowicz also produced a very useful map on the complex settlement structure of the Danube Basin's ethnic entities (*Magyarország néprajzi térképe*, 1928).

Eugene Fodor (b. 1905) finished his secondary school studies in the Hungarian-language gimnázium at Losonc. He attended a series of foreign higher educational institutions, among them the Sorbonne and Grenoble where he obtained a political science diploma (1927), the Hochschule für Welthandel, Hamburg (1928), and the London School of Economics (1929). Fodor is the editor, publisher and president of the world-renowned *Fodor's Modern Guides, Inc.*, which has published both in the United States and Great Britain exhaustive and magnificently illustrated travel guides to over 50 countries with translations in French, German, Italian, Spanish, Dutch, Hungarian, etc. Since 1948 he has been a member of the World Tourist Organization, the Authors League, etc. Fodor has been the recipient of several international writers awards.

Explorers

As a rule, the Hungarian explorers of Asia shared the inspiration of theories that the ancient home of the Magyars was located somewhere on that continent. As early as the thirteenth century Julian, a Hungarian friar and outstanding explorer of his day, was sent to Asia in search of a tribe of the Magyars separated from the main body during their westward migrations three centuries before. Friar Julian did indeed locate them and had no difficulties understanding their spoken Hungarian.

Márton Szepsi Csombor (1595-1623) was an eminent figure among late Protestant humanists. Szepsi Csombor distinguished himself by his travels throughout Europe and a widely read book on his journeys under the title *Europica varietas* (1620) in which he described not only the places he visited but the differing national characteristics of European nations. Well ahead of his contemporary travel book writers, he took a firm stand— as mentioned before — on national liberty of the masses against any kind of oppression by noble classes and foreign elements.

Sámuel Teleki's (1845-1916) expedition is of great significance in the discovery of Africa. Teleki traveled to Africa in the autumn of 1886 in the company of Ludwig Höhnel, an Austro-Hungarian Navy officer from Pozsony. On April 12, 1887 they became the very first explorers ever to reach Kilimanjaro. And in October of 1887 they became first among explorers of Africa to scale the Kenya Mountains. Then came Sámuel Teleki's greatest achievement: the discovery of Lakes Rudolf and Stephanie. Sámuel Teleki and his exploring and hunting expedition traveled about 3,000 kilometers in Africa, which journey he described in minute detail in his three journals (*Tagebuch* 1: Dec. 30, 1886-Feb. 17, 1888; *Tagebuch* 2: Feb. 18, 1888-Oct. 3, 1888; *Tagebuch* 3: March 17, 1895-April 11, 1895). These journals themselves are day-by-day accounts of the expeditions, including encounters, friendly and hostile, with the native population, description of climate and topography, hardships in travel, etc.*

---

*The Sámuel Teleki materials are held by the Michigan State University Library, East Lansing, Michigan. The material was purchased from Charles Teleki by the Michigan State University's African Studies Center.

Béla Széchenyi (1837-1918), son of Stephen Széchenyi and an outstanding geographer and geologist, completed his higher studies in Berlin and Bonn. Then he traveled throughout England, France, Italy, the Balkan Peninsula, the United States and Canada. Between 1865 and 1870 Béla Széchenyi was in Africa four times as a big game hunter. His three year-long expedition to Asia began in 1877 and its most important accomplishment was the exploration of those mountain ranges which border the Tibetan plateau on three sides. The latter is all the more noteworthy because Sven Hedin in 1906 discovered the Trans-Himalayas on the basis of the results of the Széchenyi expedition. Among many other specialists, geologist Lajos Lóczy, linguist Gábor Bálint, and topographer Gusztáv Kreitner took part in the Széchenyi expedition. Twenty Hungarian and foreign scientists participated in classifying and evaluating the material collected by the expedition. Béla Széchenyi's publications include his United States travelogue (*Amerikai utam*. Pest, 1863), and the three-volume detailed, scientific description of his East Asia expedition entitled *Gróf Széchenyi Béla keletázsiai útjának tudományos eredménye, 1877-1880*) with Lajos Lóczy. Budapest, 3 vols., 1890-1897. In German: *Die wissenschaftlichen Ergebnisse der Reise des Grafen Béla Széchenyi in Ost-Asien, 1877-1880*. Wien: E. Holzel, 1893-1899. 3 vols.).

One of the world's greatest explorers of all times, archaeologist and linguist (orientalist) Sir Aurel Stein was born in Budapest (1862, d. 1943 in Kabul, Afghanistan). Having completed his higher studies in Vienna, Leipzig, and Tübingen, Aurel Stein went to England and became much influenced by the orientalist Sir Henry Rawlinson and Sir Henry Yule, the outstanding expert on Marco Polo's travels. Stein immediately entered into Great Britain's service and later became a naturalized citizen. In 1888 he took a job at the Punjab University in Lahore as professor of Sanskrit philology. In 1900 he set out on the first of his numerous expeditions. His greatest historic journey occurred in 1907 when he discovered the westernmost portion of the Great Wall of China and after making their way 200 miles eastward the expedition arrived at the "Caves of the Thousand Buddhas". His expedition found more than 900 Chinese manuscripts, many paintings and other art relics. Most of them are now housed in the British Museum at London. Stein's expeditions yielded materials of great archaeological value in exploring the Central Asian desert areas. Aurel Stein maintained unbroken contact with his native land, especially with the Hungarian Geographical Society (*Magyar Földrajzi Társaság*). Returning to Europe in 1909, Aurel Stein by the invitation of the Hungarian Geographical Society delivered a lecture in Budapest, and in 1922 was the first scholar to receive the Society's Lóczy Medal established that very year. In his will he presented his invaluable private library to the Hungarian Academy of

Sciences. Beginning with his first scholarly publication which appeared in 1894, Aurel Stein's publications were extensive and overwhelmingly in English.

Geology — Mineralogy — Hydrology . . .

Ádám Tomcsányi (1755-1831) graduated from the Institutum Geometricum founded by Joseph II in 1782 as a part of the philosophical faculty in the University of Buda. This engineers' institute fulfilled a real mission because by 1850 it had turned out 1,275 engineers. Tomcsányi, in cooperation with Pál Kitaibel (1757-1817), was the first scientist to utilize isoseismic concepts in the interpretation of earthquakes. He first applied these concepts in the analysis of the earthquake of Mór (Hungary) in 1810 which he described in his *Dissertatio de terrae motu . . . in genere, ac in specie Moorensi anno 1810* (with Pál Kitaibel, 1 map. Buda, 1814).

József Szabó (1822-1894), mineralogist, mining engineer, and the founder of the school of petrology earned world reputation for several of his accomplishments: namely, for his pioneering work concerning the trachyte system, for his investigations into Hungary's Tertiary volcanism, and for his study of the geological conditions of the Great Hungarian Plains. His several published monographs deal variously with the geological structure of the Tokaj-Hegyalja region (*Tokaj-Hegyalja és környékének földtani viszonyai*. Pest, 1866), his travels in the United States (*Északamerikai utam vonala*. Budapest, 1883), his lectures on different topics of geology (*Előadások a geológia köréből*. Budapest, 1893). Elemér Vadász evaluated József Szabó as a geologist in his treatise entitled *A magyar földtan útja Szabó József nyomában* (Hungarian geology and József Szabó. Budapest, 1967).

József Krenner (1839-1920) functioned as a professor of mineralogy and petrology from 1870 to 1894. As the head of the Hungarian National Museum's Division of Minerals, Krenner created one of the world's best mineral collections. He was esteemed as one of Europe's best mineralogists for his descriptions and definitions of minerals. He discovered many new minerals: to name but a few, a new gold-silver tellurium ore called Krennerit discovered in 1877, followed by Semsey, Lorandit and Avasit in 1881, Kornelit in 1888, Andorit in 1889, Warthait in 1909 and Schafarzikit in 1915. József Krenner summarized his work on mineralogy in *Magyarország ásványai* (Hungary's minerals. Budapest, 1908).

Aladár Vendl (1886-1971) and Miklós Vendel (b. 1896) conducted investigations into rock and ore formation in Hungary and abroad and solved many relevant problems. Both are recognized petrologists throughout the world.

Elemér Vadász (b. 1885) surveyed the geology of bauxite and coal and was the first to recognize the nature of stratigraphy and sediments of manganese ores in the Bakony Mountains. He wrote a well-documented treatise on the 150-year history of Hungary's geological research in *Magyarország földtana* (Geology of Hungary. Budapest, 1953) which was translated into Russia (*Geologiia Vengrii*. Moscow: Mir, 1964. 531 p.).

Mine surveying and geophysics were the specialties of geodesist Antal Tárczy-Hornoch (b. 1900). With his associates he constructed a superior triangulation method for geodesic area measurements. Tárczy-Hornoch and his co-workers also substantially improved the correction calculus. The following of his many publications (books and ca. 250 periodical articles published in Hungary and elsewhere) contain his noteworthy contributions: Das *Verwerfenproblem im Lichte des Markscheiders* (Berlin, 1927), *Kiegyenlítőszámítás* (Correction calculus, 1930), *A Gauss-Krügerkoordináták számítása* (Calculation of the Gauss-Krüger coordinates, with István Hazay, 1951), *Tablitsy dlia ellipsoida Krasovskogo* (dlia zony 40° do 55°—Tables for Krasovskii-ellipsoid between 40th and 55th parallels, 1959);*Markscheiderische Studien* (1963). Antal Tárczy-Hornoch has substantially improved the making of geodetic instruments and promoted the application of electronics in geodesy.

Elemér Szádeczky-Kardoss (b. 1903) completed his studies in geology and geochemistry at Budapest University and has been a university professor since 1934. He is a member of several domestic and foreign professional organizations such as the International Union of Geological Sciences, the U.S. Geochemical Society, the World Academy of Art and Science, corresponding member of the Wien Geological Society, and honorary fellow of the Mineralogical and Geological Society of the Czechoslovak Academy of Sciences, and of the Finnish and East German geological societies. He has done outstanding research in sediment (deposit) formation, formation of magnetic rocks, geochemistry and related fields. Szádeczky-Kardoss conceived an entirely new theory of rock formation based on the principle of transvaporization. As a result of his research work, new concepts were formulated as to the origin of bauxite and the localization and extension of ore deposits. He has published over 300 scientific papers in his native land and abroad. His monographs of chief importance discuss the formation, chemistry and mining of coal (*A kőszén képződése, kémiája és bányászata*, 1952), geochemistry (*Geokémia*. Budapest: Akadémiai Kiadó, 1955. 680 p.), and the structure and evolution of the earth (which is an introduction to petrology) under the title *A föld szerkezete és fejlődése; bevezetés a kőzettanba* (Budapest, 1968. 339 p.).

András Tasnádi Kubacska (b. 1902) has written 28 books, several of them in foreign languages, and over 200 articles in geology and mineralogy.

On the basis of his investigations geophysicist László Egyed (b. 1914) originated a totally new theory as to the expansion of the earth's inner structure which has attracted considerable support in the world's scientific community.

János Bogárdi (b. 1909) graduated from Budapest University of Technical Sciences, pursuing post-graduate studies at the Iowa State University (USA) from 1937 to 1938. From 1962 Bogárdi has been university professor of hydraulic engineering at the Budapest University of Technical Sciences. From 1958 to 1965 Bogárdi was the president of the European commission on hydrometeorology of the World Meteorological Organization (WMO). 1964 brought him to the United States on a year-long lecture tour. The sciences of hydrology and hydraulics, among others, have been enriched by his theory concerning the alluvial deposits of rivers (A hordalékmozgás elmélete, 1955), by his explanation of the role of subsoil waters, and a wealth of other contributions. Bogárdi has published more than 100 items in Hungarian and foreign journals along with several books. His Korrelációszámitás és alkalmazása a hidrológiában (Correlation calculus and its application in hydrology. Budapest, 1952) ranks among his standard books.

A member of the Toulouse Academy of Science, and honorary doctor of the universities of Grenoble and Padua, Endre Németh (b. 1891) has been honored by several other foreign professional institutions for his extraordinary accomplishments in hydrology, hydromechanics, hydraulic engineering and water supply. He played a pioneering role in the planning and construction of the irrigation system of the Alföld. Németh devised up-to-date hydrological methods for modern agriculture. (A korszerű mezőgazdaság vizi feladatai, 1942) and wrote a widely used handbook on hydrology and hydrometry (Hidrológia és hidrometria, 1959) and a high-level university textbook on hydromechanics (Hidromechanika, 1963).

Endre Németh and Emil Mosonyi (b. 1910) claim international repute for their solution of major practical problems in water power utilization. Mosonyi's multivolume Water power development (1963-) published in several languages is appreciated by specialists in water-power electric plans and hydraulic machinery for its innovative nature. Owing to his singular expertise, Mosonyi was chosen to be the editor of the proceedings of the International Seminar and Exposition on Water Resources Instrumentation. Organized by the International Water Resources Association in cooperation with the American Society of Engineers, the seminar was held June 4-6, 1974 in Chicago and the two-volume set of proceedings appeared under the title Water Resources

Instrumentation, etc. (Ann Harbor, Michigan: Ann Harbor Science Publishers, 1975). Emil Mosonyi also edited a polyglot dictionary of water-powered electric plans and waterways (*Vizierő-művek és viziutak*. Budapest: Terra, 1960. 204 p.)

Jenő Kvassay (1850-1919) studied at Budapest University of Technical Sciences. He made several study tours of Germany, Switzerland and France and began publishing extensively in Hungarian, German (*Wiener Landwirtschaftliche Zeitung*), and French (*Annales des Ponts et Chaussés*, Paris)—a paper in the latter language entitled "Notes sur le moulinet de Woltman" was well-received by professional circles everywhere. Kvassay played an eminent role in devising the theory of water regulation and its application. In 1879 he authored a book which was regarded as a classic in agricultural hydraulics. It was Kvassay's brainchild to establish the International Danube Commission which came into being thirty years after his death. Kvassay also wrote in 1872 about the desirability of seafaring vessels using Budapest harbor, a dream which has since been realized.

NOBEL PRIZE LAUREATES OF HUNGARIAN DESCENT

1905	Philipp Lénárd	Physics:	Research on cathode rays
1914	Robert Bárány	Physiology or Medicine:	Physiology and pathology of vestibular apparatus.
1925	Richard Zsigmondy	Chemistry:	Elucidation of the heterogeneous nature of colloidal solutions.
1937	Albert Szent-Györgyi	Physiology or Medicine:	Work on biological combustion.
1943	George Charles de Hevesy	Chemistry:	Use of isotopes as tracers in chemical research.
1961	Georg von Békésy	Physiology or Medicine:	Functions of the human inner ear.
1963	Eugene P. Wigner	Physics:	Principles governing mechanics and interaction of protons and neutrons in the atomic nucleus.
1971	Dennis Gábor	Physics:	Invention and development of holography.

PART III — THE HISTORICAL AND THE SOCIAL SCIENCES (THE HUMANITIES)

Historiography

1

The First Period of Historical Writing [1]

Up to the end of the tenth century A.D., the movements of the Magyar tribes from the northern shore of the Black Sea to the conquest of their present homeland in the Middle Danube Valley, their tenth century raids and campaigns, and their peculiar way of life, including their religion as well as their political and military system, were recorded by Arab, Persian, Greek, French, German, Italian and Slavic writers. Their interest in describing the Magyars stemmed in large part from the latter's military art, for the pagan newcomers posed a potential threat to the just established Christian order in the heart of Europe. This earliest phase of the country's history can be quite well reconstructed with the aid of medieval forms of writing such as chronicles, gestas (historias), annales, legends and like. At this time in Central and Western Europe the annalistic form dominated. Until the country's conversion to Christianity which started in the closing decades of the tenth century and climaxed during the reign of Stephen I (1000-1038), no native sources and writers had related national or even local events. Though the Magyars were keenly interested in their origins and heroic deeds and they possessed even an alphabet of their own, none of their records, if ever any existed at this time, survived. The various descriptions and biographical works in which pre-conversion events, stories and doings of the Magyars were recorded in this early phase of the Middle Ages were done by foreign authors. Thus the country's historical writing began exclusively with the products of foreign annalists, chroniclers and other compilers.

To our present knowledge, native history writings began in the first half of the eleventh century — approximately between 1019 and 1060 — with very brief annalistic notes on epochal affairs and dates especially concerned with the Benedictine Order in Hungary. These notes prepared by an unidentified monk were preserved in the Annales Posonienses written around 1195 and reflect contemporary Western pattern. These annalistic notes are of importance only for their chronology of some national and local events.

The first Hungarian legend dating from the same period is a brief sketch of the life of two Poles, Zoerard and his disciple, Benedict.

Zoerard and Benedict are regarded to be among the earliest apostles of Christianity in Hungary. The author, Bishop Maurus of Pécs, compiled a typical, brief legend which also contained a few data on cultural history. Then and for decades to come, legends and vitae dominated historical interest. These forms of writing mirrored a characteristic medieval transcendentalism. Miracles abounded and, as in the ancient plays with deus ex machina, a sudden intervention by Providence was a recurrent feature. Naturally, legends and vitae had little value with respect to describing historical reality except when the subjects of these legends and vitae were the saint-members of the House of the Árpáds and were thus connected with the life of the royal court and contributed to the charismatic power of the dynasty. The legends of Hungarian saints (Legenda Minor S. Gerardi; Legenda Maior S. Gerardi; Legenda Minor S. Stephani Regis; Legenda Maior S. Stephani Regis; Hartvic's Life of St. Stephen; Legenda S. Emerici Ducis; Legenda S. Ladislai, etc.) bore some relationship to contemporary narrative writings, chronicles, and in the light of textual criticism they occasionally complemented each other.

In this initial phase of historical writing, the country's literature lagged far behind its Western counterparts. The then so modish narrative writings — annales, chronicles and gestas — were not produced by native authors until after the end of the twelfth century. Historical writing by native authors, as I have mentioned previously, appeared much later and for centuries bore many signs of foreign influence. At this time the way of historical narration had already been paved methodologically by such great names as Jordanes, Paulus Diaconus, Liudprand, and later Otto of Freising, and many others in the West.

Because Christianity was disseminated in Hungary by foreign priests, there were many foreign scholars active in that country and some Hungarians attended foreign schools. But Western cultural influence came to fruition only around the turn of the twelfth and thirteenth centuries. The first narrative work at the Western level was written around 1091-1092 by an unnamed native writer. His *Gesta Ungarorum* is rightly regarded as the principal source for all later works during the Age of the Árpáds and even afterwards for the duration of the Middle Ages. Anonymus' *Gesta Hungarorum* is one of its continuations. The fact that his *Gesta Hungarorum* has come down in a single manuscript whose first leaf is missing is responsible for the uncertainty surrounding the date and identity of the author. Anonymus' *Gesta* was first published in 1746 and since then a continuing debate has mobilized a series of Hungarian and foreign historians to solve the many relevant problems. Anonymus was schooled at the University of Paris and was employed at the time of writing as a notarius, presumably in the court of Béla III (1173-1196). He made use of primary sources and to a certain degree even employed some form of source criticism when condemning "the false tales of peasants and the naive songs of joculators." His critical judgment is best demonstrated in the chapter on the Conquest which can even today be considered as a masterpiece of objective narration and description. Not only Anonymus but all other writers up to Simon Kézai entitled their works *Gesta Hungarorum* and quoted *Gesta Ungarorum* which was compiled during the last years of the reign of St. Ladislas (1077-1095) as their principal source. The text of this earliest Gesta was lost and never found to this day.

Simon Kézai's *Gesta Hungarorum* consists of a history of the Magyars from earliest times to the historian's day. His *Gesta* is dedicated to Ladislas IV (1272-1290) whose "faithful clerk" he styles himself. Two of the greatest narrative chronicles of the Middle Ages, the *Chronicon Budense* and the *Chronicon Pictum Vindobonense*, used Kézai's *Gesta* as their main source. The *Chronicon Budense* gives the country's history up to the middle of the fifteenth century. Printed by András Hess at Buda in 1473, the text is the first book printed in Hungary.

Among the continuations of Kézai's *Gesta* under the name of Chronicle is the *Chronicon Pictum Vindobonense* written in 1358 by Márk Kálti, a canon of Székesfehérvár. This magnificently illuminated codex, which property gave the text its name, was made between 1374 and 1376. Following Kézai's pattern, Márk Kálti also divided the country's history into two parts: the history of the Huns and of Magyars, that is, prima et secunda cronica hungarorum.

The last chronicler of medieval Hungary was János Thúróczy. His work also relied heavily upon the works of predecessors, including Kézai's *Gesta*. In the chapter following the death of Louis the Great of Anjou (1342-1382) the *Chronicle* is quite independent, and is a very reliable, substantial source material with respect to the Age of the Hunyadis. The Thúróczy manuscript was printed twice in 1488: in Brünn and in Augsburg.

2

The Age of the Renaissance and the Turkish Yoke

From about the last quarter of the fifteenth century the naive, medievally styled narration of historical past could no longer satisfy even the sparse readership of the time. Therefore, under the influence of antique historiography, the humanists searched for new guidelines to be applied in their studies. Instead of the transcendent attitude so characteristic of medieval literature, these Renaissance historians labored in the service of national politics based upon dynastic interests. This dynasty-oriented interpretation of history had some deep roots, as I have already pointed out, in Hungary's gesta and chronicle literature. Therefore, the transition from medieval traditions to the new requirements occurred relatively rapidly and smoothly.

Antonio Bonfini's (1434 ?-1503) *Rerum Ungaricarum decades . . .* was first printed in Basel, in 1543 by Márton Brenner, its first complete edition having been prepared by Zsámboki (Sambucus), also in Basel, in 1568. In conformity with the new trend, Bonfini tried to prove in minute details King Matthias Hunyadi's Roman descent as well as Latinizing the country's personal and place names. Bonfini also searched for and found entirely new, heretofore never used source material thereby eliminating the naive, obsolete medieval practice of chronicles. Bonfini was the first historian who fully laicized the country's past to do service to his ruler, King Matthias I (Hunyadi) upon whose commission he undertook this task. Bonfini located new sources which had never before been available to chronicles and gesta writers. His depiction of the age of the Hunyadis is especially valuable and was regarded for the next two centuries as significant chiefly for its character-painting style and for Bonfini's clear-cut efforts to establish causal relationships.

Another Italian humanist who affected Hungarian historical science was Petrus Ransanus (1420 ?-1492). As the envoy of Naples, Ransanus stayed in Hungary during 1488. Using a chronicle text, Ransanus rewrote, also in a humanistic style, Hungary's history up to 1485 and titled it *Epitome rerum Ungaricarum* (Pécs, 1558). This work comprised a part of his world history. These Italian-born humanists were instrumental in launching a systematic data gathering during the second half of the reign of King Matthias Hunyadi. As a result, contemporary historians like János Thúróczy and the immediate Hungarian followers of Bonfini were satisfied no more with the previously utilized familiar chronicles, legends and vitae, but made use of foreign sources such as Rogerius (*Carmen miserabile*), Liudprand, Otto of Freising, as well as Czech and Polish chronicles, contemporary documents (diplomas), etc.

The central character of Miklós Oláh's (1493-1568)[2], main work, *Hungaria et Atila* (Vindobonae, 1763; its newest critical edition appeared in 1938 under the editorship of László Juhász and Kálmán Eperjessy in L. Juhász, *ed.*, Bibliotheca scriptorum medii recentisque aevorum, XVI), was also Matthias I (Hunyadi), the Renaissance king.

The last and most significant representatives of humanistic historiography were Miklós Istvánffy (1538-1615) and István Szamosközy (1570-1612). No vestiges of either medieval ideology or methods existed in their works. Miklós Istvánffy sided with the Habsburg dynasty in the interpretation of events. He related especially those events which occurred between 1490 and 1606 giving a more detailed account of the post-1547 national affairs. Istvánffy's main contribution was published under the title *Historiarum de rebus Ungaricis libri XXXIV* (Cologne, 1622). A prominent public figure, Miklós Istvánffy was Vice Palatine, and secretary to Miklós Oláh in addition to being a relatively well trained, part-time historian.

István Szamosközy (Zamosius, 1570-1612) was the first professional historian who from his youth prepared seriously for his chosen profession and could not be diverted from his youthful aspiration. Szamosközy studied at Padova, Italy, where his first work on Transylvania's Roman inscriptions entitled *Analecta lapidum vetustorum et nonnularum in Dacia antiquitatum* appeared in 1593. This work merited for him the distinction of being the first archaeologist in Hungary. Returning home, Szamosközy was hired as the archivist of Gyulafejérvár (Transylvania), and appointed as the court historian of István Bocskay, Prince of Transylvania. Szamosközy also researched the origins of the Magyars and systematically buttressing his work with archival sources on the country's sixteenth-century history, applying a well-developed methodology truly advanced for his age. Unlike his contemporaries, Szamosközy was not a partisan chronicler of events. He drew upon well-selected source materials with scientific objectivity and criticism. Sándor Szilágyi, a noted nineteenth-century scholar issued a critical edition of Szamosközy's works in a four-volume set entitled *Szamosközy István történeti maradványai.*[3]

Unfortunately, Szamosközy, presumably due to the adversity of wartime conditions, could not create a school of disciples. His research and objective critical work remained quite an isolated phenomenon and even his valuable source collection was scattered throughout his homeland after it was used by Farkas Bethlen in the seventeenth century.

Farkas Bethlen (1639-1679) was the chancellor of Transylvania and a historiographer who wrote Transylvania's history between the crucial years of 1525 and 1609. In his *Historia de rebus Transylvanicis* Szamosközy's lost manuscript was utilized. János Bethlen (1613-1678) followed in his father's footsteps, becoming chancellor of Transylvania as well as a historian. His works, *Rerum Transylvanicarum libri IV* (Nagyszeben, 1663), and *Historia rerum Transylvanicarum ab anno 1662-73* (issued by Elek Horányi in Vienna, 1782) can likewise be regarded as important sources.

The Principality of Transylvania enjoyed independence and relative peace while Hungary, the motherland, had been divided into parts and kept under constant military pressure by the Ottoman Empire. Transylvanian writers during the Age of Turkish Yoke, which lasted up to the turn of the seventeenth and eighteenth centuries, excelled also in writing autobiographies, memoirs, diaries, and their correspondence can also be regarded as preeminent contributions to this early stage of historical scholarship. Hungary's tragic defeat at Mohács in 1526 signaled the start of a defensive struggle against the Ottoman Empire which engaged its energy full-scale for one and a half centuries. This fact in itself can explain why historical writing could not make greater progress during the periods of Reformation and Counter-Reformation. Historiographers of that era involved themselves in political and religious struggles. They were, in many instances, high-ranking office holders or statesmen who happened to be interested in the pivotal issues of the day. But in spite of their preoccupation with the daily politics this turbulent age produced very important source materials — namely, diaries, memoirs, autobiographies, and a vast political and diplomatic correspondence. It can also be stated that with the exception of a few, this age conspicuously lacked scholars whose aim would have been to conduct a systematic and organized research. Menyhért Inchofer, a Hungarian Jesuit living in Rome, was one of the few exceptions. Inchofer planned to compile the country's church history based on unpublished sources, but he completed only the first volume which related events up to the middle of the eleventh century. For this he relied heavily upon the collections of the Vatican archives in his *Annales ecclesiastici regni Hungariae* (Tomus I., Roma, 1644).[4]

3

The Founding of Scientific Historiography
1700-1825

Gábor Hevenesi (1656-1715), the Rector of Pazmaneum in Vienna, Austria, was the first scholar to engage in full-fledged systematic and well-organized historical research. In his *Ungariae sanctitatis indicia* (Nagyszombat, 1692), Hevenesi made use of the data and material of the Bollandists relating to Hungary's past. It was through his handwritten guide entitled *Modus materias conquirendae pro Annalibus Ecclesiasticis regni Hungariae continuandis a P. Gabriele Hevenesi compositus et typis datus* that Hevenesi carved his niche as the initiator and pioneer organizer of systematic historical research in Hungary. *Modus materiae* . . . surveyed and condemned the backwardness in church history research and the destruction by war of archives, and exhorted scholars to participate in a systematic data-gathering service, instructing them how to collect and copy manuscript and other documents and treat and select reliable oral traditions, in order to carry on and improve Inchofer's unfinished work. The new enterprise was intended by him to be a synthesis of church as well as national affairs as reflected in unpublished sources. Hevenesi's plan was adopted by Count Leopold Kollonics, Archbishop of Esztergom. The Archbishop ordered the heretofore inaccessible official and church archives to be opened to researchers. Hevenesi's handwritten collection for two centuries remained a treasury for historical research. He succeeded in founding a school whose most important scholars were Sámuel Timon (d. 1736), István Kaprinai (1714-1786), György Pray (1723-1801), and István Katona (1732-1811). Kaprinai significantly enlarged Hevenesi's 140-volume handwritten collection of sources to 323 volumes and planned to publish at least a part of it accompanying it with critical notes.[5] In addition, Kaprinai was the first scholar who was interested in and laid down the foundation of a Hungarian numismatics.

Sámuel Timon compiled a detailed index to Hevenesi's collection, continued his source-gathering activity, and between 1714 and 1719 completed a work on the history of Hungary. Its second edition appeared in 1736 under the title *Epitome chronologica rerum Hungaricarum*. Timon's lifework was of epochal significance since he redirected his disciples' attention from the domination of church affairs to the primacy of political history in the nation's past and present life.

Mátyás Bél (1684-1749) saw a relationship between history, public law, and geography and wanted to write a work which would have included the universal knowledge (history, politics, physical geography, ethnography, linguistics, economics, medicine, etc.) of his country. In his main work, *Notitia Hungariae novae historico-geographica* (Vienna, 1735-1742), he became a world-renowned representative of the German polyhistor school. Bél also began recording Hungary's narrative sources in his *Adparatus ad historiam Hungariae* (I. decas: Posonii, 1735, II. decas: 1745, 1746) which was the first important, well-arranged source publication in Hungary. Bél also prepared the Preface to his Austrian disciple's really substantial source collection. This is Johann Georg Schwandtner's *Scriptores rerum Hungaricarum veteres ac genuini* (Tomi I-III, Vienna, 1746-1748) which included the first edition of Anonymus' *Gesta Hungarorum*, the most vehemently debated source publication in the country's historiography.

György Pray (1723-1801) already during his university years studied Hevenesi's source collection and became influenced especially by the works of Sámuel Timon and Mátyás Bél. His great work, *Annales regum Hungariae ab A. 997 ad A. 1564*. (I-V, Vienna, 1763-1770), was based on well-selected primary sources whose authenticity was critically analyzed in the most important synthesis of Hungary's history written during the eighteenth century. Pray succeeded in grouping historians around himself and his school of critical historiography was substantially superior to the one-sidedness of the old church-affiliated historiographical trends. Pray and his collaborators — among them Károly Wagner; István Schönwisner, the founder of Hungarian archaeology and numismatics (concerning the latter discipline Kaprinai also pioneered), Károly Ferenc Palma, the first collector of heraldic monuments; as well as Dániel Cornides — were appointed professors of auxiliary sciences of history at the University in Pest. His correspondence was so prolific that it substituted at that time for periodical literature. The influence of Pray's school of historical criticism lasted about half a century and affected the elite of the native historians such as István Katona, Dániel Cornides, Márton György Kovachich.

The largest critical synthesis of this period was written by István Katona entitled *Historia critica regum Hungariae* (Vols. 1-42, Pest, 1779-1817) which was also an excellent source collection to be used for generations to come and is valuable even to the present.

Apart from the source-gathering activity of Márton György Kovachich (1744-1821), he proposed to organize a historical society with its own library and archives. After such preparations at the outset of the nineteenth century, several multi-volume national histories were written, among them the most significant being Ignác Aurél Fessler's ten-volume synthesis.

It is worth mentioning that between 1711 and 1800, when scientific, critical historiography was founded, 509 volumes of historical works were published in toto in Hungary, an overwhelming 78 per cent of which (397 volumes) were the products of Hungarian printing house.[6]

At the turn of the eighteenth and nineteenth centuries it became quite evident that Hungary had already entered the transition period from semifeudalism to capitalism—more aptly phrased, to a bourgeois socioeconomic order. Its intellectual life seemed to be interwoven more and more with the threads of the philosophy of the Enlightenment and the ideas of the French and American revolutions. These foreign influences helped shape the concept of the nation as a historical entity and put it in the focus of scholarly as well as public attention. Many a new literary product affected by the progressive movements of the contemporary West expressed also to some degree anti-clerical mentality. The first such works which reflected this new, bourgeois attitude were written by Ignác Aurél Fessler (*Die Geschichte der Ungern und ihrer Landsassen*. Leipzig. Vols. I-X, 1815-1825), who used the volumes of I. Katona's *Historia critica*; Johann Christian Engel (*Geschichte des ungarischen Reichs und seiner Nebenländer*. Halle. Vols. I-IV, 1797-1804); and Benedek Virág (*Magyar Századok* which was published in parts from 1808).[7]

4

Stagnation in the Age of Reforms
1825-1848

The central issue of these years was the struggle for self-fulfillment of all ethnic entities across the Habsburg Empire and especially in Hungary. All nations and ethnic minorities happened to be more or less involved in these self-realization movements. And all wanted to materialize their political aims primarily through the promotion of their native languages and literatures. Naturally, emotional prejudices against each other came to the fore in public life and even well-trained professional historians like István Horvát (1784-1846), and his friend György Fejér (1766-1851), director of the University Library in Pest, rather served illusory goals fostered by a national romanticism. It would have been urgent to rewrite the country's history in an objective and up-to-date manner at such a time, but all the more because scholarly research and publication had for decades been at a standstill. Far from doing so, István Horvát especially threw himself into solving the origins of the Magyars by inventing fantastic hypotheses in order to satisfy public demand as well as the self-centeredness of a rapidly elevating fever of nationalism.

The romantic interest in discovering the ancient home and the origins of the Magyars ran so high in those decades that Alexander Kőrösi Csoma (1784-1842), the famous founder of Tibetan philology, as early as his student years decided to visit the remnants of the "Asiatic Magyars" in the heart of that continent. He, as it is known, was unsuccessful in his quest to locate those Magyars on his romantic journey.

István Horvát's *Rajzolatok a magyar nemzet legrégibb történeteiből* (1825) expressed the national pride of the masses and shortly thereafter the historian himself became a symbol of national romanticism and consciousness for generations.

Otherwise, István Horvát's source collection comprised several hundreds of handwritten volumes, though he was not really interested in publishing them or making notes on them. He published only a few documents which he equipped with some explanatory remarks. Horvát was the best known historian of the Reform Age and the first scholar of bourgeois descent who systematically dealt with the auxiliary sciences of history as a professor at the University of Buda.

Through applying a naive etymological method, Horvát strove to demonstrate that Magyars played a role in the most significant occurrences of world history. This unscholarly method was all the more inconsistent on his part because his philosophy of history as depicted in his diaries mirrored a really advanced system of historical knowledge. Despite his errors, Horvát exerted valuable influence upon a series of his disciples, including such names as László Szalay, Ferenc Toldy, and even József Eötvös. Horvát also affected Pál Vasvári whose essays on the philosophy of history revealed a prominent, historically-minded thinker.[8]

György Fejér collected and published with notes an enormous quantity of medieval sources under the title *Codex diplomaticus Hungariae ecclesiasticus ac civilis* (Buda, Vols. I-XLIII, 1829-1844). Because of his uncritical approach to documents, Fejér's collection should be treated very cautiously. Otherwise, his *Codex diplomaticus* was the largest source-publishing enterprise throughout the Age of the Reforms. During these years there were but a few source publications. Even the leading scholarly journal, *Tudományos Gyűjtemény* (founded 1817 by Gy. Fejér), sparsely published historical documents. It should also be noted that it was József Weszerle who in 1816 started collection of sources of Hungarian numismatics.

Following the examples of the eighteenth-century pioneers, József Kemény began collecting sources relating to the history of Transylvania and Hungary, a small part of which was published between 1835 and 1845. Similarly, Antal Gévay collected and published important sources of the Turkish yoke, and László István Endlicher issued the laws, statutory provisions and other sources pertinent to the early Middle Ages in his *Rerum Hungaricarum Monumenta Arpadiana* (Sankt Gallen, 1849).

In spite of the fact that the newly created organization, the Hungarian Academy of Sciences (Magyar Tudós Társaság), was founded in 1825 and began its variegated activities at the outset of the 1830's, it failed to promote social and historical sciences because of its preoccupation with linguistics and literature and with the political aspects of the Magyar language. The change in the policies of the Academy came only after the defeat of the Uprising of 1848-1849.

Before closing this chapter of the evolution of Hungary's historical thought, a brief reference should be made to József Teleki's accomplishment. His monumental portrait of the age of the Hunyadis seems to be the most scholarly work of the period. President of the Hungarian Academy of Sciences, József Teleki lived from 1790 to 1855. His multivolume *Hunyadiak kora Magyarországon* has proven to be of extraordinary value even for the researchers of today by virtue of its having been written on the basis of well-selected unpublished documents and in an amazingly objective manner. In preparation for decades, only its first four volumes were published during the author's lifetime (Pest, 1852-1854). This monumental contribution was the first detailed portrait of an entire period (the age of the Hunyadis) in the country's historical literature.

5

Prelude to Organized Science

The Uprising of 1848-1849 ended in complete defeat for Hungary. The war had its aftermath of realizations. Hungarians became preoccupied with regaining their independence until the Austro-Hungarian Compromise of 1867. Owing to the lessons drawn from this political struggle for independence, it dawned on the intelligentsia that there had accumulated by then numerous shortcomings in cultural policy. The Academy's activity, for instance, was one-sidedly philological. Now they saw clearly that the social and historical sciences had been neglected for decades. Psychologically it was natural that after the devastating defeat politicians and scholars riveted their eyes upon the more fortunate and glorious periods of history, and started organizing a centralized mode of research for the first time in history.

Though the Academy of Sciences had its own historical division since its founding, it failed to mobilize individuals and existing organizations for systematic work. In 1854, the Academy finally organized its first permanent section, the Committee on Historical Sciences (Történettudományi Bizottság). According to its By-laws, the Committee is entrusted to issue systematically the most important sources on national and local history. For this purpose, the Committee launched the *Magyar Történelmi Tár* (Hungarian Historical Collection, later *Történelmi Tár*) which periodical served successfully for decades the cause of source-publishing and interpretation. The Committee also issued the well-edited volumes of *Monumenta Hungariae Historica*, by now the largest source publishing enterprise, following the pattern of *Monumenta Germaniae Historica*. The *Monumenta Hungariae Historica* consisted of the following parts: First class (Scriptores), 32 volumes; Second class (Diplomataria), 26 volumes; Third class (Documents of the National Assembly), 9 volumes; Fourth class (Diplomatic documents), 7 volumes.

Between 1855 and 1877 the periodical *Magyar Történelmi Tár* appeared in 25 large volumes. The Committee was instrumental in issuing many other source publications in these decades. Its organizational work surpassed all expectations.[9]

Not only well-arranged and edited source publications but some highly comprehensive and synthetic new works characterized this period: first of all, Ferenc Toldy's history of Hungarian literature (*A magyar nemzeti irodalom története*. Pest, 1851, 1852), the first such synthesis, and László Szalay's (1813-1864) truly scholarly synthesis of Hungary's history (*Magyarország története*. Vols. I-IV, Leipzig, 1852-1854, Vols. V-VI, Pest, 1857-1859) — another first — for which he twice was honored with the Grand Prize of the Hungarian Academy of Sciences. Very characteristically, both of them used much unpublished material and applied up-to-date methodology. For its objectivity and structural excellence Szalay's masterpiece can largely satisfy even present-day scholarly requirements.

Mihály Horváth (1809-1878), like Szalay, prepared several important works while in exile after the 1848-1849 events. Horváth significantly enlarged the scope of research to embrace the history of the peasantry, economic conditions, and made a masterful description of the Age of Reforms (*Huszonöt év Magyarország történetéből 1823-1848*. Vols. I-III, Geneva, 1865) and the Revolution itself (*Magyarország függetlenségi harcának története 1848 és 1849-ben*. Vols. I-III, Geneva, 1865, Pest, 1871).

In comparing the two pioneers of modern Hungarian historiography, László Szalay and Mihály Horváth, there seems to be some justification to state that Szalay purposefully tried to be as objective as a practicing historian can be, while Horváth interpreted events, personalities and institutions on the value scale of liberty. Though both scholars possessed talent for historical research, both turned to become historians only by chance. Szalay originally was a brilliant jurist, and Horváth a Catholic priest.[10]

Inspired and encouraged by the rapid advance of historical scholarship, many just established organizations even outside the nation's capital devoted their full energy to research and publication. Thus under the guidance and supervision of Károly Ráth, Arnold Ipolyi, and Flóris Rómer, the Dunántúl Society for Archaeology and History in Győr (Dunántúli Régészet- és Történetkedvelők) issued between 1865 and 1880 a seven-volume then exemplary set of source publication entitled *Hazai Okmánytár*.

Partly as a result of the work of the Toldy-Szalay-Horváth trio, scholarly organizations, churches, administrative units, and many individuals set up a demanding objective: to continue and finish the great eighteenth-century enterprises by (1) searching for and collecting and publishing a possible cŏmplete set of Hungary's historical sources, national and local alike, and (2) by compiling a new, modern synthesis of the country's historical past. These new truly challenging undertakings began to take shape in the next epoch of rapidly increasing and multifaceted scholarly activities.

6

Towards Positivism in the Era of Specialization
1867-1918

The founding of the Hungarian Historical Association (Magyar Történelmi Társulat) and its periodical *Századok* (The Centuries), both of which were established in 1867, proved to be the most decisive steps in the organization of historical sciences. It is singularly noteworthy that both the Association and its journal have by now successfully withstood all political crises the country has undergone since, and that they still constitute an organic part of the historical profession.

The newly established Association brought about meaningful changes in research trends. While the Academy's Committee of Historical Sciences worked under the guidance and supervision of the old generation and failed to modernize itself, the leaders of the Association and the editors and contributors of *Századok* belonged to the promising younger generation of scholars who devoted themselves to important reforms in conformity with contemporary Western, chiefly German, scientific movements.

In addition to Mihály Horváth, Arnold Ipolyi (1823-1886) also became a Vice-President, and the younger scholars formed a decisive majority in the Association's leadership. Thus the Association's most active members were the relatively young ones and it was they who determined the direction of research and publication in the next fifty years. Among them Arnold Ipolyi, Sándor Szilágyi, Károly Szabó, Nándor Knauz, Ferenc Salamon and especially Gyula Pauler and Vilmos Fraknói played eminent roles.

The government acknowledged the efforts of this younger generation and appointed its leading figures to university chairs of history, Ferenc Salamon, Károly Szabó, and Flóris Rómer being among them. Rómer simultaneously was appointed as head of the Division of Archaeology of the Hungarian National Museum. Vilmos Fraknói was named head of the National Széchényi Library, Sándor Szilágyi became the director of the University Library in Budapest, and the most talented — Gyula Pauler — headed the National Archives.

Within a short while these young scholars exerted influence even on the policies of the Academy. Already in 1871 the Academy's Second (Historical) Division elected the then twenty-eight-year old Vilmos Fraknói as its secretary, subsequently as the rapporteur of the Academy's Committee of Historical Sciences. Fraknói and other young scholars in high positions paved the way for young historians who after the death of Ferenc Toldy in 1875 took over the leadership in both institutions: the Hungarian Academy of Sciences and the Hungarian Historical Association.

The takeover meant more than a change in influential figures. It amounted to a thorough reshaping of professional organization. It meant new possibilities for training historians in specialized fields. It signaled the end of the age of autodidacts and polyhistors. This new generation of historians made very careful preparations for their chosen profession and devoted full energy to it. They believed that a professional historian should be well-trained in methodology, should base his findings on a variety of archival sources and should be versed, among others, in critical philology and the like.[11] This group of historians through conscious division of labor became highly specialized. Under the guidance of Gyula Pauler and Vilmos Fraknói they pursued their research on the grounds of positive facts and data and not on theorizing as their predecessors were inclined to do. Through analytical criticism of sources they tried to determine historical truth in an objective way. They published many volumes dealing in details with heretofore ignored topics of economic and social history.

Many a historian approved the philosophy and methodology of positivism. But, in this conjunction, it should be noted that as practicing historians they did not rigidly apply Comte's system or any other theorem; they refused to accept or apply *a priori laws*. Their positivistic approach meant rather an untiring search for unpublished sources, new documentary evidence.

Gyula Pauler (1841-1903) ranked high among the positivists. Since he was the first in Hungary to advocate positivism the historians' community has regarded him as the father of the Hungarian version of positivism. He investigated its effects on historiography and discussed Auguste Comte's views on history.[12]

But Pauler did not accept positivism as a whole. He as a practicing historian refused to approve any theoretical standpoint at the expense of induction. Pauler's brand of positivism emphasized that researchers should take into consideration only individual phenomena of history, facts, data, and only then, if possible, should they try to abstract from historical reality appropriate laws.

Pauler stressed his widely accepted main thesis in the following: "Our task, therefore, is not speculation but narration . . . In order to depict realistically and completely historical phenomena it is necessary to consider all aspects of historical life . . . Only through this practice can science attain its true objective: to be the picture of the past and key to the future . . . "[13] Pauler adhered to these precepts in his two-volume, well-footnoted main work (*A magyar nemzet története az Árpádházi királyok alatt*. Budapest, 1893) for which the Hungarian Academy of Sciences granted him its Grand Prize in 1895. I would conclude that

Pauler stood nearer to "factography" than to any form of theoretical positivism. As the first head of the Hungarian National Archives he ordered the arrangement of its collections chronologically and by subject matter. Though Pauler could not establish a school of followers in the traditional sense of the word, his influence lasted for decades and some of his works stirred the interest of the historians even during the interwar period.

Positivism through the works of French philosopher and critic, Hippolyte Taine, and English historian Henry Thomas Buckle greatly affected Hungarian historians in the last quarter of the nineteenth century. Buckle's chef d'oeuvre, *History of civilisation in England*, was not only translated into Hungarian (1873-1875) but there appeared several affirmative reviews in contemporary literature about his realistic philosophy of history. On the other hand many others severely criticized Buckle's work as dangerous for its materialistic approach.[14]

Undoubtedly, positivism helped pave the way to economic and social history writing as well as drawing attention to material culture in general. Henrik Marczali (1856-1940) already in 1881 emphasized the importance of economic and social studies, and Ignác Acsády (1845-1906) focused his attention on historical statistics. Acsády's work on the history of serfdom is useful even now for its great quantity of data and its impartiality. Already in 1893, Károly Tagányi as editor-in-chief, and Ignác Acsády as chief contributor, launched, first such work in Europe, a periodical dealing exclusively with economic history. It was entitled *Magyar Gazdaságtörténelmi Szemle* (Hungarian Review of Economic History). Owing to the general political climate of the Age of Dualism (1867-1918) the majority of scholars engaged themselves rather in constitutional matters and other topics with a political overtone — an orientation already clearly expressed in the proceedings of the First Congress of Hungarian Historians in 1885.

The First Congress of Hungarian Historians[15] held in Budapest, 1885, and arranged by the Hungarian Historical Association aimed to be the first survey of the country's historiography. Several lectures were delivered dealing mostly with methodology, auxiliary sciences, archivistship and the teaching of history at secondary and college level. Arnold Ipolyi (1823-1886), then President of the Hungarian Historical Association, in his opening address spoke about a new trend intended to raise historiography to the rank of exact sciences through enormously increasing the quantity of source materials. Ipolyi regarded Niebuhr and Ranke as ideals for historiographers. He stressed that historiography for educational purposes should reflect the national spirit.

This Congress indicated — perhaps for the first time — that German science had already made headway in the country's historiography. By contrast and prior to this, Voltaire, Rousseau, and Montesquieu and similar thinkers exerted influence upon Hungarian intellectuals.

In line with the rising German influence, Gyula Lánczy's lecture on historical methodology vigorously questioned the value of positivism. By rejecting Auguste Comte's and H. T. Buckle's positivism, Lánczy accepted the anti-positivist teachings of Humboldt and Droysen. Deeply affected by them, Lánczy argued that spiritual-intellectual factors are of primary importance—so much so that without them there is no history at all. Lánczy made even more direct reference to German historiography when stating that Germans presented a rigorous political education (eine strenge politische Ausbildung) in the context of their historical science. Lánczy's reasoning like that of Ipolyi's was interwoven with current nationalistic tendencies.

Lajos Thallóczy (1857-1916) spoke on the use of archival materials; László Fejérpataky (1857-1923), an internationally famous scholar of auxiliary sciences; and Henrik Marczali, the author of *Hungary in the Eighteenth Century* (Cambridge, 1910) on teaching of history in colleges and universities. All lecturers at the Congress emphasized the significance of using source materials and of archival research and thereby helped prepare the next generation for applying scientific methodology. Henrik Marczali's congressional lecture, to which I have already referred, singled out several highly interesting topics on research methodology and didactics. Marczali stressed that Hungary's past should be related within the framework of universal history because it was a country which had never occupied a central place in universal development. Similar to Fejérpataky's idea, Marczali also regarded it important to organize a historical institute to face the problems of reevaluation and advancement.

Congressional lectures inspired a series of debates between the old and the new schools. Characteristically, Árpád Horváth (1820-1894), professor of diplomatics at the University in Pest and a member of the old school, vehemently attacked Fejérpataky's lecture, especially its allegedly pro-German tone. Fejérpataky's reply, on the other hand, sounded very objective, far from being emotionally motivated. Fejérpataky strictly dealt with the desired reforms relating to research and teaching of diplomatics.[16]

This first really scholarly dispute foreshadowed the famous Erdélyi-Tagányi and Szekfű-Ballagi debates prior and during World War I. In these and similar debates the rising tide of nationalism frequently intervened and only a handful of political historians were able to remain impartial.

The Millenium of Hungary's Conquest provided an excellent opportunity for strengthening national consciousness by means of historiography. It also substantially accelerated book and periodical publishing in local history and stimulated the activities of local historical societies. Evidently, the Millenium by its nature served Hungaro-centric purposes. And it is all the more interesting that its representative work proved to be a quite objective enterprise. Under the editorship of Sándor Szilágyi (1827-1899), who was perhaps the best organizer of that period, a ten-volume collective work appeared entitled *A magyar nemzet története* (History of the Hungarian nation) issued upon the commemoration of the nation's one thousand years' history in 1896. The work was rather moderate in tone. Although this multivolume set is an uneven work of leading historians it should be regarded as the most important synthesis up to the publishing of the Hóman-Szekfű's *Magyar történet* (1929-1933).

In this period of time some branches of auxiliary sciences were in full swing. Nándor Knauz's *Kortan* (Chronology), even now can be considered as the best guide to Hungary's medieval chronology. László Fejérpataky laid down the foundations for modern diplomatics, and József Csoma did the same for heraldry, János Karácsonyi for genealogy, and László Réthy for numismatics. The intensive source-publishing enterprise sponsored by the Academy and the Historical Association made this magnificent revival of auxiliary sciences possible without which the up-to-date methods of textual criticism and critical philology could not have been employed.[17]

Positivism helped auxiliary sciences and historiography in general flourish. But starting at least with the Millenium, nationalism, as I have already indicated, clashed with historical thought and delayed scientific progress.

In the first two decades of the twentieth century, current politics deeply penetrated once again even in the fields of medievalists. László Erdélyi (1868-1947) and Károly Tagányi discussed medieval social history topics in the pages of *Történelmi Szemle* (1913-1916). Tagányi expressed an intransigent standpoint against Erdélyi's "Slavophile" opinion. Gyula Szekfű's (1883-1955) dispute with Aladár Ballagi (1853-1928) on the eve of World War I on the personality of Prince Ferenc Rákóczi divided the whole nation into two: the kuruc (Hungarocentric) and labanc (Habsburg loyalists) camps. This famous debate was the first in the country to result in mass meetings passionately interfering with historiographic topics. Only the events of World War I could deviate the public attention from the Rákóczi debate.

In a few years, the same Gyula Szekfű published another book *A magyar állam életrajza* (German ed., Berlin, 1917, Hungarian translation, Budapest, 1918) which seemed to be a pro-German philosophy of Hungarian history. Despite all of its shortcomings this book represented perhaps the highest achievement of historiography in this period and seemed to be an early earmark of the slowly evolving trend of Geistesgeschichte. This chapter cannot be closed without a short mention of the work of Árpád Károlyi (1853-1940). Károlyi happened to be the first Hungarian historian trained in Vienna in Sickel's Institut für Österreichische Geschichtsforschung. He was admittedly a positivist and, as the director of the Austrian State Archives (1909-1913), and after 1920 as the director of the Hungarian Historical Institute in Vienna (Bécsi Magyar Történeti Intézet) he published documents relating to the history of Austria and Hungary. Mentor of Gyula Szekfű and many other Hungarian scholars attending Vienna institutions, he was directly responsible for issuing a series of source publications based on Vienna archival collections. Károlyi is a never-surpassed master of essay literature.[18]

7

In the Sphere of Geistesgeschichte
1918-1945

This trend appeared as a direct reaction to positivism and historical materialism. Its philosophical precursor was Wilhelm Dilthey (1834-1911). As a Kantian, Dilthey dealt with theoretical questions raised by historical studies. His theory of the reliving (Nacherleben) of psychological processes deeply impressed some historians in Hungary because they believed it opened new vistas in the interpretation of history. This anti-materialistic view, seasoned with the thoughts of theologian-philosopher Ernst Troeltsch (1865-1923) and influenced also by Ortega y Gasset's (1883-1955) statements on the revolt of the masses ؟ and the significance of the elite, captivated the minds of Hungarians. They believed that the new orientation could prevent or reduce the influence of materialism. Their chief reason in adopting Geistesgeschichte so hastily was of a politico-ideological nature.

The political regimes between the wars not only in Hungary but in all bourgeois countries of Central and Eastern Europe dreaded the spread of the Marxist revolutionary ideas. The memories of the short-lived and bloody Hungarian Soviet Republic of 1919 determined above all the new historiographic orientation. This political climate so characteristic of the interwar period also encouraged historians to downgrade material forces (class warfare, labor movements, etc.) as primary history-making factors. The keynote works in this spirit were written by Gyula Szekfű (1883-1955), the most talented Hungarian historian of all times. Szekfű was a methodologically well-trained scholar with an excellent command of several foreign languages. Having graduated from the Péter Pázmány University in Budapest (1904), he worked in the

Hungarian National Museum, National Archives, and the Austrian State Archives in Vienna. His most important works include *Familiárisok és serviensek* (Budapest, 1912), a brilliant study on medieval social stratification; *A száműzött Rákóczi* (Budapest, 1913) which incited, as I have already referred to, the most emotional debate dividing the whole country into pro- and anti-Habsburg camps; and *A magyar állam életrajza* delineating the evolution of the country's political philosophy in a pro-German, idealistic (Geistesgeschichte) style. This last work, as I have already said, should be regarded as the very first step in the direction of Geistesgeschichte. But it is his *Három nemzedék* (Three generations. First ed. publ. 1920) which definitely set the tone for the new course and became the Bible for most historians up to the end of World War II. It expounded the standpoint that liberal theory meant progress only in the history of thought but as a political practice seemed to be detrimental. In Szekfű's reasoning, liberalism via the stage of radicalism led directly to revolutions, as in fact was Hungary's case during the proletarian dictatorship in 1919. This Bolshevik-type revolution in Szekfű's judgment represented the lowest point in Hungary's history. This opinion alone can explain why Szekfű carved such a spectacular career during the Horthy times.

His *Három nemzedék* exerted an enormous influence upon the intelligentsia and public figures alike. Szekfű reevaluated the country's past and present in line with Stephen Széchenyi's Christian ethics. The acceptance of Széchenyi's moral philosophy prevented Szekfű from following the path of German chauvinism. On the contrary, Szekfű's attitude towards ethnic minorities was tolerant if not liberal. His vast knowledge of facts, his superb ability to keep enormous quantity of published and unpublished sources under his firm control, made his art of writing especially convincing. There was a period, namely, between 1925 and 1935, when Szekfű's views echoed, unchallenged, on all sides of the ideological spectrum. His research methods, his unique art of reliving past events through data-based intuition, as well as his beautiful literary style helped spawn a huge school of imitators. His influence can be perceived even in post-1945 publications. Many of his best disciples have filled key positions in the universities, research institutes, archives and libraries even in the new Hungary.

Szekfű's unique art of writing was instrumental in convincing the reader to accept his main thesis that progressive conservatism and not liberal-radical revolutionary characteristics are the true concomitants of the nation's history. Until about the mid-thirties his philosophy did not evince changes. Somewhat later, touched by the brutal execution of the Anschluss in 1938, Szekfű's pro-German viewpoints completely disappeared and his conservative philosophy started showing more and more liberal elements already at the outset of the Second World War. But his real metamorphosis came as an aftermath of the war. His postwar writings (*Forradalom után*. Budapest, 1947; "Az értelmiség átállása a felszabadulás idején," posthumously publ. in *Csillag*, 1955) indicated that the new constellation was a natural outgrowth of historical circumstances and should be taken as the permanent, unchangeable state of affairs in the whole Danube area.

The most significant accomplishment of the interwar period was written by Bálint Hóman and Gyula Szekfű. Their joint work, the multivolume set of *Magyar történet* (first publ. in 1929-1933 in seven volumes, then in five volumes in many consecutive editions), an indisputably high-level synthesis, was heretofore unparalleled in historiography. It was the first synthesis in the country which fully utilized modern methods of source and textual criticism and to a lesser extent the up-to-date results of historical epistemology. Bálint Hóman prepared the medieval parts up to 1458, while Szekfű dealt with the modern age. Hóman succeeded in infusing the volumes of *Magyar történet* with the achievements of his oustanding research. I refer especially to his pioneer research in Hungarian numismatics (*Magyar pénztörténet 1000-1325*. Budapest, 1916) and economic history (*A magyar királyság pénzügyei és gazdaságpolitikája Károly Róbert korában*. Budapest, 1921) to mention only two of his numerous publications.

Hóman's contribution to *Magyar történet* in fact did not reflect the influence of Geistesgeschichte, except in some of the phrases he used to serve the spiritually-oriented, anti-Marxist political course. Hóman by his portrayal of medieval Hungaria as a great power tried to promote certain political objectives of the regime.

Szekfű's contribution to *Magyar történet* affected the professionals and the reading public alike much more deeply. He believed that the only proper way of development is progressive conservatism and that in his nation's past class warfare and other Marxist concepts were reflexly excluded as decisive history-making forces. Both authors concluded that their country and its peoples, Magyars and non-Magyars alike, chose the Western way of civilization and that Hungary for centuries fulfilled its mission of being "the bulwark of Christian civilization" against the pagan invaders from the East. Prodigious amount of data, including the use of heretofore unpublished documents, characterizes this monumental synthesis. It is interesting to note that since its first publication, *Magyar történet* has continuously been used as a reference tool and even Marxist historians are acknowledging some of its outstanding features.

One of the most gifted disciples of Bálint Hóman was József Deér (1905-1972) who more or less followed his master's ideology. In reevaluating the country's past in line with the requirements of Geistesgeschichte, Deér introduced the thesis of charismatic leadership which had not been a familiar topic in writings on the Middle Ages. Deér went even further by reasoning that charismatic elements played an important role in the medieval formation of the nation. For this and similar views Deér was viciously attacked after the war by Ernő Gerő and Emma Léderer which forced him to emigrate to Switzerland where he was appointed director of the Medieval Institute at the State University of Switzerland at Bern and continued his methodologically well-based research and prolific publishing activity dealing with Hungarian and universal medieval topics.

Very few individuals opposed the official trend represented by Bálint Hóman and Gyula Szekfű. Elemér Mályusz (1898-) belonged to this small group of dissenting historians. He succeeded Hóman in the Chair of the History of Medieval Hungary at the Péter Pázmány University in Budapest in the early thirties. Even Mályusz accepted in general the principles and standpoints expressed in *Magyar történet*. Together with Sándor Domanovszky, another opponent, he criticized the Hóman-Szekfű synthesis only from a religious (Protestant) angle.

Mályusz pioneered in working out the objectives and methodology of local history at the beginning of the thirties. His concept was that local history and ethnic studies (more correctly Siedlungskunde, history of ethnic settlements in his interpretation) were closely related issues. Regarding the methodology of these related issues, Mályusz learned much from Volkstumskunde and Auslanddeutschtum research organizations. Mályusz formulated and submitted a detailed proposition to organize a central research institute affiliated with the Hungarian National Archives to deal with local history and the development of ethnic settlements. His plan did not materialize.[19]

Mályusz succeeded in launching a new era in local history research. Until his pioneering work local history writing was colored by local patriotism and the overwhelming majority of local historians was not well-trained methodologically. Inspired chiefly by his works, Jenő Házi, Ambrus Pleidell, Kálmán Eperjessy and several others considered local history research as a lifetime professional undertaking and all published first-class scholarly works.

Research in local history and ethnic settlements after the Nazi takeover of 1933 reflected increasingly anti-German attitudes, and in the second half of the thirties as a fast-growing movement such research embraced almost all the significant branches of the humanities climaxing in settlement history, sociography and essay literature.

Sándor Domanovszky (1877-1955) remained a positivist and dealt chiefly with economic and social history topics. In addition, Domanovszky wrote several well-footnoted, detailed studies on chronicle and gesta literature. He edited, with moderate success for decades up to 1943, the *Századok*, the official journal of the Hungarian Historical

Association, in addition to a useful monographic series entitled Studies on the History of Hungarian Agriculture (Tanulmányok a magyar mezőgazdaság történetéhez).

The political and intellectual climate, as I have pointed out previously, did not favor any deviation from the official line of the philosophy of history embodied in Hóman-Szekfű's *Magyar történet*. It can be said that István Hajnal (1892-1956), professor of modern world history at the Péter Pázmány University, alone opposed diametrically the official trend of Geistesgeschichte. His theory of historical knowledge in principium opposed any "philosophizing" in history. Therefore he explicitly rejected all theorizing efforts including Geistesgeschichte and historical materialism. He took the stance that objective historical research can be based on primary sources only and its goal should be the concrete investigation into the forms of culture (civilization) so that in the center of inquiry would stand human labor (work). Thus in Hajnal's concluding remarks, the history of technical development (progress) and the comparative history of writing should be in the focus of investigation. Labor (work) as the central concept of human evolution seemed to be the mainstay of his epistemology which he tried to illustrate in his highly interesting university lectures and foreign language publications.[20]

Hajnal was deeply convinced that he had opened new vistas in historical research through giving a central role to human "work" in man's evolution.[21]

Interwar historiography cannot be properly measured without reviewing its second main product: a collective work of the nation's eleven leading historians. This book bore the title *New Ways of Hungarian Historiography* (*A magyar történetírás új útjai*. Budapest: Magyar Szemle Társaság, 1931. 464 p.) under the editorship of Bálint Hóman. Delineating the more important guiding principles historians applied in their works, it also gives some insights into the workshops of scholars. With the sole exception of Tivadar Thienemann's article on literary history, the German-styled Geistesgeschichte had little room in the authors' theoretical foundation of history writing. Every one of them, including Hóman and Szekfű, took all the history-making factors into consideration. István Dékány, like all co-authors of this volume, rejected historical materialism and argued against any form of monism, contending that economic and social historians should base their opinions exclusively on documentary evidence. Ferenc Eckhart reiterated the principle that legal and constitutional institutions should also be viewed solely on the grounds of sources and sub specie historiae but stressed that more attention should be paid to the viewpoints of Geistesgeschichte. Imre Szentpétery's survey of auxiliary sciences in Hungary and abroad pointed out that methodologically well-trained scholars had never believed in the applicability of any monistic theory, that diplomatics had always ranked high among auxiliary disciplines, and he evaluated Nándor Knauz' *Kortan* (Chronology) as well as József Csoma's works on heraldry (1903, 1913) as being still viable contributions.

Archaeology during this period leapt the tremendous gap from typology (József Hampel, Béla Posta, Árpád Buday, etc.) to scientific synthesis. This progress was represented above all by the achievements of the world-renowned András Alföldi whose research on Roman antiquities assured him an outstanding place among the world's best archaeologists. János Banner, his disciple Mihály Párducz, Sándor Gallus and several others excelled in archaeology in this time and laid down the foundations for the post-1945 progress.[22]

During this period two very significant organizations came to being: in 1920, the Hungarian Historical Institute of Vienna, Austria (Bécsi Magyar Történeti Intézet) and in 1941 the Hungarian Institute of Historical Sciences (Magyar Történettudományi Intézet). The Hungarian Historical Institute of Vienna awarded scholarships to talented young historians, giving them an opportunity to use the rich archival and library collections of Vienna and to get acquainted with modern research methods and thus insuring the continuation of positivism in a time of flourishing idealism. Fortunately, all the directors of this Vienna institute (Árpád Károlyi, Dávid Angyal, Gyula Miskolczy) represented the best traditions of historiography and were far removed from the sway of any one-sided approach.

The Hungarian Institute of Historical Sciences was the first institute of historical research in Hungary: It was a section of the Pál Teleki Scientific Institute. Its members, though prey to the censorship of the governments during World War II, succeeded in publishing some outstanding volumes in ethnic studies.

Several useful source publications were issued at this time. Under the editorship of Imre Szentpétery the exemplary *Scriptores rerum Hungaricarum* contained medieval narrative sources excellently edited and utilizing the latest accomplishments in the auxiliary sciences. A leading authority on medieval Latin, László Juhász founded and edited the *Bibliotheca scriptorum medii recentisque aevorum*, publishing late medieval and early modern narrative sources relating to Hungary and equipped with critical philological notes. Sponsored by the Hungarian Historical Association the volumes of *Fontes historiae Hungaricae aevi recentioris* focused on the first half of the nineteenth century, devoting several volumes to sources relating to Stephen Széchenyi, Louis Kossuth, and the nationality question. Among monographic series, the volumes of the *Handbook of Hungarian Historical Science* (*A magyar történettudomány kézikönyve*, edited by Bálint Hóman) attained the highest peak in surveying such important fields as source publications, historiography, auxiliary sciences, the philosophy of history, etc.

In the thirties new directions in teaching history appeared in educational publications and debates. The new methods of teaching originated heated debates about the tasks, methods, and means of historiography as well as history teaching.[23]

In this quarter-century, the history of the nationality question in the Middle Danube Valley ranked high on the agenda. Most of the relevant publications were prepared by using valuable unpublished documents and their results seemed to be impressive. But in the final analysis these publications, with very few exceptions, for being politically motivated failed to recognize the specific, self-centered character of the nationality movements.

On the threshold of World War II, it was already obvious that the older generation and its scholarship could no longer satisfy the requirements of the changing times. Hence, already in the mid-thirties new enterprises were being born, among them a periodical, *Történetírás* (Historiography), designed to be a counterpart of *Századok*, the official journal of the Association. Many a dissatisfied young scholar, including the writer of this review, grouped around *Történetírás* and challenged the older generation's idealistic views. *Történetírás*, founded and edited by János Belitzky, a Domanovszky disciple, ceased to exist after a few years, due in part to financial difficulties, as did many other opposition movements in the turbulent years of the war.[24]

8

Marxist-Leninist Reevaluation
1945-

Also as an aftermath of World War II, Hungary fell into the Soviet Union's sphere of influence and became one of its neighbors. The new constellation not only determined the fate of the country but its intellectual orientation as well. It is an established fact that up to this point in time there had been no direct, if any, lasting Russian effect on Hungary's cultural life which had heretofore developed exclusively under Western influence.

Since the conclusion of the war, the country's intellectual development precisely mirrored the main phases and characteristics of the political changes taking place there and in the Kremlin-dominated area as a whole. Directives issued by the Central Committee of the Hungarian Communist Party have triggered all political and cultural changes and historians have been compelled to make research and rewrite history accordingly. Interestingly enough, the Marxist-Leninist rewriting of history, as did so many other enterprises in the country's scholarship, began with Gyula Szekfű's activity. His series of lectures delivered at the Budapest headquarters of the Free Trade-Union of Hungarian Educators (Magyar Pedagógusok Szabad Szakszervezete) in the early spring of 1945 initiated the process of reevaluation.[25] Szekfű modified his previous, antimaterialistic views, condemned the exaggerations of Geistesgeschichte and the by-now exclusive Western attitude. Szekfű's first postwar public appearance thereby heralded the beginning of an entirely new era in conducting social and historical research. He also stressed in these historic lectures that Hungary ought to find its place in the new foreign policy constellation through indicating an Eastern orientation and forging a sincere friendship with all of its neighbors, above all with the USSR. This new state of affairs should be considered, Szekfű reasoned, immutable and therefore final. But his words proved to be a voice in the wilderness. Historian Erzsébet Andics, a Moscow-trained leader of the new orientation as early as 1948 said with resignation that "The writers and editors of the *Századok* (the chief organ of the Hungarian Historical Association) failed to notice the Soviet Union even in 1948; there was not a single article or communication in the *Századok* which would have made the most remote reference to Soviet historiography. The Soviet Union and its mighty historical science simply did not exist for the *Századok* in 1948."[26]

In order to eradicate the bourgeois science and to create in its place a Marxist-Leninist approach, the Party's Central Committee from time to time has issued guiding principles to promote an all-out revolution. As a result social and historical sciences have undergone significant changes in four phases, each in full coordination with the major currents of political development. The first phase, the preparatory one, lasted approximately up to 1948-1949; the second one, known as the Stalinization (Rákosi) period, culminated in the first postwar Congress of Hungarian Historians held in Budapest, June 1953. The third stage represented a relative liberalization process reaching a peak during the Imre Nagy regime and the Petőfi-Circle debates preceding the October 1956 events; while the fourth phase has been in continuous effect since the defeat of the 1956 Revolution.

Research and interpretation in all four phases of the above-outlined historiographic development have suffered in varying degrees from the same simplistic vision of the past which stemmed from the coercive application of historical and dialectical materialism. Prior to scrutinizing postwar literature let us make a brief survey of some more important structural changes the historical profession has undergone since the end of the war.

In 1949 and the years immediately afterwards, the whole of scientific life, and within its framework the historical profession, was thoroughly reorganized in line to varying extents with the Soviet pattern. The Division of Social and Historical Sciences, and the Institute of Historical Research, both affiliated with the Hungarian Academy of Sciences, were reshaped to become the country's top professional institutions. Their members, as well as university professors, leading archivists, and museologists, now constitute the elite of the historical profession.

Since the war the reorganization of archives, museums and libraries has been geared to the practical needs of historians. Archivistship especially since 1945 has enjoyed a high level. The first references to the preservation of documents of the royal chancery go back to the period of King Béla IV (1235-1270). In 1273 a law was promulgated which prescribed that all public documents of national interest be kept in the archives of the country, the universale archivum regni, under the jurisdiction of the Palatine. Since the Palatine relinquished these rights in 1756 the National Archives was established which for the most part retained its feudal character until its reorganization in 1875. The new Archives Law providing for uniform organization of the archives was enacted in 1950, its most important provision being the setting up of the National Center of Archives (Levéltárak Országos Központja) to supervise the archival network.[27]

The Hungarian National Archives in Budapest has five departments. Its masterfully knowledgeable guides are part of the program to facilitate use of the records in its custody. The Budapest State Archives, nineteen county archives, and numerous church and private archives all belong to the state-controlled system of archives in addition to the National Archives. Nowadays, archives are concentrating on promoting the auxiliary sciences of history, historical statistics, history of public administration and source publication.[28]

The Museum Act of 1949 (amended in 1963) made possible a large-scale development by creating a state-controlled network of museums. The largest and oldest among them, the Hungarian National Museum (founded in 1802) in Budapest, has five departments, its Department of Archaeology being the most important. It boasts a most rich and variegated collection of objects from the different cultures of the continent. All of Hungary's archaeological excavations are coordinated under the Museum's supervision. The Museum's well-edited *Folia Archaeologica* publishes papers in numerous foreign languages.

Valuable objects are deposited in the Christian Museum (Keresztény Múzeum) of Esztergom, the Museum of Contemporary History (Legújabbkori Történeti Múzeum), the Museum of Military History (founded in 1918), and the Museum of Theatrical History (founded 1952) all in Budapest.

The reorganized library system, also under state control, helps in many ways to promote the goals of the historical sciences. The oldest library extant is the Benedictine Monastery's at Pannonhalma whose inventory dating back to 1090 has been preserved. The largest is the National Széchényi Library (founded in 1801), having about five million items. The Library of the Hungarian Academy of Sciences, the Library of Loránd Eötvös University, as well as the Library of the National Assembly, all seated in Budapest, possess valuable collections too, especially in their manuscript divisions.

Among ecclesiastical libraries, the Library of the Esztergom Cathedral (better known as the Bibliotheca of Esztergom) has world-renowned medieval collections.

No serious study of the immense postwar literature[29] can be made without first depicting some characteristics of its ideological background.

Substantial theoretical studies prepared by Erik Molnár, Erzsébet Andics, Dezső Nemes, and Aladár Mód have tried to determine the objective of historical writing. In their consensus, historical writing is an educational means in the service of the socialist transformation of the society and accordingly historical writing should reflect the spirit of socialist patriotism and its inseparable concomitant: proletarian internationalism. Fortunately, this nonhistorical approach has fully materialized only in a few instances though its spirit more or less affected many historians.

It is interesting to note that the treatment of pre-1526 topics has been more objective than the analysis of the issues of the later centuries, especially than that of the period of late feudalism. For instance, the social unrest of feudal peasantry in the sixteenth-eighteenth centuries has been so magnified and distorted in Marxist-Leninist literature that there seems to be no distinction at all between the anti-feudal goals of peasant movements and the national objectives of the Hungarian nation as a whole. Feudal peasantry has been described most unprofessionally from a historical vantage point as the flagbearer of national independence movements, though the peasantry of that period lacked any semblance of a well-developed national consciousness suitable for leading a nation's struggles for independence. This task was exclusively consigned in history to the nobility. But many a historian has idolized the role of the peasantry in conformity with the Russian *narodnik* views which confused class warfare of the peasantry with the national independence movements.[30]

To identify the class warfare of the peasantry with the national independence movements led by the nobility was all the more possible because historians and sociologists up to about 1963 failed to define the concepts of the nation, nationality, fatherland, etc., much less to view them historically. They knew only the Marxist-Leninist concept of the nation and they forcibly applied it in all periods of history which resulted in a distorted picture of the nation and all of its relevant concepts. Due to the unhistorical notion of the nation and nationality Endre Arató's otherwise well-documented studies of the nationality question cannot be considered a historically well-based, realistic portrayals.

In 1963, and the following years, the historical concept of the nation attracted the attention of many outstanding specialists. Among them Ágnes R. Várkonyi, László Benczédi, and Károly Vígh especially contributed positively to the realistic portrayal of the nation concept which, as they correctly pointed out, varied from period to period.[31]

Some of the practicing historians have remained unaffected from the Party-minded views and rather benefited from the official trend of historical and dialectical materialism — benefited to that extent that in opposition to bourgeois idealism their works based strictly on archival sources more realistically depicted life. As a result they enlarged the scope of investigation so that they were able to prepare quite well-balanced synthetic works on the country's history giving adequate space to political, cultural, and above all economic (chiefly industrial) development. They have quite successfully depicted Hungary's history within the framework of East Central Europe and in some instances injected the country's historical occurrences into the framework of world affairs.[32] All this has partly been a natural reaction to the Hungaro-centrism of the preceding generation.

In line with this anti-idealist trend, the labor movement has also come to the fore. It is all the more important because prewar research neglected this question in addition to social and economic issues in general. A series of documentary volumes relating to social history and the workers movement has been recently published. Though the selection of sources and their explanatory notes have been in many instances partial, they should nonetheless be regarded as positive contributions to historiography, as should the multivolume set of the *Magyar Munkásmozgalom Története Válogatott Dokumentumai* (Selected Documents Relating to the History of Hungarian Labor Movement).

The *Párttörténeti Közlemények* (1955-), the official journal of Párttörténeti Intézet (Institute of Party History) illuminated several topics of the heretofore ignored labor and Party movement but its militant phraseology and attitude, and the counterselection of documents in most instances exaggerated anti-labor events in order to discredit completely the activities of the pre-1945 regime in the fields of social insurance, labor laws and legislation. Naturally, this one-sided approach could be materialized only at the expense of historical truth.

Source publications and interpretations issued by the Institute of Historical Research of the Hungarian Academy of Sciences are, in general, useful enterprises, as are the well-edited volume of *Magyarország és a második világháború* (Hungary and World War II. Budapest: Kossuth Könyvkiadó, 1959) and the similarly well-prepared series entitled *Diplomáciai iratok Magyarország külpolitikájához 1936-1945* (Diplomatic documents relative to Hungary's foreign policy 1936-1945). They contain some startling revelations. Final conclusions are often in line with Marxist-Leninist ideology and flagrantly disregard some basic facts so convincingly expressed in the sources. The New Series (Új sorozat) of *Értekezések a történeti tudományok köréből* contains monographic treatises concentrating heavily on nineteenth- and twentieth-century topics, Hungarian and foreign. Up to 1972, sixty-three books have appeared in this New Series.

Acta Historica, a foreign language quarterly issued also by the Hungarian Academy of Sciences is perhaps the most useful serial publication after *Századok*, a bimonthly, and *Történelmi Szemle*, a quarterly publication of the Institute of Historical Research.[33]

It is common knowledge that bibliography in the humanities and social sciences is in a state of crisis. The information explosion makes it virtually impossible for most individuals to keep abreast of new developments.[34] These maxims cannot apply to postwar Hungary where the science of bibliography has advanced enormously. Historical periodicals, almost without exception, carry well-edited book review sections and current bibliographies. The Budapest-based *Magyar Nemzeti Bibliográfia* (Hungarian National Bibliography) is an excellent tool for keeping the relatively huge book production under firm bibliographical control. There have been several bibliographical undertakings geared to the needs of historians. For example, the four-volume Hungarian historical bibliography, *Magyar történeti bibliográfia 1825-1867* (Budapest: Akadémiai Kiadó, 1950-1959) issued by the Institute of Historical Research of the Hungarian Academy of Sciences is a useful aid to scholars specializing in the whole Middle Danube Valley and even the Balkan Peninsula. Its contents: Volume 1, General Part, 5,654 entries; Volume 2, Economy, 15,855 entries; Volume 3, Politics, Law, Education, Science and Humanities, Press, Religion, 24,698 entries; and Volume 4, Non-Hungarian Peoples — Nationalities contains 26,682 entries, the largest bibliography ever compiled on the topic of ethnic minorities. References are made to monographs and periodical articles in Hungarian, Slavic, and West European languages. Up to now this is the largest collective undertaking in historical bibliography in Hungary.

Among individual efforts two bibliographical undertakings should be mentioned. First off, there is the two-volume set compiled by János Banner and Imre Jakabffy entitled *A Közép-Dunamedence régészeti bibliográfiája 1960-1966.*[35] Secondly, Domokos G. Kosáry's bibliographical enterprise is to be the most comprehensive work in historical bibliography under the title *Bevezetés Magyarország történetének forrásaiba és irodalmába* (Introduction to the sources and literature of Hungary's history. vol. 1. Budapest: Tankönyvkiadó, 1970. 900 p.). Four additional volumes are planned. The encouraging first volume gives a critical evaluation of Hungarian bibliographies pertinent to history and related sciences and discusses all important bibliographies published abroad.[36]

Among auxiliary sciences diplomatics has always ranked high. But auxiliary sciences in general could not reach that level which characterized them during the interwar period under the leadership of Imre Szentpétery. Like diplomatics, historical statistics has also been an outstanding domain of research. Already in the sixteenth century a useful Hungarian statistics was prepared by Miklós Oláh.[37]

Thanks to the pioneer works of Elek Fényes, Károly Keleti and some others in the nineteenth century, historical statistics has advanced greatly in the post-1945 period. First and foremost among its numerous postwar representatives the works of József Kovacsics should be mentioned.[38] The majority of postwar works in this field have been compiled on the grounds of archival sources and with the close cooperation of the National Archives staff. Similarly, owing to the scholarly collaboration of the National Archives researchers, great progress has also been made in historical geography. The most eminent contributor to historical geography has been György Győrffy, member of the Institute of Historical Research, Hungarian Academy of Sciences, whose multivolume set, *Az Árpádkori Magyarország történeti földrajza* (Historical geography of Hungary during the Age of the Árpáds. Budapest: Akadémiai Kiadó, 1963-), is the result of painstaking archival research. Regarded as an exemplary accomplishment in the methodology of historical geography in and outside of Hungary, Győrffy's monumental undertaking indeed embodies the continuation and improvement of the best traditions since Dezső Csánki's epochal work (*Magyarország történelmi földrajza a Hunyadiak korában*. Budapest: Magyar Tudományos Akadémia, 1890-1913. 7 vols.).

Historical geography and local history research developed interdependently in Hungary where scholars were simultaneously engaged in both of these fields. Local history specialists specifically emphasized the necessity of the concentration of knowledge including such disciplines as economics, sociology, demography, archaeology, art, history, etc. This principle of concentration was advocated in a report[39] prepared by Elemér Mályusz, Lajos Ruzsás and Jenő Szűcs for the January 10, 1966 session of the Committee of Historical Sciences, Hungarian Academy of Sciences. This report also stressed that a synthetic work on

Hungary's city history can be prepared only as a result of decades-long teamwork. Published in 1971, Kálmán Eperjessy's just quoted synthesis of the country's city history is all the more worth mentioning because it was done as a one-man project. Its singularly important feature is that it is absolutely free from nationalistic prejudice. Up to now very few authors in Central and Eastern Europe have been able to purge themselves of this traditional bias. Eperjessy and a few others, basing their stand on archival materials, have refuted the old school's dogmatic views and have proven that not only Germans and Hungarians but Slavs and several other ethnic elements had a hand in the establishment of cities in the Middle Danube Valley. Professor Eperjessy has also convincingly proven in the light of primary sources that no German or any other nation's exclusive priority in land settlement can be accepted concerning the area as a whole. This problem, in Dr. Eperjessy's judgment should be treated individually to highlight significant regional differences.

Local archives have done much to discover important regional features in the nation's history. More recently, the Hajdú-Bihar County Archives excelled in issuing two huge volumes of heretofore unpublished documents, published with interpretive studies to illuminate the county's role in the national developments.[40]

Interestingly, only very few professional historians have left the country since the conclusion of the Second World War, the world-renowned Károly Kerényi (1897-1973) and András Alföldi (1895-) being among them. Kerényi distinguished himself as an expert on antique civilization, mythology, humanism and the history of Europe's intellectual life, while Alföldi who was for years a member of the Institute for Advanced Study in Princeton, New Jersey, earned an international reputation in Roman history and archaeology and the culture of Eurasian nomads. József Deér (1905-1972), for years the Director of the Medieval Institute at the State University of Switzerland, Bern, broadened his previously Hungary-oriented research to include some medieval topics of the Holy Roman Empire.

Alexander Gallus (Australia) switched at least one and a half decades ago from archaeology to anthropology. Ludwig von Gogolák (Vienna, Austria) has been lecturer at several historical meetings in Austria and published several items on Hungarian-Slovak relationships.

Astrik Ladislas Gábriel (1907-) achieved international fame through his numerous articles and papers on medieval subjects, primarily on medieval universities. István Deák, Director of the Institute of East Central Europe, Columbia University, New York, N.Y., specializes in the Habsburg, German, and Hungarian history; George Barany, University of Denver, Colorado, in the political biography of Stephen Széchenyi.

Stephen Foltiny (Princeton, New Jersey) has been active in the archaeological research of the Carpathian Basin, while Tibor Baráth (Montreal, Canada) has centered his activities on the origins of the Magyars. Francis S. Wagner's (Library of Congress, Washington, D.C.) scholarly interests focus on the nationality problem, and diplomatic history of World War II, and the theory of historical knowledge, subjects on which he publishes and lectures extensively.

Stefan Lorant (b. 1901, Budapest) achieved fame in America as an author popularizing U.S. history. His major publications include *Lincoln, His Life in Photographs* (1941); *F.D.R., a pictorial biography* (1950); *The Life of Abraham Lincoln* (1954); *The Life and Times of Theodore Roosevelt* (1959); *The Glorious Burden: The American Presidency* (1968).

Stephen Borsody (b. 1911), Béla K. Király (b. 1912), and especially John A. Lukacs (b. 1923) are quite well-known among American college teachers dealing with modern — primarily twentieth-century Central European — topics; and, in December 1976, John Lukacs was elected president of the American Catholic Historical Association.

The British Carlile Aylmer Macartney (1895-), the Czech Josef Macurek (1901-), and the Slovak Daniel Rapant, occupy unique places among the foreign historiographers of Hungary. All three have devoted a lifetime to study this country's past. Macartney embraced several topics ranging from medieval historiography and social history to the nationality question. He also authored a historical synthesis (*Hungary: a short history*. Edinburgh: University Press, 1962. 262 p.) Josef Macurek's main work *Dejiny Madaru a uherského státu* (Prague: Melantrich, 1934. 344 p.) immediately aroused the interests of his Hungarian colleagues, chiefly for the reason that he tried to prove that Hungarian statehood was not solely the achievement of the Magyars. Macurek as the head of the Committee on Hungarian Studies of the Czechoslovak Academy of Sciences, has been very active and a prolific author since the war. Both Macartney and Macurek have successfully demonstrated objectivity. The scholarly well-trained Daniel Rapant has not been able to reach the same level of objectivity due partly to his sensitive subject matters, the history of Magyarization, the Revolution of 1848-1849, and the Slovak-Hungarian historical relations.

There is only one high-level professional organization functioning abroad: the Hungarian Institute in Munich, Germany, under the directorship of Tamás Bogyay, himself a distinguished specialist on the Middle Ages. The Institute has been responsible for systematic research and publishing in the field of Hungarian studies.

Taking a bird's eye view of the centuries-long development of historical thought in Hungary, one should logically conclude that from the times of the chronicle and gesta literature, politics has been the salient feature in historical writing. One of the main reasons for this is the simple fact that the country lies in East Central Europe, at the crossroads of historic East-West conflicts. Historians could not insulate themselves and their science from the frequently experienced events of oppressive power politics. Under such circumstances the nation and its historians automatically resorted to nationalism as a quite natural means of resistance and self-preservation.

Needless to say the rising waves of nationalism helped distort the picture of the past. Historians affected by it were more or less inclined to reconstruct the past in an anachronistic way — that is to say, in the image and likeness of their own age. This has been to some degree a recurrent defect in Hungary and until the end of the last world war led to a Hungarocentric presentation of events. The situation has since improved and Hungary's history has more or less been presented within the context of Central and Eastern Europe and even world history. This is indisputably a significant accomplishment.

But current historiography has not been able to solve the problems stemming from nationalism either. In order to free themselves from nationalistic bias historians overrate the roles of class warfare and radical revolutionary movements in the history of a rather conservative nation. They ignore the once significant roles of the nobility and the middle classes in order to demonstrate a relationship between the progressive traditions of the past and the present system. Marxist-Leninist scholars, overly captivated by the dogmas of dialectical materialism, do not view this problem historically—on the basis of source materials. They are, therefore, unable to perceive the nation as a historical product of many centuries. Nor can they see that the genesis and further evolution of nationalism paved the way to self-fulfillment of the nation, including its ethnic minorities, a nation whose evolutionary processes could not run parallel with the interests of German or Russian or any other national developments.

A large group of historians judged correctly the state of affairs in the field of their science when they had a free — the first and last such occasion since 1945 — discussion on May 30, and June 1, 1956, in Budapest, arranged by the revolutionary Petőfi-Circle in the wake of the 20th Congress of the Communist Party of the Soviet Union.[41] The nearly one thousand participants almost unanimously agreed that the common source of their mistakes and falsifications was the subjective, sectarian and forced application of Party directives, directives adhering to the changing requirements of the personality cult of Stalin and Rákosi.

Undoubtedly since then the situation has been bettered to the extent that now not Stalin but the relatively moderate Lenin is quoted in history books and papers as the highest authority. This practice has produced again the counterselection of sources and Party-minded, though somewhat modified, views.

In contrast, those fields which are not directly affiliated with political history have demonstrated significant progress in the last two decades or so. Among them archaeology, art (Dezső Dercsényi) and local history, ancient history (János Harmatta), Byzantine studies (Gyula Moravcsík, 1892-), historical bibliography (Domokos Kosáry), archivistship (Győző Ember), etc., have been rapidly developing fields of historical scholarship.

One of the main factors contributing to progress since 1953 has been the exchange of scholars between Hungary and the socialist countries, later also with the West. 1953 was the year of the first postwar Congress of Hungarian Historians, held in Budapest, which was attended by many delegates from European socialist countries as well as China.[42] Since then Hungarians have participated in over one hundred international conferences in the socialist countries and some in the West. Obviously, these international meetings have made possible the exchange of experiences and raised their professional level, particularly in methodology, helping also to uncover new, unpublished sources.

Noteworthy is the fact that since the beginnings of scientific historiography in about the eighteenth century, the dominant characteristic of Hungarian historians has been their frequent use of unpublished (archival) materials to substantiate their theses. This source-oriented tradition since then has saved them from professing any monistic philosophy of history because in the light of documentary evidence they have seen the complex history-making factors which form the prism of reality.

Sociology

The disciplines of both sociology and economics in Central Europe grew primarily out of the historical sciences. Prior to the last quarter of the nineteenth century social and economic history appeared only within the framework of political history and not even a separate chapter was devoted to social and economic phenomena. Around the turn of the past century, due to the influence of Hegel, Comte and Marx, historical materialism as well as positivism came to the fore of historical research and simultaneously triggered the socioeconomic interpretation of history. Sociologists and economists invented new systems of periodization in history and analyzed the typical instead of the individual phenomena in human evolution. This new trend advocated that only one social class be regarded as the real and only history-making factor. This monistic standpoint was in total conflict for instance with the views of earlier Gergely Berzeviczy (1763-1822) and other contemporary social and economic philosophers. Gergely Berzeviczy, one of the best economists and social philosophers of his age, refuted the monistic stance and evidenced a high esteem for the functions of the middle class by declaring that: the tiers état is that noteworthy and outstanding class of the society which resides in cities and whose characteristic way of life is urbanism.*

Historical materialism was the driving force of the intellectuals who belonged to the following two institutions during the first two decades of the twentieth century: the Galilei Kör (Galilei Circle), representing a rather small percentage of Budapest University students and professors, and the *Huszadik Század* (Twentieth Century), the official journal of the Sociological Society which under the editorship of Oszkár Jászi coordinated the activities of many radical thinkers of the Habsburg Monarchy. Representing this latter group, Ervin Szabó (1877-1918) analyzed the country's Uprising of 1848-1849 from a point of view of Marxist sociology in his *Társadalmi és pártharcok a 48-49. nagy forradalomban* (Vienna, 1921).

Péter Ágoston (1874-1925) also belonged to the leadership of the *Huszadik Század* and emphasized the role of economic factors in describing and evaluating the functions that the owners of large landed estates fulfilled in the nation's past (*A magyar világi nagybirtok története*. Budapest, 1913).

The best known Hungarian sociologist up to now has been Karl (Károly) Mannheim (1893-1947). Mannheim who spent his youth in Hungary and experienced the revolution and counter-revolution in his native land, went to Germany in 1919 then in 1933 fled Germany and spent the remainder of his career in Great Britain teaching sociology at the London School of Economics. He devoted his entire career to the development of a sociology of knowledge, which branch of science has since been associated with his name. In Karl Mannheim's interpretation, knowledge is a social product and is related to the social status of the individual. In spite of Mannheim's and others' efforts, the sociology of knowledge has remained an unsolved issue of epistemology. As an architect of the sociology of knowledge, he reluctantly conceded that objective knowledge of reality was impossible. For details see his *Wissenssoziologie; Auswahl aus dem Werk* (Berlin, 1964. 750 p.).

---

*On economy, 1819. From Latin manuscript. C.F. Jenő Gaál, *Berzeviczy Gergely élete és művei*. (Budapest 1902. pp. 41-42); and István Dékány, "Gazdaság- és társadalomtörténet", in Bálint Hóman, ed., *A magyar történetírás új útjai*. (Budapest, 1931. p. 224).

Oscar Jászi (1875-1957, Oberlin, Ohio, USA) studied, besides Budapest University, in France and England. The nationality question and its federalist solution were central issues in his lifework. After the proclamation of the Hungarian Soviet Republic in March, 1919, Jászi first emigrated to Vienna then to the United States. In 1925 he was appointed professor of sociology at Oberlin College, Ohio, where he earned wide recognition. His literary works deal with quite a number of subjects, including sociology, history, political science, to mention just a few. Oscar Jászi published two main works in the United States: *The Dissolution of the Habsburg Monarchy* (Chicago, 1929) and *Against the tyrant; the tradition and theory of tyrannicide* (with John Donald Lewis as joint author. Glencoe, Ill., 1957).

During the period between the wars, István Dékány (1886-1965) was a prominent figure in promoting social philosophy which he taught at the Budapest University up to 1946. Dékány also exercised wide influence on sociological research as the secretary general of the Hungarian Philosophical Society and as president of the Hungarian Sociological Association. Using an eclectic approach, István Dékány developed his own system of sociology based on the categories of social philosophy. His treatise prepared for delivery at the 14th (Bucharest, 1939) International Congress of Sociology dealt with the problem of social groups (*Communautés et organisations; essai sur la classification des groupements sociaux* (Paris: Domat-Montchrestien, 1940. 96 p.) He published a multitude of monographs on interpsychical cognition (*Bevezetés az interpszihikai megismerés elméletébe.* Kolozsvár, 1919), social philosophy (*A társadalomfilozófia alapfogalmai.* Budapest, Hungarian Academy of Sciences, 1933), and a high-level, really scholarly introduction to social sciences (*A mai társadalom. Bevezetés a társadalomtudományokba.* (2d ed., Budapest) as well as a well-organized dictionary of sociology (*Szociológiai műszótár.* Budapest: Pantheon, 98 p.).

In post-1945 Hungary, Sándor Szalai (b. 1912) has ranked high among Marxist sociologists. Szalai's research has dealt chiefly with methodological topics and social implications of socialist industrialization. Author of several monographs in these fields, Szalai in recent years has held an important position in the International Sociological Association and in the United Nations Institute for Training and Research (UNITAR). It is worth stating that between the wars, the movement of the people's writers (népi írók mozgalma), especially the works of Géza Féja, Ferenc Erdei and Imre Kovács, culminated in a very specific form of Populism. Its sociological by-product proved to be a characteristic, never-before-used interdisciplinary approach through which the writers were able to make a highly effective description of the socioeconomic, political and cultural phenomena of individual places and regions.

Economics

Gergely Berzeviczy (1763-1822) began his economic research under the influence of Adam Smith (1723-1790). In his first significant work (*De commercio et industria Hungariae*. Lőcse, 1797) Berzeviczy advocated the principle of free foreign trade and disapproved of any form of Viennese mercantilism. At the beginning of the nineteenth century he frequently exchanged letters with leading German scholars and in 1802 was elected member of the Göttingen Academy. In order to expand foreign trade towards Northern Europe Berzeviczy traveled to Warsaw and Danzig to study this problem on the scene. As a result of his study trip Berzeviczy wrote a treatise (*Die Erweiterung des nordischen Handels*. Vienna, 1814) which was submitted to the Congress of Vienna. As early as 1808 Berzeviczy wrote a well-documented study (*Ansichten des asiatisch-europäischen Welthandels*. Pest, 1808) in which, far ahead of his time, Berzeviczy discussed intercontinental foreign trade relations. In his *De conditione rusticorum in Hungaria* (1809) Berzeviczy condemned the system of serfdom and argued for economic liberalism. His purely theoretical work *Oeconomia Publico Politica* was written in 1818 and remained in manuscript form until 1902, when Jenő Gaál published it in Hungarian translation.

Economists and historians of later decades looked back upon Gergely Berzeviczy as a model for progressive social and economic philosophers. Consequently it was not surprising that Károly Tagányi and Ignác Acsády, who as early as 1893 issued the *Magyar Gazdaságtörténelmi Szemle* (Hungarian Review for Economic History), should be the first in Europe to actualize such an enterprise.

A Budapest University professor, Gyula Kautz (1829, Győr—1909, Budapest) played a leading role in the field of economics, even outside of the Habsburg Monarchy. Kautz' chief theoretical and historical work on national economy (*Theorie und Geschichte der Nationalökonomie*. 2 vols., Vienna, 1858-1860) hastened his brilliant career which culminated in his appointment as governor-general of the Austro-Hungarian Bank from 1892 to 1900. There is a consensus among economic historians that Gyula Kautz' literary activity was superior to that of his contemporaries.

University professor István Varga (1897-1962) was in close harmony with the traditions of the country's economic thought. Having gained experience in the Central Statistical Office and in a financial institution from 1927 to 1949, István Varga was the head of the Hungarian Institute for Economic Research (Magyar Gazdaságkutató Intézet, Budapest) where he trained an elite cadre of economists. His publications appeared in several languages. With Mátyás Matolcsy (1905-1953) he published *The national income of Hungary, 1924/25-1936-37* (London: P.S. King & Son, 1938) and his standard work on profit appeared under the title *Der Unternehmungsgewinn; ein Beitrag zur Theorie der Vermögensverteilung* (Berlin: Duncker & Humblot, 1957). One of his last publications entitled *Money in Socialism. International Economic Papers* (London, 1958) appeared also in English.

Similar to István Varga, Theo (Tivadar) Surányi-Unger (b. 1898) is known in Eastern and Western circles alike. Surányi-Unger's seminars at the University of Szeged also trained outstanding economists. After World War II, he taught economics and conducted research at several U.S. and West German universities. A very prolific author, Surányi-Unger, in addition to his native Hungarian, wrote a number of monographs in German and English — to single out two, his book on price regulation *(Nationale und internationale Preisspolitik.* Jena, 1938) and on the history of economic philosophy *(Geschichte der Wirtschaftsphilosophie.* Berlin, 1931). Through his numerous English language publications Surányi-Unger undoubtedly acquired world fame as an authority on economic policy, comparative economics, as well as economic philosophy. His relevant books include *Private enterprise and governmental planning; an interpretation* (1st ed., New York: McGraw-Hill, 1952. 628 p.), and *Economic philosophy of the twentieth century* (DeKalb, Ill.; Northern Illinois University Press, 1972. 357 p. Translation of *Wirtschaftsphilosophie des 20. Jahrhunderts*).

Béla Csikós-Nagy (b. 1915) graduated from Szeged University and was a member for years of Surányi-Unger's seminars. After World War II, Csikós-Nagy specialized in socialist economy while during the war years he had occupied himself with elucidating Hungary's economic role in the German lebensraum. Csikós-Nagy is considered the greatest authority on price regulation in the socialist bloc of countries. In recent years he has been the chairman of the National Board of Materials and Prices. Csikós-Nagy's main work, *Árpolitika az átmeneti gazdaságban* (Price policy in a transitional economy), is still considered a model work and was translated into Russian *(Problemy tsenoobrazovaniia i politika tsen.* Moscow: Izd-vo sotsialno-ekon. lit-ry, 1960. 476 p. According to D.D. Kondrashev's introductory essay Csikós-Nagy's is a supreme authority on price policy in the socialist camp. Csikós-Nagy's *Socialist economic policy* (New York: St. Martin's Press, 1973. 238 p.) is based on his *Bevezetés a gazdaságpolitikába* (Introduction to economic policy). His study on the foreign exchange problem in the communist countries appeared in Italian *(Problemi monetari del Cemecon.* Triest: ISDEE, 1974. 100 p.).

Jenő (Evgenii) Varga (1879, Nagytétény — 1964, Moscow) was a leading Soviet economist who published 75 books and brochures and about 500 scientific papers, overwhelmingly in Russian. Between 1927 and 1947 Varga was the director of the Moscow-based Institute of World Economy and World Politics.

Among Marxist economists in present-day Hungary, István Friss (b. 1903) is internationally acknowledged for his analysis of the country's economic mechanism *(Reform of the economic mechanism in Hungary; nine studies*, 1969, in Russian: *Reforma khoziaistvennogo mekhanizma v Vengrii*, 1968).

For many years József Bognár (b. 1917) was deeply engaged theoretically as well as practically in economic assistance planning especially for the new states of Africa.

Otto E. Thur (b 1928, Dárda, Hungary) is professor of economics at the University of Montreal, Canada, and a member of the Economic Council of Canada. He has published many articles in Belgian, German, Italian, as well as Canadian professional journals.

Aranka E. Kovacs, professor of the University of Windsor, Canada, is a leading authority on labor problems in Canada. Among many other awards, she has been granted the Canada Council Award, and has contributed articles, reports and book reviews to major professional journals in the field.

Anthropology and Ethnology

University professor Lajos Bartucz exerted great influence on the inter-war anthropological research in Hungary and neighboring countries. His investigations into the anthropometry of ninth century and pre-Conquest Magyars were considered substantial. See his "Adatok a honfoglaló magyarok anthropológiájához" *(Archaeológiai Értesítő,* 1931). In his *Fajkérdés, fajkutatás* (Race question, race research. Budapest, 1941. 322 p.) he discussed in a very objective manner the highly explosive questions of race research and cautiously refuted the then so popular Nazi race myth. At the First Congress of Finno-Ugrists held in Budapest in 1960 Bartucz delivered a paper entitled "Die Finnisch-Ugrischen Beziehungen der ungarischen Anthropologie" which described anthropological ties between the Magyars and other members of Finno-Ugrians.

János Nemeskéri is one of the most talented of present-day anthropologists. Nemeskéri has conducted research on modern topics as well, a case in point being his *Demographic and physical-developmental study of those who applied for admission to universities, higher schools in 1966* (Budapest, Central Statistical Office Demographic Research Institute, 1970). Nemeskéri with György Acsády as joint author wrote a comparative study entitled *History of human life span and mortality* (Budapest: Akadémiai Kiadó, 1970. 346 p.).

Pál Lipták (b. 1914) has been a co-worker of János Nemeskéri for decades. Having published a great many papers in Hungarian, as well as Slavic and numerous Western languages, professor Lipták prepared an exemplary handbook on physical anthropology, human evolution, and prehistoric man (*Embertan és származástan* (Budapest; Tankönyvkiadó, 1969. 283 p.).

István Győrffy (1884-1939) did valuable spadework in ethnography, especially in the study of peasant settlements and traditional farming methods.

Sándor Solymossy (1864-1945) was for years professor of ethnology at Szeged University between the wars and achieved substantial results in collecting and interpreting folk tales and ancient beliefs.

Gyula Ortutay (b. 1910) was the student of Sándor Solymossy at Szeged University in the first half of the thirties. Since his university years Ortutay has been especially prolific author. Scores of his works have been translated into foreign languages. His more important publications include the *Kis magyar néprajz* (Short Hungarian ethnography. 3d rev. and enl. ed., Budapest, 1958, for a German ed, see *Kleine ungarische Volkskunde*. Weimar: Böhlau, 1963. 229 p.), *Hungarian folk tales* (Selected and with an introduction and annotations by the editor, Gyula Ortutay), and *Új magyar népköltési gyűjtemény* (New anthology of folk poetry. Budapest: Akadémiai Kiadó, 1953-). Up to 1963 eleven volumes, mostly folk tales classified by regions were published under the editorship of Gyula Ortutay. He has been concerned primarily with universal and comparative folklore and folk ballad and folk tale research. In recognition of his scholarly activities, Gyula Ortutay was elected member of the Finnish Academy of Sciences, the Sicilian Academy of Sciences, the presidium of the International Union of Anthropological and Ethnological Sciences and the presidium of the International Society for Ethnology and Folklore.

Zsigmond Bátky (1874-1939) dealt with objective Hungarian ethnography, while Béla Gunda (b. 1910) conducted ethnological research on various ethnic entities of the Danube Valley.

Sándor Bálint (b. 1904, Szeged) graduated from University of Szeged where he lectured on the ethnography of the people of the Alföld from 1934 up to his retirement. Bálint is an internationally well-known scholar of the religious life and customs of the peoples living in the Middle Danube Valley. His major works include *A szegedi tanyák népe* (1936), *A parasztélet rendje* (1943), *A szegedi népélet szakrális gyökerei* (1943), *A magyar népballada* (1947), *Szegedi szótár* (2 vols., Budapest: Akadémiai Kiadó, 1957).

Linguistics – Oriental Studies

1

Hungarian linguists were creatively present at the dawn of modern linguistics. Precisely as early as around the turn of the eighteenth and nineteenth centuries, three Hungarian linguists advocated comparative as well as historical methods in the analysis of linguistic phenomena. János Sajnovics (1735-1785) while in Lapland on an astronomical expedition collected linguistic data, and by using comparative methods he firmly demonstrated the relationship between the Hungarian and Finno-Ugrian languages in his pioneering *Demonstratio Idioma Hungarorum et Lapponum idem esse*, (1770). Sámuel Gyarmathi (1751-1830) in his *Affinitas* (1799) helped lay down the foundations of Finno-Ugrian comparative linguistics by proving the relationship between the Hungarian and Finno-Ugrian tongues, while Miklós Révai (1750-1807) created and applied a new branch of linguistics, that is, historical philology, in his Latin-language *Elaboratior Grammatica Hungarica* (1806).

Later in the nineteenth century, the relationship between the Hungarian and Finno-Ugrian languages was studied more methodologically, chiefly by Antal Reguly (1819-1858). Jointly sponsored by the Hungarian Academy of Sciences and the Russian Academy of St. Petersburg, Reguly toured Lapland, the Ural region and Siberia studying the way of life and languages of the Finno-Ugrian peoples. Pál Hunfalvy (1810-1891) and the German-born József Budenz who from 1858 on made his home in Budapest initiated a new stage in the Finno-Ugrian comparative linguistics which since then has remained the official line of the country's linguistic research, though there have always been efforts to stress Turkish (by Ármin Vámbéry, Gyula Németh, et al.) and other (Sumerian, for instance) linguistic affinity.

Among the linguists of international fame, Gábor Szarvas (1632-1895) and Zsigmond Simonyi (1850-1919) are worthy of note for they published — among many other items — a model historical dictionary of the Hungarian language (Magyar nyelvtörténeti szótár) and because Gábor Szarvas began dialectological research.

József Szinnyei (1830-1913), an outstanding follower of the Finno-Ugrian school, published a still indispensable multivolume encyclopedia of Hungarian authors (Magyar írók élete és művei. Budapest, 1890-1914).

Zoltán Gombocz (1877-1935) founded the internationally highly esteemed Budapest school of linguistics, and compiled with the aid of János Melich (1872-1964), a noted Slavicist, the etymological dictionary of the Hungarian language (Magyar etymológiai szótár). For this latter achievement Gombocz and Melich were awarded the Grand Prize of the

Hungarian Academy of Sciences in 1921. His methodologically exemplary investigations included many domains of linguistics: general linguistics, Finno-Ugrian and Altaic philology, Hungarian phonetics and phonology, etc. Gombocz published quite a number of monographs and periodical articles which were well received by critics in Hungary and abroad especially his *Zur ungarischen Phonetik* (with E.A. Mayer, 1909) and *Die bulgarisch-türkischen Lehnwörter in der ungarischen Sprache*. Dezső Pais (b. 1886) conducted widely recognized research into many fields of linguistics — general as well as comparative, phonology and lexicology, to mention a few. Similarly, Géza Bárczi (b. 1894) also embraced many topics of linguistic research. Miklós Zsirai (1892-1955) in Finno-Ugrian philology and István Kniezsa (1898-1965) as a researcher of the etymology of medieval place-names, history of orthography, and Slavic philology likewise distinguished themselves.

Kniezsa's famous predecessor in Slavic studies was Oszkár Asbóth (1852-1920) who attended Budapest, Leipzig, Berlin and Göttingen universities. In 1882 and 1889 Asbóth did research work in Russia then was appointed professor of Slavic philology at Budapest University in which capacity he functioned between 1882 and 1919. During this period Oszkár Asbóth helped introduce Slavic studies into Greater Hungary. He was the first linguist who conducted methodologically well-prepared investigations into the Slavic loanwords of the Hungarian language (*Szláv jövevényszavaink*. Budapest, 1907). Asbóth's treatises appeared in the Hungarian and German languages in Hungary and elsewhere. One of his earlier major works, entitled *Die Umwandlung der Themen im Lateinischen*, had already been published in 1875 in Leipzig. Asbóth systematically exchanged letters with Russian and Ukrainian linguists. Their valuable correspondence is preserved in the Leningrad Archives of the Academy of Sciences of the Soviet Union and the manuscript divisions of the Moscow Museum of History and the Lenin Library.*

John Lotz (1913, Milwaukee, Wis., USA — 1973, Washington, D.C.) was a second-generation scholar who completed his education in Hungary, at the Lutheran Gimnázium of Bonyhád (1931) and at Budapest University (1937). For years John Lotz was professor of linguistics at Columbia University, New York, and the director of the Center for Applied Linguistics, Washington, D.C. Lotz was instrumental in initiating several important linguistic projects in the United States and Hungary, among them The Hungarian-English Contrastive Linguistics Project. He contributed to several scholarly journals and collective works in the United States and Europe.

---

*For details see "Asbóth Oszkár orosz nyelvű útinaplója" in János Váradi-Sternberg's *Utak, találkozások, emberek: írások az orosz-magyar és ukrán-magyar kapcsolatokról*. (Uzhgorod: Kárpáti Könyvkiadó, 1974. pp. 258-266).

Under the guidance of Géza Bárczi a group of unusually well-trained linguists produced a six-volume linguistic atlas of Hungarian dialects *A magyar nyelvjárások atlasza* (Budapest: Akadémiai Kiadó. Parts 5 and 6 are in preparation) which is an absolutely unique enterprise as to its methodology. They masterfully applied a most modern methodology and introduced an entirely new phase, unknown to this day in the making of linguistic atlases. This new phase means that the linguists introduced the "on-the-spot" control of data. This innovation was never before used as a workphase in the history of linguistic atlases.*

2

Sándor Kőrösi Csoma (1784, Kőrös—1842, Darjeeling, India) received a British scholarship when he was fifteen years old to study Oriental languages at Göttingen University. In order to find the ancient home of the Hungarians, Kőrösi Csoma traveled to Asia. He did not succeed in this romantic endeavor but, instead, under the influence of W. Moorcroft, an English traveler, he immersed himself in Tibetan studies and as a result prepared and published the first grammar of the Tibetan language. (*A Grammar of the Tibetan language in English*. Calcutta, 1834), along with the first English-Tibetan dictionary (*Essay towards a Dictionary Tibetan and English*. Calcutta, 1834). Both works are regarded as milestones in Oriental linguistics. In 1837, Sándor Kőrösi Csoma was appointed librarian of the Asiatic Society in Calcutta. Here in Calcutta he compiled glossaries for sixteen European and Oriental languages. The Asiatic Society erected a monument above his tomb in Darjeeling. Kőrösi Csoma's papers were collected and issued by Tivadar Duka under the title *Kőrösi Csoma Sándor dolgozatai* (Budapest, 1885). As the founder of Tibetan philology, Kőrösi Csoma opened up entirely new vistas for Oriental studies.

Ármin Vámbéry (1832-1913) distinguished himself as a traveler in the Middle East and Central Asia and as an authority on those regions. His reputation was especially outstanding in contemporary Great Britain and Russia. Vámbéry's *Bokhara története* appeared in several languages including Russian (*Istoriia Bokhary . . .* St. Petersburg, 1873) and in English (*History of Bokhara*. London: H. S. King, 1873, which was reprinted by Arno Press, New York, 1973). His *Etymologisches Wörterbuch der turko-tatarischen Sprachen* (Leipzig: F. A. Brockhaus, 1878) proved to be so useful that it was republished in 1972 by Biblio-

---

*For details see A Magyar nyelvjárások atlaszának elméleti-módszertani kérdései. Edited by László Deme and Samu Imre. (Budapest: Akadémiai Kiadó, 1975. 345 p.).

Verlag (Osnabrück, XXIV, 228 p.). Vámbéry's views of the Eastern question (Central Asia) were in the focus of debates in England in the last decades of the nineteenth century, particularly his relevant monographs, *Central Asia and the Anglo-Russian frontier question; a series of political papers* (London, 1874. VIII, 385 p.), and *The coming struggle for India, being an account of the encroachments of Russia and Central Asia, and the difficulties sure to arise therefrom to England* (London, 1885. VIII, 214 p.).

Ignác Goldziher (1850, Székesfehérvár—1921, Budapest) received his education in Budapest, Berlin, Leiden and Leipzig where he obtained his doctorate. From 1873 to 1874 Goldziher was on a study trip to Syria, Palestine and Egypt. Between 1894 and 1921 he taught at the Budapest University and was recognized as one of the greatest scholars of Semitic philology. In 1889 at the Stockholm International Congress of Orientalists he was awarded the Gold Medal for his scholarly achievements and was elected member of the Berlin, St. Petersburg, Göttingen, Amsterdam and Copenhagen academies. Most of his treatises were published in his lifetime not only in Hungarian but in German, French, English, Russian, Swedish, Serbian as well as Arabic languages. According to Soviet Russian orientalist M. A. Batunskii, Ignác Goldziher positively influenced the development of czarist Russian and Soviet Oriental studies and this is why Goldziher was reelected in 1922 to the Soviet Academy of Sciences.*

Goldziher was the first scholar who employed modern, critical methods in the historiography of Islamic civilization. Several of his works have recently been republished. See his *Études islamologiques; traduction analytique* par G. H. Bousquet (Leiden: E. J. Brill, 1962. 133 p., reprinted from *Arabica*, t. 7-9), his *Gesammelte Schriften* (edited by Joseph de Somogyi. Hildesheim: G. Olnis, 1969-1973).

Gyula Germánus (b. 1884) studied history, Latin, Oriental languages, Arabic and Turkish literatures at Budapest, Constantinople (Istanbul), Vienna and Leipzig universities, and in 1907 worked in the Library of the British Museum. Germanus acquired international fame as an authority on the cultural history of Mohammedan peoples and on Arabic literature. He made numerous trips to the Middle East and published extensively—chiefly in English—on his topics. Interestingly, most of his writings have been published abroad by foreign publishers: for example, *Lecture on Turkish Popular Literature* (Lahore, 1931); *The role of Turks in Islam* (Hyderabad, 1933-1934); *The Awakening of Turkish Literature* (2 vols., Hyderabad, 1933); *Sulle orme di Maometto* (Milano, 1938); *Mahmoud Teymour and Modern Arab Literature* (London, 1950);

---

*Cf. M. A. Batunskii, *K voprosy o znachenii nauchnogo naslediia I. Goldziera.* (Izvestiia Akademii Nauk Uzbekskoi SSR, 1960. pp. 50-58.).

Sources of the Arab Nights (London, 1951); *Unknown Masterpieces of Arab Literature* (Hyderabad, 1952); *Arab Geographers* (London, 1964); *Trends of Contemporary Arab Literature* (London, 1957-1958); *The Berber-Arab Literature of Morocco* (Hyderabad, 1964); *Ibn Khaldum, the Philosopher* (Lahore, 1967); *Arab Poets and Critics* (Delhi, 1967); *New Arab Novelists* (Lahore, 1969). Evidently, Germanus was instrumental in informing English-speaking intellectuals about Islamic civilization, his focus being the history of Arabic literature.

Ervin Baktay (1890-1963) concentrated his scholarly activities on the problems of Indic religions, philosophy, art, as well as social life and customs. In 1928 Baktay successfully located the most important places of Sándor Kőrösi Csoma's journey, which Baktay summarized in his monograph, *Kőrösi Csoma Sándor* (Budapest, 1962). In 1956 and 1957 at the invitation of the government of India, Ervin Baktay again made a study tour of India. Baktay's books include treatises on Rabindranath Tagore (1922); a two-volume set about India (1931); *Kashmir* (1934); and an art history of India (1958) which in 1963 was translated into German (*Die Kunst Indiens*. 494 p., illus., col. plates).

Lajos Ligeti (b. 1902) studied at Budapest University, the Sorbonne, and the Collège de France. Between 1928 and 1931 Ligeti made a study trip to Mongolia (see his *Rapport préliminaire d' un voyage d' exploration fait en Mongolie chinoise, 1928-1931*. Leipzig, 1933). During the years 1933 to 1935 Ligeti lectured at the École des Langues Orientales, Paris. In 1936 and 1937 Ligeti conducted research work in Afghanistan. He is a member of the Mongolian Academy of Sciences and several other learned societies including the Leipzig and the French academies. For years he has been the editor of *Acta Orientalia*, a journal issued by the Hungarian Academy of Sciences. Lajos Ligeti has contributed to many areas of Oriental studies but primarily dealt with the languages of Central Asia and Altaic philology. Ligeti's *Az ismeretlen Belső Ázsia* (The unknown Central Asia. Budapest, 1940) was translated also into Turkish (*Bilinmiyen Ic-Asya*. Istanbul, 1946. 261 p.). Ligeti's *Catalogue du Kanjur mongol imprimé* (Budapest. Bibliotheca orientalis Hungarica, 3) was continued by Biambyn Rinchen's *Catalogue du Tanjur Mongol imprimé* (New Delhi, International Academy of Indian Culture, 1964-). He has written quite a number of books and scholarly articles for domestic and foreign journals and edited *Histoire secrète des Mongols* (Text in Mongolian. Budapest, 1971. Monumenta linguae Mongolicae collecta, 1), and *Mongolian studies* (Amsterdam: Grüner, 1970. 590 p.), furthermore *Studia turcica* (Articles in English, French, German, Russian, and Turkish. Budapest, 1971. 498. Bibliotheca Orientalis Hungarica, 17). Lajos Ligeti is regarded as one of the greatest living experts in his fields.

Literary History Writing

The first comprehensive summary of Hungarian literary history was written as early as 1851 by Ferenc Toldy (1805-1875) and this has earned him the title of "father of Hungarian literary history". But literary criticism in the form of essays had flourished even before 1851, especially in the works of József Bajza (1804-1858). Subsequently, literary criticism as practiced by Pál Gyulai (1826-1909), Jenő Péterfy (1850-1899), Frigyes Riedl (1856-1921) and some of their contemporaries attained a level of excellence meeting European standards. Some literary journals like the *Nyugat* (The West) along with the chairs of literary history at universities helped advance literary scholarship in the twentieth century.

János Horváth (1878-1961) was the most important single factor responsible for the extraordinary progress the country's literary scholarship has made in our century. Above all, János Horváth was an unsurpassable writer of literary essays which were based on modern textual criticism and aesthetics. In 1901 and 1902 he attended the École Normale Supérieure in Paris on scholarship. Between 1923 and 1948 János Horváth functioned as professor of Hungarian literary history at Budapest University and trained with impressive results the next generation of literary historians and critics. His monumental works include *A magyar irodalmi műveltség kezdetei: Szent Istvántól Mohácsig* (last ed., Budapest: Magyar Szemle Társaság, 1944. 330 p.) in which he depicted the beginnings of Hungarian literary culture and masterfully analyzed the multinational character of the Middle Ages. His *Az irodalmi műveltség megoszlása* (last ed., Budapest: Magyar Szemle Társaság, 1944. 318 p.) is a lasting monument to the transition period during which vanishing medievalism was superseded by Renaissance culture and Latin language by the vernacular. Horváth's poetics (*Magyar vers*. Budapest: Magyar Tudományos Akadémia, 1948. 314 p.) is the best work ever written on poetry in Central Europe.

Mihály Babits (1883-1941) and Antal Szerb (1901-1945) surveyed European and world literature. Mihály Babits' work *Az európai irodalom története*, 1760-1925 (Budapest: Nyugat, 1935. 352 p.) has two German editions entitled *Geschichte der europäischen Literatur* (Zürich: Europa Verlag, 1949; Wien: Europa Verlag, 1949). Antal Szerb's *A világirodalom története* (History of world literature. Budapest, 1941, 1962, 1973. 1013 p.) is a brilliant synthesis of the history of world literature. Both authors discussed Hungarian literature as a part of European and world trends and currents.

In post-1945 Hungary Gábor Tolnai (b. 1910) has been very active as literary historian and critic. His fields of specialization include twentieth century Hungarian and Spanish literature.

István Sőtér (b. 1913) majored in Hungarian and French philology at Budapest University where he is presently professor of literature. In 1935 and 1936 Sőtér received a scholarship to study at the École Normale Supérieure in Paris. Professor Sőtér is the director of the Institute of Literary History of the Hungarian Academy of Sciences and from 1970 to 1973 was the president of the International Comparative Literature Association. In 1973 he was awarded an honorary doctor's degree at the Paris University. He is a many-sided scholar, writing studies, essays, itineraries, novels and short stories. Sőtér's monographs on French-Hungarian cultural relationships (*Francia szellem a régi Magyarországon*. Budapest, 1940); *Magyar-francia kapcsolatok*. Budapest, 1946), on József Eötvös (*Eötvös József*. Budapest, 1963), and on Imre Madách (*Álom a történelemről: Madách-tanulmány*. Budapest, 1965) are works of importance. István Sőtér was one of the general editors of a colossal, six-volume synthesis of Hungarian literary history (*A magyar irodalom története*. Budapest: Akadémiai Kiadó, 1964-1966).

Tibor Klaniczay (b. 1923) has been the deputy director of the Institute of Literary History of the Hungarian Academy of Sciences since 1956. In 1967 he spent a year in Paris as a guest professor of literary history at the Sorbonne. Since 1964 Klaniczay has been a member of the International Comparative Literature Association. He is an internationally recognized authority on the comparative literature of Central and Eastern Europe. One of his major works (*Zrínyi Miklós*. Budapest, 1954, 1964) elucidated the character and literary significance of Miklós Zrínyi (1620-1664), a frequent topic in Central and Eastern European literature. Tibor Klaniczay (in cooperation with József Szauder and Miklós Szabolcsi) authored the *Kis magyar irodalomtörténet* (Budapest: Gondolat, 1961. 493 p.) which work was translated into English (*History of Hungarian literature*. London: Collet's, 1964. 361 p.) and several other languages including French and Russian.

Mihály Czine (b. 1929) is one of the best-trained literary critics in present-day Hungary. Besides being associated with Budapest University, professor Czine has been working in the Institute of Literary History of the Hungarian Academy of Sciences since 1956. His main field of interest is twentieth century literature. He is the co-author of *A magyar irodalom története* (History of Hungarian literature. Vols. 5, 6. Budapest, 1965, 1966). His monographs on modern writers (*Móricz Zsigmond útja a forradalmakig*, 1960; *Móricz Zsigmond*, 1968; *Szabó Pál*, 1971) are many-sided interpretations based on the writers' life, work and surrounding historical circumstances.

The best known Hungarian literary critic from a world vantage point is György Lukács (1885-1971). He is indeed a world authority on German literature, Shakespeare and Balzac. Naturally, scholars in the West have always paid special attention to the activities of György

Lukács and their attitude towards him has often been very critical, especially when they scrutinized Lukács' concepts of literary realism, socialist realism and the like. As an aftermath of the two world wars, a modern migration of nations has taken place on all continents. New states have been founded all over the world and we are witnessing a never before experienced rebirth of national consciousness. This development is of importance all the more because there is not a single country in the world where, in some form or another, the signs of national revival would not appear on the scene. The problem of majority versus minority has come to the fore in almost every country, be it great or small. The study of inter-ethnic relations is now a priority one topic on the agenda of many countries. But to most people it is not patently obvious that literary research is capable of revealing the basic nature of ethnic entities and of helping solve in practice the most complex of interethnic relations. To remedy this, a unique work has been done by those literary historians, critics and writers of Hungarian descent who live in minority status in the succession states. All in all, these works of minority scholars and writers clearly mirror the varying degrees of symbiosis of co-existing ethnic entities, the assimilation and dissimilation and all the other essential facets which help determine the quality of their coexistence. Let us single out just a few of the scholars who in the past decades have been engaged in this pioneering mission.

In Czechoslovakia, Sándor Csanda (*Első nemzedék; a szlovákiai magyar irodalom keletkezése és fejlődése*. Bratislava, 1968. 305 p.; *Harmadik nemzedék; kritikák, tanulmányok*. Bratislava, 1971. 246 p.; *A törökellenes és kuruc harcok költészetének magyar-szlovák kapcsolatai*. Budapest, 1961. 223 p.) and Lajos Turczel (*Két kor mezsgyéjén; a magyar irodalom fejlődési feltételei és problémái Csehszlovákiában 1918 és 1938 között*. Bratislava, 1967. 311 p.) developed a new methodology for describing Hungarian-Slovak-Czech literary ties in a changing political climate.

In Romania, László Szabédi (1907-1959) published several books (among them *A magyar ritmus formái*. Bukarest: Állami Irodalmi és Művészeti Kiadó, 195?, 231 p.; *Szabédi László legszebb versei*. Válogatta és az előszót írta Kántor Lajos. Bukarest: Albatrosz, 1972. 147 p.) and numerous essays in the service of Romanian-Hungarian coexistence in Transylvania. And when the minority university at Kolozsvár-Cluj (Transylvania) was abolished in 1959 by the order of the majority authorities, Szabédi's reaction was suicide.

The literary activities of the still very active Edgár Balogh (b. 1906) are models for the analysis of a minority's behavior in bourgeois and Communist Romania as well as in Czechoslovakia. Nowadays Edgár Balogh is working on a unique enterprise: a multi-volume encyclopedia to historically survey all facets of the life of the Hungarian minority in Romania (Transylvania). No such work has been initiated before in the field of ethnic studies.

Imre Bori lives in Yugoslavia and can be listed among the top literary historians of present-day Central and Eastern Europe. In his methodology he is doubtless a follower of János Horváth. Bori is the best observer of literary interactions in the Danube Valley. He wrote several monographs on literary trends on a comparative basis (*A szecessziótól a dadáig* . . . Újvidék: Forum, 1969. 322 p.; *A szürrealizmus ideje* . . . Újvidék: Forum, 1970. 302 p.).

Philosophy – Psychology (Psychiatry)

The flourishing Renaissance culture which culminated in the court of King Matthias I (1458-1490) came to a sudden end as a consequence of the Battle of Mohács in 1526. The trend of humanism, which had up to that point of time provided some unity to knowledge fell apart in the subsequent movements of the Reformation and the Counter-Reformation. In 1635 Cardinal Péter Pázmány (1570-1637) founded the Nagyszombat University: the hotbed of scholastic philosophy. He himself was an outstanding philosopher and a close associate of Cardinal Bellarmine. A follower of Aristoteles, Péter Pázmány investigated the nature of universals and categories in his *Dialectica* and wrote several other philosophical treatises. This trend of thought revealed conspicuous affinities with the Italian and Austrian schools of philosophy, while Hungarian Protestants turned toward German and Dutch universities. János Apáczai Csere (1625-1659) was the first Hungarian to receive a doctor's degree from a Dutch (Hardwijk) university and published the first Hungarian-language philosophy book, *Magyar Encyclopaedia* (Utrecht, 1653-1655), expressing a universal-pansophic philosophy. His book on logic, *Magyar Logikátska* (Fejérvár, 1654), was issued in Transylvania.

István Márton (1760-1831), an early follower of Immanuel Kant (1724-1804), expounded his master's thoughts in his *Systema Philosophiae Criticae* (1820).

In the nineteenth century, Hegel, Comte and Neo-Scholasticism provided stimulus to the activities of the country's philosophers and simultaneously the idea of creating a national philosophical system appeared on the scene. It is, therefore, quite understandable that already between 1835 and 1845 a three-volume set of prize-winning philosophical works were prepared in native Hungarian (*Philosophiai pályamunkák*. Pest: Eggenberger, 1835-1845). These essays which were awarded prizes in competitions sponsored by the Hungarian Academy of Sciences (then Magyar Tudós Társaság), were concerned with the historical development and contemporary status of philosophy, including psychology and educational theory in Hungary and elsewhere. Subsequent to such preparatory efforts, individual philosophers of European fame a short while later began their many-sided activities.

Károly Böhm (1846-1911) studied at Pozsony, Göttingen as a disciple of H. Lotze and H. Ritter, and in 1896 was appointed professor of philosophy at Kolozsvár University. In 1881 Böhm founded the *Magyar Philosophiai Szemle* (Hungarian Philosophical Review) to which Böhm contributed several essays. He was the first Hungarian philosopher who developed an independent system of philosophy and into it he incorporated some elements of the philosophies of Kant and Comte. Böhm contributed studies to philosophical anthropology (*Az ember és világa*. 3 vols., Budapest-Kolozsvár, 1883-1906), to axiology (*Az értékelmélet feladata és alapproblémái*. Budapest, 1900), to logic, and to experimental psychology, as well as to the theory of knowledge. He founded a flourishing school of philosophy among whose followers were Béla Tankó and György Bartók.

The greatest Hungarian philosopher, Ákos Pauler (1876-1933), was born into an intellectual environment. His father was well-known historian, Gyula Pauler. Ákos Pauler's first published work appeared in 1893 in a scholarly journal, *Bölcseleti Folyóirat*. In this article the highschool student Pauler argued in defense of metaphysics. Years later, influenced by Imre Pauer, his philosophy professor, Ákos Pauler for years became a defender of positivism. Having obtained his doctorate (1898), Pauler continued his studies at Leipzig and at the Sorbonne. Afterwards Pauler rejected positivism and remained a lifelong adherent of objective idealism. Pauler continued research work in several domains of philosophy. In the order of the chronology of his monographic publications Pauler: elucidated the concept and the tasks of the philosophy of nature (*A természetfilozófia fogalmáról és feladatairól*. Budapest, 1898); he discussed the psychological foundations of epistemology (*Az ismeretelmélet lélektani alapjairól*. Budapest, 1898); determined the problem of the concrete in modern philosophy (*A magánvaló problémája az újabb filozófiában*. Budapest, 1901); dealt with the relativity of cognition and of concept-forming in mathematics (*Az ismerés viszonylagossága és a matematikai fogalomalkotás*. Budapest, 1902); analyzed the sources, subjects and limits of knowledge (*Ismeretelméleti tanulmányok*. Budapest, 1903); and clarified in a supremely logical way the notion of epistemological categories (*Ismeretelméleti kategóriák*. Budapest, 1904). His philosophical propaedeutic (*Bevezetés a filozófiába*. Budapest, 1920. 1st ed., *Grundlagen der Philosophie*. Berlin-Leipzig: W. de Gruyter & Co., 1925) has always been regarded as an innovative act for its unique division of philosophy and because important philosophical issues were put into historical perspective by Pauler. In Pauler's opinion, logic is the most significant part of philosophical studies. His relevant monograph is indeed a standard work in the literature of pure logic (*Logika*. Budapest, 1925, in German: *Logik. Versuch einer Theorie der Wahrheit*. Berlin-Leipzig: W. de Gruyter & Co., 1929).

Pauler succeeded in clarifying many theretofore obscure topics. He threw new light on the Aristotelian interpretation of Plato's theory of ideas. Besides the fact that Pauler succeeded in elaborating a quite independent system of philosophy, he greatly contributed to several spheres of philosophical thinking. As a highly esteemed logician, the advocate of pure logic, Pauler added his "reductive method" to the classical forms of inference, that is, to induction and deduction. He significantly enriched the field of logical principles by adding to them his own principium classificationis according to which everything is classifiable at least in the category of unclassifiables. Pauler's metaphysics relies on the so-called substances which are the centers of self-activity. All substances strive toward the principle of self-liberation, that is, toward the Absolute. The ontological basis of substances is their striving toward the Absolute. This reasoning gives a uniform metaphysical background to Pauler's worldview. The majority of philosophers in twentieth century Hungary and the Middle Danube area have looked upon Ákos Pauler as a great authority of philosophy in general and of logic and epistemology in particular. His system has attracted many a thinker, among them József Somogyi (1898-1947) and Béla Brandenstein. Recently Pauler has been acknowledged more and more outside his native land and his name has been entered in internationally well-known professional encyclopedias while more and more references have been made to his scholarly activities in monographic literature.

Between the wars the official trend of Neo-Scholasticism flourished. Antal Schütz (1880-1953), József Trikál (1873-1950) and to a certain extent József Somogyi, can be listed as its main representatives. Gyula Kornis (1885-1958) excelled in the service of supplying a political philosophy for the conservative regime.

Endre Ivánka (b. 1902) was professor of philosophy at Vienna University and published several standard books and articles on ancient Greek philosophy and the Byzantine civilization (*Plato Christianus; Übernahme und Umgestaltung des Platonismus durch die Väter*. Einsiedeln: Johannes Verlag, 1965. 495 p.).

Béla Brandenstein, likewise his master, Ákos Pauler, extended his investigations almost to the entire domain of philosophy. Born in Budapest (1901), he graduated from the local university and obtained doctorate in philosophy in 1923. Between 1928 and 1945 Brandenstein taught philosophy at Budapest University and was the president of the Hungarian Philosophical Society. After World War II he was appointed professor of philosophy at Saarbrücken University, Germany where he taught until his retirement. Prior to 1945 Brandenstein wrote several monographs, including *Bölcseleti alapvetés* (Philosophical foundations. Budapest, 1935. 546 p.) and a monumental volume on *Nietzsche* (Budapest, 1942. 503 p.) as well as numerous essays in *Budapesti Szemle*. But his main contributions to philosophy appeared in the post-1945 years. His lifework was summarized in the six-volume *Grundlegung der Philosophie* (Munich, 1965-1970). In this grand synthesis Brandenstein examines the all-important problems of ontology, logic, philosophy of mathematics, metaphysics, theory of science, epistemology, aesthetics, ethics, and many borderline problems of philosophy. In the last decades Brandenstein has published well over a dozen books, all in German. In his latest monograph Brandenstein returned to two of his favorite topics: logic and ontology (*Logik und Ontologie*. Heidelberg: Winter, 1976. 120 p.). A remarkable logical thinker, Béla Brandenstein has demonstrated himself to be an independent philosopher with a strong leaning toward the traditional.

Primarily since the conclusion of World War II, many a Hungarian philosopher has left his native land and worked abroad, chiefly in Western countries. Imre Lakatos (1922-1974) acquired world fame as an authority on the philosophy, methodology and history of science. His works appeared in Western languages (*Historia de la ciencia* . . . Madrid, 1974; *Proofs and refutations*, 1976; *Problems in the Philosophy of science* (papers delivered at the International Colloquium in the Philosophy of Science, Bedford College, 1965. Edited by Imre Lakatos).

Ervin László's career is one of the most interesting ones. Born in Budapest (1932), he was first known as an accomplished pianist. László received U.S. citizenship when 21 years old. Interestingly, in 1962 he worked as a scientific collaborator at the Institute of East-European Studies at the University of Fribourg. László's field of specialization is of an interdisciplinary nature. His studies are concerned with systems theory and philosophy. He prepared widely known treatises such as *System, structure and experience; toward a scientific theory of mind* (New York: Gordon and Breach, 1969. 112 p.), *The system view of the world; the natural philosophy of the new developments in the sciences* (New York: G. Braziller, 1972. 131 p.), *A strategy for the future; the systems approach to world order* (New York: G. Braziller, 1974. 238 p.). Ervin László edited an important collective work, *The world system; models, norms, applications* (New York: G. Braziller, 1973. 215 p.) containing the lectures delivered at the first Systems Philosophy Symposium, arranged by the State University of New York in 1973.

The Austrian-born and -educated (Innsbruck and Vienna universities) Ludwig von Bertalanffy (1901-1972), a renowned expert on theoretical biology, was also deeply engaged in general systems theory.

See Ervin László's "Introduction: the origins of general systems theory in the work of von Bertalanffy," in *The relevance of general systems theory: papers presented to Ludwig von Bertalanffy on his seventieth birthday* (Edited by Ervin László. New York: G. Braziller, 1972. VIII, 213 p.).

Arthur Koestler (1905, Budapest) is the best known Hungarian philosopher of non-Marxist orientation. First he was known as a novelist, journalist, and political scientist, but then in the late fifties Koestler turned to philosophy and has become one of the most celebrated philosophers of the Western world. Koestler has philosophically analyzed such subjects as art, science, and society. His investigations in the field of philosophical anthropology startled the world by his unconventional approach as is demonstrated in *The Sleepwalkers* (1959) in which he scrutinized man's changing role in the universe, while in *The Ghost in the Machine* (1968) Koestler convincingly argued against the mechanistic interpretation of man's nature.

In postwar Hungary dominant themes and main currents reflect Marxist thought. There has not been enough time to educate a series of eminent scholars of philosophy whose influence would be conspicuous beyond the national borders. Presently, József Szigeti (b. 1921) seems to be in a key position to train the new generation, for he has held leading posts since the late forties. Szigeti frequently refers to György Lukács (1885-1971), the best known Marxist philosopher of today. Born in Budapest into a rich family Lukács was educated at the Budapest University and later studied under Georg Simmel at Berlin and under Max Weber at Heidelberg. Between 1933 and 1944 Lukács worked at the Institute of Philosophy of the Soviet Academy of Sciences in Moscow, and from 1945 to 1956 at the University of Budapest as professor of aesthetics and the philosophy of culture.

With the defeat in the War of Independence of 1848-1849, Hungary completely lost its constitutional institutions and its cultural elite suffered in every respect. A weighty percentage of the intelligentsia was imprisoned, executed or left the country. During this Era of Habsburg Absolutism (1849-1867) systematic cultural movements completely died out. It was the Austro-Hungarian Compromise (Ausgleich) of 1867 that rung down the curtain on this period of stagnation and ushered in a cultural revival never before seen in the country. Hungary once again resumed active participation in Europe's intellectual efforts. The school system above all was modernized at all levels in order to create quality education based upon the pillars of educational and child psychology. This new, psychology-grounded school system produced several generations of cultural elite up to the end of World War II. Scientists, scholars and artists who were educated in these new schools promoted mankind's civilization. As already stated, educational psychology and child study played a decisive role in this widely recognized progress. More than anyone else László Nagy (1857-1931) helped develop a new method applied in child study and educational psychology. In 1881 László Nagy began teaching at Budapest Teachers Training Institute where in 1909 he founded the first laboratory for educational psychology. In 1916 he commenced lecturing in experimental psychology at Apponyi College (Budapest) where professors as 1903 the country's teachers training institutes were educated. As early as 1903 László Nagy was instrumental in founding the *Gyermektanulmányi Társaság* (Society for Child Study), later organizing and heading the psychological laboratory of *Székesfővárosi Pedagógiai Szeminárium* (Pedagogic Seminar of the City of Budapest). That same year he also founded a periodical entitled *A gyermek* (The child) which for decades remained a distinguished forum for psychologists and educators engaged in child study. In addition László Nagy was at the vanguard in the founding of the Budapest-based *Gyermektanulmányi Múzeum* (Museum of Child Study). He was among the first theorists to stress as a basic principle of education that the child should be the center of education: that the whole teaching process — curriculum and methods of instruction — should be adjusted to the nature and requirements of children. He was also among the first of the reform thinkers who methodically discussed the significance of children's drawings in education. László Nagy's then innovative didactics was built up on direct observation, practical exercises as well as on systematic studies of school children's activities. With his pedagogic views László Nagy was well ahead of contemporary educational theorists. He worked out the psychology of the range of children's interests (*A gyermek érdeklődésének lélektana*. Budapest, 1908) which guided teachers the country over.

Károly Schaffer (1864-1939), neurologist and psychiatrist, completed his medical studies in Budapest and from 1901 up to his retirement was professor of neurology and psychiatry there. He conducted research in the morphology of nerve cells, the morphological bases of hereditary nervous and mental disorders, and hypnotism, to mention but a few of the scientific fields within his interest for which he received international recognition. Károly Schaffer's main works include the *Über das morphologische Wesen und die Histopathologie der hereditär-systematischen Nervenkrankheiten* (Berlin, 1926), *Az elmebetegségek és kapcsolatos idegbetegségek kórtana* (Pathology of mental diseases and their related nervous disorders. Budapest, 1927), *Anatomische Wesenbestimmung der hereditär-organischen Nerven-Geisteskrankheiten* (With Dezső Miskolczy. Szeged, 1936), *Histopathologie des Neurons* (Budapest-Leipzig, 1938).

Pál Ranschburg (1870-1945), a noted psychiatrist, neurologist and psychologist graduated from Budapest University and established the first psychophysical laboratory as early as 1890 and in 1928 the Hungarian Psychological Society, both in Budapest. Ranschburg devised and applied several new measuring methods and devices for investigating intellectual functions. His research on association and memory is still held important. Pál Ranschburg dealt extensively with children's intelligence, and the psychology of reading and writing. Besides his several Hungarian-language monographs he wrote a still very useful German-language book on the psychology of reading and writing and related intellectual-cognitive development (*Die Lese- und Schreibstörungen des Kindesalters; ihre Psychologie, Physiologie, Pathologie, heilpedagogische und medizinische Therapie*. Halle a.S., 1928. 314 p.).

Sándor Ferenczi (1873-1933), one of the giants of psychoanalysis, at the outset of his career was profoundly engaged in organizational activities. In fact, it was partly attributable to Sándor Ferenczi's initiative that already prior to World War I psychoanalysts from many European countries convened for yearly meetings. In 1909 at a meeting in Nuremberg Ferenczi made the motion to organize the International Psycho-Analytical Association, and in 1918 was elected to its presidency. In 1913 Ferenczi and three colleagues formed the Hungarian Psycho-Analytical Society of which he remained permanent president the rest of his days. During an eight month visit to the United States beginning in 1926 Sándor Ferenczi gave a series of lectures at the invitation of the New School of Social Research in New York City. Ferenczi was a devoted friend and ardent co-worker of Sigmund Freud. He wrote a great number of papers on his theories of personality, personality disorders, and a wide range of psychoanalytical topics. The last of the therapeutic theories he formulated can be summarized in one sentence: "The indispensable healing power in the therapeutic gift is love."*

Many of the books and voluminous papers by Sándor Ferenczi are now available in the English translation. These include *Sex in Psychoanalysis* (New York: R. Brunner, 1950), *First contributions to psychoanalysis* (London: Hogarth Press, 1952), *Further contributions to the theory and technique of Psycho-analysis* (London, 1926, 1950, 1951; New York, 1952, 1953). His complete works have been issued in French under the title *Oeuvres complètes* (Paris: Payot, 1968-).

Lipót Szondi was born in Hungary in 1893 and graduated in 1919 from Budapest University. Following his graduation he served until 1926 as assistant in experimental psychology under professor Pál Ranschburg at the Institute of Psychology of the Budapest University. Before World War II Szondi headed the Institute of Physiology and

---

*De Forest, Izette, *The leaven of love; a development of the psychoanalitic theory and technique of Sándor Ferenczi.* (Hamden, Conn., 1965. p. 6.).

Pathological Psychology at the Training College for Teachers of Handicapped Children (Gyógypedagógiai Tanárképző Főiskola, Budapest). It was during the years 1927 to 1941 that Szondi developed a new branch of science, the so-called schicksal (fate, destiny) psychology. He worked out a system of depth psychological analysis that has been designated as schicksal analysis. The Szondi-Test system is frequently used in psychiatry and neurology. Topics covered by him include mental deficiency (*A fogyatékos értelem*. Budapest, 1925), *Constitutioanalysis és értelmi fogyatékosság*. Budapest, 1931), and anthropometric norms (*Magyar antropometriai normák*. Budapest, 1929). Szondi acquired a world reputation chiefly through his numerous Western language publications among which we should list at least the following few: *Experimental diagnostics of drives* (New York: Grune & Stratton, 1952. Translation of *Experimentelle Triebdiagnostik; tiefenpsychologische Diagnostik im Dienste der Psychopathologische, Kriminal- und Berufpsychologie, Charakterologie und Pädagogik*. 2 vols., Bern, 1947); *The Szondi-test; in diagnosis, prognosis, and treatment* (Philadelphia: Lippincott, 1959. 309 p.). On leaving Hungary he first lived in Switzerland then in the USA and finally resettled in Switzerland.

Dezső Miskolczy (b. 1894) was a close collaborator of Károly Schaffer. He graduated from the Faculty of Medicine of the Budapest University. During 1924 and 1925 Miskolczy continued his research work at the Cajal Institute in Madrid. He taught at the universities of Szeged (1930-1940), Kolozsvár (1940-1945), Marosvásárhely (1945-1964), and from 1964 up to his retirement at the Budapest University of Medicine. Miskolczy published several books and about 100 papers on the structure of the cerebellum, schizophrenia and relevant topics. He was elected member of the Hungarian Academy of Sciences, the Leopoldina, the Romanian Academy of Sciences and several other international societies. His highly esteemed monograph on the overlapping questions of internal medicine and neurology (*A bel- és ideggyógyászat határterületi kérdései*) was translated into German (*Grenzgebiete der inneren Medizine und Neurologie in Klinik und Praxis* (Frankfurt am M.: J. A. Barth, 1972. 224 p.).

Thomas Stephen Szasz (b. 1920, Budapest) has challenged many traditional notions which has triggered a chain of repercussions and reassessments in the field of law as well in psychiatry. He received his M.D. from the University of Cincinnati in 1944, and has been teaching psychiatry at the State University of New York at Syracuse since 1956. In his opinion mental illness is only a "myth". Szasz is founder and board chairman of the American Association for the Abolition of Involuntary Mental Hospitalization. His writings include *The Myth of Mental Illness* (1961), *Psychiatric Justice* (1965), *Ideology and Insanity*

(1970). His books are included in the curricula of countless institutions of higher education the world over.

Géza Révész (1878-1955) achieved renown for his studies in acoustic sensation. He was for years head of the Amsterdam Psychological Institute and editor of a well-known monographic series there under the title *Psychologische bibliotheek*. Its first volume which was written by him and entitled *De beteekenis der psychologie voor de wetenschappen en voor de practijk* (Amsterdam, 1945) was translated into German (*Die Bedeutung der Psychologie für die Wissenschaft, für die Praxis und die akademische Ausbildung der Psychologen*. Bern, 1947). In this widely acclaimed book Géza Révész discusses the role of psychology in scientific research ad introduced some reformative ideas to improve the university training of psychologists. His book on the psychology of genius also met with great success (*Creatieve begaafdheid*. Den Haag: Servire, 1946. 138 p.).

During the inter-war years, László Benedek (1887-1945) was one of the best known psychiatrists and neurologists in Hungary. Professor of psychiatry and neurology at Debrecen and later at Budapest University, he was highly esteemed for his publications on hydrophobia (*Über die Entstehung der Negrischen Körperchen*. Berlin, 1921), paralysis (*Der heutige Stand der Behandlung der progressiven Paralyse*. Berlin, 1926), and on his own individual method for cranial percussion (*Über die Schädelperkussion*. Berlin, 1932). His book on insulin shock was discussed at several international meetings.

In the sphere of pediatrics Pál Gegesi-Kiss (b. 1900) followed the best traditions as represented decades ago by János Bókay (1858-1937) and Pál Heim (1875-1929), both pioneering pediatricians. In recent years Gegesi-Kiss shifted his concentration to psychological topics and together with Lajos Bartha (b. 1927) developed completely new methods in experimental psychology. Gegesi-Kiss' monumental work on childhood disorders of personality appeared in German as well under the title *Persönlichkeits-Störungen im Kindesalter* (Budapest: Akadémiai Kiadó, 1969. 597 p.).

Studies in psychology were promoted by the establishment of special education schools. The first such school, the Institute for the Deaf, was founded at Vác in 1802 by a local lawyer, András Cházár. The establishment of the internationally recognized Training College for Teachers of Handicapped Children, (Budapest, 1922) gave impetus to the development of several branches of experimental psychology.

Dennis Szabó (b. 1929, Budapest) has for years been on the staff of the University of Montreal and is the director of its International Center of Comparative Criminology. He is an internationally acknowledged authority on criminal psychology and criminal justice. One of his best known monographs is *Criminologie* (Montreal, 1965. 565 p.).

Musicology

During the first decades of the nineteenth century, litterateurs already recognized that their art could be rejuvenated by means of folk literature. János Erdélyi (1814-1868) collected folk songs and legends (*Népdalok és mondák*. 3 vols., 1846-1848), the preponderance of his work being so folk literature oriented that it included not more than twelve folk melodies. Although years later István Bartalus (1821-1899) in his seven-volume folk song collection (1873-1896) included music scores, it did not arouse much interest in genuine folk melodies. The real breakthrough came in 1895 when Béla Vikár (1859-1945) using Edison's phonograph recorded for the very first time folk songs. Vikár's collection of folk music material was acclaimed by international representatives of the profession at the Paris World Exhibition in 1900. It is interesting to note that Béla Bartók himself later transcribed Vikár's phonographic material. Béla Bartók and Zoltán Kodály found it vital to develop a precise, scientific methodology for collecting folk songs. Kodály began a tour for the purpose of collecting folk songs in 1905, placing emphasis on genuine folk melodies. Zoltán Kodály's doctoral dissertation on the strophic structure in the Hungarian folk song which appeared in 1906 was a decisive step in the right direction. That same year he and Bartók started their lifelong collaboration in ethnomusicology which revolutionized not only Hungarian music but the entire field of the music of the Western world. They proved in a series of treatises that the pentatonic (five-tone) scale is the ancient, genuine foundation of Hungarian folk music. The pentatonic scale has since become the wellspring for many Hungarian composers who were to follow the traditions of Bartók and Kodály. Their collaborative efforts formed the keystone for the research of the many composers and musicologists who have subsequently devoted their research to ethnomusicology.

Béla Bartók laid the foundations for comparative ethnomusicology in his *Népzenénk és a szomszéd népek népzenéje; 127 dallammal* (Our folk music and the folk music of neighboring peoples; with 127 melodies. Budapest, 1934). In *Népzenénk* Bartók comparatively examines genuine folk songs of the Middle Danube Valley nations while determining their ethnic origins and the relative degree and extent of mutual influences. This invaluable contribution to comparative ethnomusicology and folklore has been translated into German as *Die Volksmusik der Magyaren und der benachbarten Völker* (Berlin: Walter de Gruyter, 1935), and Russian as *Narodnaia muzyka Vengrii i sodernikh narodov* (Moskva: Muzika, 1966).

A multivolume set entitled *A magyar népzene tára* (Thesaurus of Hungarian folk music. Budapest: Akadémiai Kiadó, 1951- illus.) has been published under the names of Béla Bartók and Zoltán Kodály. The volumes published thus far appear to be the best compiled folk music collections ever: I. *Gyermekjátékok* (Children's games, 934 p.); II. *Jeles napok* (Special days, 1245 p.); III A/B. *Lakodalom* (Weddings, 1089, 704 p.); IV. *Párosítók* (Pairing songs, 905 p.); V. *Siratók* (Laments, 1139 p.). Future volumes will not be restricted to but a single genre of song. This enterprise is regarded as one of methodological excellence replete with appropriate ethnomusicological interpretations.

There are at least forty to fifty learned ethnomusicologists working in present-day Hungary. Among them are László Lajtha (1892-1963) who focused on Bartók's works on musical folklore and forms of folk music, András Szőllősy who examined ancient Hungarian folk music and comparative musical folklore, and Bence Szabolcsi (b. 1899) who occupied himself with comparative studies of the peoples who evolved and used the five-tone scale as opposed to those who did not, as well as with studies of Hungarian and universal histories of music. Dénes Bartha (b. 1908) has published extensively on such topics as the eighteenth-century folk song, Johann Sebastian Bach, and universal music history both instrumental and vocal.*

The following two works on the history of Hungarian music merit special mention: *A magyar zene krónikája; zenei művelődésünk ezer éve dokumentumokban* (Chronicle of Hungarian music; a thousand years of our musical culture in documents. Budapest: Zeneműkiadó, 1962. 535 p.) edited by Dezső Legány, and *A magyar zene története* (A history of Hungarian music. Budapest: Zeneműkiadó, 1959. 2 vols.) by István Szelényi (b. 1904).

The most recently published *A magyar népballada és Európa* (Budapest: Zeneműkiadó, 1976. 2 vols.) by Lajos Vargyas, is also a high-level comparative treatment of the subject.

Hungarian musicologists have also written monumental works of excellence in fields related to ethnomusicology. In closing this chapter let us mention a few of them: *Studia Musicologica* (1961- Budapest, biannual); *Magyar Zene* (Hungarian Music, 1960- Budapest, bimonthly); *Magyar Zenetudomány* (Hungarian musicology, 1953- Budapest, annual), and *Monumenta Hungariae musica* (1963- Budapest), a well-edited monographic series.

---

*For a more complete survey see Jaap Kunst, *Ethnomusicology: A study of its nature, its problems, methods and representative personalities to which is added a bibliography*. (The Hague: Martinus Nijhoff, 1974.).

¹For more details see the following publications: Gyula Pauler and Sándor Szilágyi, *eds.*, *A magyar honfoglalás kútfői* (Sources relating to the Hungarian Conquest) (Budapest: Magyar Tudományos Akadémia, 1900), 877 p. Publishes most important Western as well as Oriental sources in the original language and in Hungarian with commentaries and bibliography; Henrik Marczali, *ed.*, *A magyar történet kútfőinek kézikönyve* (Handbook of

THE HISTORICAL AND SOCIAL SCIENCES

sources relating to Hungarian history) (Budapest: Atheneum, 1901), 967 p. Collection of most important sources from the pre-Conquest times up to the third quarter of the nineteenth century, including Law No. XXX of 1868. Greek and Latin sources are published also in Hungarian translation; Carlile Aylmer Macartney, *The medieval Hungarian historians; a critical and analytical guide*. (Cambridge: The University Press, 1953), 190 p. — Perhaps the best survey of chronicle and gesta literature can be found in János Horváth's *A magyar irodalmi műveltség kezdetei, Szent Istvántól Mohácsig*. (Budapest: Magyar Szemle Társaság, 1944), 330 p. Bálint Hóman's treatises are even now indispensable readings on the development of historical writing especially that up to the end of the eighteenth century. See his *Történetírás és forráskritika* (Historiography and source criticism) in vol. 2 of *Hóman Bálint munkái* (Budapest: Magyar Történelmi Társulat, 1938). Relevant studies by Sándor Domanovszky, Elemér Szentpétery, Péter Váczy and József Deér are very useful, and especially those of Elemér Mályusz who in his more recent publications made an excellent critical survey of medieval writings by using up-to-date historicophilological methods of textual criticism. Cf. Elemér Mályusz, *A Thúróczy-krónika és forrásai*. (Budapest: Akadémiai Kiadó, 1967), 206 p. (Tudománytörténeti tanulmányok, 5), and his *Az V. István-kori gesta*. (Budapest: Akadémiai Kiadó, 1971), 151 p. (Értekezések a történeti tudományok köréből. Új sorozat, 58).

For the whole subject matter as expressed in the title of this treatise see Emma Bartoniek, *comp., Magyar történeti forráskiadványok* (Hungarian historical source publications) (Budapest: Magyar Történelmi Társulat, 1929), 203 p. (A magyar történettudomány kézikönyve, I.3/b). Contains 3,109 entries, partly annotated, covering historical Hungary and Transylvania inclusive from the Conquest up to the Compromise of 1867. Also lists guides to domestic (Hungarian) and foreign archives storing documents relating to the country's history.

Domokos G. Kosáry's tripartite *Bevezetés a magyar történelem forrásaiba és irodalmába* (Introduction to the sources and literature of Hungarian history) (Budapest: Közoktatásügyi Kiadóvállalat, 1951-1954) has been revised and enlarged to become a five-volume edition entitled *Bevezetés Magyarország történetének forrásaiba és irodalmába* (Introduction to the sources and literature of Hungary's history) (Budapest: Tankönyvkiadó, 1970-). This seems to be an excellent and almost complete reference tool for specialists of the history of historiography, dealing also with all the relevant topics. It is very easy for a user to determine where the sources, manuscripts are stored, for instance, and lists also the most essential literature on them. Cf. George Barany's review in *Slavic Review*, vol. 31, no. 3, 1972, Pp. 718-719.

For sources of legal and constitutional development consult the volumes of *Corpus Juris Hungarici*. Sándor Flegler's monograph *A magyar történetírás történelme* (History of Hungarian historiography) (Budapest, 1895) can be useful for its many data but not for its interpretive notes.

²Cf. József Szemes, *Oláh Miklós* (Esztergom, 1936), and Pál Schleicher, *Oláh Miklós és Erasmus*. (Budapest, 1941).

³Budapest, 1876-1880. *Monumenta Hungariae Historica*. II., 21.I. Rerum Ungaricarum libri IV. 1566-1586; II. Rerum Transylvanicarum Pentades, 1598-1599; III. Hebdomades. 1603; IV. Hungarian diary notes, Latin poems. — I. Szamosközy as the first professional historian is characterized by Gyula Szekfű, *Adatok Sz. I. munkáinak kritikájához* (Budapest, 1904).

⁴For the period of the Renaissance see János Horváth, *Az irodalmi műveltség megoszlása*. (Budapest, 1935 and 1944); Tibor Kardos, *A magyarországi humanizmus kora* (Budapest: Akadémiai Kiadó, 1955), 463 p.; Péter Kulcsár, *Bonfini-forrástanulmányok* (Szeged, 1963); Tibor Kardos, *Renaissance tanulmányok* (Budapest: Akadémiai Kiadó, 1957), 542 p.

⁵Both the Hevenesi and Kaprinai collections are housed in the Budapest University Library (Egyetemi Könyvtár).

⁶Cf. Bálint Hóman, "Adalék a magyar nyomdászat XVIII. századi történetéhez," in his *Történetírás és forráskritika*. (Budapest: Magyar Történelmi Társulat, 1938), p. 381.

⁷Cf. Emma Léderer, *A magyar polgári történetírás rövid története*. (Budapest: Kossuth Könyvkiadó, 1969), p. 26. See also B. Hóman's work already referred to.

⁸E. Léderer, *Op. cit.*, p. 27, and Éva V. Windisch, *Az OSZK könyvtárosai a reformkorban* (Tanulmányok Budapest múltjából, 1961).

⁹Mrs. János Fráter surveys in details the activity of the Committee in her useful work *A Magyar Tudományos Akadémia Történettudományi Bizottságának működése (1854-1949)* (Budapest: MTA Könyvtára, 1966), 61 p. (M.T.A. Könyvtárának közleményei, 52).

¹⁰Cf. Gyula Szekfű, "A politikai történetírás," in Bálint Hóman, *ed., A magyar történetírás új útjai.* (Budapest: Magyar Szemle Társaság, 1931), Pp. 421-426.

¹¹Cf. Bálint Hóman, *Történetírás és forráskritika.* (Budapest: Magyar Történelmi Társulat, 1938), Pp. 428-429.

¹²Cf. Gy. Pauler's articles "A positivismus hatásáról a történetírásra," *Századok,* 1871, Pp. 527-645, 624-641; "Comte Ágost s a történelem," *Századok,* 1873, Pp. 226, 391, 462.

¹³Gy. Pauler, "A positivismus hatásáról a történetírásra," *Századok,* 1871, p. 641.

¹⁴For Buckle's effect on Hungarian bourgeois historiography see Ágnes R. Várkonyi's treatise "Buckle és a magyar polgári történetírás," *Századok,* no. 3, 1963. Pp. 610-646.

¹⁵Proceedings of the First Congress of Hungarian historians held in Budapest, 1885, are published in the volume *A Magyar Történelmi Társulat 1885. július 3-6. napjain Budapesten tartott Congressusának irományai.* A Választmány megbízásából szerkeszti Szilágyi Sándor titkár. (Budapest, 1885).

¹⁶Cf. Árpád Horváth, "A budapesti Diplomatikai Tanszék, a szemináriumi oktatás és a felállítandó Történelmi Intézet," *Századok,* 1886. Pp. 747-787, and L. Fejérpataky, "A történeti kongresszus utóhangja," *Századok,* 1886, Pp. 896-907.

¹⁷For a fuller account see Albert Gárdonyi, *A történelmi segédtudományok története.* (Budapest: Magyar Történelmi Társulat, 1926), 36 p. (A magyar történettudomány kézikönyve. II. köt. - 1. füzet), and Imre Szentpétery, "Történelmi segédtudományok," in B. Hóman, *ed., A magyar történetírás új útjai.* (Budapest: Magyar Szemle Társaság, 1931), Pp. 321-352.

¹⁸For a more complete analysis of historiography in the period of 1867-1918, see Tibor Baráth, *L'historie en Hongrie (1867-1935).* Paris, 1936. 170 p.; Emma Léderer, *Op. cit.,* Péter Gunst, *Acsády Ignác történetírása.* Budapest, 1961 (Tudománytörténeti tanulmányok, 2); Ervin Pamlényi, *Horváth Mihály.* (Budapest, 1954); József Szigeti, *A magyar szellemtörténet bírálatához.* (Budapest, 1964); Zoltán Varga, *A Széchenyi-ábrázolás fő irányai a magyar történetírásban 1851-1918.* Budapest, 1963 (Tudománytörténeti tanulmányok, 3); Ágnes R. Várkonyi, *Thaly Kálmán és történetírása.* Budapest, 1961 (Tudománytörténeti tanulmányok, 1).

¹⁹Cf. Elemér Mályusz, "A népiség története," in B. Hóman, *ed., A magyar történetírás új útjai.* (Budapest: Magyar Szemle Társaság, 1931), Pp. 237-268; and Rózsa Varga, *A népi írók bibliográfiája; művek, irodalom, mozgalom, 1920-1960.* (Budapest: Akadémiai Kiadó, 1972), 940 p.

²⁰See his *Vergleichende Schriftproben zur Entwicklung und Verbreitung der Schrift im 12-13 Jahrhundert.* (Budapest, 1943), and *L'enseignement de l'ecriture aux universités medievales* (Budapest, 1954), etc.

²¹For more details see Károly Irinyi, *Hajnal István történetszemlélete.* A Debreceni Kossuth Lajos Tudományegyetem évkönyve, 1962.

²²Cf. János Banner and Imre Jakabffy, *A Közép-Dunamedence régészeti bibliográfiája a legrégibb időktől a XI. századig.* (Budapest: Akadémiai Kiadó, 1954), 581 p., containing 17,590 entries.

²³Péter Szebenyi, *Feladatok - módszerek - eszközök; Visszapillantás a hazai történelemtanítás múltjára.* (Budapest: Tankönyvkiadó, 1970), 247 p.

²⁴For a more detailed survey of the historiography of the period 1918-1945, see the chapter *Kútfők és Irodalom* (Sources and Literature) at the end of each of the five volumes of B. Hóman and Gy. Szekfű, *Magyar történet* (Budapest: Egyetemi Nyomda, 1943); furthermore, Tibor Baráth, *Op. cit.,* Emma Léderer, *Op. cit.,* József Szigeti, *Op. cit.,* and Gyula Mérei, "Szekfű Gyula történetszemléletének bírálatához," *Századok,* vols. 1-3, 1960, Pp. 180-256; József Szigeti, *A magyar szellemtörténet bírálatához* (Budapest, 1964).

²⁵Cf. Francis S. Wagner, *A magyar történetírás új útjai, 1945-1955.* (Washington, D.C., 1955) p.1, and Sándor Győrffy, "Marxista történetírásunk új eredményei," *Társadalmi Szemle,* vol. 6, 1951.

²⁶*Ibid.*

[27]See Győző Ember, "A kétszázéves Országos Levéltár", *Levéltári Közlemények*, vol. 27, 1956. Pp. 3-30.

[28]Cf. Gy. Ember, "Les archives et l'historiographie en Hongrie,"*Acta Historica*, vol. 4, nos. 1-3, 1955. Pp. 319-343.

[29]See *A magyar történettudomány válogatott bibliográfiája, 1945-1968*. (Budapest: Akadémiai Kiadó, 1971) 856 p., compiled by the Institute of Historical Research, Hungarian Academy of Sciences, which contains 8,840 entries written by Hungarian authors and published in Hungary. Since all important scholarly works are listed, the volume can be regarded as a reliable quantitative measurement of the country's historiographic production. See also its review by Francis S. Wagner in the *Slavic Review*, vol. 31, no. 3, September, 1972.

[30]Cf. Erik Molnár, "Válasz a nacionalizmus kérdésében írt vitacikkekre," *Új Írás*, vol. 3, nos. 8, 9, 1963.

[31]In addition to periodical articles of the sixties, see the following monographs dealing with the historical evolution of nationalism and class warfare in Hungary: *Vita a magyarországi osztályküzdelmekről és függetlenségi harcokról*. Az elő- és utószót írta: Pach Zsigmond Pál. (Budapest: Kossuth Könyvkiadó, 1965), 463 p., Aladár Mód, *Sors és felelősség; tanulmányok*. Budapest: Magvető, 1967), 541 p., Jenő Szűcs, *A nemzet historikuma és a történetszemlélet nemzeti látószöge; hozzászólás egy vitához*. (Budapest: Akadémiai Kiadó, 1970), 127 p.; *Nemzetiség a feudalizmus korában; tanulmányok*. (Budapest: Akadémiai Kiadó, 1972), 204 p. (Értekezések a történeti tudományok köréből. Új sorozat, 64).

[32]I refer to some chapters of the university textbooks and the two-volume*Magyarország története*. (Budapest: Gondolat Könyvkiadó, 1971. 3rd ed., 1971), in general.

[33]For a detailed bibliographic guide to 84 historical periodicals and related serial publications see Margit Szekeres' and Francis S. Wagner's chapter "Hungary" in Eric H. Boehm, *ed., Historical Periodicals: An Annotated World List of Historical and Related Serial Publications*. (Santa Barbara, California - Munich, Germany, 1961), Pp. 253-263.

[34]Eric H. Boehm, "Bibliography: Current state and prospects," in Lyman H. Legters, *ed., Russia. Essays in History and Literature*. (Leyden: Brill, 1972), p. 152.

[35]I already referred to its first volume. The 2nd volume (Budapest: Akadémiai Kiadó, 1968), 242 p., contains 5,938 entries.

[36]See also footnote No. 1 on Kosáry's bibliography.

[37]Cf. Martin Schwartner, *Statistik des Königreichs Ungern; ein Versuch*. (Budapest: Trattner, 1798), p. 29.

[38]József Kovacsics, *Város- és községstatisztika*. (Budapest: Statisztikai Kiadóvállalat, 1954), 268 p., J.K., *ed., A történeti statisztika forrásai*. (Budapest- Közgazdasági és Jogi Könyvkiadó, 1957), 460 p. written by György Acsádi et al, and J.K., *ed., Magyarország történeti demográfiája; Magyarország népessége a honfoglalástól 1949-ig*. (Budapest: Közgazdasági és Jogi Könyvkiadó, 1963), 441 p. written by István Bakács et al.

[39]"A várostörténeti kutatás helyzete és feladatai,"*MTA. II. Oszt. Közleményei*, 15, 1966. For its interpretation see Kálmán Eperjessy, *Városaink múltja és jelene*. (Budapest: Műszaki Könyvkiadó, 1971), Pp. 7-8, 291, 293.

[40]See György Komoróczy,*A helytörténetírás levéltári forrásai*. (Debrecen: Déri Múzeum Baráti Köre, 1972), 2 vols. (A Hajdú-Bihar Megyei Levéltár Közleményei, 3-4).

[41]See its detailed description in "Történészvita a Petőfi-Körben,"*Századok*, no. 3, 1956. Pp. 425-440.

[42]See *Magyar Történész Kongresszus, 1953. június 6-13*. (Budapest: Akadémiai Kiadó, 1954), 688 p. See also Francis S. Wagner, "Political historiography and its bibliography in post-1945 Central and Eastern Europe,"*Studies for a New Central Europe*, no. 1, 1971-1972, Pp. 73-92.

PART IV — THE ARTS

The systematic conversion of the people to Christianity began with the reign of King Stephen I (1000-1038). It was a long-lasting process during which period the art of the Hungarians was subject to various foreign, chiefly Western, influences. Hungarian disciples of foreign masters proved to be very talented and many of them were deservedly held in great esteem by their contemparies.

Architecture

Inspirations for medieval architecture in Hungary came from several centers of the West. The Romanesque style was most closely linked with South Germany, Austria and Northern Italy. The Italian style is reflected in the grand Cathedral of Pécs with its four towers whereas the abbey churches of Ják, Lébény and Zsámbék reveal the German Romanesque influence.

The construction in the Gothic style of the Matthias Church (Mátyás templom) in Budapest began in the second half of the thirteenth century and was completed during the reign of Matthias I (1458-1490). Internationally speaking, the reign of King Matthias and the decades following boasted the most outstanding phase of the country's architecture. The King was a patron of famous Italian masters and preferred the new style in architecture. In church art, the beautiful Bakócz Chapel (1507) in Esztergom Cathedral (Basilica) also evinces the Italian influence.

A number of churches were built in these centuries which now deservedly are tourist attractions. Among them are the Church of St. Michael (14th century, Kolozsvár), the Parish Church of the Inner City (14th century, Belvárosi templom, Budapest), and the impressive St. Elizabeth's Cathedral (early 15th century, Kassa).

In the sixteenth and seventeenth centuries the monuments of the Turkish occupation (mosques, minarets, baths, etc., at Pécs, Eger, Budapest) appeared and presented a vivid contrast to Western art. Although during this period some fortresses were erected (at Győr, etc.) after the new Italian models, following the Turkish yoke it was the Austrian and Bohemian Baroque which dominated the stage in architecture. Among the most representative of the Baroque style are the Esterházy Palace at Kismarton (Eisenstadt, Austria) across the Austrian border (1663-1672), the huge Esterházy Palace at Fertőd (1764) and the Lyceum at Eger (1765-1785). Very soon Neo-Classicism triumphed over the Baroque style. The remarkable Cathedral at Vác

(1763-1777) is one of its masterpieces. The motifs of Neo-Classicism culminate in the strikingly beautiful Cathedral of Esztergom (1822-c. 1850) built by János Packh (1796-1839) and József Hild (1789-1867). A creation likewise representative of neo-classic style is Mihály Pollack's (1773-1885) Hungarian National Museum (1836-1845) in Budapest. Mihály Pollack was the leading classicist of his age. He studied in Milan under his brother, Leopoldo Pollack (1751-1806), who was assistant to Piermarini. Mihály Pollack built several private and public buildings, completing the Theatre and Assembly Room in Warsaw in 1832 and building the Ludoviceum in Budapest from 1829 through 1836.

The richly embellished and Italianate Opera House in Budapest (1875-1884), a supreme artistic achievement of Miklós Ybl (1814-1891), marks the peak of eclecticism. Similarly, the world-renowned Parliament Building in Budapest (1885-1902), a work of Imre Steindl (1839-1902), is the apex of nineteenth-century eclecticism and the late revival of Gothic architecture. After a while the movement of Art Nouveau revolted against eclecticism. Ödön Lechner (1845-1914) was one of the most brilliant craftsmen of Art Nouveau architecture. He also advocated the creation of a national (Hungarian) architecture. The attractive Postal Savings Bank in Budapest (now called the Hungarian National Bank) is one of Lechner's many artistic designs.

The Fishermen's Bastion (Halászbástya, 1901-1902) in Budapest, a highly picturesque style of architecture, was designed by Frigyes Schulek (1841-1919) who was influenced by medieval art so deeply that he applied his craftsmanship primarily to the restoration of historic monuments.

In postwar years, the country's leading architects conformed their art to the eclectic style then to Classicism, which trends have gradually disappeared in the past two decades. As of now, the most interesting work is being done in the realm of industrial architecture. The newly erected buildings of the Research Institute for Iron and Metals designed by Jenő Lauber and József Szendrői, the Warehouse of Pharmaceutical Products at Kőbánya (1954-1957) designed by Jenő Juhász, the Hotel "Aranyhomok" at Kecskemét built after the designs of István Janáky, the Office Block of Chemolimpex in Budapest designed by Zoltán Gulyás, and the monumental People's Stadium designed by Károly Dávid demonstrate that the country's architecture has clearly chosen a new trend by embracing the universal idea of modern architecture.

In addition to the preceding brief survey, the following biographical sketches of some of the outstanding master builders may help elucidate the progressive traditions so characteristic of the Hungarian methods of training architects.

László Warga was born on November 21, 1878 in Jászberény. He was brought up in Kolozsvár and studied at József Nádor Műegyetem

(Budapest University of Technical Sciences). While an employee of the city of Budapest from 1902 to 1927, he was invited to become the first professor at the newly created chair for urban design at the József Nádor Műegyetem. He retired from that position in 1934, but for two years subsequently he contributed his full-time service without pay. He died on June 19,1952. As a young man he was an employee, later the leader, of the section for urban design at Budapest. His plan for the Tabán (a section of Budapest) won general acclaim at the International Exhibition for Urban Design in Berlin (1910). Those of his plans dating from 1912-1913 already clearly evidence his independent approach. In 1913 in his plans for Kelenföld (Budapest) he applied for the first time—and years in advance of anyone else—the principle of garden city construction as a general method of city development which later became generally accepted by modern city planners all over the globe. His plans were noted for their balance between requirements of traffic flow and economics on the one hand, and aesthetic and health considerations on the other. Warga emphasized the well-proportioned distribution of parks and even insisted that these areas form a continuous chain of green areas, later generally referred to as "green belts". His plans allowed every part of the whole to have a direct link to "open nature" parks or water surfaces. His ideas had a determinant effect on city planning all over the world.

László Warga participated with great success in urban design competitions within Hungary (plans for Kassa (now Kosice, Czechoslovakia), Miskolc, Székesfehérvár, Szombathely, Salgótarján) as well as abroad, for example in the international competitions for the redevelopment of the inner city in Canberra (Australia) and Birmingham (England), the fortress area in Antwerp (Belgium, 1910), the city of Brassó (now Brasov, in Transylvania, 1911) and the city of Belgrade (1922). Warga mailed his plan for Belgrade from Paris instead of Budapest in order to avoid the anti-Hungarian prejudice rampant in Belgrade after World War I. When he won first prize and his identity was finally revealed, it caused a sensation.

His plans were acclaimed at the International Exhibition for Urban Design in London (1924) and in Tokyo (1925). His new approach motivated several large cities (New York, Tokyo, Milan among them) to send a group of experts to study the methods of city planning employed in Budapest. Warga prepared with special care and love the plans for Kolozsvár (Cluj, in Romania). He donated his time for this work free, even after this overwhelmingly Hungarian-inhabited city came under Romanian rule after World War I, and again after World War II.

Marcel Breuer (1902, Pécs, Hungary) left Hungary to become one of the best-known architects of our age. He went to London in 1935, to Harvard in 1937. Breuer's independent practice in the United States gained momentum only after World War II. In the past two decades his practice has spread to several other countries (Bijenkorf, Rotterdam, 1953; UNESCO, Paris, 1953). His New York office is a world center for widely accepted architectural innovations. Breuer designed several buildings throughout the world which are considered as true reflections of his genius. Prior to his coming to the United States Marcel Breuer worked in the Bauhaus workshop which represented a movement initiated in Germany having as its aim the integration of art and technology.

Sculpture

Among medieval Europe's artistic movements Hungarian sculpture with its bronze human figures and equestrian statues, occupied a special place. The Kolozsvári brothers, Márton (Martinus) and György (Georgius), created several such bronze figures in the second half of the fourteenth century. In 1373 they sculped the world-famous mounted figure of St. George which now stands in the courtyard of the Hradcany in Prague. Both the human figure and the horse are distinguished by vivid realism. The concept of realism being altogether unknown in that age, the two brothers introduced an entirely new mode in the universal history of sculpture.

Hungarian goldsmithery assumed the lead in Europe during the Gothic period, that is, in the fifteenth and sixteenth centuries. Every kind of technique flourished. The world-renowned *Calvary of King Matthias I* is an important sample of the goldsmith's art. The *Calvary* is exhibited at the Christian Museum in Esztergom.

Excavations in the last decades at the onetime royal castles of Buda and Visegrád unearthed a lot of outstanding stone carvings from the fourteenth and fifteenth centuries. At the Royal Court of King Matthias I mythological figures, fountains from which wine flowed, red marble ornaments, etc., represented a transition from the Gothic to the Renaissance style. Huge numbers of stone art work were to be found as well in parish churches, chapels and in the mansions of wealthy aristocrats and of the bourgeosie. But the Turkish invasion nearly put an end to the large-scale artistic evolution and as a result Romanesque, Gothic, Renaissance and Baroque sepulchral monuments are the main representatives of the various stages of sculptural development in the sixteenth and seventeenth centuries.

Parallel to the revival of patriotism in the first decades of the nineteenth century, István Ferenczy (1792-1856) carved busts in stone or marble of eminent public figures of the national revival movement. Perhaps the most artistic of these carvings is the bust of Ferenc

Kazinczy, a leading figure of literary revival. Beginning his studies in Vienna, Ferenczy continued in Rome under the masters Canova and Thorwaldsen, the greatest sculptors of that period.

Miklós Izsó (1831-1875) learned the rudiments of sculpture in the studio of István Ferenczy and continued his studies in Vienna. Partly as a reaction to the Habsburg rule, Izsó revolted against the rigid academic forms and rural themes derived from the simple life of peasant people were frequent features in his art. His *Shepherd in Grief*, is one of his many carvings exemplifying his life-like style.

The Austro-Hungarian Compromise of 1867 helped nourish intellectual life. The demand for art grew and the newly founded Budapest Academy educated many a young sculptor. Alajos Stróbl, János Fadrusz and György Zala were the most gifted among them, but Alajos Stróbl (1856-1926) was the greatest of them all.

Stróbl produced many of the best monuments in Budapest — for instance, the statues of Ferenc Liszt, Ferenc Erkel, János Arany and Mór Jókai. He also carved the sculptural decorations for the Kossuth Mausoleum at the Kerepesi Cemetery in Budapest.

The specialty of János Fadrusz (1858-1903) was the making of historical monuments. Commissioned by the city of Pozsony (Bratislava), Fadrusz carved the *Monument of Queen Maria Theresa* (1896) which, unfortunately, was destroyed after 1918. His chef d' oeuvre is perhaps the bronze *Monument of King Matthias* erected at Kolozsvár (Cluj) in 1902.

György Zala's (1858-1937) artistry lay in creating monuments for public squares. His *Equestrian Statue of Andrássy* was executed in the best traditions of sculptural art. Zala carved the majority of the statues on the Millenium Memorial which is a high priority in the sightseeing tours of Budapest.

Alongside monumental sculpture, the art of small sculpture started flourishing from the onset of the twentieth century. Having studied in Munich and Paris, Márk Vedres (1870-1961) spent the greater part of his life in Italy where he attained perfection in the fashioning of small bronze figures.

Fülöp Ö. Beck's (1873-1945) plaques and medals commanded international appreciation.

Ferenc Medgyessy (1881-1958) became famous for his reliefs. Medgyessy was awarded the Grand Prix at the 1937 Paris World Exhibition for his allegorical figures which now stand in front of the Déri Museum at Debrecen.

Béni Ferenczy (b. 1890) studied sculpture in Bourdelle's studio in Paris after which he lived in Vienna and in Moscow for a long period. In 1936 Ferenczy created his well-known bronze Bartók Medallion.

The self-trained Pál Pátzay (b. 1896) began his artist's career with small sculpture. In this stage of his artistic evolution Pátzay studied the relationships among space, planes and motion. Later he gradually turned to life-size figures and his career climaxed in the creation of the huge *Heroes' Memorial Monument* erected at Székesfehérvár in 1939. Pátzay also carved a mounted figure of János Hunyadi.

Zsigmond Kisfaludi-Stróbl (b. 1884) is considered by many to be the greatest artistic talent of this age. He studied in Vienna, Brussels, Paris and Italy. Many of his works are in private and museum collections abroad: for instance, *The birth of Venus* in California and *The Lizard* in London. High valued are his commissioned portraits of George Bernard Shaw, Queen Elizabeth II of Great Britain, etc. Kisfaludi-Stróbl's famous monument of Lajos Kossuth, erected in 1952, is seen in front of the Parliament Building in Budapest. He also sculpted a 10 foot high bronze statue of Ferenc Rákóczi II for the Millenium Memorial in Budapest.

After World War II, sculpture—monumental as well as small—has evinced certain advances inasmuch as newly erected buildings, historic houses and squares have been decorated by a rising number of gifted artists. In addition to the sculptors already noted, we should at the very least mention the names of Sándor Mikus (b. 1903), Jenő Kerényi (b. 1908), Miklós Borsos (b. 1906), and József Somogyi (b. 1916) as they have produced many sculptural works of lasting value.

József Ispánki's sculpture (b. 1906, Budapest) enjoys great success in the United States and many countries abroad. Ispánki studied under Lajos Mátrai at the Budapest School of Applied Arts and was István Szentgyörgyi's student at the College of Fine Arts in Budapest. From 1931 to 1933 he was on scholarship in Rome. He is highly esteemed as a creator of statues for public squares (*St. Stephen and Gisella*, Veszprém, 1938; *Petőfi*, Kaposvár, 1954; *Symbolic figure*, Kecskemét, 1965, etc.) as well as a designer of medals, having won many national and foreign prizes as a medalist. Since 1928 Ispánki has been exhibiting his works. His art is distinctive for its search for innovation.

In relief sculpture, Amerigo Tot (b. 1909 at Fehérvárcsurgó, Hungary as Imre Tóth) is considered one of the leading artists of the world. He studied at the Budapest School of Applied Arts and from 1929 under László Moholy-Nagy in the Bauhaus at Dessau, then in Paris as a pupil of Maillol. Since 1937 Amerigo Tot has taken an active part in Italy's artistic life, at the beginning belonging to the circle of R. Guttuso. In 1949 Tot won the contest to execute the facade reliefs for the Termini Railroad Station in Rome. His robus reliefs also decorate the Sports Palace and the Automobile Club in Rome.

Dora Pedery-Hunt (b. 1913, Budapest) of Toronto, Ont., Canada, is a noted sculptress and designer who has won many international awards. Her works are exhibited in the National Gallery of Canada, The

Art Gallery of Toronto, The Penning Cabinet, The Hague, The Royal Cabinet of Medals, Brussels, etc.

Painting

The art of painting miniatures was in vogue in Western and Central Europe throughout the Middle Ages. Hungary was no exception. Its codex literature preserved beautiful samples of miniature painting. Ecclesiastical art as well, such as panels of altars in churches demonstrated a high artistic level of this genre. No wonder that the country's greatest Gothic painter, Master M.S., appeared on the scene and enjoyed success as early as the onset of the sixteenth century. His art was firmly rooted in Hungarian soil and was superior to that of most contemporary painters in craftsmanship, richness of imagination and realistic approach. One of his paintings (*Visitation*, 1506) is housed in the Budapest Museum of Fine Arts, and four others (*The Agony in the Garden; Christ Carrying the Cross; Crucifixion*, and *Resurrection*, 1506) are in the Christian Museum at Esztergom.

It was a custom, chiefly during the years of Turkish occupation, for gifted young men to leave Hungary to complete their studies abroad. It was the case of Jakab Bogdány (1660-1724). Born at Eperjes (now Presov, Czechoslovakia), he studied in Vienna and in the Netherlands. From 1690 on Bogdány lived in England; he died in London as a court painter. Bogdány excelled in painting birds and still lifes of flowers and fruit. His paintings were bought by royalty the world over and are now exhibited in Hampton Court Palace, Kew Palace, the National Museum of Stockholm, the Museum of Fine Arts in Budapest, among others.

János Spillenberg (1628, Kassa-1679) was also a disciple of the Baroque school of painting. Although he spent most of his creative life abroad working in Venice and Bavaria he always called himself Pictor Hungaricus. *Vertumnus and Pomona*, a masterpiece of his, is in the Dresden Gallery.

One of the supreme talents in eighteenth-century Baroque portrait painting was Ádám Mányoki (1673-1757). Mányoki studied painting at Lüneburg and Hamburg with the famous German painter Scheitz. Appointed official portrait painter of the Berlin Court in 1703, Mányoki worked in this capacity until 1707. In 1709 he returned to his native Hungary and was court painter to Ferenc Rákóczi II until 1711, the year of the defeat of the Rákóczi-led War of Independence (1703-1711), when he again left Hungary. The years 1713 to 1723 found him working in Dresden and Warsaw as court painter. In 1723 Mányoki once again returned to Hungary to paint portraits of Hungarian aristocrats. In 1731 the artist returned to Dresden where he resumed the position of court painter until his death. Ádám Mányoki's *Portrait of Ferenc Rákóczi* and his *Self-Portrait as a Young Man* bear the distinction of being ranked among the most prominent portraits of eighteenth-century Europe.

During the first half of the last century two characteristics of the development of art in Hungary were salient. Firstly, artists rallied behind the concept of patriotism and at the same time they caught up with the progress of the arts in the most developed countries of Western Europe. The most popular and visible artist of that age was Károly Markó the Elder (1791-1860), a highly successful landscape painter (*Visegrád*, oil painting, 1825-1830); *The Great Hungarian Plain* (Alföld), oil painting, 1853) whose pictures turned up in the collections of Europe and the United States.

Miklós Barabás (1810-1898) specialized in portrait painting (*Ferenc Liszt*, oil painting; *Mme István Bittó*, oil painting, 1874), likewise József Boros (1821-1883), whose *National Guard (Nemzetőr*, 1848) was the most popular picture of that time.

Bertalan Székely (1835-1910) and Viktor Madarász (1830-1917) set an entirely new tone in the country's art movement. With outstandingly great talent both immortalized tragic scenes from the nation's past. The *Bewailing of László Hunyadi* by Viktor Madarász was exhibited in France at the famous Paris Salon and in 1861 was awarded the highest French artistic prize: the Gold Medal of the State. His *Zrinyi and Frangepán in Prison* is regarded by some critics as the most representative work of Hungarian historical painting. Bertalan Székely also devoted his talent to historical scenes (*Ladislaus V and Czilley; The Women of Eger*, etc.) and garnered great success. Historical painting in this superior tradition was continued by Sándor Wagner (1838-1919), who was a master of the Munich Academy. His most famous painting is *The Self-Sacrifice of Titus Dugovics*.

Károly Lotz (1833-1904) drew his inspiration and subjects from quite different sources, as illustrated by his *Sunset* (oil painting) and *The Muse* (oil painting from the 1890's). His versatile talent is evident in Lotz' numerous murals in churches and public buildings (*Aurora* and *Apollo*, murals on the ceiling of the Budapest State Opera House, 1882-1884).

Mihály Zichy (1827-1906) had the most colorful career among Hungarian painters. He was among the first pupils of painter Giacomo Marastoni (1804-1860) in Pest. In 1844 Zichy left Pest for Vienna where he joined Waldmüller's private art school. In 1847 his oil painting, *The Lifeboat*, scored such spectacular success that Zichy was invited immediately to St. Petersburg, Russia as the drawing master of Princess Jelena Pavlovna. Then from 1859 on, with the exception of a few years which he spent in Paris and Budapest, Zichy was the official painter to the Russian Imperial Court. He worked primarily in water colors and favored pencil sketches. Zichy brilliantly illustrated the works of the literary giants Goethe, Lermontov, Imre Madách, János Arany, and Sándor Petőfi. His graphics and paintings housed in Hungarian and Russian galleries still attract those visitors who enjoy works of the Romantic style.

The group of the first really modern Hungarian painters includes such masters as Mihály Munkácsy, László Paál, Pál Szinyei Merse and Géza Mészöly.

Mihály Munkácsy (1844-1900) was the country's most famous painter in the nineteenth century and one of the world's most gifted artists at that time. His tremendous success is owed mainly to his prize-winning oil paintings. At the age of twenty-six, in 1870, his painting entitled *Death Row* (1870) exhibited in the Paris Salon won the French Gold Medal. Years later another of his great compositions, *Milton*, was awarded another Gold Medal at the Paris Salon.

Munkácsy's subsequent visit to the United States in November and December of 1886 forged numerous ties between him and American intellectuals and philanthropists. Munkácsy was one of the most celebrated painters in America. More than sixty paintings of his were sold in the United States to various private and public collections. Of these paintings, *The Pawn Shop* is housed in the New York Metropolitan Museum of Art, *Milton* in the Lenox Library, New York City, while two of his biblical themes: *Christ before Pilate* (1881) and *Calvary* (1884) were acquired by John Wanamaker of Philadelphia for the highest prices ever paid in history to an artist up to that time. According to John Wanamaker's instructions these two Biblical compositions are exhibited every year during the Lenten and Easter seasons in the Grand Court of the huge Wanamaker department store in Philadelphia.*

Munkácsy's art was highly esteemed in contemporary opinion. Let us cite two such views on his famous painting *Calvary*: "This picture is certainly one of the most perfect which have been produced for many a year, combining all the majesty of classic schools with the modern and personal stamp that marks it of the nineteenth century. When one gazes on this picture and hears Munkácsy speak, one realises the feelings which the contemporaries of Rubens, Murillo or Veronese must have experienced when they conversed with those great masters who were destined to be handed down to the admiration of posterity." (*The Times*, London, January 24, 1884). Furthermore, in the March 16, 1885 issue of the *New York Times* we read the following meditative words: "The

---

*Cf. Tribute of U.S. Congress to Mihály Munkácsy entitled "The 125th Anniversary of the Birth of Michael Munkácsy, Hungarian Artist-Painter" in the *Congressional Record*. Proceedings and Debates of the 91st Congress, First Session. February 19, 20, March 20, 25, 1969).

Calvary of to-day, over which not only the world of art but the world of fashions, of thought, and of religion is at present wondering, is indeed a marvellous picture. Taking all things into consideration, it is a strange subject to offer in this century of unbelief, of scepticism, and of scoffing. Who has time now to think of the Man of Sorrows? What artist living in Christian England ever dares to offer such scenes to the critical public, and who could imagine such a subject coming from a Paris studio, where even the last rags and shreds of religion are cast scornfully to the winds?''

Subsequent to his departure from the United States, Munkácsy was conferred the title of nobility by Emperor Francis Joseph I acting as King of Hungary, and was twice recipient of the prestigious Legion of Honor, France's highest tribute rarely accorded a foreigner. Munkácsy received countless other decorations from various countries of Europe.

Munkácsy's close friend, László Paál (1846-1879), is known as one of the best landscape painters of nineteenth-century Europe. He died at the age of thirty-three leaving posterity a legacy of only about seventy paintings. Paál followed Munkácsy to Paris and settled down at nearby Barbizon to paint landscapes there.

Géza Mészöly's (1844-1887) style of representation favored minute details and small canvases depicting the landscapes of Western Hungary (the Dunántúl), the Tisza region, and the Lake Balaton and the Lake Velence. Mészöly's best known oil painting is the *Fishermen's Cottage at Lake Balaton* (1877).

Lajos Deák Ébner (1850-1934) studied in Munich and Paris and excelled in depicting village scenes. After returning from Paris, Deák Ébner worked in Budapest and then in Szolnok where he helped reestablish the local artists' colony. One of his most famous oil paintings is entitled *Harvesters Homeward Bound*.

Sándor Bihari (1856-1906) also studied in Paris. Returning home, Bihari followed the same course as Deák Ébner. Bihari's *Before the Justice of Peace* and his *Sunday Afternoon* are his oil paintings most characteristically representative of rural life.

László Mednyánszky (1852-1919), also a great landscape painter, learned the academic style of painting in Munich and Paris. The first stage of his development was characterized by his rare use of human figures in his admirably well-composed sceneries (*Marshy Landscape*, oil painting, etc.). Later he turned to portrait painting and created an impressionistic style of his own.

The oil paintings of Pál Szinyei Merse (1845-1920), however, frequently feature human figures in perfect harmony with the landscape. Szinyei Merse also studied in Munich though its fashionable trend of historical painting failed to inspire him. On the contrary, Szinyei Merse preferred nature's beauties over historical canvases. The psychological explanation for his orientation towards nature was that, his father being a landowner in a beautiful countryside, Szinyei Merse as a young artist spent much of his time outdoors. This is why his masterpiece, *Picnic in May* (oil painting, 1873), reflects the dazzling colors of nature together with the exuberant atmosphere of a sunny May. This masterfully designed setting and the picnicking human figures form a coherent unity. In the opinion of art critics, this bold initiative as manifested in the vivid coloring and audacious structural forms is a unique solution which had never before been attempted by any artist in this genre.

The same artistic harmony can be enjoyed when viewing his other major composition, *Woman in Purple* (oil painting, 1874), in which the painter's mother, a figure dressed in purple, blends perfectly with the picturesque background of this masterpiece.

Interestingly, the public has from the beginning understood and accepted the bold initiative of Szinyei Merse's art, while art critics started viewing the innovation favorably only since the turn of the century when French impressionism made an impact upon them.

Szinyei Merse as an artist and as a professor of the Budapest Academy of Fine Arts staunchly advocated as ideals progressivism in art and personally assisted the endeavors of the Nagybánya art colony.

Simon Hollósy (1857-1918) was the head of the Nagybánya group of artists. Besides him, his pupils István Réti (1872-1945), János Thorma (1870-1938), Béla Iványi-Grünwald (1867-1942) and Károly Ferenczy (1862-1917), all eminent painters, belonged to the founding members of the Nagybánya school of art. Hollósy, like most of the members, studied in Munich. Though he never visited France he later became affected with the French artistic style. While in the incipient stage of his career he selected themes from rural life and he settled into portraiture. While at Nagybánya Hollósy occupied himself with producing the first sketch to the Rákóczi March, and with book illustrations (József Kiss' poems). Then he left Nagybánya for Técső where he created his fine paintings (*Trees on the Bank of the Tisza River; Técső*) in the simple and sincere spirit of naturalism. Hollósy trained a generation of eminent painters. In 1886 he opened his famous private art school in Munich which became a center for young artists from countries all over Europe. In 1896 Hollósy decided to move his school to Nagybánya for the summer months. This was the beginning of the Nagybánya art colony and movement which educated many hundreds of gifted young artists and opened new vistas in the art of Central Europe.

It took time for the Nagybánya movement to change the course of art history because Munich academicism still exerted a heavy influence upon the majority of painters who concomitantly enjoyed government subsidization. Munich academicism also remained an influential factor for a long time because Gyula Benczúr (1844-1920), an extraordinary talent, was himself a student there. After the exhibition in 1875 of his *The Baptism of Vajk* (oil painting, Hungarian National Gallery, Budapest) Benczúr was elected professor of the Academy of Munich, all the more understandable since Benczúr has always been regarded as one of the luminaries of European historical painting. Benczúr held his distinguished position in Munich until 1883 when he accepted the appointment to be the head of the Masters' Department of the School of Model Drawing (Mintarajziskola) in Budapest.

Since his early youth Benczúr painted historical themes (*The Farewell of László Hunyadi*, 1866; *The Capture of Ferenc Rákóczi* (Bucharest Gallery, Romania). The *Recapture of Buda Castle*, created for the Millenial (1896) celebrations is esteemed by art critics as a masterpiece of European academic historicism.

Gradually the Nagybánya movement succeeded in overcoming obstacles and the Szinyei Merse method of plein-air painting, the principle of art nouveau and the widely popular European Impressionism triumphed over the rigid, tradition-bound academicism.

In 1906 Károly Ferenczy was appointed professor of the Budapest Academy of Fine Arts and very shortly thereafter other members of the Nagybánya group followed him in professorships: István Réti, Oszkár Glatz, and after 1920 István Csók, Gyula Rudnay and János Vaszary. This signified the end of the sway of Munich academicism over the training of artists. In line with the pattern of the Nagybánya movement, several other art colonies (in Szolnok, Kecskemét, Szentendre, Hódmezővásárhely, etc.) came into being as important centers of the fine arts.

Of all schools up to the present the members of the Nagybánya group had the greatest impact on Hungarian painting—especially János Thorma (1870-1938), Béla Iványi-Grünwald (1867-1942), Károly Ferenczy (1862-1957), Oszkár Glatz (1872-1958), Aurél Bernáth (b. 1895), but above all István Szőnyi (1894-1960) who was the most gifted among them. Various foreign and domestic influences can be detected in István Szőnyi's work at the beginning of his career. But in time he arrived at an independent style and reverted to a direct observation of nature. *The Bend of the Danube at Zebegény; Evening; In the Village; The Calf is for Sale* are highly successful products of Szőnyi's plein-air color tempera painting.

There are several artists who followed a more or less independent line and cannot be identified with any contemporary art centers, though they had some contact with them — above all with the Nagybánya school. Among them József Rippl-Rónai, János Tornyai, János Vaszary, Gyula Rudnay, but foremost István Csók, merit being dealt with in further detail.

József Rippl-Rónai (1861-1927) studied painting in Vienna, Munich and in Paris where he apprenticed at Mihály Munkácsy's studio. Shortly afterwards Rippl-Rónai became personally acquainted with distinguished French artists, including Maillol and Cézanne, and exhibited his works together with that of these French masters at the Paris shows of the "Nabis" group. Rippl-Rónai's paintings are part of the collections in many galleries of Europe. The *Portrait of Aristide Maillol* is in the Musée de Jeu de Paume, Paris. Experimenting with several artistic trends throughout his career, Rippl-Rónai after World War I returned to plein-air coloring and Impressionist technique (*Self-Portraits; Portrait of Mihály Babits*, etc.). His oeuvre is internationally well-known.

János Tornyai (1869-1938) worked as Mihály Munkácsy's student in the master's Paris studio. Munkácsy's influence proved to be of a lasting nature, much stronger than Tornyai's experience at the Nagybánya school. Born at Hódmezővásárhely of peasant parents, Tornyai chose the quiet atmosphere of this town of the Alföld to work in. József Egry (1883-1951), another painter of peasant origin, setled down on the shore of Lake Balaton and painted the scenic Lake and its surroundings. János Tornyai did a series of paintings depicting the monotonous yet picturesque scenes of the Great Plain (Alföld) and its peasantry (*Sad Hungarian Fate*, oil painting, 1908; *The Draw Well*, oil painting, 1912). In addition to pictures representing peasant life, Tornyai painted historical portraits (*Rákóczi at Rodostó*, 1904; *Miklós Bercsényi*, 1908). His oeuvre has always been judged very positively, mainly for its simplicity in structure and natural coloring.

János Vaszary (1867-1937), like Rippl-Rónai, was to a certain extent a representative of French orientation. Vaszary depicted rural life in the spirit of naturalism (*Old People*, oil painting in Museo Maragoni, Udine, Italy). *The Portrait of Primate Kolos Vaszary* (Christian Museum, Esztergom) shows the artist's superb craftsmanship. Almost each and every year János Vaszary made a study tour of a foreign country to become acquainted with new trends in order to enrich his own work and to utilize them in his curricula as a professor of the Academy of Fine Arts in Budapest.

Gyula Rudnay (1878-1957) also functioned as a professor of the Academy of Fine Arts. Although he studied the older masters (Goya, Rugendas, Simon Hollósy), the application of the Nagybánya principles and several other art concepts, none of them exerted a lasting influence upon him because from the outset of his career Rudnay cherished the heritage of Munkácsy. Rudnay's portraits (*The Fugitives; Attila's Feast; Man with Violin*) and his landscapes (*Street at Nagybábony; Landscapes*) are brilliantly composed and convincingly prove his high-level of individual taste.

Many art critics are of the opinion that the greatest Hungarian painter of our century and one of the world's best is István Csók (1865-1961), a born painter. Csók attended the Budapest School of Model Drawing (Mintarajziskola) under such masters as János Greguss, Bertalan Székely and Károly Lotz, furthering his education at the Munich Academy in 1886 and 1887, then at the Julian Academy in Paris under Bouguereau and Robert-Fleury in 1888 and 1889. Afterwards he resided in Munich for a number of years, during which period he won several international grand prizes with his oil paintings (*Do this in Commemoration of me*, 1890; *Orphans*, 1891). In 1903 István Csók settled down again in Paris and his work increasingly approached that of the French postimpressionists. But Csók never became a true impressionist, those pictures of his which depict nudes being generally in the studio style (*Thamar*, oil painting, 1918, in the Galleria D' Arte Moderna, Rome). He left Paris for Budapest in 1911, where his *Portrait of Tibor Wlassics* was awarded the Gold Medal.

His portraits (*Godfather's Breakfast; Züzü*—a series about his little daughter and landscapes (The Balaton-series) are bravuras of brush technique. István Csók is one of those very few non-Italian painters whose self-portrait, as an avowal of his excellence, hangs in the famed Uffizi Gallery. Csók was twice awarded the Kossuth Prize (1948, 1952), and in 1952 the title of "outstanding artist."

Hungarian painters have been part of and influenced by all the major artistic trends of the world. But regardless of their affiliations, most of them broke free to evolve more or less independent or individual styles, a fact doubtless rooted in the national character. Be it the Group of Eight, the School of Rome, or the artists' movement in which social themes dominate over any other, the art of the followers of these trends is nonetheless imbued with the stamp of individualism.

Vilmos Aba-Novák (1894-1941) started his career under the influence of István Szőnyi. Later the Nagybánya style, and—his being the most talented member of the School of Rome—some Italian influence, German expressionism, and even Cubism, had an effect on his works. But in essence, Aba-Novák followed a strikingly individual course in compositions (*The Maker of Masks*, tempera, 1935) and primarily by his large-scale works in the Votive Church of Szeged and other places. We are indebted to him by the latter for thoroughly modernizing ecclesiastical art.

Individuality of style is very much evident in the case of Jenő Barcsay (b. 1900) who taught artistic anatomy at the Budapest Academy of Fine Arts from 1945 up to his retirement. Graphic art has become the country's most advanced form of fine arts through his works. Barcsay, who has won several national and international awards (Venice, 1964, for instance), is among the world's foremost designers of mosaics (*The*

Miskolc mosaic, 1965; Mosaic mural of the Budapest National Theater; *The Szentendre mosaic*, 1970). Barcsay's beautifully illustrated monographs on artistic anatomy (*Művészeti anatómia*. Budapest), drapery (*Ember és drapéria*. Budapest, 1958), and on forms and space (*Forma és tér*. Budapest, 1964, 1966, 1967) have been translated into several languages and won him world fame.

Marcel Vértes (1895-1961) is known throughout the world as a political cartoonist and designer of posters, likewise the famous painter of the Group of Eight: Bertalan Pór (1880-1964).

János Kass' (b. 1927) activity as a graphic artist is significant. As a book illustrator he won the Silver Medal at the 1958 Brussels World Exhibition and at the 1966 Leipzig book art exhibition Kass was awarded not only the Gold Medal but "The World's Most Beautiful Book" Prize.

Artúr Halmi (1866-1933) as a painter of portraits became very popular in the United States, while Philip de László (1869-1939) received a title in Great Britain in honor of his celebrated portraiture.

László Moholy-Nagy (1895-1946), painter and architect, the renowned representative of the Bauhaus movement, founded the "New School" in Chicago.

With the work of Endre Domanovszky (b. 1907) and others, the course of the country's fine arts took a new turn after 1945. As a direct result of postwar political changes, new topics and themes from the everyday life of the working classes have inspired Hungarian artists. Domanovszky's *Furnacemen* (oil painting) and his large-scale murals (the frescoes of Dunaújváros, for example) aptly represent this new direction of art.

Joseph Domján (b. 1907, Budapest), the master of colored woodcuts, has made his home in the United States for many years now. His unique style is inspired by Hungarian decorative peasant art. Domján's works can be found in the world's important museums and galleries: the Victoria and Albert Museum, London; the National Museum, Stockholm; the Johansen Gallery, Copenhagen; and the Academies and Artists' Federations of Peking, Shanghai, Hangchow, Canton, Wuhan, Senyang, for instance. Domján was awarded the rare honor of the title, "Master of the Coloured Woodcut", in China, the classical home of this art, where this title had never before been bestowed upon anyone except the native Chi Pai-shi, the greatest authority on wood-engraving in modern times.

One of the greatest figures of twentieth century painting, Victor Vasarely is considered the founder of the op-art movement. Born in Pécs (as Győző Vásárhelyi) in 1908, he was trained in the Bauhaus tradition in Budapest under Sándor Bortnyik. He left Hungary in 1930 for Paris where he has since been living. At the beginning of his Parisian stay he worked for years as a commercial artist doing illustrations and graphics. In his inimitable style Vasarely developed a new process of ornamentation. His pictures are a harmony of geometric forms and interacting colors. In 1963 the Musée des Arts Décoratifs featured a grand exhibition of Victor Vasarely's works.

Literature

Life and literature are interdependent in the existence of small nations. It is primarily so in the case of their poetry, which eminently reflects the realities of everyday life . . . realities which stem from the fact that the options of small nations are limited because their history has always been interwoven with—to use a moderate phrase—unwanted external influences. Due to their being a permanent pawn on the chessboard of international conflicts, literature has been a major influence in the history of small nations. Characteristically, the spiritual prelude and catalyst to their main historical events has almost as a rule been provided by their writers and poets. Poets of small nations as themes frequently extol qualities their nations in reality had been rendered destitute of, themes such as liberty, independence, and security. Deprivation of these rights motivated the literary sons of small nations to adopt a tone quite often revolutionary and simultaneously fired with rebellious patriotism and a prophetic vision of a distant world in which brotherly love occupies a significant place in the mainstream of human deeds. Due to the universal appeal of such themes, many of the literary works of these small nations enjoy worldwide appreciation.

Prior to the first half of the nineteenth century, Hungarian literature did not meet the European level and was consequently unable to be empathized or identified with by the, at that time, more cultured West. Only with the appearance of the Big Three — Mihály Vörösmarty, Sándor Petőfi, and János Arany — did this situation change.

Sándor Petőfi's (1823-1849) literary creation constitutes a summit in the world's lyric poetry. In addition Petőfi is rightly held the foremost representative of the national and universal ideals that are such dominant colors in the canvas of his nation's history.

Mihály Vörösmarty (1800-1855) earned the title of being the greatest artist of romantic verse while János Arany (1817-1882) excelled as the supreme creator of epic poetry. Anton N. Nyerges* rightfully says about Arany that "Although he wrote much more, the extent of Arany's greatness will be measured by his epics. His role as a great

---

Epics of the Hungarian plain from János Arany. Tr. and introd. by Anton N. Nyerges, (Cleveland, Ohio: Classic Printing Corp., 1976. p. 217.).

contributor to this literary form is secure, if not widely familiar in the world."

Watson Kirkconnell, another brilliant interpreter of Hungarian literature and literary critic shares the same opinion about Arany and several other Hungarian poets.

Vörösmarty, Petőfi and Arany helped refine a language which became as powerful a means of expression as any other great language in world literature. In the same century several prose writers also found themselves in the forefront of the European elite. Among them were novelist and political philosopher József Eötvös (1813-1871), Mór Jókai (1825-1904) whose scintillating imagination and inexhaustible narrative talent produced exceptionally popular historical and social novels, and Kálmán Mikszáth (1847-1910) who combined sparkling humor with a realistic portrayal of human characters in his still very popular novels and short stories. These literary notables paved the way for the next generation of prose writers, including Zsigmond Móricz (1879-1942), one of the greatest writers the country has had in this century.

Playwright Imre Madách (1823-1864) is another distinguished member of this community of writers. His *The Tragedy of Man* (1859-1860) has since been translated into several dozen languages and is considered one of the greatest creations in world literature. *The Tragedy of Man* unfolds in its historical scenes the perennial and universal problems of the individual and of mankind, a really unique literary experiment to this day. Besides Madách's play József Katona's (1791-1830) *Bánk bán*, a national tragedy, which in parts rises to Shakespearean heights has inspired Hungarian dramatists.

Endre Ady (1877-1919) carried on the tradition of Petőfi's revolutionary poetry in line with social, historical and artistic requirements of the twentieth century. Ady has influenced most of the contemporary and later poets and even prose writers with his radical tone. This new trend surfaced in the poetry of Gyula Juhász (1883-1937), Attila József (1905-1937) and in somewhat other forms in the poems of Lőrinc Szabó (1900-1957), and Ferenc Juhász (b. 1928) who are the most gifted poets in this group.

Poet Gyula Illyés (b. 1902) is perhaps the most important in the country's present-day literature. Illyés won the Kossuth Prize three times, in 1965 he won the International Grand Prize of Poetry, and the Herder Prize in 1970. In addition he is outstanding as a dramatist and prose writer.

Sándor Weöres (b. 1913) and Géza Képes (b. 1909) besides being great poets are both exceptionally gifted translators and interpreters of foreign poets. Weöres translated a long series of poetry from ancient Indian texts to the works of Thomas Stearns Eliot, while Géza Képes is the artistic interpreter of Finnish, Arabic, Persian and other poets in their original forms. There are two living poets who are regarded by their foreign critics as being among the greatest artists of religious lyric poetry. János Pilinszky (b. 1921) is one of them. Pilinszky's *Selected poems* (Manchester: Carcanet New Press, 1976. 67 p.) was recently translated into English by Ted Hughes and János Csokits. The other one, László Mécs (b. 1895), received the approbation of the world-renowned French poet, Paul Valéry, in the preface to *Ladislas Mécs: Poèmes* (Paris: Horizons de France, 1944. Pp. XI-XVIII).

In prose writing several authors captured a readership outside Hungary, at first those who, like Mór Jókai or Géza Gárdonyi (1863-1922), won international literary contests. Gárdonyi wrote about peasant life and historical topics (*The Stars of Eger*, 1901; *The Invisible Man*, 1902; *The Captives of God*, 1908, etc.). Ferenc Móra (1879-1934) also described peasant life but in a more realistic vein than did Gárdonyi. Móra's historical novel, *The Gold Coffin* (1932), delineates the last days of the Roman Empire focusing on the struggle between Christianity and heathendom. Móra's historical novel is a true masterpiece in which an artistic level of the writer's craft is combined with a scholar's subject knowledge: Móra commanded an international reputation as an expert archaeologist.

István Fekete (1900-1970) is also an outstanding portrayer of village life. His writings are all the more of note because his descriptions of the beauties of nature are unexcelled.

Sándor Márai (b. 1900) gives us an insight into the life of the middle classes. Márai infuses his novels with intellectualism and his peculiar philosophy of life in such a way it leaves the reader's aesthetic pleasure unimpaired. In the last several decades he has lived in the United States and Italy.

Dezső Szabó (1879-1945) and László Németh (1901-1975) both belonged to the populist writers' movement (népi írók mozgalma) and regarded the peasantry as the alpha and omega of the nation's existence. Both were extraordinarily talented as fiction writers and essayists. In addition, Németh excelled as a playwright.

Áron Tamási (1897-1966) through both short stories and novels depicted the life of Hungarians living in Transylvania in his very unique and essentially romantic style.

Albert Wass (b. 1908), likewise Áron Tamási, selects his themes from the life of the middle class and village folks of Transylvania. Later he included more general subject matter in his widely read novels. Albert Wass has won three prestigious literary awards. After the war he emigrated to the United States where he is active also as a publisher.

Lajos Zilahy (1891-1974) in his best-selling novels analyzed social and moral problems of the Hungarian middle class, then turned to depicting the world of the Hungarian and other European aristocracy. Prior to his death Zilahy lived in the United States for decades, writing several books in English.

Unlike our previous fiction writers, Tibor Déry (b. 1894) presents rather urban stories and figures, himself being the son of a well-to-do, big city family.

All of the above discussed prose writers are well known in this day and age — some of them enjoying overwhelming popularity — in foreign lands.

The greatest literary figure during the interwar years was Mihály Babits (1883-1941), poet, novelist, essayist, translator and editor of the *Nyugat* (The West) periodical, the most important literary journal. He was also director of the Baumgarten Foundation which awarded yearly the nation's highest literary prize. Since Babits was a middle-of-the-roader, he was attacked by Left and Right alike. Dezső Kosztolányi (1885-1936), likewise multi-talented, was important as a lyric poet, essayist, translator and journalist.

Following Madách's philosophical drama, *The Tragedy of Man*, no play of international note was written for decades to come. It is all the more interesting that suddenly, in 1908, a spectacular "Hungarian invasion" of the American theater began. In New York City alone, the adaptation and production of 53 Hungarian plays written by 21 authors could be seen between 1908 and 1940. From 1923 to 1925, seventeen Hungarian plays opened on Broadway, and between 1930 and 1933, twelve. Furthermore, among statistics elucidating American-Hungarian cultural relations, we should mention that the number of produced plays from each Hungarian author during the period 1908-1940 is as follows: Ferenc Molnár (1878-1952), 16; Ernő Vajda, 5; Menyhért Lengyel, 5; László Fodor, 5; Lajos Biró, 4; Ferenc Herczeg (1863-1954), 3; László Bús-Fekete, Gábor Drégely (1883-1944), Lili Hatvany, László Lakatos, 2 each; Árpád Pásztor, Jenő Heltai (1871-1957), Imre Földes, Lajos N. Egri, Lajos Luria (Pseudonym), Imre Fazekas, Attila Orbók, Ádám Gosztony, Lajos Zilahy, János Vaszary, Dezső Szomory, 1 each.

Ferenc Molnár's plays totaled 2,148 first run performances; one reached 326 performances, four exceeded 200, and five exceeded 100 nights. The thirty-seven other plays totaled 2,900 first run performances; one exceeded 300, one 200, and eight 100 performances. The record run, however, was scored by Gábor Drégely's *A Tailor-Made Man* (398).*

---

*Emro Joseph Gergely, *Hungarian drama in New York; American adaptations, 1908-1940.* (Philadelphia: University of Pennsylvania Press, 1947. Pp. 3, 10, 141.).

During the same priod (1908-1940) most European capitals similarly adapted and produced plays written by some of the above-mentioned authors.

In addition to plays, many other forms of literature have been translated into foreign tongues. Tibor Demeter's excellent multivolume bibliographical tool entitled *Magyar szépirodalom idegen nyelven* (Hungarian belles lettres in foreign languages. Budapest, 1957-) demonstrates that the Hungarian language in essence is not so isolated since its products have always been translated into foreign languages and at a very impressive rate. Between the wars, for example, many works of a series of Hungarian authors have appeared in Italian, among them the novels of Mihály Földi, Jenő Heltai, Mór Jókai, Sándor Márai, Kálmán Mikszáth and Ferenc Molnár.*

English translations of Hungarian belletristic works published in Great Britain since 1830 were listed in Magda Czigány's useful bibliography, *Hungarian literature in English translation published in Great Britain, 1830-1968* (London: Szepsi Csombor Literary Circle, 1969. 117 p.).

It is an established fact that official Hungary has promoted the export of cultural goods much better than previous regimes did. This is one of the reasons that between 1962 and 1967 several works of 128 Hungarian writers were translated into 36 languages. In the number of translated items, the German language leads, followed by English, Polish and Slovak. Interestingly, the most popular writer, ranked quantitatively according to the number of translations, is Magda Szabó (b. 1917), a highly gifted and prolific prose writer who has blossomed fully in the past two decades. One of her novels was translated into Bulgarian, Danish, Dutch, Latvian, Italian, Spanish, Swedish, Slovak and Ukrainian languages; 2 of them into Czech, Finnish, Croatian, Lithuanian, Russian, Romanian, and Slovenian; 3 into English and Polish; 4 into French, while 8 of Magda Szabó's novels were translated into German. Endre Ady, Tibor Déry, Endre Fejes, Géza Gárdonyi, Mór Jókai, Attila József, Kálmán Mikszáth, Ferenc Móra, Zsigmond Móricz, László Németh, and Sándor Tatay are among those writers whose works have been most frequently translated into foreign languages in the period of 1962-1967. (Cf. *Idegen nyelven megjelent magyar szépirodalmi művek listája 1962-1967 között*. Budapest: Magyar Írók Szövetsége, 1968. 60 p.).

In the past fifty years Sándor Petőfi has been the most popular among the poets of small nations read in China. Most of his works have been translated into Chinese and many articles in Chinese newspapers, periodicals and anthologies have reviewed Petőfi's life and poetry. The most recent edition of Petőfi's *Selected poems* (a total of 104 poems)

---

*See the "Bibliografia" section in Antonio Villetti's *Novelle ungheresi (Roma: Sandron, 1945)*.

appeared in the People's Republic of China in 1954. This single edition has been reprinted between 1954 and 1962 in seven times and sold in more than 100,000 copies.*

It is quite convincing even from this very brief survey that Hungarian belles lettres is now a weighty constituent of world literature. This is so because Hungarian contributions to world literature mean something new, yet specific, in content and aesthetic form. No one knows at present exactly the quantity and effect of these contributions because no complete statistical surveys have been made on this topic. But there is an encouraging fact: namely, that the number of Hungarian translations into some 40-50 languages has shown a definitive tendency toward increase.

Hungarian contributions to intellectual life have as a rule coincided with the great epoch-making events of history—American, Hungarian and world—and quite naturally with large waves of immigration. Joseph Pulitzer (1847, Makó, Hungary - 1911, Charleston, S.C., USA), the father of modern journalism is one of many such immigrants. Reared in Budapest, he was inducted in Hamburg by a U.S. agent in 1864 to emigrate as a recruit for the Union Army in the Civil War (1861-1865). After the war Pulitzer went to St. Louis, Missouri, where he gained control of the St. Louis *Dispatch* (founded 1864) and the *Post* (founded 1875) and merged them as the influential *Post-Dispatch*. In New York City Pulitzer purchased the *World*, a morning paper and founded its counterpart there, the *Evening World*. Both newspapers prospered under his direction. He endowed the Columbia University School of Journalism which opened in 1912. With a gift of $500,000 he established the Pulitzer Prizes awarded annually in May since 1917 for fiction, poetry, biography, history, drama, music (since 1943) and various branches of newspaper work.

Besides the field of journalism, Joseph Pulitzer was influential in the political arena. He was elected to the Missouri state legislation in 1869. In 1871 and 1872, Pulitzer helped organize the Liberal Republican Party in his state and became one of its secretaries at its Cincinnati (Ohio) convention in 1872 which nominated Horace Greely (who was also the candidate of the Democratic Party) for president. In 1885 Pulitzer was U.S. congressman from New York.

---

*See Endre Galla, *Világjáró magyar irodalom; a magyar irodalom Kínában* (Hungarian literature in China. Budapest: Akadémiai Kiadó, 1968. p. 93).

Music

Judging from written sources, Hungarians must have had a special love for music, song and dance. Such arts played an important role not only in their special events but in their daily lives. According to musicologists, Oriental and Finno-Ugrian traditions are preserved in ancient Hungarian folk music based on the five-tone, that is, pentatonic, scale. Medieval Hungary retained its original heritage which was later colored by the musical culture of the neighboring peoples and the West. Unfortunately, their secular music prior to 1500 was not preserved in written notes, but there is ample authentication for the existence of liturgical music. Although this liturgical music cannot be identified as an independent Hungarian dialect of Gregorian style, it was interspersed with elements of popular melody and rhythm.

Already in the sixteenth century two composers and instrumentalists appeared on the scene: Sebastian (Sebestyén) Tinódi (1505?-1556) and Bálint Bakfark (1507, Brassó-1576, Padua). Tinódi's 23 melodies survived as popular church songs, and one of them was even published in a contemporary Czech songbook. Bakfark's fantasias are listed among the best of lute compositions of that century. Educated in Buda, Bakfark served as a court musician in France and Poland and was active as a musician in Vienna, Transylvania and Italy.

At the outset of the second half of the eighteenth century the "verbunkos" — a recruiting dance music — appeared. The verbunkos consisted of the elements of Hungarian folk music colored with Slavic and Levantine motifs. Through the compositions of János Bihari (1764-1827), János Lavotta (1764-1820), and Antal Csermák (1774-1822), the verbunkos style achieved great popularity in the nineteenth century both in Hungary and abroad. Even the giants of Western music were inspired by the rhythmic and melodic characteristics of the verbunkos. Haydn, Mozart, Beethoven, Weber, Schubert, Berlioz, Brahms and many others used verbunkos music in their compositions: Mozart, for instance, in his *Violin Concerto in A major*; Beethoven in his *König Stephan* and in some parts of the *Third* and *Seventh Symphonies*, not to mention Brahms' *Hungarian dances*. József Ruzitska's opera *Béla's Flight* (*Béla futása*), first performed in 1821 was considered a representative Hungarian national opera at that time due to its verbunkos style. Undoubtedly, the verbunkos enriched the country's musical treasury. Even the csárdás of today developed slowly but directly from the verbunkos and reached its peak in the compositions of Márk Rózsavölgyi (1789-1848) who was, incidentally, an outstanding violin virtuoso.

The verbunkos style to varying degrees influenced the work of many composers of the Romantic school, including Ferenc Erkel

(1810-1893), Mihály Mosonyi (1815-1870), and Ferenc (Franz) Liszt (1811-1886). Erkel's two best operas, the highly successful *Hunyadi László* (1844) and the long-popular *Bánk bán* (1861), are imbued not only with Italian and French motifs but above all with the music of the verbunkos. Erkel was the first composer to consciously develop a distinctively Hungarian musical style for his eight operas, besides which he helped found the Philharmonic Society in 1853 and was the director of the Academy of Music, both in Budapest.

Mihály Mosonyi while at first adhering to German musical traditions after 1856 joined those composers who embraced Hungarian Romanticism. His operatic work, two symphonies, four masses, etc., were written in the German style, while post-1856 works were built upon Hungarian folk tunes, the verbunkos reaching its highest peak in Mosonyi's works. When Mosonyi died in 1870 Liszt composed a funeral march in his memory.

Notwithstanding the popularity of the verbunkos, international appreciation and knowledge of Hungarian music as a whole eluded the art form until the appearance of Ferenc Liszt, the father of modern church and piano music, himself one of the greatest pianists of all time. Though Liszt and his contemporaries had not yet become acquainted with the archetypal forms of Hungarian folk music, he composed the famous *Hungarian Tunes* and *Rhapsodies* (1840-1886) and several other works based on the verbunkos and popular (but not folk) melodies. This musical style permeated the music of Liszt in his *Hungaria* (1856), *The Legend of St. Elizabeth* (1865), the *Mass of Esztergom* (1855), and especially in the *Coronation Mass* (1867). With Liszt, the leading concert pianist of his age, performing its most representative pieces everywhere on the continent, Hungarian music became popular overnight across Europe. Thus Liszt's appearance on the musical scene represented a landmark in enhancing the foreign image of Hungarian music. Interestingly, Ferenc Liszt has since become the most popular foreign composer in the United States. Bedrich Smetana (1824-1884), father of the Czech national school of composition, was an ardent admirer of the music of Liszt. Liszt was an unusually prolific genius. His collected works amount to approximately 40 volumes, his writings to 6, and his correspondence to over 10 volumes. It can rightly be said that as a result of the efforts of the three Hungarian Romantic composers — Erkel, Mosonyi and Liszt — Hungarian music emerged from isolation and turned into a "universal art" appreciated the world over.

Károly Goldmark (1830, Keszthely, Hungary-1915) followed the contemporary Viennese masters in his operatic (*The Queen of Sheba*, 1875), chamber and symphonic works, though his music bears much of the Hungarian character in melody and conception alike. This is all the more understandable because, as he relates in his memoirs, Goldmark's first determinative musical experience occurred as a child at Keszthely when he first heard strains of music coming from the local Catholic church. It was then he decided to make music his life. Goldmark was one of the most popular composers around the turn of the century. Liszt was instrumental in helping him gain acceptance by the official Viennese circles which for a lengthy period of time opposed the performance of *The Queen of Sheba*. They relented only after Liszt's favorable intervention.

Owing to the popularity of the verbunkos, many Hungarian composers even in the twentieth century cultivated that musical style to some degree, as did Jenő Hubay (1858-1937) in his operas, symphonies and violin compositions though he was rather more influenced by contemporary French and German masters.

Internationally acclaimed composers Ernő (Ernst von) Dohnányi, Béla Bartók and Zoltán Kodály further enriched our musical life by virtue of their capacities as educators and musicologists. Composer, pianist, and educator Dohnányi (1877, Pozsony-1960, New York City) notwithstanding his influence by German Romanticism he often employed Hungarian motifs in his compositions, such as *Ruralia Hungarica* (1924). Dohnányi became well-known for his *Variations on a Nursery Song for piano and orchestra*. Besides being a genius of a composer and a piano virtuoso, Dohnányi also ranked among the best as a conductor. His works include the ballet, *The Veil of Pierrette* (1910), *The Tenor* (1929), as well as symphonic, choir, chamber, piano and church music. Dohnányi was appointed director-general of the Academy of Music in Budapest to succeed Jenő Hubay after his death. After the war Dohnányi left Hungary for Argentina and from 1949 has been living in Florida as composer-in-residence at the Florida State University in Tallahassee. At Florida State Dohnányi wholeheartedly devotes himself to music education and in turn is idolized by his students. Dohnányi created several compositions in the United States including his *American Rhapsody* for orchestra (debut performance in Athens, Ohio, February 21, 1954, the composer conducting).

In the genius of Béla Bartók (1881-1945, New York City) and Zoltán Kodály (1882-1967) Hungarian tradition harmoniously merged with a universal language. Bartók composed around 100 works. The *Kossuth Symphony* (1904) was his first major work. His six string quartets (1910-1939) are considered so phenomenal that they are frequently compared with Beethoven's quartets. Bartók's sonatas and violin and piano concertos are also regularly performed selections throughout the world. His stage works, the one-act *Duke Bluebeard's Castle* (1911), and two ballets, *The Wooden Prince* (1916), and *The Miraculous Mandarin* (1919), were first performed in the Budapest State Opera House but now grace the program of the world's outstanding musical institutions. As to the influence Bartók exerted upon composers let us quote William W. Austin's words in his *Music in the 20th century from Debussy through Stravinsky* (New York: W.W. Norton & Co., 1966. p. 329): "More than Schoenberg or Stravinsky, Bartók left a source of possible pervasive influence, unsystematic, open to every direction, rooted in the many-layered past, always fresh, energetic, precise, and personal."

Among musical titans, Hungarian or foreign, Zoltán Kodály drew much more inspiration from Hungarian folk music than any other composer. His otherwise individual style was tinged with contemporary French influences and the religious music of the Italian Renaissance. Among his major works is the *Psalmus Hungaricus*, a monumental piece for tenor, chorus and orchestra completed in 1923. *The Szekler Spining Room* (*Székelyfonó*), based entirely on folk tunes, was first presented a year later. Both compositions reaped much acclaim, and in 1926 when his comic opera, *Háry János*, was performed Zoltán Kodály became an international celebrity. The *Háry János Suite* has since been assimilated into the repertoire of most of the world's major symphony orchestras. Kodály's suite consists of six movements, all of which are imbued with the ebullient spirit of Hungarian folk song and dance. It was specifically Kodály's *Dances from Marosszék* (1930) and *Dances from Galánta* (1933), as well as his *Te Deum* (1936); a concerto for orchestra (1941); *Missa Brevis* (1942); an opera *Cinka Panna* (1948) also interwoven with threads of folk music, and the *Symphony in C Major* (1961) which clinched his worldwide popularity and success. Like Bartók, Zoltán Kodály was an international authority on both ethnomusicology and the methodology of music education. Kodály made several trips to the United States.

In classical chamber music Leó Weiner (1885-1960) was a leading influence followed by many composers of the contemporary younger generation. Weiner's works are, by the way, close to the Bartók-Kodály-initiated style.

It can be said that most Hungarian composers of the younger generation before developing their independent styles imitated Bartók and Kodály along with the best foreign models. The characteristic phenomenon that all the important forms of music possess many prominent exponents is creditable primarily to the groundwork laid by Erkel, Mosonyi, Liszt, Hubay, Dohnányi, Bartók, Weiner and Lajos Bárdos (b. 1899). Present-day Hungary has several dozen outstanding composers whose works have already reached foreign audiences in Europe and elsewhere. Among operatic composers Ferenc Farkas (b. 1905), Jenő Kenessey (b. 1906), Pál Kadosa (b. 1903), György Ránki (b. 1907), and Tibor Polgár (b. 1907), to mention only a few, put Hungarian music in the context of European development. These composers have created significant works in many forms of music, Tibor Polgár for instance. Polgár who in the last two decades has been living in Toronto, Canada, has composed, in addition to his operas, chamber, string quartet, symphonic, film and dance music, songs, etc., and is an accomplished conductor, pianist, and educator as well.

Erzsébet Szőnyi (b. 1924) also enriched Canada's music life some years ago as guest professor there. Composer of operas and other genres, Szőnyi since 1960 has been head of the chair of music education at the Budapest Academy of Music. She is a council member of the International Society for Music Education.

Tibor Serly (b. 1900) was brought to the United States as a small child. In 1931 he returned to Budapest and studied composition under Zoltán Kodály. Serly graduated from the Music Academy in 1934. He became known to the general public in 1937 when the Philadelphia Orchestra played his *First Symphony*.

Following the footsteps of the older generation, Emil Petrovics (b. 1930) and Sándor Szokolay (b. 1931) achieved world renown by their operatic works which revived in modern forms the best traditions of their native land.

Sándor Veress (b. 1907) has also achieved success as composer, pianist and educator in Hungary and abroad, including Switzerland where he lives and the United States where for years he functioned as a guest professor at the prestigious Peabody School of Music in Baltimore, Maryland.

Ede Poldini (1869, Pest-1957, Switzerland) like Sándor Veress lived for decades in Switzerland. He composed the comic operas *The Vagabond and the Princess* (Budapest, 1903) and *The Carnival Marriage* (Budapest, 1924). Poldini's forte consisted of piano works which netted him much popularity abroad, especially in Great Britain and the United States.

Operettas

The verbunkos style, as I have already mentioned, infiltrated popular and folk music throughout the country. Already in the second half of the nineteenth century and afterwards a lot of popular plays were written featuring popular songs. Such a popular song was Elemér Szentirmay's (1836-1908) composition entitled *Csak egy széplány van a világon* (There is but one beautiful girl in the whole world), an ever-popular song today played under varying titles by radio broadcasting stations throughout the world, including the United States.

The transition from popular songs to operetta music was very natural. Though operetta music consisted of three different roots — Viennese, Hungarian and international — all of them in varying degrees borrowed something from the well-known motifs of the respective nation's popular songs.

Major representatives of the Viennese style were Victor Jacobi (1883-1921, New York City), Imre (Emerich) Kálmán (1882-1953, Paris), and Ferenc Lehár (1870, Komárom, Hungary-1948, Ischl, Austria). Jacobi achieved fame especially through the performance of his *Szibill* in Central Europe, Great Britain and the United States. Imre Kálmán is one of the greatest masters of this genre. He studied with Bartók, Kodály and Weiner at the Budapest Academy of Music. In his youth Kálmán had composed prize-winning sonatas, symphonic poems and other forms of serious music. But suddenly, for unknown reasons, he shifted his exceptionally great talent to the composing of light music. Having left Budapest, Kálmán resided in Paris until 1940 then came to the United States, settling in New York City and Hollywood until 1949 when he returned to Europe. Kálmán composed a series of melodious and highly successful operettas, among them the *Tatárjárás* (1908), *Cigányprímás* (1912), *Csárdás Princess* (1915), *Countess Marica* (1924). Kálmán's last work, *Arizona Lady* was performed posthumously in Bern in 1954. His music and that of Lehár has entertained hundreds of millions on five continents.

Ferenc Lehár studied at Prague Conservatory and began his career as a conductor of military bands in Losonc, Pola, Trieste, Budapest, and Vienna. His interest turned to operettas in 1902 and Lehár wrote more than 30 such stage works which were performed primarily in Vienna, Budapest, London and New York. His most resounding success, *The Merry Widow*, has had more stage performances than any other operetta in the twentieth century. Among his most famous pieces are *The Count of Luxembourg* (1909), *Gypsy Love* (1910), *Frasquita* (1922). *The Land of Smiles* (1923) has been a standard selection in the repertoires of the world's musical performing centers.

The Hungarian-type operetta is best represented by Jenő Huszka (1875-1960; *Prince Bob, Gül Baba*, etc.), Pongrác Kacsóh (1873-1923) whose *János vitéz* has been a permanent selection on the annual program of the State Opera House in Budapest, and Ákos Butykay (1871-1935).

Pál Ábrahám (1892-1960, Hamburg, Germany) cultivated the international style in his operetta compositions. Graduating from the Academy of Music in Budapest in 1928 he assumed conductorship of the Municipal Operetta Theater there. His *The Rose of Hawaii* (1931), *The Ball at the Savoy* (1932), and *Victoria* scored international successes.

Sigmund Romberg (1887, Szeged, Hungary-1951, New York City) upon arriving in the United States did a stint playing piano in local Hungarian orchestras from which he soon catapulted to a star-studded career as composer of light music for the stage. Romberg composed over 70 operettas, including such familiar favorites as *The Midnight Girl*

(1914), *The Blue Paradise* (1915), *Maytime* (1917), *The Rose of Stamboul* (1922), *The Student Prince* (1924), *My Maryland* (1927) and *Up in the Central Park* (1945).

Film Music

There are at least two musicians who have achieved eminent success in this type of composition: Tibor Polgár and Miklós Rózsa (1907, Budapest). Polgár wrote music for over 200 motion pictures and for more than 500 radio plays. Miklós Rózsa graduated from secondary school in Budapest (1925), then studied composition and musicology at the Leipzig Conservatory from which he received his diplomas with honors in 1929. His first appearance before the public took place in Leipzig that same year. From 1932 on Rózsa lived a goodly portion of his life in Paris and his compositions figured frequently in the repertoire of continental orchestras. He wrote many sorts of music: ballet dance music (*Hungaria*, 1935), choral and orchestral works, rhapsody for the cello, chamber and pianoforte music, and songs. But Rózsa is known best throughout the world for his film music. Rózsa composed music for countless motion pictures among them such American productions and film classics as *A Double Life; Kipling's Jungle Book; The Lost Week-End; Madame Bovary; Quo Vadis; Spellbound; The Thief of Baghdad;* and *Ben Hur*. In order to propagate his compositions and artistic views The Miklós Rózsa Society was formed in the United States whose quarterly publication is issued under the title *Pro musica sana* in Bloomington, Indiana.

* * *

Hungarian style has had an impact on universal music since the sixteenth century. Certain pieces of dance music in sixteenth century Europe, for example, were named "Ungaresca" while "All'Ongarese" referred to the verbunkos style at the end of the eighteenth century. It would be highly opportune and desirable for historians to trace the chronological and geographical journey of the most frequently used Hungarian motifs in foreign compositions. For instance, the *Rákóczi March* which evolved from the motifs of the eighteenth-century Rákóczi song, complete with the bugle calls used in the Rákóczi army camps from 1703 to 1711, was revived by violinist János Bihari and military band leader Miklós Scholl. The *Rákóczi March* in its next stage of development, the famous Hector Berlioz version (1846), conquered the world. It is incorporated into the *Fifteenth Rhapsody* of Liszt and its motifs have since been used in several other compositions.

In 1942 a noteworthy attempt was made by Margit Prahács of the Budapest Academy of Music to make a quantitative survey of Hungarian motifs occurring in foreign musical compositions. In her work *Magyar témák a külföldi zenében* (Hungarian themes in foreign music. Budapest: Magyarságtudományi Intézet, 1942. 88 p.) she listed several hundred composers of 15 nations whose works revealed a Hungarian influence. In her far from complete survey she enumerates 550 German and Austrian composers with 852 works among them who adopted Hungarian themes; 77 French composers with 98 works; 73 Czech with 115 compositions; 60 Englishmen with 81 works; 60 Italians with 74 works; 25 Poles with 30 works; 23 Russians with 35 works; 8 Swedes with 11 works; 7 Norwegians with 9 works; and 2 Spaniards, 2 Finns, and 2 Dutchmen numbering 9 compositions each.

Hungarian style has been systematically adopted by foreign composers since Joseph Haydn (1732-1809). No foreign composer has drawn so much and so often from the wellspring of Hungarian music than did Johannes Brahms (1833-1897). Among the hundreds of composers influenced by Hungarian music are such names as Ludwig van Beethoven (1770-1827), Hector Berlioz (1803-1869), Wolfgang Amadeus Mozart (1756-1791), Franz Shubert (1797-1828), Johann Strauss (1825-1899), Karl Maria von Weber (1786-1826) to mention just a few.

The popularity of Hungarian music has not declined since. On the contrary, it can safely be stated that since the sixteenth century Ungarescas rising numbers of authentic Hungarian folk tunes have sounded in foreign compositions. In a parallel phenomenon, Hungarian composers have enjoyed an upsurge in foreign popularity. In 1966, for example, 31 contemporary Hungarian composers' 91 works were broadcast by 164 radio stations abroad. (See *Information Hungary*. Oxford: Pergamon Press, 1968. p. 648).

Conductors

For decades it seemed to be a custom that noted composers participated in the country's musical life also in the capacity of conductors. Ferenc Erkel, for instance, helped found the Budapest Philharmonic Society in 1853 and conducted its concerts until 1870. Ernő Dohnányi was also the conductor of the Budapest Philharmonic between the world wars and was also guest conductor throughout Europe. It can be said that the best conductors have been members of the Budapest Opera House. In several instances, it was their stepping-stone to achieving world fame.

János Ferencsik (b. 1907) started his career at the Budapest Opera in 1927 where he has been conductor since 1930. Ferencsik worked as a musical assistant at the Bayreuth Wagner Festivals in 1930 and 1931.

Since 1936 he has made tours to Europe, the United States and the Far East, and was twice (1938, 1950) a guest conductor of the Vienna State Opera House.

György Lehel (b. 1926) has been the chief conductor of the Symphonic Orchestra of Hungarian Radio and Television since 1964 and made several foreign tours during the past two and a half decades.

Lajos (Ludovít) Rajter up until the very end of World War II was associated with the Academy of Music and the Hungarian Radio in Budapest. After 1945 Rajter was instrumental in reorganizing Slovakia's musical culture and became the chief conductor of Slovenská Filharmónia.

Ferenc Fricsay (1914-1963) received his music education at the Budapest Academy where Kodály and Bartók were among his teachers. First he conducted at Szeged (1936), then at the Budapest Opera from 1945, and between 1945 and 1949 he made several guest appearances in Vienna, Salzburg, the Netherlands and in South America. For years Fricsay remained in Berlin as principal conductor of the RIAS Symphony Orchestra and until 1958 as general music director of the Berlin City Opera. From 1956 to 1958 Fricsay was general music director of the Bavarian State Opera House in Munich. He made his American debut with the Boston Symphony Orchestra on November 13, 1953. In 1954 he was engaged as conductor of the Houston Symphony Orchestra, but due to serious disagreements on musical policy Fricsay resigned after only a few concerts and returned to Europe. In his last years he conducted the Berlin Radio Symphony Orchestra and was guest conductor and artistic adviser of the new German Opera in Berlin. Fricsay was a great interpreter of the masterworks of Haydn, Mozart, Brahms, and especially that of Kodály and Bartók. Fricsay made many recordings and was in great demand at most of the great musical festivals in Europe due to the precision and brilliance of his conducting. In 1947 during the Salzburg Festival when sudden illness made it impossible for Otto Klemperer to conduct the world premiere of Gottfried von Einem's opera, *Danton's Death*, Fricsay took over at the last moment and saved the performance. This proved to be his golden break and gave Fricsay a scintillating world reputation overnight.

One can hardly find a single country on the globe without Hungarian conductors and the United States seems to be their favorite gathering place. Let us open our review of the long line of American-Hungarian conductors with Fritz (Frigyes) Reiner (1888, Budapest-1963, New York City). After his diploma from the Academy of Music in Budapest he conducted in Budapest, Laibach, Dresden, Hamburg, Berlin, and Vienna. In the United States Reiner was conductor of the Cincinnati Symphonic Orchestra (1922-1931) and several other orchestras, and in 1949 became conductor of the famous "Met" . . . the New York Metropolitan Opera. Reiner's last permanent post was that of conductor of the Chicago Symphony Orchestra (1953-1963). Reiner was a master of the technique of conducting.

George Széll (1897, Budapest-1970, Cleveland, Ohio) conducted at the Metropolitan Opera House from 1942 to 1946 and in 1946 was engaged as permanent conductor of the Cleveland Orchestra.

A child prodigy, Eugene Ormándy (b. 1899, Budapest) entered the Budapest Academy of Music at the age of five and began studying violin with Jenő Hubay receiving an artist's diploma for violin in 1914. He came to the U.S. in 1921 and subsequently held positions as concertmaster then as conductor. In 1936 Ormándy became associate conductor of the Philadelphia Orchestra (with Leopold Stokowski) and from 1938 on as permanent conductor. Ormándy is a brilliant interpreter of the works of Beethoven, Schumann, Richard Strauss, etc. He conducts all his scores from memory. He has recorded innumerable singles and albums.

Antal Doráti (b. 1906, Budapest) studied with Bartók and Kodály at the Academy of Music, and at the age of 18 conducted at the Budapest Opera House. Then he conducted opera in Dresden (1928), in Münster (1929-1932), and was the conductor of the Ballet Russe de Monte Carlo (1934-1940) with which he toured Australia. He made his American debut with the National Symphony Orchestra in Washington, D.C., in 1937. Following the war Doráti was appointed conductor of the Dallas and Minneapolis Symphony orchestras. In recent years, he was the music director of the National Symphony Orchestra, and was just appointed conductor of the Detroit Symphony Orchestra. Doráti has constantly appeared as guest conductor in Europe and the United States. In addition to being a foremost conductor he is known to have composed at least one major work each year.

Georg Solti (1912, Budapest) studied at the Academy of Music with Ernő Dohnányi (piano) and Zoltán Kodály (composition). From 1933 to 1939 he conducted at the Budapest State Opera House, then in Zürich, Munich, as well as in Frankfurt am Main. In 1953 he made his American debut with the San Francisco Opera. At present Solti is the musical director of the Chicago Symphony Orchestra.

Violinists

Because violin is the principal orchestral instrument of verbunkos music, this boosted violin playing throughout the country. This atmosphere produced first-rank virtuosos very soon, among them Ede (Eduard) Reményi (1828, Miskolc-1898, San Francisco, USA). From 1852 to 1853 Reményi toured Germany taking Brahms with him. The *Hungarian Dances* by Brahms were composed under the influence of

Reményi. In 1853 Reményi visited Liszt, who became his friend and promoter, in Weimar. Next year Reményi was appointed solo violinist to Queen Victoria. In 1885 he came to the United States where he stayed until 1860 when he obtained amnesty for his participation in the 1848-1849 Hungarian Uprising and returned to his native land. Repeated tours in Germany, France, England, the Netherlands, and Belgium spread his fame. In the autumn of 1878 Reményi permanently resettled in America. In 1887 he undertook a world tour during which he received many distinctions as a leading virtuoso of the world. Ede Reményi died in 1898 during a concert he was playing in San Francisco.

József (Joseph) Joachim was born near Pozsony (Bratislava, 1831-Berlin, 1907). He began playing violin at the age of five and his extraordinary talent was immediately recognized, soon affording him a series of concert appearances with ever-mounting success in Germany and England. In 1853 Joachim accepted the post of concertmaster and solo violinist to the King of Hanover and in 1868 became the head of a newly founded department of the Royal Academy of Arts in Berlin. He was admired for his technique by the musical world and received many distinctions, among them orders of knighthood from German and other royal dynasties and in 1877 the honorary degree of Doctor of Music from the University of Cambridge. His most important composition is the *Hungarian Concerto* for violin and orchestra (Op. 11). In expansion of the vistas of his musical endeavors he founded a string quartet (Joachim Quartet) in Berlin in 1869.

Shortly afterwards the time became mature for the establishment of a Hungarian school of violin playing. This was done by Jenő Hubay (1858-1937) who studied violin under his father and from the age of thirteen for five consecutive years under Joachim in Berlin. In 1878 Hubay appeared with great success at the Pasdeloup concerts in Paris and made a lifelong friendship with Vieuxtemps. In 1882 he accepted a position to teach violin at the internationally famous Brussels Conservatoire. In 1886 he returned to Budapest and accepted a professorship at the Academy of Music. He toured most European countries as a soloist and was acknowledged as one of the world's greatest performers. Both in Brussels and Budapest Hubay formed quartets, and as a quartet leader he was enthusiastically praised by Brahms. Highly successful as educator, his pupils included Szigeti, Vecsey, Erna Rubinstein, Eddy Brown, Telmányi, Stefi Geyer, and Ede Zathureczky.

Franz (Ferenc) von Vecsey (1893, Budapest-1935, Rome) received his first instruction from his father and at the age of 5 became Hubay's pupil. He studied also with Joachim. Vecsey made concert tours from his tenth year on, appearing in Berlin (1903), London (1904), and New York (1905) and touring Italy, Scandinavia, Russia, Germany, and the Far East. He composed brilliant violin pieces, *Valse triste* among others.

Joseph Szigeti (1892, Budapest-1973) studied with Jenő Hubay at the Academy of Music and started concert tours at the age of 13. Szigeti was an internationally appreciated interpreter of classical and modern works, especially of those of Bartók, Ravel, Stravinskii, Prokofiev. He made two world tours during which he performed with all the great symphonic orchestras of the world. Szigeti's autobiography (*With Strings Attached: Reminiscences and Reflections*. London, 1949) reveals the development of his talent and says much about the vitality of his playing.

Also a pupil of Hubay, Emil Telmányi (b. 1892) toured Europe and America in 1911. In 1919 he settled in Copenhagen and from 1940 was on the staff of the Aarhus Conservatory. Telmányi created a special "Bach bow" for use in playing the violin music of Bach.

Ede Zathureczky (1903-1959, Bloomington, Indiana) toured Europe and the United States. Between 1929 and 1957 he was associated with the Budapest Academy of Music first as professor then as its general director. Zathureczky was an outstanding performer of romantic and modern (especially Bartók's) works. From 1957 he has been on the staff of the Indiana University of Bloomington.

Sándor Végh (b. 1905), a graduate of the Academy of Music in Budapest, won the Hubay and Reményi prizes in Hungary and was one of the winners at a Viennese competition for violinists. As a solo virtuoso Végh toured Europe and the United States. In 1935 he was one of those who formed the Hungarian String Quartet. The quartet successfully toured most of Europe and in honor of its excellence several modern composers dedicated their works to it. In 1940 he established his own, the Végh, quartet.

Róbert Virovai (b. 1921) after finishing his studies with Hubay commenced concert tours. In 1937 Virovai won first prize at the International Contest in Vienna for violinists and cellists. In 1938 he made his American debut with the New York Philharmonic-Symphony Orchestra playing the *Violin Concerto No. 4 in D Minor* by Vieuxtemps.

Johanna Martzy (b. 1924, Temesvár) at the age of sixteen won the Reményi Prize and at seventeen the Hubay Prize. In 1943 she was soloist with the Budapest Philharmonic under Mengelberg. In 1947 Martzy captured the First Prize of the Concours International d'Exécution in Geneva, Switzerland. She subsequently toured Europe then performed in the United States in 1957.

Martha Hidy, also a graduate of the Budapest Music Academy, started her career in her teens. Her wide repertoire includes classical as well as modern compositions. She is a follower of the best traditions of violin playing. For the past several decades she has made her home in Toronto, Canada.

Dénes Kovács (b. 1930) studied under Ede Zathureczky at the Budapest Academy of Music. From 1951 to 1960 he was the concertmaster of the Budapest State Opera. In 1955 Kovács won the Flesch Contest in London. Since 1957 he has taught violin at the Budapest Academy of Music where since 1968 he has been director general. He has widely toured Europe and China as outstanding interpreter of Bach, Mozart, Beethoven and Bartók compositions.

* * *

János Starker (1924, Budapest) following the death of Pablo Casals has been hailed as the greatest living cellist of our time. He first performed as a soloist at the age of ten. Having graduated from the Budapest Academy of Music he became the first cellist of the Budapest Opera orchestra. In the United States Starker has held the position of first cellist with the Dallas Symphony Orchestra, the Metropolitan Opera orchestra, the Chicago Symphony Orchestra, etc. In 1958 he was appointed professor at Indiana University in Bloomington. János Starker has widely toured Europe and the United States as solo recitalist.

Pianists

In addition to being one of the greatest composers of all time, Ferenc Liszt as a piano virtuoso was recognized as the unequaled master of his instrument. In 1875 Liszt undertook not only the presidency of the newly founded Academy of Music in Budapest but the simultaneous heading of its piano department. Thus Liszt was in a position to exert influence upon generations of Hungarian musicians, above all pianists. Among his first disciples was Géza Zichy (1849-1924). Zichy lost his right arm in an accident in 1863. Despite such a staggering handicap, Zichy industriously pursued left-handed exercises on the pianoforte to become a unique phenomenon: the most distinguished one-handed virtuoso in the history of piano playing.

Ernő Dohnányi toured Europe and America and cemented a reputation as one of the best piano virtuosi of his day. His brilliant technique, pure style of interpretation, and unparalleled memory were highly appreciated by the musical world.

Concert pianist Andor Földes (b. 1913, Budapest) studied with Dohnányi at the Music Academy in Budapest. He won the International Liszt Prize at a piano contest in Budapest in 1933. Földes has given concerts in Europe and the United States.

Annie Fischer (b. 1916) has widely toured Europe and given several concerts in America. She is well-known performer of Beethoven and Mozart compositions and has made many recordings.

Gyula Károlyi (b. 1914) has made several tours in Europe. The American debut of Károlyi took place at Carnegie Hall in New York City at the beginning of the fifties.

Béla Böszörményi-Nagy was already an established concert pianist in Europe when he arrived in Canada in 1948 for a concert tour. For the past decades he has been living in the United States and has been engaged in teaching piano at the college level.

Dohnányi's favorite pupil was Géza Anda (1921, Budapest-1976, Switzerland). Simultaneously, he attended the Budapest State Teachers College, where for four years I was his literature professor, and the Academy of Music under Dohnányi's tutelage. Anda was recognized to be so outstandingly gifted by school authorities that Dohnányi was permitted to arrange for Anda to spend the whole of every Thursday for years at the music academy under his sole instruction although there was neither legal basis nor precedent to absolve a college student from compulsory daily attendance. Interestingly, he received his artist's diploma a few weeks earlier than his teacher's diploma. During this same period he won the Liszt Prize.

Géza Anda appeared with major symphony orchestras throughout Europe and the United States and made innumerable recordings. In 1955 Anda made his American debut with the Philadelphia Orchestra. From the middle of World War II Anda lived in Switzerland, and subsequently gave numerous recitals in Europe and America. He excelled as an interpretative musician and a virtuoso and was especially successful in the works of Brahms, Liszt, Mozart, Grieg, and Bartók.

György Cziffra (b. 1921) was a child prodigy. He studied at the Budapest Academy with Dohnányi and György Ferenczy. He has done concert tours since 1950. Boasting a versatile repertoire, Cziffra is most successful in interpreting romantic compositions, especially those of Liszt. He is one of the most highly esteemed pianists of our day. Since 1957 he has been living in Paris.

Tamás Vásáry (b. 1933, Debrecen) was encouraged by Dohnányi to continue his studies at the Budapest Academy of Music and shortly thereafter won the Liszt Prize. In 1956 he settled in Switzerland, and within a short time he began giving concerts in Belgium, the Netherlands, Great Britain, Italy, Brazil, and the United States. He played with the Berlin Philharmonic for the first time in 1959, and rendered his debut performance at London's Royal Festival Hall in 1961. Tamás Vásáry's interpretations and the bravura quality of his piano playing have garnered the unanimous accolades of his critics.

Among organists Dezső Antalffy-Zsíros (1885-1945, Monticello, New York) and Sebestyén Pécsi (b. 1910) are internationally highly esteemed. Antalffy-Zsíros taught from 1910 on at the Academy of Music in Budapest. In 1921 he toured the United States and joined the staff of the Eastman School of Music in Rochester, New York after which he was commissioned by Max Reinhardt to be his composer and conductor. From 1935 to 1942 he was the organist and composer of the Radio City Music Hall in New York, and member of the New York Philharmonic. Sebestyén Pécsi also taught at the Academy of Music and since 1945 has been giving concerts all over Europe.

Singers

The teaching of singing in Hungary did not reach the level of Italian and German or Austrian methodology for decades. This is why the majority of outstanding singers learned their art from foreign, especially Italian, masters, at the beginnings of singing instruction in the first half of the nineteenth century and afterwards. Coloratura soprano Kornélia Hollósy (1827-1890) studied in Vienna (under M. Salvi) and Milan (under F. Lamperti). She sang operatic roles in Corfu, Torino, Bucharest, Vienna, and Warsaw and performed the role of Melinda at the 1861 premiere of *Bánk Bán* at the Hungarian National Theater.

Soprano Aurelie Révy (1879, Kaposvár-1957, Toronto, Canada) studied in Budapest and London. She sang at Covent Garden (1898-1900, 1902, 1904). In 1900 she became an operetta singer at the Theater an der Wien. Révy made guest appearances in Berlin, Zürich, and Russia.

Maria Basilides (1886-1946) had a beautiful contralto voice. A graduate of the Budapest Academy of Music, she was a member of the Hungarian State Opera House from 1915 until her death. As an outstanding interpreter of Schubert, Mahler, Bach, Gluck, Handel, Wagner, Bartók and Kodály she was regularly invited to Berlin, London, Paris, Vienna, Dresden, Copenhagen, Prague, and Munich, etc., between 1923 and 1946.

Soprano Anne Roselle (b. 1894, Budapest as Anna Gyenge) came to America as a child and completed her study of singing here. In 1920 she made her debut at the Metropolitan Opera as Musetta in *La Bohème*. She appeared as guest singer at the Dresden State Opera, the Budapest State Opera, and sang at Covent Garden, etc. She made several recordings.

Rosette (Piroska) Anday (mezzo-soprano, b. 1903, Budapest) first studied violin with Jenő Hubay, then began taking singing lessons with noted teachers, among them Gino Tessari. Her first professional appearance was at the Budapest Opera in 1920. In 1921 she sang *Carmen* at the Vienna State Opera and became a member of this Opera, remaining so until 1961. Anday was very successful in Vienna and at the Salzburg festivals. She appeared as guest singer at Milan's La Scala, London, Munich, Budapest, Berlin, and toured the Americas and Africa. Her voice easily mastered both opera and concert repertoires.

The voice of coloratura soprano Lujza Szabó (1904-1934) was extraordinary. She graduated from the Budapest Academy of Music and in 1927 made her debut at the Hungarian State Opera. As a guest artist she sang the role of the Queen of the Night in *The Magic Flute* under the conductorship of Bruno Walter at the Berlin City Opera in 1931 and scored a magnificent success. The same year she repeated this success in Amsterdam and on the German radio. Unfortunately, Lujza Szabó died during an operation at the age of 30 before reaching the peak of her already splendid career.

Soprano Ester Réthy (b. 1912, Budapest) studied in Budapest and Vienna. Her first performance was at the Hungarian State Opera in 1935. In 1937 she joined the Vienna State Opera where she sang until 1949. Réthy became an international celebrity at the Salzburg Festivals in the role of Susanna in *Le Nozze di Figaro* and of Sophie in *Der Rosenkavalier* (1937-1939).

Soprano Astrid Várnay (b. 1918) is an outstanding singer of Wagnerian operas. In 1941 she was featured at the Metropolitan Opera. Astrid Várnay has been permanent guest artist at the Bayreuth Festivals from 1951 on.

Hungarian men have also scored international successes in the art of singing. János Halmos (1887-1961), the virtually self-taught first tenor of the Hungarian State Opera, was exceptionally successful in guest appearances at La Scala, Florence and Breslau. Having one of the most beautiful tenor voices of his day, Halmos was remarkable in heroic parts (e.g., *Bánk bán*).

Imre Palló (b. 1891) studied at the Budapest Academy of Music and in 1917 became baritone soloist of the Hungarian State Opera remaining there until his retirement. Palló made guest appearances on most of Europe's operatic stages singing in *Rigoletto, Háry János, Bánk bán*, etc. He was one of the best interpreters of Bartók and Kodály.

Zsigmond Pilinszky (b. 1891, Budapest) studied at Budapest, Leipzig, and Berlin. Between 1913 and 1927 he was a member of the Budapest Opera. Pilinszky became internationally well-known as one of the best Wagnerian tenors when he joined the Berlin City Opera. In 1930 and 1931 Pilinszky sang the title role in *Tannhäuser* at the Bayreuth Festivals. He was eminently successful as guest artist in Vienna, London, Chicago, and San Francisco.

Kálmán (Koloman) Pataky (1896-1964, Los Angeles, California) graduated from the Music Academy in Budapest. Between 1921 and

1926 he was a member of the Hungarian State Opera House, after which until 1938 he sang at the Vienna State Opera, always in leading roles. His brilliant career culminated in Vienna from where he made frequent guest appearances at La Scala, Berlin, Munich, etc. As an outstanding Mozart tenor Pataky was highly applauded at the Glyndebourne and Salzburg Festivals. In 1936 he sang Florestan in *Fidelio* at Salzburg, followed by an engagement at La Scala where he sang in 1939 and 1940, then in South America.

Recently, Hungary had two world-renowned bass singers: Mihály Székely and Endre Koréh. Mihály Székely (1901-1963) took private lessons in singing from Géza László. At 22 Székely became a member of the Budapest State Opera and remained so until his death. His guest appearances, primarily in Mozart and Bartók operas, took him through most countries of Europe and the United States. He took part in the 1937 Salzburg Festivals, and in the Glyndebourne Festivals each year between 1951 and 1961. Székely was guest soloist of the New York Metropolitan Opera between 1946 and 1950. Perhaps his best fitting role was that of Bluebeard in Bartók's *Duke Bluebeard's Castle* in which he was warmly applauded at the Holland Festivals and throughout Europe.

Endre Koréh (1906-1960, Vienna) was a leading bass singer of the Budapest State Opera, and between 1946 and 1960 the first bass of the Vienna State Opera. Koréh sang leading roles in 1948 at the Salzburg Festivals and in Florence at the Maggio Musicale. He made frequent guest appearances throughout Europe, especially at La Scala, in London, and in 1953, at the New York Metropolitan. Koréh was an international star in Mozart, Wagner, Verdi, Puccini, and Richard Strauss operas.

The best known Hungarian baritone to date, Sándor (Alexander) Svéd (b. in Budapest in 1906) learned his art in Budapest, Italy and Germany. He became a member of the Budapest State Opera in 1927. Between 1935 and 1939 he starred at the Vienna State Opera and made guest appearances at Berlin, Munich, Dresden, Milan, Rome, Paris, London, and Buenos Aires opera houses. For years until 1951 he was a celebrated baritone of the New York Metropolitan Opera. Sándor Svéd was exceptionally successful in Verdi, Puccini and Wagnerian operas.

Tenor Gábor Carelli (b. 1915, Budapest), still another student of the Music Academy in Budapest, started his brilliant career at the New York Metropolitan Opera in 1951 where he remained for several years.

Critics unanimously agree that Sándor Kónya (b. 1923, Sarkad, Hungary) is one of the world's best tenors. He studied singing in Budapest, Detmold (Germany) and in Milan. Kónya was a member of several West German opera houses including the Berlin City Opera where he made his debut in 1951. Kónya appeared at the 1956 Edinburgh Festival and at the 1958 Bayreuth Festivals in the title role of *Lohengrin*, and subsequently on all the important stages of the world. Kónya has also appeared as guest singer at La Scala, the Paris Opera, the Rome Opera, in Budapest, and many of the larger stages in Germany and elsewhere. He also made concert tours in Spain, Portugal, and the United States. Since 1961 Kónya has been a member of the New York Metropolitan Opera Company.

The Hungarian methodology of vocal instruction, as already mentioned, was not of as high a calibre as that of Italy or Germany, which is why a substantial number of Hungarian singers learned their art abroad, especially in Italy. Now it can safely be said that the situation as to the methodology of music education has greatly improved. Since about the middle of the twenties the level of music education has gradually risen, with heavy emphasis being placed on the methodology of singing by Zoltán Kodály, Artúr Harmat (1885-1962), Zoltán Vásárhelyi (b. 1900), and more recently by Erzsébet Szőnyi who laid the foundations of a very high-level choral culture and education. Their principles are actualized in the Singing Youth Movement and several other similar organizations with mass memberships, as well as in the public schools. In present-day Hungary, music (singing) education starts at the kindergarten level upon which general and secondary school relevant curricula are based. There are several highly specialized secondary schools devoted exclusively to the art of music and singing which apply the Hungarian methodology developed by Kodály which is touted by art critics as a model worthy of emulation.

The opening of the Budapest Opera House in 1884 has proven advantageous for ballet music and dance alike. Since the sixties, the ballet ensemble of the Budapest State Opera House and the Ballet Sopianae (of the National Theater of Pécs) have had tour engagements of many countries, including Britain, Scandinavia, and the Soviet Union. The Budapest State Opera House ballet ensemble won the Golden Star Medal at the 1963 Paris International Festival. Its solo dancers have frequently guested on foreign stages in Europe and the United States. At the 1965 Varna (Bulgaria) competition Ivan Nagy who was one of the medal winners was invited to join the National Ballet of Washington. After leaving the National, he was briefly associated with the New York City Ballet before joining the American Ballet Theatre of which he is now a star performer. According to Lillie F. Rosen's most recently (undated) published pictorial brochure entitled *Ivan Nagy* (dance Horizons Spotlight Series): "In his steady development Nagy has earned plaudists around the world." (p.6).

It is fitting that we mention here the work of Gusztáv Oláh (1901, Budapest-1956, Munich). For decades the stage manager and scenic designer of the Budapest State Opera House, Oláh also lent his talents as stage manager and set designer to many European theaters, including some in Sweden, the Soviet Union and East Germany. His production of Respighi at the Maggio Musicale in Firenze drew international acclaim. Oláh also participated in the production of the first performances of the Szeged Open-Air Theater, a well-known pioneering enterprise.

Theater and Cinema

by Christina Maria T. Wagner

Prior to the Turkish occupation, Hungary's theatrical culture kept pace with European developments. But with the Battle of Mohács in 1526, the country's theatrical art fell behind that of the West, with the exception of theater in Transylvania which enjoyed semi-independence and where the influence of the Italian Renaissance and humanism remained alive. During the period of Turkish occupation — for about a century and a half — there were only school productions organized in Hungary. Professional theatrical performances restarted only in the eighteenth century when the Eszterházy princely family built theaters at Eszterháza, a center of musical and theatrical life for three decades, where, among others, their protégé composer Joseph Haydn contributed to cultural enrichment. At least twenty more theaters were built by Hungarian aristocrats across the country in that same century and theatrical touring companies were organized nationwide.

The first really professional company was formed under the directorship of László Kelemen (1760-1814) and staged its first performance in Buda on October 25, 1790. It is characteristic of the country's early Shakespearean cult that *Romeo and Juliet* was being played as early as 1793 and 1794, and somewhat later *Hamlet*. With the financial aid of the Hungarian aristocrats of Transylvania, the second Hungarian company was set up in Kolozsvár (Cluj) in 1792. But the real progress in theater came with the establishment of the Hungarian Theater of Pest, precursor of the present-day National Theater, in 1837. The National Theater thrived under the management of Ede Szigligeti (1814-1878), himself a noted playwright, and Ede Paulay (1836-1894). Such actresses as Madame Déry (Róza Széppataki, 1793-1872), Mari Jászai (1850-1926) and Emília Márkus (1862-1949) elevated the art of acting to a Western European level. As a consequence, Hungarian provincial theatrical troupes were provided with permanent homes in Kassa (Kosice), Kolozsvár, Miskolc, Debrecen, Arad, Székesfehérvár, Szeged and Pécs. 1884 brought the opening of the Budapest State Opera House which has since ranked among the first three operatic ensembles on the continent. Around the turn of the century the Gaiety (Comedy) Theater (Vígszínház, 1896), the Magyar Theater (1897), and the first operetta theater, the Király Theater (1903) — the Budapest Operetta Theater was only founded in 1922 — were all established in the nation's capital. This network of permanent theaters indicated the rising interest of theatergoers and guaranteed constant artistic improvement. It is of interest to note that in 1964 there were 16 permanent theaters operating daily in Budapest (among them two operatic companies) and 14 in the countryside, some of them with first-class operatic ensembles.

At the outset of our century the short-lived Thalia Company (1904-1908) under the guidance of László Márkus and Sándor Hevesi (1873-1939) became a milestone in the history of Hungarian theater. László Markus who in 1935 was appointed director of the Budapest State Opera and Sándor Hevesi who directed the National Theater for a decade beginning in the early twenties, along with several of their contemporaries, purposefully strove to achieve realism on the stage. As a result, the rigid, declamatory style gradually disappeared from the stage. Hevesi and subsequent directors of the National Theater continued to stage Shakespeare dramas in the National Theater and elsewhere. Because of their success, Hevesi was invited by London University in 1929 to deliver a series of lectures about the vigorous Shakespeare cult in Hungary. This Shakespearean cult was all the more possible because high-level translations of the playwright's dramas had been prepared by Hungary's best poets: Mihály Vörösmarty (*Julius Caesar; King Lear*), Sándor Petőfi (*Coriolanus*), János Arany (*King John; Midsummer Night's Dream; Hamlet*), et al.

Very soon, entirely new names appeared on the scene and Budapest, with Vienna and Prague, became a world center of theater. It seems quite impossible to even list all the names of those hundreds who have taken part in establishing Hungary's position in the theatrical world. Successive generations of actors since then have been educated on the principles of realism evolved by these actors. The greatest artists of this new style of acting were numerous. Among them, Gyula Csortos (1883-1945), a member of the National Theater, excelled in the plays of Shakespeare, O'Neill, Chekhov, Ibsen and Hauptmann. Tragicomic roles best fitted his character. Perhaps the greatest actor of that epoch and in Hungarian history was Artúr Somlay (1883-1951). For the most part a member of the Gaiety Theater (Vígszínház) and after 1945 of the National Theater, he performed leading roles in the dramas of Shakespeare, Schiller, Ibsen, Strindberg, Hauptmann, Gorki, etc. He was phenomenal in classical and modern roles alike. Between 1920 and 1922 Somlay toured Western European countries and worked as a film actor in Berlin and for years was guest actor of the Kammerspiele in Vienna.

Gizi Bajor (1893-1951) was a member of the National Theater from 1914 up to her death. Her technique was so superb that according to Sándor Hevesi she was capable of solving the unsolvable in stage acting.

The repertoire of the National Theater under the directorship of Hevesi was built on the talent of Gizi Bajor. She was so jubilantly received by the audience that any play she had a role in was performed well over one hundred times. Unfortunately, owing to the shortcomings of theatrical policy, the talent of Gizi Bajor, Tivadar Uray (1895-1962) and Kálmán Rózsahegyi (1873-1961), all outstanding members of the National Theater, were not adequately used.

Among the pillars of stage acting mention should be made of Anna Tőkés (1898-1966), Klári Tolnay who is still active, as well as Éva Szörényi and Zita Szeleczky both enormously popular members of the National Theater and both of whom performed leading parts in many motion pictures. Éva Szörényi and Zita Szeleczky now live in California.

The late Kálmán Latabár (b. 1902) acquired international fame first as an acrobatic comedian who between 1927 and 1933 with his brother, Árpád, toured most of the European countries and Africa. Most of his career as an unsurpassable comedian and dancer was spent on the stage of the Budapest Operetta Theater but he also acted in many films.

Antal Páger (b. 1899) started his career as a comic actor then switched to modern dramatic roles. He became famous in the thirties as a stage and screen actor alike. After the war Páger emigrated to Argentina (1945-1956) then returned to Budapest's Gaiety Theater where he has been captivating audiences ever since. For his extraordinary talent, Antal Páger received the country's highest award, the Kossuth Prize, and the title of "outstanding artist." Páger received the prestigious Cannes Film Festival's (1964) award for best actor.

Since about the thirties, but especially since the late fifties, there has been a frequent and growing trend in cultural exchange between Hungarian and foreign theaters. The ensembles of the Hungarian State Opera, the National Theater and the Madách Theater have appeared several times before foreign audiences with impressive success. The Budapest Operetta Theater in recent years has toured with enthusiastic reception Austria, Czechoslovakia, Italy and the Soviet Union.

The newly organized College of Dramatic and Cinematic Arts takes care of training young artists, while the Department of Theatrical History of the National Széchényi Library and the Institute of Theatrical Research (the Hungarian center of the International Theater Institute) help develop theatrical culture. The Institute of Theatrical Research is a member of the FIRT (Fédération Internationale pour la Recherche du Théâtre). Hungary of late has also been an active participant in UNESCO's film exchange program. It is quite understandable that Budapest has become a hotbed of European theater where many great artists, directors and producers of foreign stages, including that of Hollywood, started their splendid careers.

185

Cinema

The history of the country's motion picture art goes back to 1896, the year of the Millennial Exhibition in Budapest commemorating the founding of the Hungarian state. On this occasion a number of shots were made of King Francis Joseph I as he attended the celebrations, among them a shot of the King as he viewed Munkácsy's famous painting, *Ecce Homo*. It cannot be overemphasized that this was the very first attempt in the world to use films for documentation and to shoot current events (newsreels). In 1898 a feature film, *The Adventure of Siófok* (screenplay by Jenő Heltai), was made by a French company. The first original Hungarian film was shot in 1901 under the title, *A Tánc (The Dance)*. Gyula Pekár's 500m illustrated lecture on the history of dance featuring Lujza Blaha, Emília Márkus, Irén Varsányi, Gyula Hegedűs and several other great artists of that time. Hungary was the first in Europe to produce educational films. The first such film was made in 1913 at the Pedagogic Film Studio in Budapest.

The expertise of Jenő Janovics (1872-1946), director of the Hungarian National Theater in Kolozsvár, proved to be a turning point in the world of film-making. Feature film production in Hungary grew tremendously as a direct result of the successful motion pictures of Janovics. In 1914 he directed the *Bánk bán* starring Mari Jászai and Mihály Várkonyi (d. 1976 in California) who in the twenties under the name of Victor Varconi became a star of Hollywood silent films. Several producers and directors like Sándor Korda (Sir Alexander Korda), Mihály Kertész (Michael Curtiz), Márton Garas, cameraman Árpád Virágh, etc., also launched their careers under the guidance of Jenő Janovics at the National Theater in Kolozsvár. As a result of the educational and inspirational work of Jenő Janovics 45 directors produced motion pictures prior to 1918 in over 30 major and 7 smaller studios in Hungary.

Between the wars, partly because of the 1929 economic world crisis, film production did not advance significantly. Naturally, there were several feature films which enjoyed sweeping success like *Hyppolit the Butler (Hyppolit a Lakáj*, 1931) directed by István Székely (Steve Sekely) with comedian Gyula Kabos, who later emigrated to the United States, and Gyula Csortos. Like *Hyppolit the Butler*, the twenty-fifth Hungarian sound film, *The Dream Car* (Meseautó, 1934) directed by Béla Gaál, had extraordinary success, with Zita Perczel, Jenő Törzs, Gyula Kabos, and Klári Tolnay in the leading roles. The success of *The Dream Car* positively affected the import of Hungarian feature films. While in 1934, according to *Variety*, an American trade paper, only 4 Hungarian motion pictures were screened in the United States out of 147 European films, three years later 18 Hungarian motion pictures reached American shores out of 240 imports, thereby raising Hungary to fourth place in America's film import. The 240 imported films included 67 German, 50 British, 23 French, 18 Hungarian, 17 Italian, 15 Soviet, 10 Polish, 10 Swedish products and 1 or 2 films from other countries. (Cf. István Nemeskürty, *World and Image: history of the Hungarian cinema*. Budapest: Corvina Press, 1968, p. 94). The popular actresses of that era were Zita Szeleczky, Klári Tolnay, Éva Szörényi, Piri Vaszary, Lili Muráti, and later Katalin Karády. During this time Antal Páger, Pál Jávor, Artúr Somlay, Gyula Csortos, Tivadar Uray, and comedians Gyula Kabos, Gerő Mály, Tivadar Bilicsi and Kálmán Latabár also rose to tremendous popularity.

Film critics unanimously agreed that the *People on the Mountains* (*Emberek a Havason*) was the greatest interwar production. Directed by István Szőts, it was awarded the Grand Prize at the 1942 Biennale of Venice. The screenplay was based on the short stories of József Nyírő (*Kopjafák*) and the leading roles were played by Alice Szellay, János Görbe, and József Bihari.

During the war years the screening of American films was prohibited in Hungary in 1942, with French and British pictures being banned much earlier. In the early forties, Bulgaria, Scandinavia, and the Balkans bought large numbers of Hungarian films. In 1940 Yugoslavia purchased 150 Hungarian films and Italy bought that year's entire production. Characteristically, Germany almost completely boycotted Hungarian-made motion pictures as it had during World War I. (See István Nemeskürty, *Op. cit.*, p. 111).

Between 1948 and 1965 Hungarian feature, and full-length and short nature, films won more than 130 prestigious international awards at various film festivals — Locarno, Karlovy Vary, Venice, Moscow, San Francisco, Boston, Cannes, Edinburgh, Rome, Paris, Montevideo, Bucharest, Santiago de Chile, Oberhausen, Leipzig, Padua, Mannheim, Melbourne, Bergamo, Adelaide, Vancouver, Vienna, to mention just a few. (For details see the relevant tables showing all data about the prize-winning films between 1948 and 1965 in *Cultural Life in Hungary*, ed. Zoltán Halász. Budapest; Pannonia Press, 1966, pp. 208-214).

Critics ranked motion pictures that were directed by Géza Radványi (*Somewhere in Europe*, 1947), Zoltán Fábri (*Merry-Go-Round*, 1955; *Professor Hannibal*, 1956), Félix Máriássy (*Budapest Spring*, 1955), László Ranódy (*Abyss*, 1956; *Skylark*, 1963), Károly Makk (*The House under the Rocks*, 1958) and Miklós Jancsó (*Cantata*, 1962) among the highest artistic achievements. At the 1964 Cannes Film Festival the prize for the best actor went to Antal Páger for his part in *Skylark* (*Pacsirta*). Director Károly Makk's *The House under the Rocks* was awarded the prize for the best film at San Francisco in 1958. *Love*, another import directed by Makk, starring a cast of three headed by Lili

Darvas was acclaimed by the *New York Times* as one of the ten best films of 1973. The *Times* acclaimed *Love* as a "very precise, moving, and fine-grained" film with "three superb performances". Lili Darvas, by the way, numbers 3 American films among her credits: *The Affairs of Maupassant* (1938), *Meet Me in Las Vegas* (1956) and *Cimarron* (1961). In the category of short films several Hungarian productions have won international awards, among them *Overture* (*Nyitány*) directed by János Vadász which won the Oscar and the Grand Prix for short films at the Cannes Film Festival in 1965.

The outline of cinematographic production cannot omit nature or educational films, least of all those of István Homoki-Nagy's prize-winning *The Kingdom of the Waters* (Karlovy Vary, 1952, prize for best cinematography), *From Blossom Time to Autumn Frost* (Venice, 1953, 1st prize for popular science films) and Ágoston Kollányi's *Aquarium* (Cannes, 1954, film technicians' prize; Karlovy Vary, 1954, prize for the best educational film). Gyula Macskássy is an eminent master of animated films. His cartoon, *Párbaj* (Duel), and other works have influenced a generation of young cartoonists in recent years.

Film Theoreticians

In the domain of film aesthetics or the philosophy of art there are several pioneering works by Hungarian authors. Sir Alexander Korda, about whom we will elaborate under the subheading of "Producers and Directors", was among the historic first to advocate the film theory that the motion picture is, above all, art. Korda edited three motion picture journals in Budapest during the formative period of film aesthetics: *Pesti Mozi* (*Movies in Pest*, 1912), *Mozi* (*Movie*; 1913) and Mozihét (*Movie Weekly*; 1915-1918). Interestingly, a Benedictine monk later turned educational philosopher at the University of Pécs, Cecil Bognár, published an article in the December 15, 1915 issue of the *Budapesti Hirlap* which argued that the film is not only an art but a form of communication as well. Bartók's librettist, Béla Balázs (1884-1949), ranks among the first developers of modern film theory by means of his widely quoted work *Der sichtbare Mensch* (*The Visible Man*, 1924). In recent literature much credit has been given to Béla Balázs for his theoretical work. A major portion of Dudley J. Andrew's book *The Major Film Theories: an introduction* (London, New York: Oxford University Press, 1976) is devoted to the analysis of the lifework of Béla Balázs.

Up to this point in our chapter on *Theater and Cinema* we have constructed a contextual framework within which to insert the subject of Hungarian artists in America. Hungarian-born talent has been a prominent and multi-faceted jewel in the crown of motion picture art.

Cinematographers

Cinematographers have long been unsung heroes of the motion picture art. Although space and scope of this work do not allow for exhaustive treatment or even cataloguing of these neglected artists, we can nonetheless pay substantial tribute.

According to noted American film scholar, Leonard Maltin, one reason that cinematography in Hollywood sparkled at its zenith in the 1920's was "the European boom during the 1920's. Many homegrown filmmakers were put to shame by such imports . . . of European cinema." (*Behind the Camera. The Cinematographer's Art* by Leonard Maltin, A Signet Book from New American Library, N.Y., 1971; p. 21). Furthermore, this "foreign invasion spurred many domestic filmmakers (often by 'request' of studio heads) to improve their own product, imbue it with the continental touch that audiences seemed to be enjoying so much. The competitive spirit asserted itself and was in large part responsible for Hollywood's own pictorial golden age." (*Op. cit.*, p. 22). Thus, in yet another field, the tiny population of Hungary contributed overwhelmingly more than its share to making motion picture history.

Ernest László ranks as one of the world's foremost masters of cinematography. His numerous credits include *Hell's Angels* (1930) starring Jean Harlow, *Judgment at Nuremberg* (1961), *Ship of Fools* (1951), *Fantastic Voyage* (1966), and *Airport* (1970).

Andrew László, one of the contemporary generation of Hungarian-born cinematographers in Hollywood, was born January 12, 1926 in Zombor in what is now Yugoslavia. A few of his more recent achievements include *You're A Big Boy Now* (1966) with a cast featuring Geraldine Page and Julie Harris, *The Night They Raided Minsky's* (1968) starring Jason Robards, *Popi* (1969), *Lovers and Other Strangers* (1970), *The Out-of-Towners* starring Jack Lemmon, and the 1970 *The Owl and the Pussycat*.

Highly prolific László Kovács is still another of the new breed of geniuses upholding the good name of the Hungarian dynasty in Hollywood. A refugee of the 1956 Hungarian revolution, he came to Hollywood where he has garnered rave reviews ever since. While associated with American International Pictures he photographed several of their motorcycle gang films which were resoundingly panned by the critics, although their unfortunate quality with respect to acting and shortcomings of dialogue and plot remained powerless to blight recognition of Kovács' talented contribution. *Variety*, one of America's top three show business trades, in a review of one such film photographed by Kovács deplored that "the most depressing thing . . . is that such first-rate color camerawork was thrown away on such trivia . . ." The trades abounded in rave reviews of Kovács' cinematography. *Easy*

189

Rider, the 1969 controversial motorcycle film hit which catapulted actor Jack Nicholson to superstardom, is yet another case in point. Although the picture drew decidedly mixed reviews, *Variety* dubbed Kovács' work "brilliant". His *Five Easy Pieces* (1970, starring Jack Nicholson) moved the director to dub him "fantastic". Some of László Kovács' more recent accomplishments include *Paper Moon* (1973) starring Ryan and Tatum O'Neal and *What's Up, Doc?*, the 1972 Barbra Streisand-Ryan O'Neal picture.

A likewise prolific, contemporary cinematographer is Vilmos Zsigmond. As in the case of László Kovács, Zsigmond's vehicles have not always attracted favorable reviews nonetheless reviews of his work triumphed unscathed. Among his credits are numbered *McCabe and Mrs. Miller* (1971) starring Julie Christie and Warren Beatty, *The Hired Hand* (1971) with Peter Fonda, *The Long Goodbye* (1973) with Elliott Gould, *Scarecrow* (1973) featuring Al Pacino and Gene Hackman, *The Sugarland Express* (1974) with Goldie Hawn, and *The Girl From Petrovka* (1974) starring Hal Holbrook and Goldie Hawn. Vilmos Zsigmond is especially renowned for his spectacular nature photography, an especially notable example being the 1972 *Deliverance* starring Jon Voight and Burt Reynolds.

Producers and Directors

Adolph Zukor was born in Hungary January 7, 1873. Orphaned at the age of 7, he ventured to the United States as a 16-year-old with $25 stitched into the lining of his coat. He quickly exchanged his first job of sweeping floors for that of penny arcade entrepreneur in New York City. In short order he founded the Famous Players Film Company in 1913 for the purpose of making films of successful plays such as *The Count of Monte Cristo, The Prisoner of Zenda* and *Tesse of the D'Ubervilles*. His first production, *The Prisoner of Zenda*, was the first feature-length film made in the United States.

In 1917 he founded Paramount Pictures. Zukor is responsible for introducing cinema immortals Mary Pickford, Douglas Fairbanks, Sr., William S. Hart and Pola Negri to audiences throughout the world. Other stars appearing under the Paramount symbol of the snow-capped mountain were Greta Garbo, Gloria Swanson, Rudolph Valentino, and Maurice Chevalier. Zukor's production of *Wings* won the very first Academy Award for best picture in 1928, the year the American Academy of Motion Picture Arts and Sciences was founded. Among the early classics supervised by Zukor were the original *Ten Commandments, The Sheik*, and *The Covered Wagon*.

He was honored in 1949 with a special Oscar for having rendered inestimable services to the motion picture industry over a period of 40 years. Board chairman emeritus of Paramount Pictures, Inc. he put in a full day's work every day well into his eighties. Adolph Zukor died June 10, 1976 at the age of 103.

Joe Pasternak was born in 1901 in Szilágysomlyó. His 30-year career as a top echelon producer included such greats as *The Flame of New Orleans* (1941) with Marlene Dietrich; the Deanna Durbin-Charles Laughton picture, *It Started With Eve* (1941); *Duchess of Idaho* (1950) with Esther Williams and Van Johnson; *The Great Caruso* (1951) starring Ann Blyth and Mario Lanza; *The Merry Widow* (1952) with Lana Turner and Fernando Lamas; *The Student Prince* (1954) starring Ann Blyth and Edmund Purdom; and the comedy, *Please Don't Eat the Daisies* (1960) starring David Niven and Doris Day.

Sir Alexander Korda (born Sándor Korda) is perhaps known to most of us as a producer, although he directed films over the period 1927-1948 . . . as a matter of fact he directed Laurence Olivier and Vivien Leigh in the 1948 production, *That Hamilton Woman*. Among the pictures Korda produced are *The Scarlet Pimpernel* (1935) co-starring Leslie Howard and Merle Oberon; *Knight Without Armor*, a 1937 Marlene Dietrich picture; *The Thief of Bagdad* (1940) with Conrad Veidt; and the 1948 epic, *Anna Karenina* with Vivien Leigh and Ralph Richardson. A great deal of Alexander Korda's films were products of Great Britain.

Born Iván Törzs in Budapest on June 12, 1916, Ivan Tors emigrated to the United States in 1940 where he anglicized his name to the present less complex spelling. He rose from Hollywood screenwriter (the hit television series of the recent past, *Sea Hunt*, starring Lloyd Bridges is one of the many feathers in his cap) to world-famed producer of masterful wildlife television shows and motion pictures. Ninety per cent of all animal scenes in Hollywood are the domain of his animals. A few of his veteran motion picture stars beloved by a cross-section of audience generations are "Gentle Ben" the bear, "Clarence the Cross-Eyed Lion", "Namu the Killer Whale" and "Flipper" the dolphin. Other seasoned alumni and apprentice actors in his ensemble include monkeys, elephants, snakes, and tarantulas, among other exotic talents. Ivan Tors trains his protégés with his special brand of "Affection training" at "Africa, U.S.A.", a 260-acre preserve he owns outside Los Angeles.

Michael Curtiz' directorial career in America spanned 5 decades and embraced close to 100 pictures. In his native Hungary Curtiz (Mihály Kertész) had been a director as well as a cinematographer. He was esteemed as a dynamic man with a superb artistic instinct, an ever-bubbling fountain of creative ideas. A partial roster of his films includes *God's Gift to Women*, the 1931 Joan Blondell-Frank Fay picture;

The Adventures of Robin Hood (1938), *The Case of the Curious Bride* (1935), *Captain Blood* (1935) and *The Sea Hawk* (1940), all starring the then international heartstopper of the silver screen, Errol Flynn; *Front Page Woman* (1935) starring the incomparable Bette Davis; *Angels With Dirty Faces* (1938) featuring Cagney and Bogart; *Yankee Doodle Dandy* (1942) with James Cagney and Joan Leslie; *Casablanca* (1942) with a star-studded cast including Humphrey Bogart, Ingrid Bergman, Peter Lorre, and Claude Rains; *Life with Father* (1947) featuring William Powell, Irene Dunn, and Elizabeth Taylor; *White Christmas* (1954) with Bing Crosby, Danny Kaye, and Rosemary Clooney; *The Proud Rebel* (1958) with Alan Ladd and Olivia de Havilland; and *A Breath of Scandal* (1960) with Italian screen goddess Sophia Loren and the French Maurice Chevalier.

Born in Budapest on April 1st, 1918, Jan Kádár is hailed as a brilliant director with an avid following in the United States. After the Battle of Budapest he fled to Czechoslovakia where he turned out such works as the 1965 Oscar winner for best foreign film, *The Shop On Main Street* (sometimes referred to under the variant translation, *The Shop on the High Street*, 1964), *Kidnap* (1956), *Death is Called Engelchen* (1958), *The Accused* (1964), *The Angel Levine* (1969), *Adrift* (1971), and *Lies My Father Told Me* (1975).

André De Tóth was born in Hungary as Endre Tóth. His film career was launched in Europe in 1931 and his Hollywood affiliation in 1940. Like many other directors, the first rung in his career ladder was that of cinematographer. He was associated with Bavarische Piktura in Germany until 1931 then with Hunnia Films in Hungary until 1939. In 1940 he was assistant to Sir Alexander Korda. André De Tóth has directed films in Great Britain, Hungary, and the United States.

One of his earliest pictures was screened in the United States in 1939 under the title, *Wedding in Toprin*. Made in Hungary, it starred Pál Jávor, "the Magyar screen's 'matinée idol'". De Tóth was ultra-progressive for his time — according to a *New York Times* review (November 6, 1939).

Among De Tóth's U.S. motion picture credits are: *Dark Waters* (1944) with Merle Oberon and Franchot Tone, *Dishonored Lady* (1947) starring Hedy Lamarr, *Ramrod* (1947) with Joel McCrea and Veronica Lake, *Other Love* (1947) co-starring Barbara Stanwyck and Richard Conte, *Pitfall* (1948) with Dick Powell and *Slattery's Hurricane* (1949) with Richard Widmark and Veronica Lake.

He directed several Westerns, including the Gary Cooper picture, *Springfield Rifle*, and *The Man In The Saddle* with Randolph Scott and Joan Leslie, both 1951 releases. His *House of Wax* (1953) starring Vincent Price is most memorable for being the first 3-D (three dimensional) film ever produced by a major studio.

Some of De Tóth's later efforts include *Day of the Outlaw* (1959), *Morgan the Pirate* (1961) starring Hungarian-born muscleman Steve Reeves, and *Play Dirty* (1968). The latter was reviewed in New York's *Village Voice* (March 6, 1969) as being exemplary of De Tóth's "directorial personality which has always revealed an understanding of the instability and outright treachery of human relationships." According to film scholar Leonard Maltin, André De Tóth's films are currently the subject of a cult among the young generation of American directors and cinemaphiles.

Screenwriters

Born László Faragó on September 21, 1906 in the tiny town of Csurgó, Ladislas Farago is a multitalented individual. In addition to giving us the fruits of his talent as a best-selling author and journalist, the motion picture industry is also indebted to him, hence the liberty taken of discussing him in the Theater-Cinema chapter of this book.

Subsequent to earning a degree from the Royal Academy of Commerce in Budapest, his positions included special Associated Press correspondent for Ethiopia, foreign editor of the *Sunday Chronicle* in London, editor of *Corps Diplomatique*, senior editor of *U.N. World* and the staffs of Radio Free Europe and of the *New York Times-Wide World Bureau* in Berlin.

Farago's string of best-sellers include *Palestine at the Crossroads* (1937), *Psychological Warfare* (1940), *Axis Grand Strategy* (1942), *Behind Closed Doors* (1950), *War of Wits* (1954), *Strictly from Hungary* (1962), and *It's Your Money* (1964). His *Patton: Ordeal and Triumph* (1964) was made into the 1970 Academy award-winning movie, *Patton*, starring George C. Scott and *The Broken Seal* (1967) was made into the 1970 *Tora Tora Tora* starring an international cast of Martin Balsam, Joseph Cotten, E.G. Marshall, Jason Robards, Yamamura, Takahira Tamura, and Tatsuya Mihashi. Movie rights were also purchased to Ladislas Farago's *The Game of the Foxes* (1971).

Actors

Lya de Putti (appearing under the stage name of Lia Putty in Hungary) was one of the first silent film stars. She played lead parts in several early Hollywood pictures (*Variety*, 1926; *The Sorrows of Satan*, 1926; *The Prince of Tempters*, 1926; and *Manon Lescaut*, 1926.) Born in 1897 in Vecse, Hungary, she died in New York in 1931.

Vilma Bánky was a brunette sweetheart of the silent screen and the early talkies. She co-starred with Ronald Colman in *The Dark Angel* (1925), *The Night of Love* (1927), *The Magic Flame* (1927) and *Two Lovers* (1928), while with Rudolph Valentino she starred in *The Eagle* (1925) and *The Son of the Sheik* (1926). In *The Winning of Barbara Worth* she headed a cast featuring Ronald Colman and Gary Cooper. In *A Lady To Love* (1930) Edward G. Robinson shared billing with her, while in *The Rebel* (1933) she starred with fellow Hungarian, Victor Varconi. Her acting ability was always glowingly critiqued, even when the vehicle wasn't quite up to snuff. A *New York Times* review of the 1929 production *This Is Heaven* and entitled "Vilma Banky's Voice" reports that "Samuel Goldwyn's lovely Hungarian star . . . (who) for the first time speaks her lines . . . has a charming accent . . . Whether she is silent or talking, Miss Banky is always radiant. She really gives a clever performance in this piece of fluff."

Victor Varconi (1891-1976), a protégé of American motion picture mogul, Cecil B. De Mille, masterfully relates his colorful Hollywood career in his posthumously released autobiography entitled *It's not enough to be Hungarian* (Denver: Graphic Impressions, 1976. 192 p.) Performing in Hungary as Mihály Várkonyi, Victor Varconi's Hollywood career encompassed principal or lead roles in some 50 pictures including *The Volga Boatman* (1926), *The King of Kings* (1927), *Roberta* (1935), *Suez* (1938), *Strange Cargo* (1940) and *For Whom the Bell Tolls*, the 1943 adaptation of the Hemingway novel.

The career of lovely, elegant and blonde Ilona Massey (born Ilona Hajmássy) lasted nearly a quarter of a century. Her performances include *Balalaika* (1939) and *Invisible Agent* (1942) with Peter Lorre. She died in 1974.

The superb character actor who appeared in innumerable films in his native Hungary under the professional name, Szoeke Szakall, modified his stage name to S.Z. Sakall in the States where he amassed an equally formidable roster of credits: 39 films between 1940 and 1951 with nary a minor role among them. His performances were consistently praised — as a matter of fact, in discussing the casting of roles in a major picture he appeared in, the *New York Times* exclaimed "who else" but Sakall could have been satisfactorily cast in a particular part.

Paul Lukas was born Pál Lukács in 1895 in Budapest. In America alone his career spanned 40 years and totalled 77 films — more than the prolific Peter Lorre — not to mention numerous television performances. On Lukas' list of credits we can enumerate *The Shopworn Angels* (1929), *Halfway to Heaven* (1929), *Strictly Dishonorable* (1931), *A Passport to Hell* (1932), *Little Women* (1933), *The Three Musketeers* (1935), *Dinner at the Ritz* (1937), *Confessions of a Nazi Spy* (1939), *Strange Cargo* (1940), *They Dare Not Love* (1941), *Watch on the Rhine* (1943), *Berlin*

Express (1948), *20,000 Leagues Under the Sea* (1954) and *Tender Is the Night* (1962).

Éva Bartók was born Márta Szőke in Budapest in 1929. She starred in such British films as *Her Crime Was Love*. Over the period from 1952 to 1965 her Hollywood credits included co-starring with Burt Lancaster in *The Crimson Pirate* (1952), with Gina Lollobrigida in *A Tale of Five Women* (1953), with Richard Todd in *The Assassin* (1953), and with Jack Hawkins in *Front Page Story* (1955). She was a smash success in *Ten Thousand Bedrooms*, the 1957 farce with Walter Slezak, Dean Martin and Anna Maria Alberghetti. She also made two pictures with Curt Jurgens: *The Last Walt* (1958) and *Circus of Love* (1958).

A Béla Lugosi cult flourishes in perhaps every corner of the world. Best known for his characterization of Count Dracula, he also played Frankenstein, not to mention the variety of straight dramatic and comedic roles he undertook. Lugosi's film appearances include *The Rejected Woman* (1924), *Murders in the Rue Morgue* (1932), *Chandu the Magician* (1932), *Best Man Wins* (1935), *The Mysterious Mr. Wong* (1935) and *Ninotchka* (1939).

Peter Lorre was a character of near legendary magnitude whose devotees included Error Flynn, Humphrey Bogart, and still include director-actor John Huston. Born in Hungary June 26, 1904 as László Loewenstein he was a highly individual character actor who already in 1935 was touted by Charlie Chaplin to be "the greatest living actor". In 1922 with a group of Viennese actors he pioneered the technique of improvisational acting. He made his first films in Germany, attracting international notice with "M" (1933). After two films in Britain he settled mainly in Hollywood where upon his arrival he vowed never to work rather than be typecast as a murderous character — as the cliché goes, "the rest is history . . . ".

One of the screen's classic criminals, off screen the little 5'3" Hungarian enjoyed popularity as a cordial fellow exercising a keen sense of humor. He was a good friend of Béla Lugosi, another delight off screen. Lorre's credits of some 70 films include 8 "Mr. Moto" films, *Strange Cargo* (1940) with Paul Lukas and *Mr. District Attorney* (1941). He was a mainstay in the star-studded cast of the 1942 *Casablanca*, and appeared in *The Maltese Falcon* (1941), *Invisible Agent* (1942), *Passage to Marseille* (1944), *Arsenic and Old Lace* (1944), *The Chase* (1946), *Casbah* (1948), and *The Buster Keaton Story* (1957). He died of a stroke March 24, 1964 at the age of 59 in his Hollywood home. His last picture, *Torn Curtain*, was released in 1966.

References

American Film Institute Catalogue. Feature Films, 1921-1930. New York-London:, R.R. Bowker Co., 1971.

American Film Institute Catalogue. Feature Films, 1961-1970. New York-London: R.R. Bowker Co., 1976.

Celebrity Register. Ed. by Earl Blackwell. New York: Simon & Schuster, 1973.

Filmed Books and Plays. A List of Books and Plays from which Films have been made, 1928-1974. By A.G.S. Enser, Andre Deutsch Ltd., Great Britain, 1971.

Filmgoer's Companion. 3d ed. Ed. by Leslie Halliwell. London: MacGibbon & Kee, 1970.

Filmlexicon Degli Autori E Delle Opere. Roma: Centro Sperimentale di Cinematografia, 1959.

Maltin, Leonard, *Behind the Camera: the cinematographer's art*. New York: New American Library, 1971.

Nemeskürty, István, comp., *A film ma*. Budapest: Gondolat, 1971.

Nemeskürty, István, *Word and image; history of the Hungarian cinema*. Budapest: Corvina Press, 1968.

New York Post, March 24, 1964 (Obituary of Peter Lorre).

New York Times, November 6, 1939 (Review of *Wedding in Toprin*, film of Andre De Toth).

The New York Times Directory of the Film 1920-1970. New York: Arno Press-Random House, 1971.

The New York Times Film Reviews. Subtitles: 1920-1939; 1940-1959; 1960-1969; 1971-1972; 1973-1974. Semicolons designate separate volumes.

Newark Evening News, March 29, 1964. (Obituary of Peter Lorre).

Screen World. Ed. by John Willis. New York: Crown Publishers, 1976.

Village Voice, March 6, 1969. Review by A. Sarris (Used for information on Andre De Toth).

Who's Who in the Theatre. Ed. by Freda Gaye. 14th jubilee ed. Pitman Publishers, England, 1962.

Literature on *Theater* is listed in *SELECTED BIBLIOGRAPHY*.

Folk Art

by Christina Maria T. Wagner

Far from being merely a popular avocation or a charming and decorative pastime, Hungarian folk art is a multiform, high calibre manifestation of professional artistry.

Hungarian folk art embraces the fine arts of painting, sculpture, music and the dance as well as the applied arts of metalwork, including, gold-, silver-, iron- and coppersmithery; leatherwork; carving from stone, wood, bone, and horn; the making of stained glass windows; embroidery, spinning and weaving, and a multitude of others. Of them all it is textile work and ceramics which have attained the highest degree of perfection. In present-day Hungary the Sárköz region is the richest in folk art.

As with every folk art, the diverse forms of Hungarian folk art mirror the emotions of its people; in the case of the Hungarian people, an ineradicable sense of humor, an irrepressible joie de vivre, an enthusiastic love of ceremony, and a profound appreciation of the aesthetic. The fusion of functionalism and aestheticism is a hallmark of the Hungarian artistic temperament. Again as with any folk art, Hungarian folk art is an outgrowth of the people's lifestyle, which in turn is molded by the country's history. As such, the two historical factors leaving the deepest imprint on her art were the Turkish occupation of Hungary from 1526 to 1686 and the Italian Renaissance. The Turkish influence was especially strong in embroidery. However, strong national tradition amalgamated with artistic ability made it possible to meld two such different artistic styles as Eastern and Western into a balanced, harmonious unity which was distinctly Hungarian in character.

As early as the ninth century we have written and other documentation of the fact that decorative arts flourished among the Hungarian people — the Magyars — at a relatively high level. Although they were a seminomadic, equestrian people at the time, decoration of clothing was a widespread occupation. Contemporary eyewitnesses expressed amazement at the Magyars' proficiency and imagination in fabricating and embellishing armor and at their mastery of the decorative branches of the metal crafts and leather craft. Ninth century bridles, trappings, harnesses, stirrups, arrowheads, sword blades and other artifacts bear witness to the Hungarian philosophy that what is functional need be simultaneously aesthetic.

Such craftsmanship is but the precursor of Hungarian folk art . . . a sort of rudimentary folk art. So when did the formal advent of Hungarian folk art occur? When it became widespread among the people, diversified in form, and of high quality. This took place during the reign of King St. Stephen which began in the year 1000.

Who are the practitioners of the folk arts? The general peasantry, along with artisans or specialists. These specialists are also of the peasantry and usually pursue their artistic activities alongside their regular occupations. The specialists fall into two categories: those who exercise their skills when the occasion calls for it and without accepting monetary compensation, and those who earn a living from it. Included in the latter category are needy people, the handicapped, and those commissioned to produce works of art for purposes of domestic consumption and foreign trade. Folk artists who inhabit certain regions of the country and certain communities are famed for producing works of art which even professionals are unable to surpass.

It is impossible to do a comprehensive, in-depth survey of the Hungarian folk arts herein nor is one intended, so let us touch upon a few specific art forms. Proceeding with a thumbnail sketch of the fine arts and considering music, it behooves us to point out that such internationally renowned giants as Ferenc Liszt, Zoltán Kodály, and Béla Bartók are indebted to the ancient folk melodies and harmonic patterns of their homeland which form the basis of their compositions.

Among the wealth of folk dances the internationally best known and loved is the national dance of Hungary: the regal, dynamic, and explosively passionate *csárdás* (pronounced Char'dahsh).

Painting embraces, among other representatives, the exquisite freehand adornments of the interior as well as the exterior walls of peasant homes. These cheery, vividly multicolored works of art are especially evident in the town of Kalocsa near the southern tributary of the Danube.

The designs in decorative folk art are predominantly floral, the most favored being tulips, lilies, and carnations, with profusions of petals as space-fillers. Other motifs include fruits, such as the pomegranate, and animals, with birds, especially the peacock, being the most popular. Human figures are rarely depicted. Also characteristic are the preference for certain colors, especially red, and the rare use of others, such as yellow and purple.

Carving is a most versatile art. It is the herdsman's art. The materials he employs are generally wood, bone, and horn. He embellishes countless objects of his métier as well as personal use, including the handle of his herdsman's whip, his pipe, matchbox, and flute. Herdsmen excel at carving because the long, uneventful hours spent minding their flocks afford the opportunity for much practice. But carving is by no means restricted to the herdsman or the media he utilizes. Cases in point are furniture, buildings — including details on peasant cottages such as arcaded porches, gables, roofs — ceilings and belfries of churches, gates and other structures which exhibit elaborate carvings. Indeed, in Transylvania the very shovel used for digging graves is splendidly decorated with carvings, not to mention grave markers. Also, it is a matter of record that in a prison of old a peasant carved on a laundry mangleboard the story of how he had clobbered a tax collector and the malice of the judges had landed him in the pokey.

Embroidery is one of the most interesting of the folk arts. Its origins can be traced back to the eleventh century when Queen Gisela, wife of Stephen I, the first king of Hungary, maintained a workroom for embroidery. As early as the fourteenth century professional craftsmen were producing embroidery which was renowned throughout Hungary and abroad. As a matter of fact, the master embroiderer of the king of France between 1384 and 1417 was a man named Étienne de Hongrie, which is translated Stephen of Hungary. In the sixteenth century Hungary created a new style of embroidery which was a merger of Eastern and Western motifs yet characteristically Hungarian.

Items embroidered are endless, including bookmarks, saddles, boots, pillows and bedclothes, cloaks and mantels, tablecloths, and aprons. As a matter of fact, in the seventeenth century, Hungarians were ardently embroidering practically everything they could get their hands on, including ladies' lingerie and gentlemen's underclothing.

Embroidery and native costume-making are interdependent and perhaps the most symbolic and expressive of the Hungarian way of life. A symmetrically arranged flower cluster or vine constitutes the dominant motif of Hungarian embroidery, with a different flower usually growing from every branch of the stem. There are many variations on this motif, some including fruits. About 25 stitches are known. Among the materials used for embroidering are gold and silver threads, coral, pearls, lace, silk, taffeta, satin and brocade.

Depending on the colors, fabric, style, embroidery, and the particular article of clothing, the observer of the Hungarian native costume is able to ascertain the wearer's sex, age bracket, socioeconomic status, possibly his occupation, the region of the country he hails from, marital status, and the occasion for which he is attired. For example, older women wear more sparsely embroidered clothes and more somber colors than younger women, the fiery red of youth gradually giving way with the passage of time to green, blue, then finally black. Unmarried girls generally go bareheaded but on festive occasions wear a wreath-like headdress called a *párta* (pahr'tuh). Older women wear coifs or kerchiefs, while young married women without children sport the most sumptously ornate headdresses of all. Another example of the story native costume tells is the wearing of a certain handkerchief to reveal that a young man is engaged. Called a betrothal handkerchief and made for him by his fiancée, each of its 4 corners is embroidered in a different pattern and each Sunday the young man wears it to church he will display a different corner.

In style there is no difference between the garb of the rich and poor. The only variance is that a wealthy person would have a greater quantity of costumes and they would be fashioned of more expensive and richly decorated materials.

Pottery is one of the most varied and colorful branches of folk art. The Great Hungarian Plains (Alföld) is the seat of pottery-making. There are two basic types of pottery: multicolored, glazed ceramics and unglazed, smoked black earthenware. Design and shape, of course, vary according to occasion and use.

What used to be the Zsolnay Factory is now called the Pécs Porcelain Factory. It began as a small chinamaker's shop around the middle of the nineteenth century. In just a few years, under the artistic leadership of Vilmos Zsolnay (1828-1900), this little shop was transformed into a topnotch factory. The Zsolnay Factory used the eosin formula invented by Vince Wartha in decorating its objets d'art. This innovation made the Zsolnay products famous in most European countries by the last quarter of the nineteenth century. Since the Zsolnay porcelains were awarded the Grand Prix at the Paris World Exhibition in 1900 they have gained popularity the world over. The artistic achievements of the Zsolnay Factory have resulted in a continuous chain of international successes which are well documented in A Zsolnay Család (The Zsolnay Family. Budapest: Corvina Press, 1974. 240 p., 48 illus.) written by Teréz Zsolnay and Margit Zsolnay Mattyasovszky.

It would be sacrilegious to speak of the Hungarian folk arts, much less of pottery, without mentioning the world-famous porcelains of Herend. They are the crowning glory of the folk art of pottery. Because of its exceptional craftsmanship, beautiful and numerous hues, and imaginative wealth of designs, it became sought after by international connoisseurs of art and those with exquisite taste.

The Herend factory has been in existence since 1839. Herend porcelain won acclaim at many international and national exhibits. Here in America at the 1853 N.Y. Exhibition of Industrial Art the director of the Herend factory was awarded a diploma and medal in recognition of the porcelain's superb quality. At the 1855 World's Fair in Paris, every single piece of Herend porcelain was sold.

Queen Victoria of England ordered a very large Herend table service for Windsor Castle. Needless to say, the English aristocracy flocked to follow suit and ownership of Herend became all the rage. The 14th president of the United States, Franklin Pierce, also joined the ranks of the many illustrious owners of Herend. Austrian Emperor Franz Josef, still another customer, gifted his mother, the Archduchess Sophia, with a tea set. Other celebrated figures in the course of history to own Herend china include the Russian czar, Alexander II; King Victor Emmanuel of Italy; King Edward VII of England; and one of the Rothschild scions whose family name is now borne by the famous design made especially for him.

Herend porcelain is increasingly prized today, a major reason being that it continues to hold out as the only major porcelain factory in the world which has refused to tarnish its artistry by "going commercial", so to speak, and adopting assemly line methods and fully mechanized production. On the contrary, one has the assurance that every piece of Herend china is hand painted by individual artists and masters, each specializing in a respective technique.

Although the second half of the nineteenth century saw the golden age of folk art, it is far from stagnant. The characteristic features of ancient Hungarian folk art live on to be enriched by ever-evolving new materials, new objects, and new styles to meet the demands of the times.

*   *   *

Literature on *Folk Art* is listed in *SELECTED BIBLIOGRAPHY*.

PART V — SPORTS AND GAMES

In this chapter, as in the rest of this book, I include only first-generation Hungarians. The achievements of second-generation Hungarians are outside the scope of this book. Furthermore, it would be statistically mammoth and interminable task even to enumerate the successes of all Hungarian-born athletes, not to mention those of such second-generation greats as golfer Julius Boros, football stars "Broadway Joe" Namath and Larry Csonka, and many, many others.

One of the reasons Hungary has produced so many European- and world-calibre champions is the fact that its official circles have most of the time supported sports and physical education almost since the Middle Ages. And even in the Middle Ages fencing was widely practiced among knights and soldiers. As early as the seventeenth and eighteenth centuries physical education was taught, although at a rudimentary level, in many of the country's schools. The most decisive step in this direction was taken in the century of the Enlightenment when in 1777 the *Ratio Educationis* prescribed certain measures relating to the teaching of physical education in Hungarian schools. Fortunately, the most popular leaders of the Reform Era (1825-1848), namely, István Széchenyi, Lajos Kossuth and Miklós Wesselényi, were themselves practicing athletes. What's more, Széchenyi and Kossuth belonged to the founding members of the well-known Physical Training Institute in Pest. No wonder that when international competition was begun decades later Hungary immediately entered the field. Seven Hungarian athletes participated among those of thirteen nations at the first modern Olympic Games in Athens in 1896 and won 2 gold, 1 silver, and 2 bronze medals.

One of the main factors underlying the spectacular achievements in sports has been the College for Physical Education (Testnevelési Főiskola) founded in Budapest in 1925. This is a four-year college for physical education teachers and offers a three-year curriculum for coaches. Physical education is compulsory in all schools and more than a million people participate in a variety of athletic activities. The government promotes sports with generous subsidies. All these circumstances are responsible for the country's outstanding rankings in the unofficial point scoring of nations entered in the Olympic Games. For instance, Hungary won third place in Berlin in 1936, London in 1948 and Helsinki in 1952; fourth place in Melbourne in 1956; fifth place among 85 nations competing in Rome in 1960; sixth place out of 94 nations in Tokyo in 1964; and fourth place in Mexico City in 1968.

The number of countries participating in the Olympic Games and the number of competitors has since risen significantly and so has Hungary's role in international sports events — Olympic, world, and

European. This upward tendency is convincingly illustrated in the following statistical columns which show the achievements of Hungarian athletes on a comparative basis:

Summer Olympic Games

	I	II	III	IV	V	VI
1896 Athens	2	1	2	1	—	—
1900 Paris	1	2	3	3	3	—
1904 St. Louis	2	1	1	1	—	—
1908 London	3	4	1	5	1	2
1912 Stockholm	3	2	3	3	1	2
1924 Paris	2	3	4	2	5	4
1928 Amsterdam	4	5	—	3	3	3
1932 Los Angeles	6	4	5	3	5	2
1936 Berlin	10	1	5	7	6	4
1948 London	10	5	12	10	8	2
1952 Helsinki	16	10	16	6	6	7
1956 Melbourne	9	10	7	10	10	6
1960 Rome	6	8	7	9	6	4
1964 Tokyo	10	7	5	7	14	6
1968 Mexico City	10	10	12	4	6	2
1972 Munich	6	13	16	9	9	10

In the Olympic Games at Montreal in 1976 Hungarian competitors turned in a moderate performance but even so won 21 medals — 4 gold, 5 silver, and 12 bronze — to attain a most respectable 10th place overall. Among gold medal winners, Miklós Németh, son of Imre Németh the gold medalist in the hammer throw at the 1948 games, won the gold medal in javelin competition. He set a new Olympic and world record in javelin throw (94,58 m.). In all-time medal placings for the games of I to XXI Olympiads inclusive, held 1896 through 1976, Hungary with a total of 106 gold, 95 silver, and 117 bronze medals ranks eighth among the nations.

Besides the Olympic Games, Hungarian athletes have regularly participated with amazing success in world as well as European championships, winning gold, silver and bronze medals in a great many events. Thus, between 1945 and May 31, 1976, they took 143 gold, 174 silver and 180 bronze medals at world championships and 140 gold, 154 silver and 202 bronze medals at European championships. During the same period Hungarian athletes won 22 gold, 23 silver and 33 bronze medals in table tennis at world championships and reaped great success in world competition canoeing with a total of 32 gold, 31 silver and 32 bronze medals in the latter. Naturally, they could boast superb accomplishments in their traditionally best-fitting sport, fencing (sabre), winning 36 gold, 43 silver and 35 bronze medals at world championships also in the aforementioned period. They were also highly rated in water polo, soccer, wrestling and swimming to mention a few others.

For the lack of space we can mention but a few athletes out of several hundreds who have made extraordinary contributions to the world of sports.

As early as 1896, the year of the first Olympiad, Hungarians made a good showing in Olympic swimming: Alfréd Hajós swam a gold medal performance in the 100-meter freestyle as well as the 1200-meter freestyle. Zoltán Halmay won two gold medals for the 100-meter freestyle and the 50-yard freestyle, both in 1904. In water sports the name of István Bárány (b. 1907) is notable since he was the first in Europe and the second in the world after the American Johnny Weismuller, to swim 100 meters freestyle in less than a minute. Bárány was second after Weismuller at the Amsterdam Olympic Games in 1928. In 1936 it was Ferenc Csík who followed the precedent of a gold medal in the 100-meter freestyle. Csík (1913-1945), a medical doctor, was first in the 100-meter freestyle at the Paris Grand Prix in 1934 and in that same year he won the European championship in the same event at Magdeburg. In 1935 Csík set a new European record of 57.8 seconds, a record he improved by two-tenths of a second to win the gold medal in the 1936 Olympics.

1952 was a record year for the Hungarian women's Olympic swimming team. They scored an across-the-board win in all swimming events offered with the sole exception of the 100-meter backstroke. Katalin Szőke won the 100-meter freestyle gold medal, Valéria Gyenge the 400-meter freestyle, Éva Székely the 200-meter breaststroke and the team of Ilona Novák, Judit Temes, Éva Novák and Katalin Szőke clinched the 4 X 100-meter freestyle relay.

In water polo tournaments there have been many Hungarian sportsmen whose names are worth noting. The accomplishments of Márton Homonnai, János Németh (his nickname was James), Dezső Gyarmati, István Szívós (father and son) and that of many others are listed in the annals and history books of water polo. Out of the 17 times water polo has been on the Olympic program, Hungary has won the gold medal 6 times: in 1932, 1936, 1952, 1956, 1964 and 1976.

Hungary has a long, distinguished record in boxing in a surprising variety of classes. László Papp (b. 1926) was a history-maker, being the only person up to now ever to win three gold medals consecutively. Papp captured the gold medal in the 1948 middleweight boxing event in London, the 1952 light middleweight event in Helsinki and the 1956 light middleweight event in Melbourne. He was a member of the national team 95 times and also won several European amateur as well as professional championships.

In Olympic competition Hungary's performances in Greco-Roman wrestling demonstrate an edge over those in free-style wrestling. Over the years, free-style gold medals have been won in the bantamweight, lightweight and heavyweight classes, while in the Greco-Roman event which has an identical number of classes, gold medals were won in the bamtamweight, featherweight, lightweight, welterweight and heavyweight classes. Most of Hungary's Greco-Roman championships have been in the heavyweight class, with István Kozma being two-time consecutive gold medalist in 1964 and 1968.

Hungarians have always maintained a respectable record in men's gymnastics. István Pelle (b. 1907) rose to world's best on the parallel bar at the world championship of 1930. Pelle participated in three Olympic Games in 1928, 1932, and 1936, his most successful accomplishment being the Los Angeles Olympic Games of 1932 where he obtained 2 gold medals in floor exercises and pommelled horse gymnastics, along with 2 silver medals (parallel bars; combined exercises, individual), 2 fourth places (horizontal bar; combined exercises, team) and 1 sixth place (long horse vault). He is very much responsible for the country's present-day excellence in gymnastics. After World War II, Pelle emigrated to Argentina where he has been living since. In 1976 the gold medal in the pommelled horse again went to a Hungarian: Zoltán Magyar who treated judges and spectators to a performance of unique, inimitable exercises.

Prefatorially it should be pointed out that women use exclusively the foil, while men use a variety of foil, epée and sabre. Fencing seems to be one of the sports best befitting the Hungarian temperament, male and female alike. Among the greatest international amateur fencers in history are Aladár Gerevich, Pál Kovács and Rudolf Kárpáti. Aladár Gerevich (b. 1910) and Pál Kovács (b. 1912) are regarded as the best sabre fencers. Gerevich took part in six Olympic Games between 1932 and 1960 and was awarded the bronze medal in 1936, the gold in 1948 and the silver in 1952. He was a six-time member of the gold-winning team and an eleven-time member of the world champion team. Kovács participated in five Olympic Games, each time as a member of the gold medalist Hungarian team, while in 1952 he won the individual championship in Helsinki.

The title of greatest woman fencer of all time probably belongs to Ilona Elek of Hungary who was Olympic champion in 1936 and 1948 and world champion in 1934, 1935 and 1951.

The following table shows the accomplishments of the world's most successful fencers in terms of the numbers of gold medals won at Olympic and world championships:

	Individual	Team
Aladár Gerevich	4	16
Pál Kovács	3	12
Rudolf Kárpáti	4	9
Ilona Elek (women's foil)	5	8
Endre Kabos	3	6
György Jekelfalussy Piller	3	5

A 5-day contest comprising athletics, the equestrian arts, fencing, shooting and swimming, the modern pentathlon is one of the most challenging and grueling of Olympic competitions, if not the most difficult. Hungary boasts a distinguished record in this field. Hungary in the persons of Ferenc Németh (1960), Ferenc Török (1964), and András Balczó (1972) has won first place in 3 of 14 years' competition and as a team won first place on 3 occasions (1952, 1960 and 1968) out of a total of 7.

Hungarians have garnered medals in a wide variety of events in shooting, but Károly Takács (b. 1910) will long be remembered as a unique symbol of willpower combined with phenomenal talent. He was already a famous shooter when at the 1938 military exercises a hand grenade shattered his right hand. But the totally handicapped Takács doggedly pursued his training in shooting with his left hand and soon attained the excellent form enabling him to win 76 competitions between 1940 and 1944. It is moving to contemplate the monumental willpower which led Károly Takács to become Olympic champion in rapid-fire pistol (silhouette) shooting (25 meters) in London (1948) and in Helsinki (1952), setting new Olympic and world records.

Hungarian soccer teams have won many international — Central European, European, Olympic and world — championships since the thirties. For example, Hungary's Olympic team won three gold medals (1952, 1964 and 1968). Soccer players like György Sárosi and Géza Toldi — at present both are internationally recognized coaches living outside of Hungary — became legendary personalities during the interwar period. After the war, László Kubala and Ferenc Puskás along with dozens of others embodied the best traditions of soccer playing. In recent years, László Kubala has been the captain as well as coach of the Spanish national soccer team. Ferenc Puskás (b. 1927) was on the Hungarian national team eighty-four times and scored goals on eighty-three occasions. Puskás left Hungary in 1956 and joined the Real Madrid playing several times on the national selected team of Spain.

Football holds the unofficial title of America's national sport. Charlie (Károly) and Pete (Péter) Gogolak are two brothers who contributed to its history and popularity. Born in Budapest on April 18, 1942, Pete fled Hungary with his brother and their family after the 1956 Hungarian uprising. Pete graduated from Cornell University and was drafted as a kicker by the Buffalo Bills in 1964. Named All-American kicker in 1965, Pete Gogolak played AFL championship games in 1964 and 1965. He signed with the N.Y. Giants professional team in 1966 and became their top scorer in 1972 with 97 points. Charlie Gogolak was born December 29, 1944 in Rábahidvég, Hungary and graduated from Princeton University. While a place-kicker for Princeton from 1963 to 1965 he popularized the soccer-style place-kick in American football, and set 7 National Collegiate Athletic Association records. He holds the distinction of ranking 5th in the career of kickscoring with 170 points. He played with the Washington Redskins in the 1966-1968 seasons, becoming the first kicker the Redskins ever drafted on the first round.

Coaches

Hungarian coaches have immortally emblazoned their names on the honor roll of the world arena of sports in the service of their native as well as adopted homelands, especially the United States. Hungarian-born coaches have long been a part of the fabric of the American sports scene. They have helped bring America to glory as the leading medal winner in the history of the modern Olympic Games — 1896-1976. Among the earliest of them was Joseph Őszy who coached the 1936 U.S. Olympic team in men's gymnastics. All these coaches are accomplished athletes in their own right and they perpetuate the tradition of excellence by their dedication to actualizing the promise of the young American athletes in their charge.

Nicholas Tóth was born March 22, 1908 in Hungary. He was coach-trainer in the pentathlon for the 1956 U.S. Olympic team and functioned as a member of the Modern Pentathlon Committee of the United States Olympic Committee in 1968.

Sándor Ferenczy was born in Szolnok, Hungary on September 18, 1925. He was co-head coach of the 1968 and 1976 women's athletic (track and field) team for the Olympic competitions and head coach of the 1973 U.S. first junior team in Europe. He was also assistant coach of the 1970 National Amateur Athletic Union team in Europe. Testimony to Ferenczy's coaching abilities are one Olympic, 5 Pan-American and 43 National AAU championships.

Bertalan de Némethy was born in Győr, Hungary on February 24, 1911. A former Olympic rider of Hungary and former international competitor in cavalry riding, de Némethy has been chef d'équipe of the U.S. Olympic equestrian team since 1956. He has also coached the U.S. show team in the 1959, 1963, 1967, and 1975 Pan-American games, leading them to first place in the 1959 and 1963 games and second place in 1967. An instructor and permanent coach of the U.S. Equestrian Team, Bertalan de Némethy has molded such superb jumpers as Bill Steinkraus, who in 1968 became the first and only American thus far to win the Olympic gold medal for show jumping, and Kathy Kusner, who among other distinctions captured first place in the 1967 Women's European championships and second prize in the Ladies' World Championships.

Stephan Von Visy was born in Hungary on August 1, 1906. He was U.S. Olympic Equestrian Team coach for the Three-Day Event in 1964 and for the same event at the 1967 Pan-American Games.

Hungarians have established a time-honored tradition of coaching the U.S. Olympic Fencing Team, beginning with the world-famed George Santelli in 1928, 1932, 1936, 1948, and 1952, followed by Lajos Csiszár in 1956 and the current coach, Csaba Élthes from 1960 to 1976. Élthes, born in Csikszereda, Transylvania on March 10, 1912 also coached the Pan-American team in 1959, 1967, 1971 and 1975, along with the World Championship Team in 1958, 1963, 1967, 1973 and 1975. This boundlessly talented, devoted and energetic man has also been affiliated as fencing master with the New York Athletic Club, the New York Fencers' Club, Pace College in New York City and St. Peter's College in Jersey City, New Jersey.

Béla Károlyi dominated the limelight among coaches in the most recent Olympic Games in Montreal. He is the coach of the Romanian women's gymnastic team and of the 14-year-old child wonder of the 1976 Olympics: Nadia Comaneci.

The one-time brilliant player of the Hungarian Olympic water polo team, Dezső Lemhényi is coach of Canada's national water polo team.

Chess

In the light of contemporary chronicles and other sources we can trace the beginnings of chessplaying in Hungary back to the late Middle Ages. Beatrix, the wife of King Matthias I, was considered one of the best chess players in the second half of the fifteenth century. In modern times, József Szén finished fifth at the first international chess tournament arranged in London in 1851. Géza Maróczy (1870-1951) captured the title of international grand master with his victory in Hastings in 1895. Afterwards, Maróczy won first place at several international chess tournaments (in Monte Carlo in 1902 and 1904, in Munich in 1903, in Ostende in 1905, etc.). Under the leadership of Géza Maróczy the Hungarian team won gold medal at the 1927 London World Championship and defended its title in the Chess Olympics at the Hague and again took first place in the 1936 Munich World Championship. Since the end

of World War II, the Hungarian team has generally attained second
place — right behind the Soviet Union — in international chess tournaments.

Primary Sources
Books Referred to and Briefly Quoted

Antal, Zoltán, *A magyar sport kézikönyve*. Budapest: Sport, 1972.

Antal, Zoltán, *Világ-és Európa-bajnokságok, 1893-1973*. Budapest: Sport, 1974.

Benagh, Jim, *Incredible Olympic Feats*. New York: McGraw-Hill Company,
1976. For a detailed evaluation of the accomplishments of Aladár
Gerevich, Pál Kovács, Dezső Gyarmati, and László Papp, see pp. 39,
73-74, 75-76.

The Encyclopedia of Sports. 3d rev. ed. By Frank G. Menke. New York: A.S.
Barnes and Co., 1963.

Information Hungary. Editor-in-Chief Ferenc Erdei. Oxford: Pergamon Press,
1968.

Kamper, E., *Encyclopedia of the Olympic Games*. 1st ed. New York: McGraw-
Hill, 1972.

A magyar sport - The Hungarian Sport. Issued by the Hungarian Olympic Committee. Budapest, 1976. pp. 4-56.

Newsweek, August 2, 1976.

Szily, József, *Maróczy Géza élete és pályafutása*. Budapest, 1957.

U.S. Olympic Committee. *1968 Olympic Committee Book*. Published by the U.S.
Olympic Committee.

U.S. Olympic Committee. *1972 Olympic Committee Book*. Published by the U.S.
Olympic Committee.

U.S. Olympic Committee. *1976 Olympic Committee Book*. Published by the U.S.
Olympic Committee.

U.S. Olympic Committee. *U.S. Olympic Committee Quadrennial Review of Activities for the Period 1965-1969*. Presented April 18-20, 1969 at the Quadrennial Meeting of the United States Olympic Committee, Denver, Hilton
Hotel, Denver, Colorado.

Who's Who in Football. Ed. by Ronald L. Mendell, 1974.

PART VI — CONCLUSION

The preceding work based on documentary evidence and historical fact
has tried to outline the birth and growth of a nation's cultural heritage
and aspirations from its primitive stages up to the present. Quite evidently Hungarian culture has from its beginnings been many-hued, and
the core of it colored by Oriental and Western elements alike. The
decisive turning point came at the end of the tenth century when the
country's historic conversion to Western Christianity began and im-
planted the seeds of an entirely new civilization.

Neither the Tartar invasion of the thirteenth century nor the long-
lasting Turkish occupation of the sixteenth and seventeenth centuries
could deflect the course of cultural events: Hungary has undergone —
with some delay — the same stages of cultural development as Western
Europe. Although Hungarians followed Western patterns, they some-
how succeeded in preserving the basic characteristics of the contents
and forms of their ancient, original culture which are so manifest in their
folk music, folk art and folk literature.

The high level of development of statecraft in medieval Hungary
should be listed among those factors which helped evolve Hungarian
culture in the multinational Danube Valley. An early indicator of this
precocious statesmanship was King Andrew II's "Bulla Aurea". Issued
in 1222, it was preceded by the English Magna Charta of 1215 by but a
few years. Both these documents proved to be milestones in European
constitutionalism. Politics and culture already figured as interdependent
notions in the conception of Hungary's civilization, which symbiosis
has remained a fact of life since.

Due to Hungary's elastic concept of nationhood, many non-
Hungarian elements were assimilated and made important contributions
to all segments of life. These elements, once non-Hungarian by origin,
had accepted for centuries as their own the country's political and
cultural values and enriched them significantly. They even figured in the
establishment of city settlements, principally in the Danubian Basin,
which were cradles of modern civilization. In recent decades an ever-
proliferating number of published sources, in a refutation of the old
school's dogmatic views, have been instrumental in proving that not
only the Germans but also the Hungarians, Slavs, and other ethnic
elements had a hand in establishing and developing cities in East Central
Europe. It can also be convincingly proven in light of the individual
cultural histories of the area's nations that neither Germany nor any
other nation had exclusive priority in establishing Central Europe's
culture, though Germany had an indisputable role concerning the area as
a whole. In our judgment, the modus operandi in approaching this

question should involve zeroing in on significant regional differences existing within the area. Hungary's role in East Central Europe seems analogous to that Americans of English descent have played in the founding and nurturing of the North American civilization.

As a rule, during the years of foreign oppression, mathematical and natural sciences flourished greatly while historical and social sciences suffered severe setbacks. This is mirrored in the intellectual life of the sixteenth and seventeenth centuries. It is truly amazing that so many naturalists and physicians functioned in this era of the Turkish subjugation. Interestingly, German progress rather affected mathematicians and natural scientists, while French, English, and American influence can be detected mostly in the branches of the humanities. This foreign influence in the humanities can be traced from the outset of the nineteenth century when the ideals of the American Revolution began to be infused into the minds of thinkers in Central Europe.

Because so many conflicting ideals gushed into the heart of Europe under such varried circumstances and either at the same time or in rapid succession, no exclusivity can be claimed with regard to any intellectual or political trends. Anti-German feeling appeared on the scene many times in reaction to the Habsburg rule. It affected many thinkers of the past two centuries in that area. This political attitude determined even the artistic directions taken by Béla Bartók and Zoltán Kodály prior to 1918.

From the outset of history, Hungary's population has lived in a buffer zone between two conflicting worlds: the East and the West. The conversion to Christianity was, therefore, not a simple event but a process lasting for several centuries. But by the time the country and its population fell under the control of the Ottoman Empire for one and a half centuries after the Battle of Mohács in 1526, Hungary had already been firmly attached to the sphere of Occidental civilization and sloughed off any effects of Islamic culture on the intellect of the local population. This immunity stemmed from two main factors: (1) the strength of the local spirit fortified by centuries-old Western traditions and (2) the indifference of the Islamic Turks who for all their religious beliefs were not interested in the conversion of Christian nations. Thus the Turkish rule left the souls of the Hungarian people essentially untouched and now only a few Turkish loanwords remind us of those otherwise intolerable years. Following liberation from the Turkish yoke, Western trends and principles — first and above all the French and American cultures — were gradually instilled into the minds of intellectuals in nineteenth-century Hungary. These fertile years mark the beginning of Hungary's systematic and well-planned contributions to world civilization. According to data available on the history of cultural exchange, the United States has been one of the principal beneficiaries of Hungarian efforts. As we pointed out earlier, this cultural contribution commenced in December 1832 when a fruitful relationship was established between the Hungarian Academy of Sciences and the American Philosophical Society of Philadelphia. Since then, thousands of Hungarian scientists, scholars, artists and sportsmen have rendered their services in all phases of America's cultural and intellectual life. It is well known that after the events of October 1956 more than fifteen hundred Hungarian university and college graduates arrived in the United States. (According to a reliable source, about the same number of physicians are practicing or are engaged in research work in North America.) Besides these, several hundred well-educated artists and sportsmen now work and make their homes outside of Hungary on five continents, most of them in the United States.

It had never before happened that the Hungarian cultural elite made simultaneous contributions to two conflicting spheres of civilization. While official Hungary is implementing the Marxism-Leninism-based socialist culture, its intellectuals outside of the Soviet orbit are positively strengthening their Occidental heritage. One question arises from this ambivalent state of cultural affairs and awaits an appropriate answer: namely, how this supposed duplicity of thought can or will affect Hungarian and world civilization as a whole. The world's intellectual picture also reflects this dilemma to a never-before-occurring intensity.

There are some reliable symptoms enabling us to arrive at our earlier diagnosis concerning the state of cultural affairs in East-West relations. It is an undeniable fact that the more liberal wing, up to now at least, has triumphed over the extreme dogmatism of the Soviet world. The rising number of dissidents seems to be a concomitant phenomenon of this slowly changing situation. But it would be a mistake to draw far-reaching conclusions and to envision the twilight of their yet unfinished civilization . . . reality forbids it. The international exchange of ideas is a two-way street. Consequently, visitors can take a close-up look at the Western world and become thoroughly acquainted with at least two shortcomings of Western civilization: its rapidly declining morality and the conspicuous lack of initiatives in handling international affairs. Both phenomena have stirred great disillusionment in the minds of a significant part of Eastern European intellectuals. Both phenomena are rapidly extinguishing the belief in the supremacy of the Western world that was once their ideal. And there are only a few remnants from their past beliefs which are still capable of kindling their enthusiasm: above all, American superiority in technology, and the concept of liberty.

All these circumstances set the stage for the intellectual activities of creative Hungarians at home and abroad alike. In this fast-changing world they seem to be in the mainstream of mankind's universal thinking by favoring a development of an anthropocentric civilization in which basic research will command its proper place and the currently exaggerated appetite for material well-being won't stand as the unchallenged alpha and omega of the scale of human values.

PART VII — SELECTED BIBLIOGRAPHY

Ábrahám, G., "Bartók and England." *Studia Musicologica Acad. Sc. Hung.*, vol. 5, nos. 1-4, 1963.

Adams, W.H.D., *"In perils oft"*: *romantic biographies*. New York, 1886.

Aggházy, M., *Early wood carvings in Hungary*. Budapest: Akadémiai Kiadó, 1965.

Albert, G., "Selected bibliography of Shakespeare's works published in Hungarian." *The New Hungarian Quarterly*, vol. 5, no. 13, 1964.

Az alföldi festészet kérdései. Hódmezővásárhely: Tudományos Ismeretterjesztő Társulat Csongrád Megyei Szervezete, 1960.

Allodiatoris, I., "Frivaldszky Imre." *Élővilág*, no. 6, 1963.

Allodiatoris, I., "Herman Ottó." *Élővilág*, no. 3, 1964.

Andritsch, J., ed., *Ungarische Geisteswelt, von der Landnahme bis Babits*. Gütersloh: Bertelsmann Lesering, 1960.

Antal, Z., *Alberttől Zsákig*. Budapest: Sport, 1968.

Antal, Z., *A magyar sport kézikönyve*. 2d rev. ed. Budapest: Sport, 1972.

Antal, Z., *Világ- és Európa-bajnokságok, 1893-1973*. Budapest: Sport, 1974.

Apponyi, S., *Hungarica*. Ungarn betreffende im Auslande gedruckte Bücher und Flugschriften. München: J. Rosenthal, 1903-1927. 4 vols.

Argan, G.C., *Marcel Breuer, disegno industriale e architettura*. Milano: Görlich, 1957.

Asbóth, O., *Az első helikopter*. Budapest: Népszava, 1965.

Asboth, O., *Géprepülés*. Budapest: Zrínyi Kiadó, 1957.

Ashbrook, J., "The reputation of Father Hell." *Sky and Telescope*, vol. 21, no. 4, 1961.

Babits, M., *Geschichte der europäischen Literatur*. Tr. of *Az európai irodalom története*. Zürich: Europa Verlag, 1949.

Bako, E., *Guide to Hungarian studies*. Stanford, California: Hoover Institution Press, 1973. 2 vols.

Baktay, E., *Kőrösi Csoma Sándor*. Budapest: Gondolat, 1962.

Balázs, B., *A távíró és távbeszélő története*. Budapest, 1952.

Balázs, E.H., *Berzeviczy Gergely a reformpolitikus, 1763-1795*. Budapest, 1967.

Ballagi, G., *A politikai irodalom Magyarországon 1825-ig*. Budapest: Franklin Társulat, 1888.

Ballér, E., *Elmélet és gyakorlat egysége Nagy László munkásságában*. Budapest: Tankönyvkiadó, 1970.

Barande, I., *Sándor Ferenczi*. Paris: Payot, 1972.

Baranyai, E., *Nagy László munkásságának neveléstudományi eredményei*. Budapest, 1932.

Bárczi, G., "The Hungarian language." *The New Hungarian Quarterly*, vol. 4, no. 12, 1963.

Barlai, K., "Kövesligethy Radó." *Élet és Tudomány*, no. 6, 1955.

Bán, I., "Szepsi Csombor Párizsban." *Irodalomtörténeti Közlemények*, 1956.

Banner, J., "A magyar őskorkutatás történetéhez." In: *A Herman Ottó Múzeum Évkönyve*, Miskolc, 1958.

"*Bauhaus*" szám. Editor: Antal Kampis. Budapest: Múzeumok Központi Propaganda Irodája, 1963.

Bayer, J., *A nemzeti játékszin története*. Budapest: Hornyánszky Viktor, 1887. 2 vols.

Benagh, J., *Incredible Olympic feats*. New York: McGraw-Hill, 1976.

SELECTED BIBLIOGRAPHY

Bencze. J., "Hutÿra Ferenc." *Orvosi Hetilap*, no. 52, 1964.
Bendefy, L., *Magyar utazók Afrikában*. Budapest, 1934.
Benedek, I., *Semmelweis és kora*. Budapest: Gondolat, 1967.
Berényi, Gy., "Hungarians on foreign scholarships." *The New Hungarian Quarterly*, vol. 7, no. 21, 1966.
Berkovits, I., *Illuminated manuscripts from the library of Matthias Corvinus*. Budapest: Corvina, 1963.
Bessenyei, A.-Molnár, I., "The reconstruction of the Polytechnical University and the scientific and technical work of its instructors after the liberation, 1945-1948." *Periodica Polytechnica, Engineering*, vol. 7, no. 1, 1963.
Blake, P., *Marcel Breuer, architect and designer*. New York, 1949.
Boda, M.P., "Péch Antal." *Élet és Tudomány*, no. 23, 1960.
Bóka, L., *Tegnaptól máig*. Budapest, 1958.
Bókay, J., *Die Geschichte der Kinderheilkunde*. Berlin: Springer, 1922.
Bolyai, F. - Bolyai, J., *Bolyai-levelek*. Válogatta, a bevezető tanulmányt írta, és a jegyzeteket összeállította Benkő Samu. Bukarest: Kriterion, 1975.
Boncz, K. - Gink, K., *Herend China*. Budapest: Pannonia Press, 1962.
Bonola, R., *Non-Euclidean geometry; a critical and historical study of its developments* . . . New York: Dover Publications, 1955.
Borbándi, Gy., *Der ungarische Populismus*. Mainz: v. Hase & Koehler, 1976.
Boros, A., "Professeur I. Győrffy." *Revue Bryologique et Lichénologique*, 1959.
Boros, I., "Földi János és az első magyar állattan." *A Magyar Tudományos Akadémia Biológiai Osztályának Közleményei*, 1952.
Borsody-Bevilaqua, B., *Régi magyar világjárók*. Budapest: Művelt Nép Kiadó, 1954.
Borsos, B., *Glassmaking in old Hungary*. Budapest: Corvina, 1963.
Boskovits, M. - Mojzer, M., Mucsi, A., *Das Christliche Museum von Esztergom*. Budapest: Verlag der Ungarischen Akademie der Wissenschaften, 1964.
Bradford, G., *The history and analysis of the supposed automaton chess player of M. de Kempelen, now exhibiting in this country by Mr. Maelzel; with lithographic figures, illustrative of the probable method by which its motions are directed*. Boston: Hilliard, Gray, 1826.
Breuer, M., *Sun and shadow, the philosophy of an architect*. New York: Dodd, Mead, 1955.
British Olympic Association. *Official report of the Olympic Games 1972: XXth Olympiad*, Munich, August 26-September 11 . . . London: Sportsworld, 1973.
Brück, A., *Vasarely-Analysen; Methoden, Ziele und Möglichkeiten zeitgenössischer Kunstbetrachtung*. Hamburg, 1970.
Budapest. Műszaki Egyetem. Gépészmérnöki Kar. *A Budapesti Műszaki Egyetem Gépészmérnöki Karának centenáriumi emlékkönyve, 1871-1971*. Editor: József Varga. Budapest, 1971.
A Budapesti Műszaki Egyetem oktatóinak tudományos és műszaki alkotásai. Budapest, 1952.
Carbonara, C., "Akos von Pauler e logica della filosofia dei valori." *Logos*, vol. 3, 1931.
Carbonara, C., *Saggi di storiografia e critica filosofica*. Napoli: Libreria scientifica editrice, 1972. 2 vols.
Cholnoky, J., "Lóczy Lajos." *Földrajzi Közlemények*, 1920.
Cholnoky, J., "Teleki Pál gróf." *Földrajzi Közlemények*, 1939.
Cholnoky, J., *Teleki Sámuel útja Kelet-Afrikában*. Budapest, 1937.
Clark, W.R., *Explorers of the world*. Garden City, N.Y.: The Natural History Press, 1964.

215

Corradini, D., *Karl Mannheim*. Milano: Giuffre, 1967.
Cotel, E., "Kerpely Antal hatása a vaskohászati tudományokra és a magyar vaskohászat fejlődésére." *Magyar Tudományos Akadémia Matem. és Term. tud. Értesítő*, 1937.
Csillag, I., "The first Hungarian textbook of surgery — 200 years old." *Acta Chirurgica Acad. Sci. Hung.*, vol. 4, no. 1, 1963.
Csók, I., *Emlékezéseim*. Budapest, 1945.
Csonka, P., "Csonka János élete és munkássága." *A Magyar Tudományos Akadémia Műszaki Osztályának Közleményei*, nos. 1-4, 1960.
Cwierawa, G.K., "Ányos Jedlik — wegierski pioner elektrotechniki." *Kwartalnik Historiki Nauk i Techniki*, no. 2, 1971.
Czigány, L., *A magyar irodalom fogadtatása a viktoriánus Angliában, 1830-1914*. Budapest: Akadémiai Kiadó, 1976.
Czigány, M., *Hungarian literature in English translation published in Great Britain, 1830-1968; a bibliography*. London: Szepsi Csombor Literary Circle, 1969.
De Forest, I., *The leaven of love; a development of the psychoanalytic theory and technique of Sándor Ferenczi*. Hamden, Conn., Atchon Books, 1965.
Deák, P., "The development of radiological institutes in Hungary." *Medicor News*, no. 5, 1964.
Demeter, T., *Magyar szépirodalom idegen nyelven. Hungarian literature in foreign languages*. Budapest, 1957 — Multivolume set.
Dénes, I.Z., *A realitás illúziója; a historikus Szekfű Gyula pályafordulója*. Budapest: Akadémiai Kiadó, 1976.
Dercsényi, D., *Kunstführer durch Ungarn*. Budapest: Corvina Verlag, 1974.
Destouches, L.F., *Semmelweis, 1818-1865*. Paris: Gallimard, 1952.
Dewasne, J., *Vasarely*. Paris, 1952.
Diccionario de filosofia contemporánea. Dirigido por Miguel A. Quintanilla. Salamanca: Sigueme, 1976.
Dictionnaire universel de la peinture. Paris: S.N.L.-Dictionnaire Robert, 1975. 6 vols.
Diehl, G., *Vasarely*. Tr. from the French. New York, 1972.
Dienes, I., *A honfoglaló magyarok*. Budapest: Corvina Kiadó, 1974.
Divald, K., *Old Hungarian art*. London, 1931.
Dizionario di filosofia: 2500 voci, 700 bibliografie, tavole cronologiche. 1st ed. Milano: Rizzoli, 1976.
Domanovszky, S., *ed., Magyar művelődéstörténet*. Budapest: Magyar Történelmi Társulat, 1942. 5 vols.
Duczynszka, I., *ed., The plough and the pen; writings from Hungary, 1930-1956*. Edited by Ilona Duczynszka and Karl Polanyi. With a foreword by W.H. Auden. London: P. Owen, 1963.
Duka, T., *Life and works of Alexander Csoma de Kőrös*. New Delhi: Manjusri Pub. House, 1972.
Eckhardt, S., *A francia forradalom eszméi Magyarországon*. Budapest, 1925.
Ecrivains hongrois d' aujourd'hui. Paris: Julliard, 1964.
Edwards, P., *ed., The encyclopedia of philosophy*. New York, 1967. 8 vols.
Ember, M., *Hungarian domestic embroidery*. Budapest: Corvina, 1963.
Eősze, L., *Zoltán Kodály: his life and work*. London: Collet's, 1962.
Erményi, L., *Petzval József élete és érdemei*. Budapest: Mathematikai és Physikai Társulat, 1906.
Evans, H.R., *Edgar Allan Poe and Baron von Kempelen's chess-playing automaton*. Kenton, O.: International Brotherhood of Magicians, 1939.
Fábián, E., *Apáczai Csere János*. Kolozsvár-Napoca: Dacia, 1975.

Faller, J., *A magyar bányagépesítés úttörői a XVIII. században. Hell Máté Kornél és Hell József Károly főgépmesterek élete és munkássága*. Budapest: Akadémiai Kiadó, 1953.

Farkas, J., ed., *Ungarns Geschichte und Kultur in Dokumenten*. Wiesbaden: O. Harrassowitz, 1955.

Farkas, Z., *Csók István*. Budapest, 1957.

Fehér, Zs.D., *Magyar festészet a XX. században*. Ö.G. Pogány, joint author. Budapest: Corvina, 1971.

Fekete, J. — Mikola, S., *Eötvös Loránd élete és munkássága*. Budapest, 1918.

Fekete, S., "Semmelweis as seen by his contemporaries and the posterity." *Therapia Hungarica, Hung. Med. J.*, vol. 13, no. 4, 1965.

Fél, E., *Hungarian peasant embroidery*. London: B.T. Batsford, 1961.

Fél, E. — Hofer, T., *Saints, soldiers, shepherds; the human figure in Hungarian folk art*. Budapest: Corvina Press, 1966.

Fél, E. — Hofer, T. — Csilléry, K., *Hungarian peasant art*. Budapest: Corvina, 1958.

Felvinczi Takáts, Z., "Dr. Baktay Ervin." *Művészettörténeti Értesítő*, no. 1, 1964.

Ferenczi, Z., *List of the translations of Jókai's works into foreign languages*. Budapest: R.T. Kiadása, 1926.

Film kislexikon. Edited by Péter Ábel. Budapest: Akadémiai Kiadó, 1964.

Fitz, J., *A magyar nyomdászat, könyvkiadás és könyvkereskedelem története*. Budapest: Akadémiai Kiadó, 1957-1967. 2 vols.

Fitz, J. — Kéki, B., *A magyar könyv története*. Budapest: Magyar Helikon, 1959.

Fodor, F., *Balla Antal élete és műszaki munkássága, 1739-1815*. Budapest, 1953.

Földes, B., "Kautz Gyula." (*Magyar Tudományos Akadémia Emlékbeszédek*, XV. Budapest, 1911)

Földvári, F., "Nékám Lajos." *Bőrgyógyászati és Venerológiai Szemle*, no. 2, 1967.

Fröhlich, I., ed., *Eötvös-emlékkönyv*. Budapest, 1930.

Gaál, J., *Berzeviczy Gergely élete és művei*. Budapest, 1902.

Gabriel, A.L., *Garlandia. Studies in the history of the mediaeval university*. Frankfurt a.M.: Knecht, 1969.

Gabriel A.L., *The mediaeval universities of Pécs and Pozsony; commemoration of the 500th and 600th anniversary of their foundation, 1367-1467-1967*. Notre Dame, Ind.: Mediaeval Institutte, University of Notre Dame, 1969.

Gádor, E. — Pogány, Ö.G., *Hungarian sculpture*. Budapest: Corvina, 1955.

Gál, I., *Angol-magyar történelmi kapcsolatok*. Budapest: Magyar Királyi Állami Nyomda, 1942.

Gál, I., *Babits és az angol irodalom*. Debrecen, 1942.

Gál, I., *Bartóktól Radnótiig*. Budapest: Magvető Kiadó, 1973.

Gál, I., *Magyarország, Anglia és Amerika, különös tekintettel a szláv világra; vázlatok a nemzetközi vonatkozások köréből*. Budapest: Officina, 1944.

Gál, I., ed., *Magyarország és Keleteurópa, a magyarság kapcsolatai a szomszédnépekkel*. Budapest: Officina, 1947.

Galla, E., *Világjáró magyar irodalom; a magyar irodalom Kínában*. Budapest: Akadémiai Kiadó, 1968.

Gauss, K.Fr., *Briefwechsel Carl Friedrich Gauss und Wolfgang Bolyai . . .* Leipzig: B.G. Teubner, 1899. (New York: Johnson Reprint Corp., 1972).

Genthon, I., ed., *Magyarország művészeti emlékei*. Budapest: Képzőművészeti Alap Kiadóvállalata, 1959-1961. 3 vols.

Genthon, I., *A régi magyar festőművészet*. Vác: Pestvidéki Nyomda, 1932.

Gerevich, T., *Magyarország románkori emlékei*. Budapest: Műemlékek Országos Bizottsága, 1938.

Gerézdi, R., *Janus Pannoniustól Balassi Bálintig; tanulmányok*. Budapest: Akadémiai Kiadó, 1968.

Gergely, E.J., *Hungarian drama in New York; American adaptations, 1908-1940*. Philadelphia: University of Pennsylvania Press, 1947.

Gerő, L., "Hungarian architecture through the ages." *The New Hungarian Quarterly*, vol. 4, April/June, 1963.

Gershkovich, A.A., *Sovremennyi vengerskii teatr*. Moskva: Izd-vo Akademii Nauk SSSR, 1963,

Gömöri, B., "Hetényi Géza." *Magyar Tudomány*, no. 4, 1959.

Gohér, M., "100 éve született Bláthy." *Elektrotechnika*, 1960.

Gombocz, E., *A magyar botanika története*. Budapest, 1936.

Gombosi, O., *Bakfark Bálint élete és művei, 1507-1576*. Budapest: Országos Széchényi Könyvtár, 1935.

Gortvay, Gy., *Semmelweis élete és munkássága*. Imre Zoltán, joint author. Budapest: Akadémiai Kiadó, 1966.

Gulya, J., "Some XVIII. century antecedents of the XIX. century linguistics." *Acta Linguistica Acad. Sc. Hung.*, vol. 15, nos. 1-2, 1965.

Gulyás, P., *Magyar írók élete és munkái*. Budapest: Magyar Könyvtárosok és Levéltárosok Egyesülete, 1939-1944. 6 vols.

Gyárfás, M. — Hont, F., eds., *Nagy magyar színészek*. Budapest: Bibliotheca, 1957.

Hajduska, I., *Tudósok közelről: ötven magyar akadémikus portréja*. Budapest, 1975.

Hajós, K., "Korányi Frigyes és kora." *Országos Orvostörténeti Könyvtár Közleményei*, no. 29, 1963.

Halász, Gy., *Öt világrész magyar vándorai; magyar felfedezők Benyovszkytól napjainkig*. Budapest: Grill K., 1936.

Halász, Z., *Cultural life in Hungary*. Budapest: Pannonia Press, 1966.

Halász, Z., *Romvárosok a sivatagban; Stein Aurél belső-ázsiai utazásai*. Budapest, 1966.

Halasy-Nagy, J., *Pauler Ákos, 1876-1933*. Budapest, 1933.

Halmai, J., "Winkler Lajos." *Orvosi Hetilap*, no. 26, 1963.

Hanák, T., *Die marxistische Philosophie und Soziologie in Ungarn*. 1st ed. Stuttgart: Enke, 1976.

Hankiss, J., comp., *Anthologie de la prose hongroise*. Lipót Molnos, joint comp. Paris: Éditions du Sagittaire, 1938.

Hankiss, J., *A magyar géniusz*. Budapest, 1941.

Hankó, V., "A legnagyobb magyar borkémikus (Preysz Mór)." *Borászati Lapok*, 1908.

Haranghy, L., *Semmelweis betegsége. Die Krankheit von Semmelweis*. In Hungarian and German. Budapest: Medicina Könyvkiadó, 1965.

Haraszthy, Á., *Grape culture, wines, and wine-making. With notes upon agriculture and horticulture*. New York: Harper, 1862.

Haraszthy, Á., *Utazás Éjszakamerikában*. 2d ed. Pest: Heckenast G., 1850. 2 vols.

Haraszti, E., "Hungary and the Great Exhibition in 1851." *The New Hungarian Quarterly*, vol. 3, no. 5, 1962.

Harmatta, J., "Baktay Ervin, 1890-1963." *Antik Tanulmányok*, nos. 3-4, 1964.

Héberger, K., *The Hungarian higher education*. Budapest: Tankönyvkiadó, 1966.

Herland, L.J., *Dictionary of mathematical sciences*. London: Harrap, 1966. 2 vols.

Hetényi, G., "Megemlékezés Korányi Sándorról." *Magyar Tudományos Akadémia Orvostudományi Osztályának Közleményei*, no. 1, 1950.

A hetvenötéves magyar Állami Operaház, 1884-1959. Budapest: Révai-nyomda, 1959.

Historical Periodicals: An annotated world list of historical and related serial publications. Editors: Eric H. Boehm and Lalit Adolphus. Santa Barbara, California — Munich, Germany, 1961. (Hungary, pp. 253-263.)

Höhnel, L., *Discovery of Lakes Rudolf and Stefanie; a narrative of Count Sámuel Teleki's exploring & hunting expedition in eastern equatorial Africa in 1887 & 1888*. London: Longmans, Green and Co. 1894. 2 vols.

Höhnel, L., *Count Teleki and the discovery of Lakes Rudolf and Stefanie*. London: Macmillan, 1960. (Early travelers in East Africa)

Hóman, B., *ed.*, *A magyar történetírás új útjai*. Budapest: Magyar Szemle Társaság, 1931.

Horecky, P.L.,*ed.*, *East Central Europe; a guide to basic publications*. Chicago & London: The University of Chicago Press, 1969. (Hungary: pp. 443-598)

Horváth, G., "Emlékbeszéd Frivaldszky Jánosról." *Akadémiai Értesítő*, VIII, 1897.

Hungarian decorative folk art. Compiled by experts of the Hungarian Ethnographical Museum. Budapest: Corvina, 1954.

Hungarian geographers. Pécs: Magyar Földrajzi Társaság Déldunántúli Osztálya, 1971.

Hunter, Sir W.W., *The India of the queen, and other essays*. (Sándor Kőrösi Csoma). London, New York and Bombay: Longmans, Green and Co., 1903.

Huszti, J., *Janus Pannonius*. Pécs, 1931.

Idegen nyelven megjelent magyar szépirodalmi művek listája 1962-1967 között. Budapest: Magyar Írók Szövetsége, 1968.

Information Hungary. Editor-in-Chief Ferenc Erdei. Oxford: Pergamon Press, 1968.

Jakucs, I., "Segner Antal." *Fizikai Szemle*, 1955.

Jávorka, S., *Kitaibel Pál*. Budapest, 1937.

Jedding, H., *Europäisches Porzellan*. 2d ed. München: Keyser, 1974.

Jordán, K., *Chapters on the classical calculus of probability*. With a short biography by B. Gyires. Budapest: Akadémiai Kiadó, 1972.

Kamper, E., *Encyclopedia of the Olympic Games*. 1st ed. New York: McGraw-Hill, 1972.

Kampis, A., *The history of art in Hungary*. Tr. of *A magyar művészet története*. London: Collets, 1967.

Kampis, A.,*A magyar művészet a XIX. és a XX. században*. Budapest: Minerva, 1968.

Kalocsay, K., *comp.*, *Hungara antologio* (Esperanto). Budapest: Literatura mondo, 1933.

Kara, Gy.,*Kőrösi Csoma Sándor*. Budapest: Akadémiai Kiadó, 1970.

Kemény, F., *ed.*, *Magyar pedagógiai lexikon*. A Magyar Pedagógiai Társaság megbízásából, Fináczy Ernő és Kornis Gyula közreműködésével. Budapest: Révai, 1933-36. 2 vols.

Kende, G.,*Magyarok Amerikában. Az amerikai magyarság története*. Cleveland: Szabadság, 1927-1928. 2 vols.

Kertész, J., "Teleki Pál gróf tudományos munkásságának repertóriuma." *Magyar Közigazgatás*, 1942.

Ki Kicsoda? *Életrajzi lexikon magyar és külföldi személyiségekről, kortársainkról*. Budapest: Kossuth Könyvkiadó, 1972.

Kirke-Rose, T., *The metallurgy of gold*. London, 1906.
Kismarty-Lechner, J., *Ödön Lechner*. Budapest, 1961.
Klaniczay, T., *History of Hungarian literature*. József Szauder and Miklós
Szabolcsi, joint authors. London: Collet's, 1964.
Koch, S., *A magyar ásványtan története*. Budapest, 1952.
Konnyu, L., *Xántus János geográfus Amerikában, 1851-1864*. St. Louis:
Amerikai Magyar Szemle, 1975.
Kornis, Gy., *Education in Hungary*. New York: Teachers College, Columbia
University, 1932.
Kornis, Gy., *Hungary and European civilization*. Budapest: Royal Hungarian
University Press, 1938.
Kornis, Gy., *A magyar philosóphia fejlődése és az Akadémia*. Budapest: Magyar
Tudományos Akadémia, 1926.
Kornis, Gy., *Új magyar filozófiai rendszer*. (Ákos Pauler). Budapest, 1922.
Kósa, L., *Apáról fiúra: néprajzi kalauz*. Budapest: Móra Könyvkiadó, 1975.
Kovalovszky, M., *Gombocz Zoltán*. Budapest, 1955.
Kreitner, G., *Im fernen Osten. Reisen des Grafen Béla Széchenyi in Indien, Japan,
China, Tibet und Birma*. Wien: A. Hölder, 1881.
Küssner, H., "Probleme des Hubschraubers. Bericht der Aerodinamischen
Versuchsanstalt Göttingen." *Luftfahrtforschung*, 1937.
Kun, A., *Tudod-e mit köszönhet a világ a magyarságnak?* Budapest: Magyarok
Világkongresszusa Állandó Szervezeti Irodája, 1935.
Kunst, J., *Ethnomusicology; a study of its nature, its problems, methods and
representative personalities to which is added a bibliography*. The Hague:
Martinus Nijhoff, 1974.
Lamatsch, S., *Kempelen Farkas két ismeretlen kéziratkötete a Fővárosi
Könyvtárban* . . . Budapest: Budapest Székesföváros Házinyomdája,
1938.
Launonen, H., *Hirvipoika: tutkielma Unkarin kirjallisuusesta*. (S. Petőfi, Ferenc
Juhász, György Lukács). Helsinki, 1976.
Lázár, B., *Mányoki Ádám élete és művészete*. Budapest, 1933.
Legány, D., ed., *A magyar zene krónikája; zenei művelődésünk ezer éve
dokumentumokban*. Budapest: Zeneműkiadó, 1962.
Lengyel, B., "Schulek Elemér." *Felsőoktatási Szemle*, no. 12, 1964.
Lesky, E., *Ignaz Philipp Semmelweis und die Wiener Medizinische Schule*. Wien,
1964.
Levenson, C.B., *Jeune cinéma hongrois*. Lyon, 1966.
Levi, H., "George de Hevesy." *Nuclear Physics*, no. 1, 1967.
Libby, B., *Stars of the Olympics*. New York: Hawthorn Books, 1975.
Ligeti, L., ed., *A magyar tudomány tíz éve, 1945-1955*. Budapest: Akadémiai
Kiadó, 1955.
Livanova, A.M., *Tri sudby*. (János Bolyai). Moskva, 1969.
Locka, A., "Than Károly." *Magyar Kémiai Lapok*, no. 4, 1960.
Lóczy, L., *A khinai birodalom természeti viszonyainak és országainak leirása, Gróf
Széchenyi Béla keletázsiai utazása alatt, 1877-1880*. Budapest, 1886.
Lóczy, L., "Széchenyi Béla." *Magyar Tudományos Akadémia Emlékbeszédek*,
XVIII.
Lósy-Schmidt, E., "Verancsics Fausztuszról és Machinae Novae című
munkájáról." *Magyar Mérnök- és Építész Egyl. Közl.*, 1925.
Lyka, K., *Nagy magyar művészek*. Budapest: Gondolat Kiadó, 1957.
Lyka, K., *Nemzeti romantika; magyar művészet, 1850-1867*. Budapest: Singer és
Wolfner, 1942.

Madarassy, L., *Művészkedő magyar pásztorok*. Budapest: Magyar Könyvbarátok, 193-?

Madarászné Zsigmond, A., *A tiszta logika alapkérdései: Pauler Ákos logikája*. Budapest, 1965.

Madden, H.M., *Xántus, Hungarian naturalist in the pioneer West*. Linz, Austria, 1949.

Magyar, B., *A magyar némafilm története, 1896-1918*. Budapest, 1966.

Magyar, M., *Ungarn-Hungary-La Hongrie. A selection of works about Hungary in 20 different languages*. Budapest: Verlag von B. Kemény, 1931.

Magyar életrajzi lexikon. Editor-in-Chief Ágnes Kenyeres. Budapest: Akadémiai Kiadó, 1968. 2 vols.

Magyar Nemzeti Bibliográfia. Bibliographia Hungarica. 1946- monthly, 1961-semimonthly. Budapest: Országos Széchényi Könyvtár.

A magyar nyelvjárások atlaszának elméleti-módszertani kérdései. Edited by László Deme and Samu Imre. Budapest: Akadémiai Kiadó, 1975.

Magyar Tudományos Akadémia. Történettudományi Intézet. *Magyar történeti bibliográfia, 1825-1867*. Budapest: Akadémiai Kiadó, 1950-1959. 4 vols.

Magyar Tudományos Akadémia. Történettudományi Intézet. *A magyar történettudomány válogatott bibliográfiája, 1945-1968*. Budapest: Akadémiai Kiadó, 1971.

Magyarok az olimpiákon, 1896-1972. Compiled by Andor Szécsi. Budapest: Sportpropaganda, 1972.

A magyarországi művészet története. Editor-in-Chief Lajos Fülep; editors: Dezső Dercsényi, Anna Zádor. 5th ed. Budapest: Corvina, 1970. 2 vols.

Major, M., *Geschichte der Architektur*. Tr. of *Építészettörténet*. Berlin: Henschelverlag, 1957-1960. 3 vols.

Malonyay, D., *A magyar nép művészete*. Budapest: Franklin-Társulat, 1907-1922. 5 vols.

Manninger, R., "Hutÿra Ferenc emlékezete." *Magyar Tudományos Akadémia Emlékbeszédek*, 1944.

Maucha, R., "In memoriam József Gelei." *Acta Biologica*, no. 5, 1954.

Mező, F., *Golden Book of Hungarian Olympic Champions*. Budapest: Sport Lap- és Könyvkiadó, 1955.

Mikó, I., *Benkő József élete és munkái*. Pest, 1867.

Miska, J., comp., *The sound of time; anthology of Canadian-Hungarian authors*. Lethbridge, Alta., Canadian-Hungarian Authors' Association, 1974.

Miskolczy, D., *Schaffer Károly*. Budapest: Akadémiai Kiadó, 1973. (A mult magyar tudósai)

Mockmore, Ch.A. — Merryfield, F., *The Bánki Water-turbine*. Corwallis: Oregon State College, 1949.

Monory, E., "Shakespeare's two centuries on the Hungarian stage." *The New Hungarian Quarterly*, vol. 5, no. 13, 1964.

Móra, L., *Zemplén Géza, a hazai tudományos szerves kémia megalapítója, 1883-1956*. Budapest, 1971.

Művészeti lexikon. Editor-in-Chief Anna Zádor, István Genthon. Budapest: Akadémiai Kiadó, 1965-68. 4 vols.

Nagy, I., *Öt világrész magyarsága*. Budapest: Magyar Szemle Társaság, 1935.

Nékám, L., *The cultural aspirations of Hungary from 896 to 1935*. Budapest, 1935.

Nemeskürty, I., comp., *A film ma*. Budapest: Gondolat, 1971.

Nemeskürty, I., *Word and image; history of the Hungarian cinema*. Tr. of *A magyar film története*. Budapest: Corvina Press, 1968.

Németh, E., *Les recherches hydrologiques en Hongrie, 1963-1966*. Budapest: Akadémiai Kiadó, 1967.

Németh, Gy., *Kőrösi Csoma Sándor célja*. Budapest: Magyar Tudományos Akadémia, 1935.

New dictionary of modern sculpture. General editor: Robert Maillard. Tr. from the French. New York: Tudor Pub. Co., 1971.

The New York Times dictionary of the theater. New York: Arno Press, 1973.

A Nobeldíjasok kislexikona. Budapest, 1974.

Nobelstiftelsen, Stockholm. *Nobel, the man and his prizes*. New York: American Elsevier Pub. Co., 1972.

Nobelstiftelsen, Stockholm. *Physics*. Amsterdam, New York, Published for the Nobel Foundation by Elsevier Pub. Co., 1964-72. 4 vols.

Nobelstiftelsen, Stockholm. *Physiology or medicine*. Amsterdam, New York, Published for the Nobel Foundation by Elsevier Pub. Co., 1964-1972.

Nouvelles hongroises; anthologie des XIXe et XXe siècles. Paris: Seghers, 1961.

Novobátzky, K., *A fizikai megismerés úttörői*. Budapest, 1959.

Oltay, K., *Genauigkeit der Lotabweichungsbestimmungen mit der Eötvös-schen Drehwage*. Budapest, 1927.

O'Reilly, M.J., "Science exhibits at the Vienna Exhibition. The battery of Dr. Jedlik, professor of physics in the University of Pesth." *Engineering*, 1873. pp. 365-366.

Országos Széchényi Könyvtár. Könyvtártudományi és Módszertani Központ. *Kiemelt szerzők az Országos Széchényi Könyvtár olvasói betürendes katalógusában*. Budapest: Népművelési Propaganda Iroda, 1974.

Ortutay, Gy., *Magyar népművészet*. Budapest: Franklin Társulat, 1942. 2 vols.

Pachner, Fr., *Za zhizn materei; tragedia zhizni I.F. Semmelweisa*. Tr. from the Czech. Moskva: Izd-vo Med. lit-ry, 1963.

Pataky, D., *Hungarian drawings and water-colours*. Budapest: Corvina, 1961.

Patakyné Brestyánszky, I., *Modern Hungarian ceramics*. Budapest: Corvina, 1961.

Pevsner, N., *A dictionary of architecture*. London: Penguin Books, 1975.

Pécsi, M. — Sárfalvi, B., *The geography of Hungary*. London: Collet's, in cooperation with Corvina Press, Budapest, 1964.

Pictura Hungarica. Hungarian panel painting today. Compiled by Tibor Szántó. Budapest: Magyar Helikon, 1971-

Podach, E. Fr., *Ignaz Philipp Semmelweis*. Berlin: Volk und Wissen, 1947.

Pogány, Ö.G., *Hungarian painting in the 19th century*. Budapest: Corvina, 1960.

Pogány, Ö.G., *Hungarian painting in the 20th century*. Budapest: Corvina, 1960.

Polinszky, K., "Emlékezés Varga Józsefre." *Magyar Tudomány*, 1957.

Poljak, L., ed., *Festschrift Leopold Szondi*. Bern: H. Huber, 1963.

Prahács, M., *Magyar témák a külföldi zenében*. Budapest: Pázmány Péter Tudományegyetem Magyarságtudományi Intézete, 1943.

Pukánszkyné Kádár, J., *A Nemzeti Színház százéves története*. Budapest: Magyar Történelmi Társulat, 1938-1940. 2 vols.

Que deram os húngaros ao mundo ? Sao Paulo, 1954.

Rácz, I., "A gyorstávíró úttörője." *Telefon*, March 30, 1965.

Radisics, E., ed., *Hungary; pictorial record of a thousand years*. Budapest: Athenaeum, 1944.

Radocsay, D., *450 Jahre Meister M.S.* Budapest, 1957.

Radocsay, D., *Gothic panel painting in Hungary*. Budapest: Corvina, 1963.

Rados, J., *Magyar építészettörténet*. Budapest, 1961.

Radzitzky, C., comp., *Visages de Hongrie*. Anthologie. Bruxelles, 1969.

Rapaics, R., *A magyar biológia története*. Budapest, 1953.

Rapaics, R., *A magyarság virágai*. Budapest, 1932.

Rásonyi, L., *Stein Aurél és hagyatéka*. Budapest, 1960.

Rearick, E.C., *Dances of the Hungarians*. New York: Teachers College, Columbia University, 1939.

Regöly-Mérei, Gy., *Akik legyőzték a betegségeket*. Budapest: Medicina Könyvkiadó, 1963. 2 vols.

Regöly-Mérei, Gy., "Lenhossék Mihály." *Orvosi Hetilap*, 1966.

"Rejtő Sándor." *Magyar Ménök- és Építész Egylet Közleményei*, 1928.

Reményi, J., *Hungarian literature*. Washington: American Hungarian Federation, 1946.

Reményi, J., *Three Hungarian poets: Bálint Balassa, Miklós Zrínyi and Mihály Csokonai Vitéz*. Washington: Hungarian Reformed Federation of America, 1955.

Reményi, J., *Hungarian writers and literature: modern novelists, critics, and poets*. Edited and with an introduction by August J. Molnar. New Brunswick, N.J.: Rutgers University Press, 1964.

Reményi, J., *Sándor Petőfi, Hungarian poet, 1823-1849*. Washington: Hungarian Reformed Federation of America, 1953.

Rempel, F.W., *The role of value in Karl Mannheim's sociology of knowledge*. The Hague: Mouton, 1965.

Renner, R.G., *Ästhetische Theorie bei Georg Lukács; zu ihrer Genese und Struktur*. Bern-München: Francke, 1976.

Réti, E., "Apáthy István." *Országos Orvostörténeti Könyvtár Közleményei*, 1962.

Réti, E., *A gyógyító ember; az orvostudomány történetéből*. Budapest: Móra Ferenc Könyvkiadó, 1963.

Réti, E., *Nagy magyar orvosok*. Budapest: Művelt Nép Könyvkiadó, 1954.

Révész, A.I. — Vargha, V., eds., *Magyar műszaki alkotók*. Budapest: Műszaki Könyvkiadó, 1964.

Rich, J., *The doctor who saved babies, Ignaz Philipp Semmelweis*. New York: J. Messner, 1961.

Rom, P., "Than Károly a magyar tudományos kémia megalapítója." *Gyógyszerész*, 1955.

Rumanovský, I., *Jozef Petzval*. Martin: Osveta, 1957.

Ruzsa, J., *A kanadai magyarság története*. Toronto, 1940.

Sándor, F., ed., *Musical education in Hungary*. London: Barrie and Rockliff, 1966.

Sándor, P., *Két magyar filozófus: Böhm Károly és Brandenstein Béla*. Budapest, 1944.

Seress, J., *Petzval József*. Budapest, 1954.

Sinclair, Sir W.J., *Semmelweis, his life and his doctrine, a chapter in the history of medicine*. Manchester: University Press, 1909.

Slaughter, F.G., *Immortal Magyar: Semmelweis, conqueror of childbed fever*. New York: Schuman, 1950.

Sőtér, I., "The place of Hungarian poetry in Europe." *The New Hungarian Quarterly*, vol. 9, no. 25, 1967.

Sőtér, I., *A sas és a serleg: akadémiai arcképek*. Budapest: Akadémiai Kiadó, 1975.

Soltz, V., "Emlékbeszéd Péch Antal felett." *Bányászati és Kohászati Lapok*, 1896.

Somogyi, J., "Die Philosophie Ákos Paulers," in *Kantstudien*, vol. 30, 1925, pp. 180-188.

Sós, J., "Hőgyes Endre." *Országos Orvostörténeti Könyvtár Közleményei*, 1959.

Spielmann, J., *A közjó szolgálatában*. Művelődéstörténeti tanulmányok. Bukarest: Kriterion, 1976. (Hungarian physicians in 16th and 17th century Transylvania).

Stäckel, P.G., comp., *Wolfgang und Johann Bolyai; geometrische Untersuchungen*. Leipzig: Teubner, 1913. (New York: Johnson Reprint Corp., 1972) 2 vols.

Stevens, H., *The life and music of Béla Bartók*. New York: Oxford University Press, 1964.

Schimanek, E., *Bánki Donát tudományos munkássága és alkotásai*. Budapest, 1954.

Schnell, J., "Emlékezés Ranschburg Pálra." *Gyógypedagógia*, no. 3, 1965.

Schöpflin, A., ed., *Magyar színművészeti lexikon; a magyar színjátszás és drámairodalom enciklopédiája*. Budapest: Országos Színészegyesület és Nyugdíjintézete, 1929-31. 4 vols.

Schulek, E., "Megemlékezés Winkler Lajosról (bibliográfiával)". *Magyar Tudomány*, 1960.

Szabadváry, F., *A kémia története Magyarországon*. Budapest, 1972.

Szabolcsi, B., *A concise history of Hungarian music*. London: Barrie and Rockliff, 1964.

Szász, P., "Fejér Lipót." *A Magyar Tudományos Akadémia Matematikai és Fizikai Osztályának Közleményei*, 1960.

Széki, T., "Gyászbeszéd Winkler Lajos r. tag ravatalánál." *Akadémiai Értesítő*, 1939.

Szelényi, !., *A magyar zene története*. Budapest: Zeneműkiadó, 1959. 2 vols.

Szénássy, B., *A magyarországi matematika története*. Budapest, 1970.

Szerb, A., *A világirodalom története*. 5th ed. Budapest: Magvető Könyvkiadó, 1973.

Szily, K., "Magyar természettudósok száz évvel ezelőtt." *Term. Tud. Közl*, 1888.

Szinnyei, J., *Magyar írók élete és munkái*. Budapest: Hornyánszky, 1891-1914. 14 vols.

Szy, T., ed., *Hungarians in America*; a biographical directory of professionals of Hungarian origin in the Americas. New York City: The Kossuth Foundation, Inc., 1966.

Tábori, P., ed., *Hungarian anthology*. London: J. Bale and Staples, 1943.

Tankó, B., *Hungarian philosophy*. Szeged, 1934.

Téchy, Ö., *Kőrösi Csoma Sándor és a tibeti buddhizmus*. Budapest: Magyar Keleti Társaság, 1944.

Telegdi-Róth, K., "A geológus Lóczy Lajos." *Földtani Közlöny*, 1949.

Teleki, P., *The evolution of Hungary and its place in European history*. New York: The Macmillan Co., 1923.

Tezla, A., *Hungarian authors; a bibliographical handbook*. Cambridge, Mass.: Belknap Press of Harvard University Press, 1970.

Tezla, A., *An introductory bibliography to the study of Hungarian literature*. Cambridge, Mass.: Harvard University Press, 1964.

Thun, R., *Fernsehen und Bildfunk*. Stuttgart, 1934.

Tompa, J., *Simonyi Zsigmond*. Budapest: Akadémiai Kiadó, 1975. (A mult magyar tudósai)

Tot, Amerigo. *Amerigo Tot kiállítása, Tihany, 1969*. Budapest: Kulturális Kapcsolatok Intézete, 1969.

Új magyar lexikon. Budapest: Akadémiai Kiadó, 1960. 7 vols.

Ungarische Dramen. Hrsg. von Georgina Baum. Berlin: Verlag Volk und Wissen, 1968.

United States. Library of Congress. *Hungarians in Rumania and Transylvania; a bibliographical list of publications in Hungarian and West European languages*, compiled from the holdings of the Library of Congress, by Elemer

Bakó and William Sólyom-Fekete. With a pref. by Edward J. Patten. Washington: U.S. Govt. Print. Off., 1969.

The universal encyclopedia of mathematics. London: Allen & Unwin, 1964.

Vadász, M.E., *A magyar földtan útja Szabó József nyomában*. Budapest: Tankönyvkiadó, 1967.

Vajda, P., "Hungarian pioneers in technics." (D. Bánki, K. Kandó, Gy. Jendrassik). *Hungarian Heavy Industries*, no. 23, 1958.

Vajda, P., *Hungarian pioneers of printing art*. Budapest: Hungarian Central Technical Library and Documentation Center, 1972.

Vajda, P., *Magyar alkotók — Creative Hungarians*. English & Hungarian text. Bibliography: pp. 82-87. Budapest: NOVEX Co. Ltd., 1975.

Vajda, P., *Mai magyar találmányok, 1945-1965*. Budapest: Táncsics Könyvkiadó, 1965.

Vajda, P., *Nagy magyar feltalálók*. Budapest, 1958.

Váli, B., *A magyar színészet története*. Budapest: Aigner Lajos, 1887.

Varconi, Victor. *It's not enough to be Hungarian*. Denver: Graphic Impressions, 1976.

Várdy, S.B., *Modern Hungarian historiography*. Boulder: East European Quarterly, 1976.

Vargyas, L., "Folk music research in Hungary." *Studia Musicologica Acad. Sc. Hung.*, vol. 1, nos. 3-4, 1961.

Vargyas, L., *A magyar népballada és Európa*. Budapest: Zeneműkiadó, 1976. 2 vols.

Varjasi, R. — Horváth, V., *Hungarian Rhapsody; the Hungarian State Folk Ensemble*. Budapest: Corvina, 1956.

Varjú-Ember, M., *Hungarian domestic embroidery*. Budapest: Corvina Press, 1963.

Vasarely, Victor. *Notes brutes*. Paris, 1973.

Végh, A., "Schulek Elemér." *Magyar Kémiai Folyóirat*, no. 11, 1964.

Végh, J., *Kolozsvári Tamás, MS. mester, Lőcsei Pál*. Budapest: Képzőművészeti Alap Kiadóvállalata, 1968.

Vendl, A.; *A Budapesti Műszaki Egyetem Ásvány- és Földtani Tanszékének története*. Budapest, 1957.

Verebélÿ, L., *Ányos Jedlik; a Hungarian pioneer of electricity*. Budapest, 1931.

"Verebélÿ Tibor." *Magyar Tudományos Akadémia Almanach*, 1941.

Vikol, J., "Cancer detection work in Hungary in the last ten years." *Medicor News*, no. 4, 1963.

Viski, K., *Hungarian dances*. London: Simpkin, Marshall, 1937.

Vogl, F., *Theater in Ungarn 1945 bis 1965*. Köln: Verlag Wissenschaft und Politik, 1966.

Wagner, F.S., *A magyar kisebbségek helyzete a szomszéd államokban*. Cleveland, 1975.

Wagner, F.S., "Széchenyi and the nationality problem in the Habsburg Empire." Reprinted from *Journal of Central European Affairs*, vol. 20, no. 3, 1960.

Weszprémi, I., *Magyarország és Erdély orvosainak rövid életrajza*. Tr. of *Succincta medicorum Hungariae et Transylvaniae biographia*. Lipsiae, 1774. Budapest: Medicina Könyvkiadó, 1960-1970. 4 vols.

Wigner, J., "Neumann János." *Fizikai Szemle*, no. 8, 1967.

Willis, R., *An attempt to analyse the automaton chess player, of Mr. de Kempelen. With an easy method of imitating the movements of that celebrated figure . . . to which is added, a copious collection of the knight's moves over the chess board*. London: J. Booth, 1821.

Young, P.M., "Hungarian music in England." *The New Hungarian Quarterly*, vol. 4, no. 10, 1963.

Young, P.M., *Zoltán Kodály, a Hungarian musician*. London: Ernest Benn Ltd., 1964.

Zádor, A., *Mihály Pollack*. Budapest, 1960.

Zelovich, K., *Kandó Kálmán emlékezete*. Budapest, 1932.

Zemplén, J.M. — Egyed, L., *Eötvös Loránd*. Budapest: Akadémiai Kiadó, 1970.

Zemplén, J.M., *A magyarországi fizika története 1711-ig*. Budapest: Akadémiai Kiadó, 1961.

Zemplén, J.M., *A magyarországi fizika története a XVIII. században; a fizika szaktudománnyá válik*. Budapest: Akadémiai Kiadó, 1964.

PART VIII — APPENDIX

A.

DOCUMENTS RELATING TO THE CULTURAL EXCHANGES BETWEEN THE HUNGARIAN ACADEMY OF SCIENCES (BUDAPEST) AND THE AMERICAN PHILOSOPHICAL SOCIETY (PHILADELPHIA):

Mr President!

In the year 1827 the sons of Hungary assembled to form a society for promoting the sciences in general and especially for the culture and diffusion of the Hungarian Language and Litterature.

The society was established and incorporated by an act of the Diet and royal sanction in the year 1829 under the denomination Hungarian Academy of Sciences.

The principal sections or branches of the academy are the following sciences

Philosophy History. Law, Astronomy and mathematics Natural History and Phisics, Philology. Belles Lettres.

The academy is constituted as follows

Patron   His royal majesty the king of Hungary Francis I.
                    Emperor of Austria
President   His royal Highness the Palatin of Hungary
                    Archduke Joseph Brother of the King)
2d President The count Joseph Teleky;
Vice president and Treasurer The Count Stephen Szechenyi
Secretary   Gabriel Döbrönley
Cashier   Michel Helmeczy,
                 and some other officers.

The honorary members are elected from the men high standing in the consideration of the nation for their patriotism and under-standing, the principal founders of the academy are among them

                                        viz

The Archduke palatin
. prince philippe Batthany
.. Count Etienne Széchenyi (Stephen)
.. Count George Andrassy
. Counts George, Stephen and Lewis Károlyi and others

Regular members are four in every Section and elected by a
majority of all votes of the grand Assembly, from the most
distinguished learned men in the country.

The Corresponding members in unlimited number are chosen from
men devoted to Sciences, and who contributed with Success
(by publishing) to promote knowledge in any part of Science

The foreign members. The academy send their Diploma to the
celebrated learned men of the known World

Weekly meetings are held, by the president and vice president
and the present Members in the City. Common and regular business
transacted.

General meetings every 3 months. The members dispersed in
the Country and the palatin are invited. and Sit eight days.

Grand Assembly every year. The palatin represents his royal majesty
the patron. all members are present. (14 days.)

The academy is situated in the City of Pest.
All dissertations and publications are in the Hungarian language

The Constitution and usages of the academy are after the model
of the academys of Paris Berlin and Petersbourg.

I can take upon myself to Declare to you, that the
Hungarian academy anxious to entertain Scientific relations

with foreign academys and learned societys, feels them duty to recommend itself in the friendly affections of the philosophical society of Philadelphia, and express its wishes for an uninterrupted connection between these two bodies, and asserts that the Hungarian academy will be the first in the communication of all its proceedings and transactions with the philosophical Society. The Hungarian Academy would be highly honoured by the friendly offer of the society, and I should me feel very happy in being the messenger of a kind mark of a such offer.

respectfully I am your most obedient servant

Philadelphia 25 Xber 1832

Charles Nagy
Member of the academy

To Mr. P. S. Duponceau Esqr president of the philosophical Society of Philadelphia!

26 Dec. 1832

A Letter from Mr Charles Nagy, stating that he is a member of the Hungarian Academy of Sciences, established at Pest, by an Act of the Diet with the Royal Sanction in the year 1829, & that the said Society is desirous of Corresponding with similar institutions throughout the World & particularly with the American Philosophical Society; Whereupon

Resolved; that Mr Nagy be informed that this Society is equally desirous of establishing a regular & constant Communication with the Hungarian Academy of Sciences, & that a Copy of the new Series of our Transactions be transmitted to him by the Librarian with a request that he will be so good as to present it in our name to the Academy, and that a Copy of this Resolution be at the same time sent to him duly attested by the Secretary.

Stated meeting

January 4th 1833

Present

President. Mr Duponceau in the chair.
V Presidents. Dr Chapman. Mr Coll.
Secretaries.
Treasurer & Librarian
Curators.

Prof Patterson .... Mr Lea.
Prof Gillies .... Dr Coates.
Mr Strickland .... Mr Lukens
Dr Horner .... Mr Tanner.
Dr Darlington. .... Lt McEwen
Dr Hays .... Mr Vaux
Dr Harris. Dr Mease Mr Gilpin

Mr Vaughan one of the tellers of the meeting for
the election of officers made the following report

January 4th 1833.

Present

Dr Chapman. Judge Hopkinson. Mr Lea & Hays
Mr Vaughan, Mr Tanner, Mr Duponceau, Mr Ord
Dr Coates Mr Hembel, Dr Mease, Maj Bache.
Messrs Tanner & Duponceau were appointed Judges
& Dr Hays & Mr Vaughan Clerks.
                The Clerks reported the following
persons to be duly elected officers of the Am Phil So
at the annual meeting held this day for that purpose
after due notice
President. Mr Duponceau
V Presidents. Dr Chapman. Judge Hopkinson. Mr Lea
Secretaries. J. Bache. J. K. Kane. G. Bache. C. D. Meigs
Treasurer & Librarian. Mr Vaughan
Curators. J. P. Wetherill. R.E. Griffith. J Lea
Counsellors for 3 years. Wm Short .... C C Biddle

The committee on accounts
made a detailed report which was accepted.
This report exhibited a bal: in favour of the Society
on account of Wittenhouse Funds _____ $270._
      Magelanic Fund. _____ 1098._
      Extra do.   do. _____ 313._

      The committee to whom was referred
the application of diff. learned Societ. of Paris, for
contributions to a monument to the memory of Cuvier
reported that they had collected the sum of $1100
which they present to this society to be transmitted
by the President to the Academy of Sciences of Paris
      The report was accepted.

Donations.

The Imperial Acad. of Russia.
The Linnean Society of Bordeaux.
Society of Antiquaries of Paris.
Mr.   Gen Parker.
Mr. J. P. Davis of Boston.
M. Nagy. of the Hungarian Acad. of sc.
Gen Parker deposited a likeness of the late Z. Collins.
Gov Cass. D. B. Warden.

      Mr. Vaughan read a letter from
M. Nagy. giving an account of the Hungarian
Acad. of Sciences.

      On motion of Mr. Vaux
Resolved. That the President be requested
to reply to the letter address'd through him to the
society to reciprocate to offers of intercourse expressed
therein

      On motion of Mr. Vaughan.
Resolved. That a copy of the Transactions of
this society (new series) be presented through Mr. Nagy
to the Hungarian acad. of sciences
      Adjourned.

To Mr. John Vaughan Esq.
Secretary and Librarian of the A. P. Society.

I received with the greatest pleasure your kind lines and hasten to answer your questions.

Mr. Stoeffel at Vienna is in my opinion the first of the living Opticians of Europe, and his Instruments are of an accomplished workmanship. Although the art of making good flintglass (for objectives) is vanished from the earth by the dead of celebrated Frauenhofer, and several attempts of very skilful chemists in Vienna to make valuable achromatic glass have failed. Mr. Stoeffel supplies the want by the far inferior english and french flint by his skill, in working the glass with the utmost mathematical accuracy; and they renders his Instruments unequalled. He published a programm and a Catalogue of his Works, wich includes all kind of optical apparatus and large astronomical Instruments for the use of Observatorys: he extends his atelier to the construction of the most subtile apparatus for philosophical experiments in dioptrics, catoptrics, perspective, the interference and polarisation of light, belonging to an entirely new theorie of the sciences he invented a new dividing machine, and he draws with the greatest accuracy the degrees minutes and seconds on silver for the Teodolites, Azimutal and horizontal circles; the construction of his Refractors is ingenious. — The most remarkable of his productions is the grand compound Mycroscope invented by him 5 years ago and much improoved since. The results of this instrument are indeed astonishing, he carries the magnification to the infinite. In the year 1830 comparative experiments were made by the celebra-

ted Baron Saquia (whose father was in america) and professor
Baumgartner of the university in Vienna, between a myeroscope
of Ploessel and a great number of the best existing myeroscopes
from amici, dollond, Troughton Ramsden frauenhofer and from
many other artists. A large assembly of learned and distinguished men — among them the archiduke Charles and prince
Metternich — pronounced without hesitation the preference
of Ploessel's who surpasses all without comparison — Of course
requests were sent from all parts of Europe for obtaining one
of his unequalled myeroscopes. — The results of this comparative enquiry are published, and I shall have the pleasure to
send you a copy together with the catalogue of Ploessel.

Mr King (prime Ward King & Co in this city) allowed
me the sending of paquets destined for the A pl Society
under his adress; and will them transmit for philadelphia.

The easiest manner to send some objects to hungary is,
by adressing them to the austrian embassy Chandoshouse
London with the note - for the hungarian academy of sciences.

Would you but prefer to send something under my
humble adress and name for Vienna Mr. Baring Brothers
in London will have the civility to forward it to me.

I am – Sir respectfully your sincere
un most obedient servant
Chy Nagy.

New York 5/1 1833.

Stated Meeting.

Present.

President. Mr. Duponceau, in the Chair.

V. Presidents. Judge Hopkinson, Mr. Ord, Dr. Chapman.

Secretaries. Dr. Mays, Mr. C. J. Buche.

Treasurer & Librarian. Mr. Vaughan.

Curators. Dr. Griffith, Mr. Lea.

Mr. Short	Col. Long
, Kimbel	Dr. Rose
J. James	Mr. Strickland
, Fisher	, Vaux
, Pickering	Dr. McEwen
Mr. Booker	, Coates
, Farner	Mr. Raynor
, Sauch	, Ficklen
Dr. Hays	Dr. Horner
, Bell	, , Morse
, Mays	Prof. DelPes , Hodge

The President reported that he had executed the duty devolved upon him in relation to the letter of . Mr. Imlay.

Donations were received from Dr. Pancoast.

A letter was read from one of the Secretaries of the Society of Antiquarians of London, acknowledging the receipt of Vols. 3. Part 2. of the Transactions of this Society.

The Committee on Finance appointed last Year were continued, viz. Messrs. C. C. Biddle, Vaux, James & Ord.

The following committees were also continued,

Committee on the Building.

Mess. Strickland, ——— Vaughan ——— and Hare

Committee of Publication,

D. Bache ——— M. Lea ——— & D. Griffith

The society proceeded to appoint a Librarian for
the ensuing year, whereupon M. John Vaughan was duly
elected,

On motion of D. Chapman resolved, that
Denon's work on Egypt procured by M. Vaughan, be pur-
-chased from him by the society.

On motion of D. Hays, resolved, that the
thanks of the Society be presented to M. Vaughan for the pains
which he has taken in relation to Denon's Egypt.

The society proceeded to ballot for New Members
and all other business having first been disposed of. The
President declared the following Persons to be duly elected
Members of this society.

Prof. Bugalsky ——— of St Petersburg
M. Marmaduke Burrough, M.D. of Philadelphia
M. W. Baldwin ——— of Philadelphia
Edwin James, M.D. ——— of Albany,
Moncure Robinson ——— of Virginia

Adjourned.

J. J. Bache Sec.

Stated Meeting

16th April 1833

Present

President — Mr Du Ponceau, in the chair

V. Presidents — Dr Chapman, Judge Hopkinson

Secretaries — Mr B- , Mr Backe, Dr Backe, Mr -

Treasurer — Librarians — Mr Vaughan

Curators — Mr Sea

Mr Rumber	Maj. Backe
Mr -	Mr Short
Swain	Nicklin
Branches	Tanner
Gilpin	Col. Biddle
Dr Bone	Dr Coates
Bird	James
Harris	Mease
Hare	Mr Biddle
Mr Vaux	Baldwin
Dr Morton	Dr Gibson
Mr Ingersoll	Mr N. Biddle
Mr H.C. Carey	Dr McEwen
Dr D. Lancey	Dr Hays	Mr Sergeant

The committee on Mr Sea's paper read March 16th 1832 and the supplement thereto read Feb. 1, 1833 reported in favor of publication, the Report was accepted.

The committee appointed to revise the Laws and regulations of the Society made a final report.

The laws and regulations reported were read, after which Mr Hare offered the following motion: viz: that the question on the enactment of the first chapter of the revised Laws, be taken at the next stated meeting of the Society.

Mr Nicklin moved the postponement of this motion, with a view to introduce the following resolution:

Resolved, that the laws and regulations reported by the Committee be laid upon the table until the next meeting, and that in the

mean time they be printed for the use of the members.
The resolution was adopted, when —

On motion of Mr. Nuttall, Resolved that a committee of two, be appointed to reduce in relation to the Printing of their resolutions. Messrs. Lea & Nuttall were appointed the committee. —

The committee in the hall to whom was referred the resolution submitted by Dr. Mease exempting the Agricultural Society from change of rent, reported that having considered the subject referred to them, they are of opinion that the resolution of Dr. Mease at the present time, would be inexpedient. —

On motion of Mr. Kane the committee was discharged from the further consideration of the subject —

Donations were received from —
The Linnæan society of Paris, the Royal Swedish Academy, the London society of Arts, Manufactures, & Commerce — H. C. B... ..., Mr. R. E. Farrins, Prof. A.D. Bache, and Mr. Jno. Pickering. —

The society proceeded to ballot for new members. —
The votes having been counted the Presdt. declared the follg. named gentlemen to be duly elected Members of this society. —

Mr. L. Laboudissière _____ of Paris _____
Chas. Nagy _____ of Pest in Hungary _____
Jacob Randolph, M.D. _____ of Philadelphia _____
Mr. Subias Francis Fisher _____ of Philadelphia. _____
Frederick Emerson M.D. _____ of Philadelphia. _____
Mr. C. Casey _____ of Philadelphia. _____

Adjourned.
A. D. Bache, Secty.

My Dear Sir, M. John Vaughan Philad.) Feb 20 of Aug 1833.

On returning from some travels in different parts of our Country, I found the letter of the secretary of the philosophical Society and your kind letter together. I feel me very greatly honored having been elected member of your highly distinguished and learned society. No greater pleasure could occur to me. My sincerest thanks to you my dear Sir, for the hearty kindness you had in proposing me.

The catalog of the optician Plössl is unfortunately out of print, but as soon as it will be reprinted (with the addition of many new instruments) I shall send you some of them. Since my return this artist made an important discovery in the construction of telescopes and improved them consequence considerably. Will the next opportunity I shall communicate to you the matter extensively. The invention consist in short "not to put more together the two pieces of glass who constitute the achromatic objectif, but in placing them very distant from each other in the interior of the tube, after the focus and the radiey of the flint glass The consequences of this arrangement are a greater accuracy with which the glasses can be prepared a greater difference and clarity of the objects regarded, a greater magnifying power (by the same dyameter of objectif), a diminution in the longitude of the tube, and lastly a much lower price in comparison with the other telescopes now in use. In this figure —————— is a) the flint glass and b) the common crown glass. A Telescope with an objectif of 22 lignes in Diameter two terrestrical and two astronomical oculars with the magnifying power from 40 to 80, tube and stand of brass all in a box costs not more than about 75 american dollars. The artist calls this instrument — Dyalitical Telescope.

The books I collected for the Library of the Society — among them
the hungarian Bible you wished for — together with some minerals I shall send probably with the same austrian frigate
who takes the unfortunate poles for america. You know
probably, that about 400 poly- all Officers from the late
revolutionary Army — who resided in austria are to be sent off
in your country: a very strange thing, without asking the
americans to send them a large number of exiled poor soldiers!!.
With the present opportunity I send you for the Society 1.° a
good Chart of Hungary — in the german tongue — a larger one
is now to be prepared, in the hungarian language, (the old ones are
not accurate enough) as soon as it is completed (in two pair of leaves,
(one sheet is published already) I shall send it for the Society.
2.° An exact copy of the moon with his mountains. It was presented to the Society of german naturalists. 3:° The Report of the X.th
congregation of the said german Society, held at Vienna past year
in September as if was in your happy country. Your countryman
D.° Frik from Baltimore was the only american present by it.
4. Some old coins.
The hungarian academy of Science will send you next time
some of it's publications, but the great meeting is not before
November, and the decisions an some of communications must be
left after the meeting.
I found a very interesting collection of minerals, almost

is beautiful Specimens, well arranged. I think we could have it as a very convenient prize. If the Society wishes to multiplicate or to grow its fine and well begun collection, I shall me feel very happy in being an instrument to contribute to its extent. If you think it apropos je vous enverrai le catalogue et le prix qu'on veut avoir pour cette collection. La voie que vous avez désignée dans votre aimable lettre sera bien sûre sous toutes les sorts de communications. Je pourrai envoyer tous ces choses par l'angleterre par l'adresse de vos chers freinds, parce que les objets de l'histoire naturelle ne payent pas rien.

You would extremely oblige me dear Sir by sending the national Gazette or an other of your best philadelphia daily papers under my adress to Mr. Black Young and Young Booksellers to the King Coventgarden Tavistockstreet London, who will pay for me and send me it every time the papers. The liners or Liverpoolpackets sail every fortnight from N. York.

My best wishes for your wellbeeing

I am with the most perfect consideration & respects,

your obedient and faithfulservant

Chs. Nagy.

My compliments to Robt & Vaux and his relations.

Az amerikai philosophiai Társaságnak Philadelphiában
üdvözletét.

Az 1825/2 beli Országgyűlésen kezdett s azóta folyt hazafiui önkéntes ajánlásokra épülése után munkálódásaihoz 1831 ben fogott magyar tudós Társaság, évkönyveinek első kötetét Uraságtoknak azon érzéssel küldi meg, melly az egész emberiséget, tudományt s művészséget szeretete által egy kis nagy lelkű ugyanságos egyesületbe vonja.

E mellett ajánlja a magyar tudós Társaság a tudományos dolgokban kész segedelmét s kikéri Uraságtoknak is iránta szíves hajlandóságát.

Ide van egyszersmind csatolva a Társaság rendszabásaiból 2 magyar s annyi latin példány a Társaságnak 1833 diki névkönyvével együtt.

Költ Pesten a magyar tudós Társaság 4dik nagy gyűlése 8dik üléséből, November 11d 1833

Gróf Teleki József
Előlülő

Döbrentei Gábor
Titoknok

Societati philosophicae Americanae, quae Philadelphiae est,
salutem.

Societas erudita hungarica, quae in comitiis annorum 182⁷/₈, sumtibus
omnino patriae salutis amore libere conferri coeptis ac dein ul-
tro continuatis instituta anno 1831 operum initia fecit, nunc
Annalium suorum volumen primum Vobis eo animi sensu
transmittit, qui universum genus humanum literarum artium-
que studiis ad communem amplam animorum cognationem con-
jungit.

Haec Societas erudita hungarica insuper officia sua in rebus literariis promtissima offerens Vestram erga se benevo-
lentiam mutuam exorat.

Huc simul adnexa sunt Statutorum Societatis exemplaria
duo hungarica, ac totidem latina, una cum libello ejusdem no-
menclatore de anno 1833.

Datum e Conventus generalis quarta Societatis eruditae
hungaricae Sessione octava, Pestini, d. 11 Novembris M.DCCCXXXIII
celebrata Comes Iosephus Teleki, Praeses Gabriel Döbrentei, Se-
cretarius.

Quatuor volumina operum Vestrorum, (Transactions)
medio Caroli Nagy, socii correspondentis Societatis eruditae hungaricae, per Praesidem Vestrum illustrem
Du Ponceau perhumane missa, grati animi sensu percepi-
mus.
                                G. Döbrentei mpr.

Stated Meeting.

19th April 1833.

Present

President. Mr Du Ponceau. in the chair.

V. Presidents. Dr Chapman. Judge Hopkinson.

Secretaries. Mr Hume. Prof. Bache. Dr Bache. Dr Meigs.

Treasurer & Librarian. Mr Vaughan.

Curators. Mr Sea.

Dr Hembel _____ Maj. Bache.

Mr Schweinitz. _____ Mr Short.

Leech. _____ Nicklin.

Bancker. _____ Tanner.

Gilpin. _____ Col. Biddle.

Dr Hare. _____ Dr Coates.

Ford. _____ James.

Horner. _____ Mease.

Kane. _____ Mr Biddle.

Dr Vaux _____ Baldwin.

Dr Morton. _____ Dr Gibson.

Mr Ingersoll _____ Mr N. Biddle.

H. C. Carey. _____ Dr McEwen.

Dr H. Sancey Dr Hays. Mr Sergeant.

The committee on Mr Sea's paper read March 16th 1832. and the supplement thereto read Feb. 1. 1833. reported in favor of publication. the Report was accepted.

The committee appointed to revise the Laws and regulations of the Society made a final report.

The laws and regulations reported were read, after which Mr Kane offered the following motion. viz. that the question on the enactment of the first Chapter, of the revised laws. be taken at the next stated meeting of the Society.

Mr Nicklin moved the postponement of this motion. with a view to introduce the following resolution.

Resolved. that the laws and regulations reported by the Committee be laid upon the table until the next meeting, and that in the for 1836 would be awarded for the most important unpublished papers in Astronomy and in Animal Physiology which have been communicated between the date of Jany 5th 1833 and June 30th 1836. _____

On motion the publication of the above letter was directed to be made in the Journal of the Franklin Institute and in Silliman's Journal, and the Secretary was directed to acknowledge its receipt. _____

On Motion of Dr. Jones. Resolved, that the Secretary in conjunction with the Treasurer be instructed to report to the Society, a list of all persons who have been elected members of this Society, noting the date of their election, whether or not they have paid their entitation fee and signed the constitution. also those who have died or resigned. _____

On Motion of Col. Biddle. the Medals presented by Mr. Hays of Hungary. were referred to the Curators of this Society to report in relation to them. _____

On application from Aly Mathew to have returned to him a paper on the "doctrine of Magnetism" laid before the society by his deceased father, was received and the Librarian was directed to return the same. _____

Dr. Bache from the Committee on Publication read a list of committees who have not reported pursuant to the requirements of the laws of the society. on motion of Prof. Bache. the Committees on the paper of Mr. Nichols on the Law of Proportion and on an offer by Dr. Lovell of Meteorological observations, were discharged; and on motion of Dr. Hays the Committee on Cheap Adams made for the prediction of fire-men was discharged. _____

Adjourned
A.D. Bache Sec.

Mr John Vaughan Esqr, Librarian of the Amphilos. Soc. to _____
_____

_____ _____ _____

of presenting to the Society this volume, I say _____ _____,
to explain its object and content. _____
This is the first Arithmetic in the Hungarian language intended
for Academies or Universities, — this science is all _____ being
teached to this day in the Latin.
There are two title-pages in the volume. _____
I assumed the classification of Ampère, by calling Arithmography the elements of Mathematics, and divided it in two dis-
tinct parts, _____ in the writing with special particular signs, _____ in
the writing with general signs. The arithmetic operates
with determined signs the numbers, and forms consequently the
first part of the arithmography; the second part writes with
general signs the letters, and is called Algebra.
This principle of the simple writing with numbers is
rigorously _____ in the volume from the commencement to the
end. The pupil (student) begins writing the ciphers, and
goes on in combining them with the different signs of operations
and signs of quality: gradually as his notions (or knowledge)
increase, the forms and combinations become more and more
complicated, and when he combines every sign is _____ _____

_____ Essai _____ philosophie des Sciences, par André Marie Ampère
Paris 1830.

$$x = \frac{(10 + 0.75).(29-3)^2 + \sqrt{37 + 81^2} - (75 + 0.190)^2}{\sqrt[4]{6.79} + \left(\frac{31}{7} - \frac{9}{10}\right)^2 - \sqrt[3]{\frac{7}{9}} + log\,0.73815 - Clg\,81}$$ and reduce

it to its most simple expression, he knows the arithmetic

perfectly well.

The volume contains

1835.   I am, Sir, your obedient and faithful servant

Vienna austria.

1004 Rue de Carinthie;   Charles Nagy

Dear Sir

The Telescope enclosed was brought to me the day of 21 [...]
and of [...] it to your Nephew [...] by [...] London, a hope
it will arrive at least to the end of [...] in a year or [...]
[I enclose] a small catalogue of names of the Hungarian
academy of sciences with the calendar for 1838.

All expenses and price of the Telescope will be paid by
your Nephew, and I draw only from London 32 [...] as
the corresponding value of [...] price and expenses.

My best and heartiest compliments to Mr [...]
Mr Backe &

I am yours faithfully

Vienna 20 May 1838

Nagy

Charles Nagy sends respectfully to the philo. Society, a copy of his calendars for 1840 with useful tables, in Hungarian, printed for the Hungarian academy of science in Pest.

Vienna 10 of August 1839.

Vienna 10 March 1841.

Dear Sir!

I send for the library 2 copies of the use of globes, the calendar for 1841 and a description of the oldest university in Hungary. The dictionary — german hungarian — is out of print and a second edition is in preparation; as soon as it appears, I shall have the pleasure to forward a copy.

Some pendulum experiments are going on under my direction. I shall have the pleasure in communicating the results to the society; the experiments closed, I would send the invariable pendulum itself to Philadelphia for continuation, you may inform me, whether this idea is agreeable to the society?

with the most cordial compliments
your faithful
Charles Nagy

To Mr Vaughan Librarian of the Society at Philadelphia

St. Meeting, Nov. 19. 1841,

Report read, and appended resolution
adopted.

    The Com. to whom was referred the letter
of Mr. Hagg of Vienna in relation to the experiments
with the invariable pendulum which he is now
making, beg leave to report;— that in their opinion
a comparison, to their making in Vienna &
a series of experiments, with the
pendulum employed by Mr. Hagg, made in Philadelphia
would be a valuable contribution to an interesting
department of science. The measures of the pendulum
made in New York by Major Sabine is often referred
to, and the verification of his results by a new
Comparison would add to the value of the former
results data. The expense of the observations necessary
cannot be considerably & the credit which would
result from them would more than repay the cost
for their outlay. The Com. therefore recommend
the adoption of the following resolution.

    Resolved that Mr. Hagg of Vienna be informed
on behalf of this Soc., that this Soc. will
be pleased to receive an account of his

pendulum records, and also the invariable pendulum with which they were made. That they will defray the expenses of the receiving & returning the instrument, & will procure a corresponding series of Observations in Philadelphia.

A. D. Bache
R. M. Patterson.

Hall A. P. J. Nov. 19/41

a. r. a.

Kiad. Nov. 5. 1852.

(· B. J·

MAGYAR ACADEMIA.

A' tudományok' magyar nemzeti Academiájának van szeren-
cséje Évkönyvei *III.* — *VII-dt*
köteteit, ugy a Magyar Nyelv-
emlékek *I.* — *III.-dt* köteteit a,
amerikai philos. Társaságnak
azon tisztelettel, mellyel illy ki-
tünö tudományos testület iránt
viseltetik, megküldeni.

Költ Pesten. *Martius 15. 1852*

Academia Scientiarum Hungarica *Societati Scientiarum*
americana, qua Philadelphia est,
Annalium suorum volumina *III. IV.*
V. VI. VII. , item Monumentorum
linguae hungaricae antiquae volumina *I. II. III.* debito tantae
societatis nomini meritisque cultu
transmittit.

Pestini, die *15. Martii, 1852.*

Toldy
Titoknok

Dr. Franc. Toldy
Acad. Hung. a Secretis

Emich és Eisenfels könyvnyomdája.

B.

LIST OF ZOLTAN BAY'S PUBLICATIONS ON THE UNIFIED STANDARDIZATION OF TIME AND LENGTH:

In the following, a detailed listing of publications of Zoltan Bay pertinent to the history of the development of the new idea of the unified standardization of time and length will be presented. Also, announcements made in the NBS Technical News Bulletin and other official organs of the U.S. National Bureau of Standards pertinent to the subject will be given. In several instances, quotations from the published material will be presented. This is done in order to provide source material for historical evaluation of an important development in experimental physics and metrology: the transition from the separate time and length standards to the unified system based on the speed of light. As already mentioned in the biographical text, this transition is not yet conclusively resolved, but the proposal that has been advocated for many years by Bay is now very close to being internationally accepted.

Bay first described the detailed theory of his new measurement method in an *Internal NBS Report* in January 1965. In *Part B* of that report, entitled "Proposal for a New Length Standard," he first outlined the practicability of the determination of optical frequencies and then he advanced the definite proposal that, owing to the new possibilities, a new standard of length should be based on the speed of light instead of on acceptance of some improved wavelength standard[1]. (The references are given at the end of the *Appendix*.) However, the leadership of NBS was reluctant .o accept the new idea and, following the old line of standardization, the emphasis in sponsoring Bureau research was put on working out a better wavelength standard based on the stabilization of the wavelengths of lasers[2].

Bay published the advances of his experiments and his theoretical investigations in several papers between 1968 and 1972. In his publications during this time Bay continually proffered the unified time-length standardization system based on the speed of light and pointed out that any newly introduced wavelength standard could only be of temporary help, while, once established in the unified system, the meter never would need to be redefined[3-7].

Since the strict constancy of the speed of light is of primary importance for future acceptance of the unified system, Bay conducted research together with J.A. White concerning the frequency dependence of the speed of light. On the basis of theory and a survey of recent experimental data they came to the conclusion that light propagation in vacuo is independent of frequency to within one part in 10^{20}, which is far above the constancy required for the practicability of the unified system[8].

255

In 1972 Bay published the results accomplished on the basis of his experimental design together with G.G. Luther and J.A. White. These included the first measurement of an optical frequency of a red laser line: this result is at present still outstanding as the only measured frequency in the visible spectrum, based directly on the frequency standard; and also a value of the speed of light surpassing for the first time in accuracy the value accepted previously for more than a decade[9]. The booklet, *Physics in 1972* (published in the annual series by the American Institute of Physics) mentioned this experiment among the few outstanding achievements during that year.

In 1972 Bay retired from the National Bureau of Standards and his experiments were discontinued[10-11]. The work of Bay, and later on that of others at NBS, was instrumental in producing resolutions by the international Committee Consultative for the Definition of the Metre. In the minutes of the June 1973 meeting, the Committee recommended a value of the speed of light and went on to urge its successors to maintain that value subsequent redefinition of the meter. This, while it still does not represent a final decision, "comes very close to fulfilling the proposal urged for many years by Dr. Zoltan Bay that the meter be defined in terms of the speed of light"[12].

The firm opinion of Bay expressed in his most recent publications is that the "the time-length measurement system unified via a defined value of the speed of light, will be the system for the future"[13-14].

Since his retirement from NBS, Bay has continued his research on the constancy of the velocity of light and a new interpretation of the special theory of relativity at the American University in Washington, D.C. Both subjects are closely related to the theoretical foundation of the new measurement system.

REFERENCES AND FOOTNOTES

[1]Z. Bay, *Internal NBS Report, January 1965* (unpublished). *Part A*: "Precision Measurement of the Velocity of Light," pp. 1-46. *Part B*: "Proposal for a New Length Standard," pp. 47-54. Quotation from page 47: *"The determination of optical frequencies. A corollary result of the experiments described in Part A is that optical frequencies can be measured with high accuracy . . . Thus, optical frequencies can be determined by measuring rf frequencies only.* To our knowledge, this is a "first" in optical experiments, made possible by the observation and measurement of high frequency photobeats. Until now optical frequencies have been determined via the wavelength and the velocity of light". Quotation from p. 53: *"The possibility of a new length standard.* The long-term stabilization of optical frequencies and the possibility of their measurement with respect to the frequency standard could, in principle, be utilized in two ways. 1) One could say that, using long time averaging processes, c can be measured with the accuracy of a few parts in 10^{12}. This approach should be discarded because of the lack of an accurate length standard. 2) One can use a defined value of c, and base a length standard on that value of c and the frequency standard. In order to be compatible with the centimeter scale, the new standard should be introduced after the following two steps. a) By the use of the frequency standard and the existing wavelength standard, one should measure c to within the accuracy of the

wavelength standard. This would result in a value, the 8th significant figure of which would be uncertain to a few units. By the collaboration of laboratories on an international basis, the 8th figure has to be agreed upon. b) All successive figures in c should be made zero . . . Thus any optical line which is generated with a good long-term stability and the frequency of which is measured with respect to the frequency standard (as outlined above) can be used for a wavelength standard."

[2]The *NBS Technical News Bulletin, 55*, p. 170, July 1971, reported the presentation of the 1971 Stratton Award (the Bureau's highest award for scientific achievements) to R.L. Barger and J.L. Hall for their work of stabilizing the He-Ne laser to an absorption line of the methane molecule and stated: ". . . the methane stabilized laser seems almost certain to be adopted as a new international standard for length." Note that this announcement was published 6 years after Bay's 1965 proposal and after his repeated arguments (see below) urging that efforts be directed towards the realization of the new concept, that of the unified system based on the speed of light. It should be noted that while NBS in 1971 was reluctant to accept the new system, some other members of the international community of the National Laboratories were strongly for it. Thus, at the 4th meeting of the Comité Consultatif pour la Définition du Mètre (Paris, September 1970), the Physikalisch-Technische Bundesanstalt, Braunschweig (Germany) stated in its report: ". . . en reliant l'unité de longueur à l'unité de temps par l'intermédiaire de la vitesse de la lumière, on créerait une définition ressemblant à un serpent qui se mord la queue." (The quotation is taken from the Minutes of that meeting published by the Bureau International Des Poids Et Mesures, Pavillon de Breteuil, F 92-Sèvres, France, page M 70; a report by Z. Bay and G.G. Luther, advocating the new system, also appeared in the Minutes, pp. M 96 — M 100.) The U.S. National Bureau of Standards began consideration of the new system as a possible alternative to the old system in 1972 after the measurements of optical frequencies at the NBS Washington, D.C. and at the NBS Boulder, Colorado laboratories started to produce numerical data. Thus, the *NBS Technical News Bulletin, 56*, p. 75, April 1972, published a statement by L.M. Branscomb (Director of NBS), concerning optical frequency measurements in the infrared spectrum by the NBS Boulder laboratories, which said: "A 30-fold more accurate determination of the speed of light should be possible, suggesting that this universal constant of nature might some day be assigned an arbitrary number, with only one standard used for both length and time measurement."

[3]Z. Bay and G.G. Luther, "Locking a Laser Frequency to the Time Standard," *Applied Physics Letters, 13*, p. 303, 1968. Quotation from page 304: "The above method of stabilization and frequency measurement is applicable to any laser line. Also, the frequency of laser lines, stabilized by other means, can be measured by these techniques. Thus, as one important application of these ideas, reference lines for spectroscopy can be established throughout the spectrum wherever laser lines are available. Another application is the evaluation of the velocity of light. It is obvious that the knowledge of the frequency in terms of the standard second and a simultaneous measurement of the corresponding wavelength in terms of the length standard results in refining the value of the velocity of light, c, in meters/second. Since it is expected that the accuracy of the frequency measurement will surpass that of the definition of the present length standard, the accuracy of c will be limited to that of the present meter, about 1 part in 10^8. A definition of c (compatible with the present meter, but otherwise arbitrary) would result in a new definition of the meter. As the above method is applicable to any laser line, reference wavelengths for precise length measurements would be available in any part of the optical spectrum without the need to define one particular wavelength as a new length standard. Also, time of flight measurements (in terrestrial and space radar) could be translated directly into distances via the definition of c."

[4]The *NBS Techn. News Bull., 53*, p. 206, September 1969 published an interim report on the measurement of light frequencies by Z. Bay and G.G. Luther. Quoting from the concluding remarks: "In the future two different approaches to the problem of improving the length standard are possible. In the first approach, the precision of the length standard can be improved by choosing one well stabilized laser line, instead of the krypton-86 line emitted by a gas discharge lamp. The second approach is to base the new definition of the meter on a specified value of c such that it is compatible with the present meter. Then all the reference lines of known frequencies can serve simultaneously as reference lines for

length measurements . . . The comparison of frequencies represents an easier task for future metrology than the intercomparison of wavelengths in distant parts of the spectrum. Therefore Drs. Bay and Luther prefer the second approach for a new and final definition of the meter."

[5]Z. Bay, "The Use of Microwave Modulation of Lasers for Length Measurements", published in *Precision Measurements and Fundamental Constants*, NBS Special Publication No. 343, edited by D.N. Langenberg and B.N. Taylor (U.S. GPO, Washington, D.C., 1971) p. 59. Quotation from page 62: "Since optical frequency comparisons and length measurements based on microwave frequencies avoid the use of a wavelength standard without any loss in accuracy, the adoption of a unified standard of time frequency and length via a defined value of the velocity of light can be advocated as soon as c is known to the accuracy of the present length standard."

[6]Z. Bay and G.G. Luther, "The Measuring of Optical Frequencies and the Velocity of Light," published in *Precision Measurements and Fundamental Constants*, NBS Special Publication No. 343, edited by D.N. Langenberg and B.N. Taylor (U.S. GPO, Washington, D.C., 1971) p. 63. Quotation from page 66: "On the basis of the foregoing conclusions the adoption of a unified standard for time interval and length via a defined value of the velocity of light is strongly advocated."

[7]Z. Bay, "The Constancy of the Velocity of Light and Prospects for a Unified Standardization of Time Frequency and Length," published in *Proceedings of the Fourth International Conference on Atomic Masses and Fundamental Constants*, Teddington, England, September 1971, edited by J. H. Sanders and A.H. Wapstra, Plenum Press, New York, 1972. Quotation from page 334: ". . . the unified standardization of time, frequency, and length via an agreed upon value of c will be preferable to a system based on a frequency standard and on a wavelength standard. Indeed, under those conditions a standard wavelength defined independently of the frequency standard, would not represent an additional advantage for the time-length measuring system . . . Besides its theoretical simplicity and its versatility, a further advantage of the unified standardization system is that in case of future improvements of the standards only one unit of measurement has to be redefined. According to what was said in Sections 4 and 5, it should be the unit of time, the second, and not the meter. The meter will be automatically refined via c for the possible use of improvements in length measuring techniques. If one of the frequency stabilized lasers turns out to be better in precision than the present frequency standard or others in prospect, and if its frequency can directly be connected to microwave frequencies, that laser could well be used as a new frequency standard. But the meter should not be tied to its wavelength. Instead, an agreed upon value of c should be adopted to be taken over as an invariable figure in future standardizations."

[8]Z. Bay and J.A. White, "Frequency Dependence of the Speed of Light in Space," *Physical Review D*, 5, p. 796, 1972. Quotation from page 798: ". . . This fact provides additional experimental support for the suggestion reviewed recently that c be used in metrology to connect the unit of time (the second) and the unit of length (the meter). The connection is made by assigning an agreed upon value to c in m/sec. The results of this paper show that in the above-mentioned broad spectrum this assignment can be made without reference to frequency. After making the connection between the two units, it is preferable to consider the unit of time and c as standards rather than the unit of length and c. The preference for time follows from the fact that in any system of inertia under steady conditions the periodicity in time (frequency) is conserved in wave propagation while the periodicity in space (wavelength) depends on the geometry of the wave propagation and changes in general from point to point. Besides the theoretical appeal and simplicity of the unified time-length measuring system, its advantages are the following: 1) The accuracies of the two units with respect to their definitions are the same and equal to that of an optical or microwave transition judged to be the best choice for a standard. 2) In case of future improvements only one unit needs to be redefined. Presumably this will be the unit of time, the second. Simultaneously the meter will be automatically refined via c for the possible use of improvements in length measuring techniques."

[9]Z. Bay, G.G. Luther and J.A. White, "Measurement of an Optical Frequency and the Speed of Light", *Physical Review Letters*, 29, p. 189, 1972. Quotation from page 192: "The ultimate accuracy of optical frequency measurements and that of length measurements by

this method is expected to be limited only by imperfections of mirror surfaces. This technological limitation is applicable also to wavelength comparisons and length measurements based on any wavelength standards, irrespective of their possible better quality. Thus, since they are applicable throughout the entire spectrum, these experiments demonstrate the possibility and practicability of a unified time-length measurement system based on a frequency standard and on a defined value of the speed of light, compatible with the present meter but otherwise arbitrary."

[10]On July 21, 1972 Bay presented a Retirement Address at a Special NBS Colloquium. His talk was announced in the *NBS Technical Calendar*, including the following statement: "The recent research" (of Zoltan Bay) "represents the application of the most modern developments in optics to the new determination of the value for one of the fundamental constants of nature, the speed of light. These and other recent developments suggest the possibility of unifying the definitions of the meter and the second by defining the value of the speed of light. Dr. Bay was the first to suggest and subsequently to perform an experiment that demonstrated the feasibility of such a unified definition". At the close of the Colloquium, Dr. E. Ambler, Director of the Institute for Basic Standards, presented a Certificate to Bay, the text of which is the following: "This Certificate is presented to Dr. Zoltan L. Bay in appreciation of the outstanding service he has rendered to the National Bureau of Standards and in recognition of his important contributions to science. His long and fruitful career, which included such achievements as the first measurement of radar echoes from the moon, had culminated in his conception and development of a technology for optical frequency measurement. This experiment has produced a new determination of the speed of light and suggests the possibility of a unified definition of length and time." The tribute was signed by Laurence M. Kushner, acting director, July 21, 1972.

[11]The *NBS Techn. News Bull.*, *57*, January 1973, reported on p. 14 the "Experimental Measurement of Optical Frequency" by Z. Bay, G.G. Luther and J.A. White, with the following concluding statement: "The success of the experiment lends further weight to the proposal previously advanced by Z. Bay that the definitions of the units of length and of time might be connected by a definition of the speed of light."

[12]Quotation taken from the booklet prepared by the NBS Optical Physics Division for the Atomic and Molecular Physics Evaluation Panel in 1973. The statement on page 2 of the Introduction says: "One of our areas of primary concern is that of the definition of the unit of length. Work in this area, both here and at the NBS Boulder laboratories was instrumental in producing several important resolutions by the Committee Consultative for the Definition of the Metre. These resolutions recommend values for the wavelength of radiations emitted by iodine and methane stabilized lasers, and recommend a new and more precise value for the speed of light. In the minutes of the June meeting, the CCDM went on to urge its successors to maintain this value of c in any subsequent redefinition of the meter. This comes very close to fulfilling the proposal urged for many years by Dr. Zoltan Bay that the meter be defined in terms of the speed of light."

[13]Z. Bay and J.A. White, "The Speed of Light and the New Meter," *Hungarica Acta Physica, 36*, p. 91, 1974. The closing sentence on page 106 is: "All this points in the direction that the time-length measurement system, unified via a defined value of the speed of light, will be the system for the future."

[14]Z. Bay and J.A. White, "The Speed of Light and the New Meter," *Physics Today*, April 1974, p. 9. The closing sentence on page 10 is: "Detailed studies of the problems involved and the successful experiments mentioned above fully justify in our opinion a decision in favor of the unified system."

C.

HUNGARIAN COMPETITORS IN THE SUMMER OLYMPIC GAMES, 1896-1968*:

TRACK AND FIELD ATHLETICS

100 m - Men
1896 Athens   3. Alajos Szokolyi 12,6

800 m - Men
1896 Athens   2. Nándor Dáni 2:11,8
1900 Paris   5. Zoltán Speidl
1908 London   4. Ödön Bodor 1:55,4

1500 m - Men
1956 Melbourne   4. László Tábori 3:42,4
1960 Rome   3. István Rózsavölgyi 3:39,2

5000 m
1956 Melbourne   4. Miklós Szabó II 14:03,4
    6. László Tábori 14:09,8

10000 m
1956 Melbourne   2. József Kovács 28:52,4

Marathon
1896 Athens   3. Gyula Kellner 3:06:35
1964 Tokyo   5. József Sütő 2:17:55,8

3000 m Steeplechase
1956 Melbourne   2. Sándor Rozsnyói 8:43,6

4 X 100 m Relay, Men
1924 Paris   4. Ferenc Gerő, Lajos Kurunczy, László Muskát, Gusztáv Rózsahegyi 42,0
1948 London   4. Ferenc Tima, László Bartha, György Csányi, Béla Goldoványi 41,6
1952 Helsinki   3. László Zarándi, Géza Varasdi, György Csányi, Béla Goldoványi 40,5

4 X 400 m Relay, Men
1908 London   3. Pál Simon, Frigyes Mezey, József Nagy, Ödön Bodor.

50 km Walk
1952 Helsinki   3. Antal Róka 4:31:27,2
1956 Melbourne   5. Antal Róka 4:50:09,0
1968 Mexico City   2. Antal Kiss 4:30:17,0

---

*(Kamper, Erich, *Encyclopedia of the Olympic Games*. 1st ed. New York: McGraw-Hill, 1972. XIX, 360 p., Szécsi, Andor, comp., *Magyarok az olimpiákon, 1896-1972*. Budapest, 1972.)

High Jump, Men
1900 Paris   3. Lajos Gönczy 1,75
1904 St. Louis   4. Lajos Gönczy 1,753
1906 Athens   2. Lajos Gönczy 1,75
1908 London   2. István Somodi 1,88
1924 Paris   5. Jenő Gáspár 1,88

Pole Vault
1900 Paris   4. Jakab Kauser 3,10

Long Jump, Men
1952 Helsinki   3. Ödön Földessy 7,30

Triple Jump
1896 Athens   4. Alajos Szokolyi 12,30

Shot Put, Men
1900 Paris   4. Rezső Crettier 12,05
1906 Athens   2. Mihály Dávid 11,83
1964 Tokyo   3. Vilmos Varjú 19,39
                 5. Zsigmond Nagy 18,88

Discus Throw, Men
1900 Paris   1. Rudolf Bauer 36,04
                 5. Rezső Crettier 33,65
1932 Los Angeles 5. István Donogán 47.08
                 6. Endre Madarász 46,52
1948 London   5. Ferenc Klics 48,21
1952 Helsinki   5. Ferenc Klics 51,13
1960 Rome   4. József Szécsényi 55,79
1964 Tokyo   5. József Szécsényi 57,23

Hammer Throw
1948 London   1. Imre Németh 56,07
1952 Helsinki   1. József Csermák 60,34
                 3. Imre Németh 57,74
1956 Melbourne   5. József Csermák 60,70
1960 Rome   2. Gyula Zsivótzky 65,79
1964 Tokyo   2. Gyula Zsivótzky 69,09
1968 Mexico City 1. Gyula Zsivótzky 73,36
                 3. Lázár Lovász 69,78
                 5. Sándor Eckschmidt 69,46

Javelin Throw, Men
1912 Stockholm   3. Mór Kóczán 55,60
1928 Amsterdam   2. Béla Szepes 65,26
1948 London   3. József Várszegi 67,03
1960 Rome   3. Gergely Kulcsár 78,57
1964 Tokyo   2. Gergely Kulcsár 82,32
1968 Mexico City 3. Gergely Kulcsár 87,06

400 m Ladies
1964 Tokyo   4. Antónia Munkácsi 54,4

800 m Ladies
1964 Tokyo   4. Zsuzsa Nagy-Szabó 2:03,5

High Jump, Ladies
1936 Berlin   1. Ibolya Csák 1,60

Long Jump, Ladies
1948 London   1. Olga Gyarmati 5,695

Discus Throw, Ladies
1968 Mexico City   3. Jolán Kleiber 54,90

Javelin Throw, Ladies
1964 Tokyo   2. Márta Rudas 58,27
1968 Mexico City   1. Angela Németh 60,36
                 4. Márta Rudas 56,38

Pentathlon, Ladies
1968 Mexico City   3. Annamária Tóth

Pentathlon, Men
1906 Athens   2. István Mudin
1924 Paris   2. Elemér Somfay

Standing High Jump, Men
1906 Athens   5. Lajos Gönczy 1,35

Discus, ancient style
1906 Athens   3. István Mudin 31,91

3000 m Walk
1906 Athens   1. György Sztantics 15:13,2

SWIMMING

100 m Freestyle, Men
1896 Athens   1. Alfréd Hajós 1:22,2
1904 St. Louis   1. Zoltán Halmay 1:02,8 (100 yards)
1906 Athens   2. Zoltán Halmay 1:14,2
1908 London   2. Zoltán Halmay 1:06,2
1928 Amsterdam   2. István Bárány 59,8
1936 Berlin   1. Ferenc Csík 57,6
1948 London   3. Géza Kádas 58,1
1952 Helsinki   5. Géza Kádas 58,6
1960 Rome   5. Gyula Dobay 56,3

200 m Freestyle, Men
1900 Paris   2. Zoltán Halmay 2:31,4

400 m Freestyle, Men

1906 Athens	4. Alajos Bruckner
1912 Stockholm	5. Béla Las Torres 5:42,0
1948 London	4. Géza Kádas 4:49,4
	5. György Mitró 4:49,9

1500 m Freestyle, Men

1896 Athens	1. Alfréd Hajós 18:22,2 (1200 m)
1900 Paris	3. Zoltán Halmay 15:16,4 (1000 m)
1904 St. Louis	2. Géza Kiss 28:28,2 (1 mile)
1948 London	3. György Mitró 19:43,2
	4. György Csordás 19:54,2
1960 Rome	5. József Katona 17:43,7

100 m Backstroke, Men

1912 Stockholm	4. András Baronyi 1:25,2
1924 Paris	3. Károly Bartha 1:17,8

200 m Butterfly, Men

1956 Melbourne	3. György Tumpek 2:23,9

4 X 200 m Freestyle Relay, Men

1906 Athens	1. József Onódy, Henrik Hajós, Géza Kiss, Zoltán Halmay 16:52,4
1908 London	2. József Munk, Imre Zachar, Béla Las Torres, Zoltán Halmay 10:59,0
1928 Amsterdam	4. András Wannie, Rezső Wannie, Géza Tarródy, István Bárány 9:57,0
1932 Los Angeles	3. András Wannie, László Szabados, András Székely, István Bárány 9:31,4
1936 Berlin	3. Árpád Lengyel, Oszkár Abay-Nemes, Ödön Gróf, Ferenc Csík 9:12,3
1948 London	2. Elemér Szathmári, György Mitró, Imre Nyéki, Géza Kádas 8:48,4
1952 Helsinki	5. László Gyöngyösi, György Csordás, Géza Kádas, Imre Nyéki 8:52,6

Highboard Diving, Men

1956 Melbourne	4. József Gerlach

100 m Freestyle, Ladies

1952 Helsinki	1. Katalin Szőke 1:06,8
	3. Judit Temes 1:07,1
1960 Rome	5. Csilla Madarász-Bajnógel 1:03,6

400 m Freestyle, Ladies

1952 Helsinki	1. Valéria Gyenge 5:12,1
	2. Éva Novák 5:13,7
	6. Éva Székely 5:17,9
1956 Melbourne	5. Éva Székely 5:14,2

200 m Breaststroke, Ladies

1948 London	3.	Éva Novák 3:00,2
	4.	Éva Székely 3:02,5
1952 Helsinki	1.	Éva Székely 2:51,7
	2.	Éva Novák 2:54,4
	4.	Klára Killermann 2:57,6
1956 Melbourne	2.	Éva Székely 2:54,8
	5.	Klára Killermann 2:56,1

100 m Backstroke, Ladies

1948 London	4.	Ilona Novák 1:18,4
1968 Mexico City	5.	Andrea Gyarmati 1:09,1

100 m Butterfly, Ladies

1956 Melbourne	4.	Mária Littomericzky 1:14,9
1968 Mexico City	5.	Andrea Gyarmati 1:06,8

4 X 100 m Freestyle Relay, Ladies

¶936 Berlin	4.	Ilona Ács, Ágnes Bíró, Vera Harsányi, Magda Lenkei 4:48,0
1948 London	5.	Mária Littomericzky, Judit Temes, Ilona Novák, Éva Székely 4:44,8
1952 Helsinki	1.	Ilona Novák, Judit Temes, Éva Novák, Katalin Szőke 4:24,4
1960 Rome	4.	Anna Temesvári, Mária Frank, Katalin Boros, Csilla Madarász-Bajnógel 4:21,2
1964 Tokyo	4.	Judit Túróczy, Éva Erdélyi, Katalin Takács, Csilla Dobay-Madarász 4:12,1
1968 Mexico City	5.	Edit Kovács, Magdolna Patóh, Andrea Gyarmati, Judit Túróczy 4:11,0

4 X 100 m Medley Relay, Ladies

1960 Rome	6.	Magdolna Dávid, Klára Bartos-Killermann, Márta Egervári, Csilla Madarász 4:53,7

50 yards Freestyle, Men

1904 St. Louis	1.	Zoltán Halmay 28,0

880 yards Freestyle

1904 St. Louis	3.	Géza Kiss

4000 m Freestyle

1900 Paris	2.	Zoltán Halmay

Water Polo

1924 Paris	5.	István Barta, Tibor Fazekas, Márton Homonnai, Alajos Keserű II, Lajos Homonnai, János Wenk, Ferenc Keserű I, József Vértesy
1928 Amsterdam	2.	István Barta, Sándor Ivády, Alajos Keserű II, Márton Homonnai, Ferenc Keserű I, József Vértesy, Olivér Halasy

1932 Los Angeles	1. György Bródy, Sándor Ivády, Márton Homonnai, Olivér Halasy, József Vértesy, János Németh, Ferenc Keserű I, Alajos Keserű II, István Barta, Miklós Sárkány
1936 Berlin	1. György Bródy, Kálmán Hazai, Márton Homonnai, Olivér Halasy, Jenő Brandi, János Németh, Mihály Bozsi, György Kutasi, Miklós Sárkány, Sándor Tarics, István Molnár
1948 London	2. Endre Győrfi, Miklós Holop, Dezső Gyarmati, Károly Szittya, Oszkár Csuvik, István Szívós, Dezső Lemhényi, László Jenei, Dezső Fábián, Jenő Brandi
1952 Helsinki	1. László Jeney, György Vízvári, Dezső Gyarmati, Kálmán Markovits, Antal Bolváry, István Szívós, György Kárpáti, Róbert Antal, Dezső Fábián, Károly Szittya, Dezső Lemhényi, István Hasznos, Miklós Martin
1956 Melbourne	1. Ottó Boros, István Hevesi, Dezső Gyarmati, Kálmán Markovits, Antal Bolváry, Mihály Mayer, György Kárpáti, László Jeney, István Szívós, Tivadar Kanizsa, Ervin Zádor
1960 Rome	3. Ottó Boros, István Hevesi, Mihály Mayer, Dezső Gyarmati, Tivadar Kanizsa, Zoltán Dömötör, László Felkai, László Jeney, András Katona, Kálmán Markovits, Péter Rusorán II, György Kárpáti, János Konrád, András Bodnár
1964 Tokyo	1. Miklós Ambrus, László Felkai, János Konrád, Zoltán Dömötör, Tivadar Kanizsa, Péter Rusorán, György Kárpáti, Ottó Boros, Mihály Mayer, Dénes Pócsik, András Bodnár, Dezső Gyarmati
1968 Mexico City	3. Endre Molnár, Mihály Mayer, István Szívós, János Konrád II, László Sárosi, László Felkai, Ferenc Konrád III, Dénes Pócsik, András Bodnár, Zoltán Dömötör, János Steinmetz

BOXING

Flyweight

1928 Amsterdam	1. Antal Kocsis
1932 Los Angeles	1. István Énekes
1960 Rome	1. Gyula Török

Bantamweight

1948 London	1. Tibor Csík

Featherweight

1936 Berlin	4. Dezső Frigyes

Lightweight

1936 Berlin	1. Imre Harangi

Light Middleweight
1952 Helsinki 1. László Papp
1956 Melbourne 1. László Papp

Middleweight
1948 London 1. László Papp

Heavyweight
1936 Berlin 4. Ferenc Nagy

WEIGHTLIFTING

Bantamweight
1960 Rome 6. Imre Földi
1964 Tokyo 2. Imre Földi
1968 Mexico City 2. Imre Földi

Lightweight
1960 Rome 6. Mihály Huszka
1968 Mexico City 6. János Bagócs

Middleweight
1960 Rome 3. Győző Veres
1964 Tokyo 6. Mihály Huszka
1968 Mexico City 3. Károly Bakos

Light Heavyweight
1960 Rome 4. Géza Tóth
1964 Tokyo 2. Géza Tóth
3. Győző Veres
1968 Mexico City 4. Győző Veres

Middle Heavyweight
1964 Tokyo 6. Árpád Nemessányi
1968 Mexico City 6. Árpád Nemessányi

Heavyweight
1964 Tokyo 5. Károly Ecsér

WRESTLING, GRECO-ROMAN STYLE

Flyweight
1948 London 5. Gyula Szilágyi
1956 Melbourne 5. István Baranyai
1968 Mexico City 4. Imre Alker

Bantamweight
1924 Paris 6. József Tasnádi
1928 Amsterdam 5. Ödön Zombori
1936 Berlin 1. Márton Lőrincz

1948 London	6. Lajos Biringer-Bencze
1952 Helsinki	1. Imre Hódos
1956 Melbourne	4. Imre Hódos
1968 Mexico City	1. János Varga

Featherweight

1928 Amsterdam	4. Károly Kárpáti
1948 London	3. Ferenc Tóth
1952 Helsinki	2. Imre Polyák
1956 Melbourne	2. Imre Polyák
1960 Rome	2. Imre Polyák
1964 Tokyo	1. Imre Polyák

Lightweight

1906 Athens	3. Ferenc Holubán
1912 Stockholm	4. Ödön Radvány
1924 Paris	2. Lajos Keresztes
1928 Amsterdam	1. Lajos Keresztes
1948 London	3. Károly Ferencz
1952 Helsinki	4. Gyula Tarr
1956 Melbourne	3. Gyula Tóth

Welterweight

1948 London	2. Miklós Szilvási
1952 Helsinki	1. Miklós Szilvási
1968 Mexico City	3. Károly Bajkó

Middleweight

1928 Amsterdam	2. László Papp
1936 Berlin	3. József Palotás
1952 Helsinki	4. Gyula Németi
1956 Melbourne	5. György Gurics
1964 Tokyo	4. Géza Hollósi

Light Heavyweight

1908 London	4. Hugo Payr
1912 Stockholm	3. Béla Varga
1928 Amsterdam	6. Imre Szalai
1948 London	4. Gyula Kovács
1952 Helsinki	4. Gyula Kovács
1960 Rome	4. Péter Piti
1964 Tokyo	5. Ferenc Kiss

Heavyweight

1896 Athens	4. Momcsilló Topavicza
1908 London	1. Richárd Weisz
1924 Paris	3. Raymund Badó
1928 Amsterdam	6. Raymund Badó
1948 London	5. József Tarányi
1960 Rome	4. István Kozma
1964 Tokyo	1. István Kozma
1968 Mexico City	1. István Kozma

WRESTLING, FREE STYLE

Bantamweight
1932 Los Angeles	2. Ödön Zombori
1936 Berlin	1. Ödön Zombori
1948 London	5. Lajos Biringer-Bencze
1952 Helsinki	6. Lajos Bencze

Featherweight
1936 Berlin	5. Ferenc Tóth
1948 London	4. Ferenc Tóth

Lightweight
1932 Los Angeles	2. Károly Kárpáti
1936 Berlin	1. Károly Kárpáti
1956 Melbourne	4. Gyula Tóth

Welterweight
1932 Los Angeles	5. Gyula Zombori
1948 London	5. Kálmán Sóvári

Middleweight
1932 Los Angeles	3. József Tunyogi
1952 Helsinki	3. György Gurics
1960 Rome	5. Géza Hollósi

Light Heavyweight
1968 Mexico City	3. József Csatári

Heavyweight
1948 London	1. Gyula Bóbis
1960 Rome	5. János Reznák

FENCING

Men's Individual Foil
1912 Stockholm	4. László Berti
1948 London	3. Lajos Maszlay
1956 Melbourne	5. József Gyuricza
1964 Tokyo	5. Dr. Jenő Kamuti
1968 Mexico City	2. Dr. Jenő Kamuti

Men's Team Foil
1924 Paris	3. László Berti, Sándor Pósta, Zoltán Schenker, Ödön Tersztyánszky, István Lichteneckert.
1952 Helsinki	3. Endre Tilli, Aladár Gerevich, Endre Palócz, Lajos Maszlay, Tibor Berczelly, József Sákovics.
1956 Melbourne	3. József Gyuricza, József Sákovics, Mihály Fülöp, Endre Tilli, Lajos Somodi, József Marosi.
1960 Rome	4. Ferenc Czvikovszky, Jenő Kamuti, Mihály Fülöp, László Kamuti, József Gyuricza, József Sákovics.
1968 Mexico City	5. Sándor Szabó, Dr. Jenő Kamuti, László Kamuti, Gábor Füredi, Attila May.

Individual Epee

1952 Helsinki	5. József Sákovics
1956 Melbourne	5. Lajos Balthazár
1960 Rome	4. József Sákovics
1968 Mexico City	1. Győző Kulcsár

Team Epee

1956 Melbourne	2. József Sákovics, Béla Rerrich, Lajos Balthazár, Ambrus Nagy, József Marosi, Barnabás Berzsenyi
1960 Rome	4. József Marosi, Tamás Gábor, István Kausz, József Sákovics, Árpád Bárány
1964 Tokyo	1. Győző Kulcsár, Zoltán Nemere, Tamás Gábor, Dr. István Kausz, Árpád Bárány
1968 Mexico City	1. Csaba Fenyvesi, Zoltán Nemere, Pál Schmitt, Győző Kulcsár, Pál Nagy

Individual Sabre

1900 Paris	4. Ámon Gregurich 5. Gyula Iványi
1908 London	1. Dr. Jenő Fuchs, 2. Béla Zulavszky, 4. Jenő Szántay, 5. Péter Tóth, 6. Lajos Werkner
1912 Stockholm	1. Dr. Jenő Fuchs, 2. Béla Békéssy, 3. Ervin Mészáros, 4. Zoltán Schenker, 6. Dr. Péter Tóth
1924 Paris	1. Dr. Sándor Pósta, 3. János Garay, 4. Zoltán Schenker
1928 Amsterdam	1. Ödön Tersztyánszky, 2. Attila Petschauer, 5. Sándor Gombos
1932 Los Angeles	1. György Piller, 3. Endre Kabos, 5. Attila Petschauer
1936 Berlin	1. Endre Kabos, 3. Aladár Gerevich, 4. László Rajcsányi
1948 London	1. Aladár Gerevich, 3. Pál Kovács
1952 Helsinki	1. Pál Kovács, 2. Aladár Gerevich, 3. Tibor Berczelly
1956 Melbourne	1. Rudolf Kárpáti, 5. Aladár Gerevich
1960 Rome	1. Rudolf Kárpáti, 2. Zoltán Horváth
1964 Tokyo	1. Tibor Pézsa
1968 Mexico City	3. Tibor Pézsa

Team Sabre

1908 London	1. Dr. Jenő Fuchs, Oszkár Gerde, Péter Tóth, Lajos Werkner, Dezső Földes
1912 Stockholm	1. Dr. Jenő Fuchs, László Berti, Ervin Mészáros, Dr. Dezső Földes, Dr. Oszkár Gerde, Zoltán Schenker, Dr. Péter Tóth, Lajos Werkner
1924 Paris	2. László Berti, János Garay, Sándor Pósta, József Rády, Zoltán Schenker, László Széchy, Ödön Tersztyánszky, Jenő Uhlyárik
1928 Amsterdam	1. Ödön Tersztyánszky, Dr. Sándor Gombos, Attila Petschauer, János Garay, József Rády, Gyula Glykais
1932 Los Angeles	1. György Piller, Endre Kabos, Attila Petschauer, Ernő Nagy, Gyula Glykais
1936 Berlin	1. Endre Kabos, Aladár Gerevich, Tibor Berczelly, Pál Kovács, László Rajcsányi, Imre Rajczy

1948 London	1. Aladár Gerevich, Rudolf Kárpáti, Pál Kovács, Tibor Berczelly, László Rajcsányi, Bertalan Papp
1952 Helsinki	1. Pál Kovács, Aladár Gerevich, Tibor Berczelly, Rudolf Kárpáti, László Rajcsányi, Bertalan Papp
1956 Melbourne	1. Rudolf Kárpáti, Aladár Gerevich, Pál Kovács, Attila Keresztes, Jenő Hámori, Dániel Magay
1960 Rome	1. Zoltán Horváth, Rudolf Kárpáti, Tamás Mendelényi, Pál Kovács, Gábor Delneky, Aladár Gerevich
1964 Tokyo	5. Péter Bakonyi, Miklós Meszéna, Attila Kovács, Zoltán Horváth, Tibor Pézsa
1968 Mexico City	3. Tamás Kovács, Miklós Meszéna, Dr. János Kalmár, Péter Bakonyi, Tibor Pézsa

Ladies Individual Foil

1924 Paris	6. Gizella Tary
1928 Amsterdam	6. Margit Dány
1932 Los Angeles	3. Erna Bógen
1936 Berlin	1. Ilona Elek
1948 London	1. Ilona Elek

Ladies Team Foil

1960 Rome	2. Tiborné Székely, Ildikó Rejtő, Magda Kovács-Nyári, Katalin Juhász-Nagy, Lidia Dömölky
1964 Tokyo	1. Ildikó Újlaki-Rejtő, Katalin Juhász-Nagy, Lidia Sákovics-Dömölky, Judit Mendelényi-Agoston, Paula Földessy-Marosi
1968 Mexico City	2. Ildikó Bóbis, Lídia Sákovics, Ildikó Újlaki-Rejtő, Mária Gulácsi, Paula Marosi

Three cornered Sabre

1906 Athens	3. Péter Tóth
	5. Jenő Apáthy

MODERN PENTATHLON

1936 Berlin	5. Nándor Orbán
1952 Helsinki	2. Gábor Benedek
	3. István Szondy
1956 Melbourne	5. Gábor Benedek
1960 Rome	1. Ferenc Németh
	2. Imre Nagy
	5. András Balczó
1964 Tokyo	1. Dr. Ferenc Török
1968 Mexico City	2. András Balczó

Modern Pentathlon, Teams

1952 Helsinki	1. Gábor Benedek, István Szondy, Aladár Kovácsi
1956 Melbourne	4. Gábor Benedek, János Bódi, Antal Moldrich
1960 Rome	1. Ferenc Németh, Imre Nagy, András Balczó
1964 Tokyo	3. Dr. Ferenc Török, Imre Nagy, Dr. Ottó Török
1968 Mexico City	1. András Balczó, Dr. István Móna, Dr. Ferenc Török

CANOEING

1000 m Kayak Singles, Men
1956 Melbourne	3. Lajos Kiss
1960 Rome	2. Imre Szőllősi
1964 Tokyo	2. Mihály Hesz
1968 Mexico City	1. Mihály Hesz

1000 m Kayak Pairs, Men
1960 Rome	2. György Mészáros, András Szente
1964 Tokyo	5. György Mészáros, Imre Szőllősi
1968 Mexico City	2. Csaba Giczi, István Timár

1000 m Kayak Fours, Men
1964 Tokyo	4. Imre Kemecsey, György Mészáros, András Szente, Imre Szőllősi
1968 Mexico City	3. Csaba Giczi, István Timár, Imre Szőllősi, István Csizmadia

1000 m Canadian Singles
1952 Helsinki	2. János Parti
1956 Melbourne	2. István Hernek
1960 Rome	1. János Parti
1964 Tokyo	4. András Tőrő
1968 Mexico City	1. Tibor Tatai

1000 m Canadian Pairs
1952 Helsinki	5. István Bodor, József Tuza
1956 Melbourne	3. Károly Wieland, Ferenc Mohácsi
1960 Rome	3. Imre Farkas, András Tőrő
1964 Tokyo	4. Antal Hajba, Árpád Soltész
1968 Mexico City	2. Tamás Wichmann, Gyula Petrikovics

500 m Kayak Singles, Ladies
1948 London	4. Klára Bánfalvi
1952 Helsinki	6. Cecília Hartmann
1956 Melbourne	4. Cecília Berkes-Hartmann
1960 Rome	5. Klára Fried-Bánfalvi

500 m Kayak Pairs, Ladies
1960 Rome	3. Klára Fried-Bánfalvi, Vilma Egresi
1968 Mexico City	2. Anna Pfeffer, Katalin Rozsnyói

10,000 m Kayak Singles
1956 Melbourne	2. Ferenc Hatláczky

10,000 m Kayak Pairs
1948 London	5. Gyula Andrási, János Urányi
1952 Helsinki	3. Ferenc Varga, József Gurovits
1956 Melbourne	1. János Urányi, László Fábián

4 X 500 m Kayak Singles Relay
1960 Rome   2. Imre Szőllősi, Imre Kemecsey, András Szente, György Mészáros

10,000 m Canadian Singles
1952 Helsinki   2. Gábor Novák
1956 Melbourne   2. János Parti

10,000 m Canadian Pairs
1956 Melbourne   3. Imre Farkas, József Hunics

ROWING

Single Sculls
1908 London   3. Károly Levitzky

Coxwainless Pairs
1936 Berlin   4. Károly Győri, Tibor Mamusich

Coxed Pairs
1948 London   3. Antal Szendey, Béla Zsitnik, Róbert Zimonyi

Coxwainless Fours
1968 Mexico City   2. Zoltán Melis, György Sarlós, József Csermely, Antal Melis

Coxed Fours
1936 Berlin   5. Miklós Mihók, Vilmos Éden, Ákos Inotay, Alajos Szilassy, László Molnár
1960 Rome   6. Tibor Bedekovics, Csaba Kovács, László Munteán, Pál Wagner, Gyula Lengyel

Eights
1936 Berlin   5. Pál Domonkos, Sándor Korompay, Dr. Hugó Ballya, Imre Kapossy, Antal Szendey, Gábor Alapy, Frigyes Hollósi-Jung, László Szabó, Ervin Kereszthy

EQUESTRIAN SPORTS

Dressage, Teams
1936 Berlin   6. Gusztáv Pados, László Magasházy, Pál Kémery

Jumping
1936 Berlin   3. József Platthy

SHOOTING

Small Bore Rifle
1932 Los Angeles   3. Zoltán Hradetzky-Soós

1936 Berlin	2. Ralf Berzsenyi
1956 Melbourne	6. Sándor Krebs
1964 Tokyo	1. László Hammerl
1968 Mexico City	2. László Hammerl

Small Bore Rifle, 3 Positions
1964 Tokyo   3. László Hammerl

Rapid-Fire Pistol or Revolver
1948 London	1. Károly Takács
1952 Helsinki	1. Károly Takács
	2. Szilárd Kún
1964 Tokyo	5. Szilárd Kún

Free Pistol (50 m)
1952 Helsinki   3. Ambrus Balogh

Clay Pigeon Shooting
1924 Paris   1. Gyula Halasy

Military Rifle (300 m)
1912 Stockholm   1. Sándor Prokopp

**Running Deer Shooting,
Single Shot - Teams**
1924 Paris   6. Gusztáv Szomjas, Rezső Velez, Elemér Takács, László Szomjas

**Running Deer Shooting,
Single and Double Shot**
| 1956 Melbourne | 4. Miklós Kovács |
| | 5. Miklós Kocsis |

GYMNASTICS

**Combined Exercises,
Individual, Men**
| 1906 Athens | 6. Béla Erődy |
| 1932 Los Angeles | 2. István Pelle |

**Combined Exercises,
Teams, Men**
1906 Athens   6. Béla Dáner, Árpád Erdős, Béla Erődy, Frigyes Gráf, Gyula Kakas, Nándor Kovács, Kálmán Szabó, Vilmos Szűcs

1912 Stockholm   2. Lajos Aradi-Kmetykó, József Berkes-Bittenbinder, Imre Erdődy, Samu Fóti, Imre Gellért, Győző Halmos-Haberfeld, Ottó Helmich, István Herczeg, József Keresztessy, János Korponai-Krizmanich, Elemér Pászty, Árpád Pétery, Jenő Réti-Rittich, Ferenc Szűts, Ödön Téry, Géza Tull

1932 Los Angeles	4. István Pelle, Miklós Péter, Péter Boros, József Hegedűs
1948 London	3. Lajos Tóth, Dr. Lajos Sántha, László Baranyai, Ferenc Pataki, János Mogyorósi-Klencs, Ferenc Várkői
1952 Helsinki	6. Dr. Lajos Sántha, Ferenc Pataki, József Fekete, Károly Kocsis, Ferenc Kemény, Sándor Réti, Lajos Tóth, János Mogyorósi-Klencs

**Parallel Bars,
Individual, Men**
1932 Los Angeles   2. István Pelle

**Floor Exercises,
Individual, Men**
1932 Los Angeles   1. István Pelle
1948 London   1. Ferenc Pataki
                    2. János Mogyorósi-Klencs

Long Horse Vault, Individual
1932 Los Angeles   6. István Pelle
1948 London   3. János Mogyorósi-Klencs (38,50)
                    3. Ferenc Pataki (38,50)

**Pommelled Horse,
Individual, Men**
1932 Los Angeles   1. István Pelle
                    5. Péter Boros

**Horizontal Bar,
Individual, Men**
1932 Los Angeles   4. István Pelle
1948 London   4. Lajos Sántha
                    6. Lajos Tóth

**Combined Exercises,
Individual, Ladies**
1952 Helsinki   3. Margit Korondi
1956 Melbourne   2. Ágnes Keleti
                    4. Olga Tass

**Combined Exercises,
Teams, Ladies**
1928 Amsterdam   4. Mária Hámos, Aranka Hennyei, Anna Kael, Margit Pályi, Erzsébet Rudas, Nándorné Szeiler, Ilona Szőllősi, Judit Tóth, Rudolfné Herpich, Irén Hennyei, Margit Kövessy, Irén Rudas
1936 Berlin   3. Margit Csillik, Judit Tóth, Margit Nagy, Gabriella Mészáros, Eszter Voit, Olga Tőrös, Ilona Madary, Margit Kalocsai
1948 London   2. Edit Vásárhelyi-Weckinger, Mária Kövi, Irén Kárpáti-Karcsics, Erzsébet Gulyás, Erzsébet Balázs, Olga Tass, Anna Fehér, Mária Sándor

1952 Helsinki	2. Margit Korondi, Ágnes Keleti, Edit Perényi-Vásárhelyi, Olga Tass, Erzsébet Gulyás, Mária Zalai-Kövi, Andrea Bodó, Irén Daruházi-Kárpáti
1956 Melbourne	2. Ágnes Keleti, Olga Tass, Margit Korondi, Andrea Molnár-Bodó, Erzsébet Gulyás-Köteles, Alíz Kertész
1964 Tokyo	5. Anikó Jánosi-Ducza, Katalin Makray, Mária Tressel, Gyöngyi Kovács, Katalin Müller, Márta Erdősi
1968 Mexico City	5. Ágnes Bánfai, Anikó Jánosi-Ducza, Katalin Schmitt-Makray, Márta Erdősi, Katalin Száll-Müller, Ilona Békési

Asymmetrical Bars, Ladies

1952 Helsinki	1. Margit Korondi
	3. Ágnes Keleti
	6. Edit Perényi
1956 Melbourne	1. Ágnes Keleti
	6. Olga Tass (18,633)
	6. Aliz Kertész (18,633)
1964 Tokyo	2. Katalin Makray

Floor Exercises, Ladies

1952 Helsinki	1. Ágnes Keleti
	3. Margit Korondi
	4. Erzsébet Gulyás
1956 Melbourne	1. Ágnes Keleti
1964 Tokyo	3. Anikó Jánosi

Horse Vault, Ladies

1956 Melbourne	3. Olga Tass

Balance Beam, Ladies

1952 Helsinki	3. Margit Korondi
	4. Ágnes Keleti
1956 Melbourne	1. Ágnes Keleti

Rope Climbing

1906 Athens	2. Béla Erődy
1932 Los Angeles	4. Miklós Péter
	5. Péter Boros

Tumbling, Men

1932 Los Angeles	4. István Pelle

Team Exercise with Portable Apparatus, Ladies

1952 Helsinki	3. Margit Korondi, Ágnes Keleti, Edit Perényi, Olga Tass, Erzsébet Gulyás, Mária Zalai-Kövi, Andrea Bodó, Irén Daruházi
1956 Melbourne	1. Ágnes Keleti, Margit Korondi, Olga Tass, Andrea Bodó, Alíz Kertész, Erzsébet Gulyás-Köteles

SOCCER

1952 Helsinki	1. Gyula Grosics, Jenő Buzánszky, Mihály Lantos, József Bozsik, Gyula Lóránt, József Zakariás, Nándor Hidegkúti, Sándor Kocsis, Péter Palotás, Ferenc Puskás, Zoltán Czibor, Jenő Dalnoki, Imre Kovács I, László Budai II, Lajos Csordás
1960 Rome	3. Gábor Török, Zoltán Dudás, Jenő Dalnoki, Ernő Solymosi, Pál Várhidi, Ferenc Kovács, Imre Sátori, János Göröcs, Flórián Albert, Pál Orosz, János Dunai, Lajos Faragó, Dezső Novák, Oszkár Vilezsal, Gyula Rákosi, László Pál, Tibor Pál
1964 Tokyo	1. Antal Szentmihályi, Dezső Novák, Kálmán Ihász, Gusztáv Szepesi, Árpád Orbán, Ferenc Nógrádi, János Farkas, Tibor Csernai, Ferenc Bene, Imre Komora, Sándor Katona, József Gelei, Károly Palotai, Zoltán Varga
1968 Mexico City	1. Károly Fatér, Dezső Novák, Lajos Dunai, Miklós Pancsics, Iván Menczel, Lajos Szűcs, László Fazekas, Antal Dunai, László Nagy, Ernő Noskó, István Juhász, Lajos Kocsis, István Básti, László Keglovich, István Sárközi

FIELD HANDBALL

1936 Berlin	4. Antal Ujváry, János Koppány, István Serényi, Lajos Kutasi, Frigyes Rákosi, Lőrinc Galgóczy, Ferenc Cziráki, Gyula Takács, Miklós Fodor, Endre Salgó, Sándor Cséfay, Tibor Máthé, Antal Bende, Imre Páli, Ferenc Velkei, Sándor Szomori

VOLLEYBALL (Men)

1964 Tokyo	6. Béla Czafik, Vilmos Iváncsó, Csaba Lantos, Gábor Bodó, István Molnár, Ottó Prouza, Ferenc Tüske, Tibor Flórián, László Gálos, Antal Kangyerka, Mihály Tatár, Ferenc Jánosi

POLO

1936 Berlin	4. Tivadar Dienes-Öhm, Imre Szentpály, Dezső Kovács, István Bethlen, Kálmán Bartalis

OLYMPIC ART COMPETITIONS

Architecture (Designs for town planning)
1924 Paris

Silver medal: Alfréd Hajós and Dezső Lauber **(Plan of a Stadium)**

Sculpture
1932 Los Angeles   Silver medal: Miltiades Manno **(Wrestling)**

Epic Works
1928 Amsterdam   Gold medal: Dr. Ferenc Mező **(History of the Olympic Games)**
1948 London   Bronze medal: Dr. Éva Földes **(The well of youth)**

PART IX — INDEX

ABOUT THE AUTHOR

Francis S. Wagner studied at the University of Szeged, Hungary, and earned his Ph.D. in history, philosophy, and literature summa cum laude in 1940. He taught at the colleges of Szeged and Budapest and served as a Slavic specialist in the Ministries of Public Education and of Foreign Affairs in Budapest. Between 1946 and 1948 he was head of the Hungarian General Consulate in Bratislava, Czechoslovakia. Since 1953 he has been on the staff of the Library of Congress.

Dr. Wagner's interests center on nationality and racial relations; the diplomatic history of World War II; the philosophy of history; U.S. foreign prestige; and the theory and workings of dialectical materialism. He has published several books on these topics in English, Hungarian and Slovak along with over 250 articles in English-, French-, German- and Hungarian-language periodicals. Among them Mr. Wagner has contributed to *Archivum Europae Centro-orientalis; Dolgozatok* (Archaeological Yearbook); *Történetírás* (Historiography); *Láthatár* (Horizon); *Nevelésügyi Szemle; Magyar Paedagogia; Revue d'Histoire Comparée; American Quarterly; American Historical Review; Slavic Review; Journal of Central European Affairs*.

The author's name has been listed in a number of biographical dictionaries including the *Directory of American Scholars; International Scholars Directory, Who's Who in the South and Southwest; Men of Achievement; Dictionary of International Biography; International Authors and Writers Who's Who*.

Currently Dr. Wagner is working on a world guide to ethnic minorities, as well as on the development of the American concept of nationhood.

His daughter, Christina, has devoted much of her time and energy to this project. A graduate of the Georgetown Visitation Preparatory School, Washington, D.C., in addition to her B.A. in philosophy she obtained an M.L.S., both from the University of Maryland. Among several positions she held in the past her assignment to the White House staff as researcher in the Office of Presidential Speechwriting was most helpful in carrying out her present task.